# THE ARMS RACE

# The
# ARMS RACE
## A Programme for World Disarmament

BY

## PHILIP NOEL-BAKER

*" Against a great evil, a small remedy
does not produce a small result, it produces
no result at all.''*—JOHN STUART MILL.

*Published by*
OCEANA PUBLICATIONS
NEW YORK

*Published in*
*The United States of America*
*by Oceana Publications, Inc.*
*80 Fourth Avenue, New York 3.*
*N.Y.*

*Published in Great Britain by*
*Atlantic Book Publishing Co. Ltd.*
*of 119 & 120 Chancery Lane, London*

*Distributed in Great Britain by*
*Stevens and Sons Limited of*
*119 & 120 Chancery Lane, London*

*Printed in Great Britain by*
*The Eastern Press Limited*
*of London and Reading*

*To the Memory*
*of*
*MY WIFE*

# Contents

## PART ONE

### THE ARMS RACE AND THE CASE FOR DISARMAMENT

## PART TWO

### NUCLEAR ARMAMENTS

## PART THREE

### THE HISTORY OF NEGOTIATIONS FOR NUCLEAR DISARMAMENT

## PART FOUR

### PROPOSALS FOR NUCLEAR DISARMAMENT

## PART FIVE

### OTHER WEAPONS OF MASS DESTRUCTION

## PART SIX

### PRACTICAL PROPOSALS FOR CONVENTIONAL DISARMAMENT

## PART SEVEN

### OTHER PARTS OF A DISARMAMENT TREATY WHICH AFFECT ALL ARMAMENTS AND ARMED FORCES

## PART EIGHT

### CONCLUSION

# Preface

THIS book is an attempt to assess the dangers of the arms race, and the importance of disarmament in national and international policy today, and to face the technical and political problems which will arise, when the governments begin the detailed consideration of how their present armaments can be reduced. It has been written principally because so little has been published on the topics with which it deals.

From first to last no difficulty has been consciously avoided. Indeed, to have shirked the difficulties would have been to defeat the main purpose for which the book was written. That purpose is to explore, as thoroughly as may be in a work intended for the general reader, the problems which arise in the drafting of a multilateral international agreement for the mutual and general reduction and limitation of national armaments; to show the complexity of these problems to those who think them simple; and to suggest solutions to those who think them insoluble. The solutions suggested may be right or wrong: the purpose of the book will be achieved if it stimulates discussion about what is now required.

Some of the proposals in the book may seem unreal to those who have not given much attention to the subject. In fact, they are founded on the author's personal experience, over more than thirty years, of international negotiations about disarmament, and of private debates among Ministers, diplomats, soldiers, sailors, airmen, scientists and other experts who have had to consider the practical realisation of a disarmament policy. It is that experience which has led him to believe that far-reaching and comprehensive proposals are most likely to succeed.

There are some chapters (*e.g.*, Chapters 4–6) which those familiar with the history of the arms race may wish to leave unread. If they do so, they can still follow the main thread of the argument by glancing at the tables in Chapter 4. These chapters have been inserted to show to those who are less familiar with past events how closely similar the present situation is to other situations which have arisen in recent decades, and how the struggle for disarmament now is not different in essential character from the struggle between the Wars.

Other chapters (*e.g.*, 33–38) contain passages about disarmament negotiations between the Wars. Readers may ask: Why rake the dead embers of failures long ago? The answer is important. The problems of conventional disarmament are identical with the problems faced by Ministers and experts between the Wars; but the discussions were then conducted at a high level of government responsibility, they were assiduously pursued, and they led to wide agreement on the technical solutions which are required for the drafting of many parts of a disarmament treaty. This work is still relevant to present problems, and the technical proposals then arrived at are still valid. It is foolish to ignore the lessons they can teach.

The opening chapters of Part Two set out the elementary facts about the production of atomic energy, which are essential to a full understanding of the rest of the nuclear section.

In some places it is said that " the close study of the records of the UN debates " leads to this or that conclusion. It is, of course, desirable that as many people as possible should make a close study of these records; but the reader should be warned that it is a formidable task, and that it is not possible, by the reading of newspaper reports, to follow what is really happening in the UN. In recent years the only serious discussions have been in the so-called Disarmament Sub-Committee. This body has had an annual session (in 1955 two sessions) lasting a number of weeks; it meets in private; but some weeks after each session is over the Verbatim Records are published, and are available to those who happen to know of their existence. In 1954 and 1955 they were reprinted by H.M. Stationery Office; they totalled 1,327 pages, with 600 words to the page; they had no index, and the proposals and other documents discussed were only printed in separate White Papers, which makes the argument very hard to follow. The records of the crucially important discussions of 1956 and 1957 were *not* printed, on the ground that it would have cost £750 (for each year) to do so. They can be seen, in many hundreds of pages of UN roneograph, in the Library of the UN Information Office in London, in the British Museum, in the Bodleian, and in some other " depository " libraries; similar arrangements are made in other countries.[1] This has made it virtually impossible for those concerned with public affairs, and for commentators and the Press, to follow what has been done. It is much to be hoped that better arrangements will be made in future to keep the public informed about discussions which are of vital importance to every citizen.

P. J. N.-B.

*April 24, 1958.*

---

[1] It is not the fault of the UN Secretariat that the Verbatim Records are not printed and widely circulated; they are not given the necessary funds in their budget.

# Acknowledgments

THE author must express his lasting gratitude to the Rockefeller Foundation who, when he began his work, made him a grant for the purchase of books and documents, for skilled assistance and secretarial help, without which the material could never have been assembled or arranged. His gratitude is more lively for the reason that the Foundation, as is its custom, placed no restriction on the expression of his opinions; and all the opinions in the book are, of course, exclusively his own.

He is also greatly indebted to the staff of the Royal Institute of International Affairs at Chatham House, and the staff of the UN London Information Centre; they have given most generous and willing help. He must record his obligation to the Controller of H.M. Stationery Office for permission to quote from Government Manuals on Civil Defence and from other Government publications. The Brighton Conference Association was formed to promote discussion of the problems of nuclear warfare, without committing itself to any particular thesis; they have kindly allowed the author to quote from their valuable collection of documents and papers on the subject.

He must express his deep appreciation of the hospitality of the Provost, Vice-Provost and Fellows of King's College, Cambridge, who have allowed him to reside in college during recent summers, in order that he might work on this book.

The author, like everyone else who is interested in armaments, owes very much to the writings of Mr. Hanson Baldwin of the *New York Times*; Dr. Vannevar Bush; Mr. Gordon Dean; Captain B. H. Liddell Hart; Sir Stephen King-Hall; M. Salvador de Madariaga, who was Director of the Disarmament Section of the League of Nations

Secretariat, and the brilliant Chairman of the Air Commission of the 1932 Conference; Mr. John Maddox, who contributes most valuable articles to the *New Scientist* and who is Scientific Correspondent of the *Manchester Guardian*; and above all to Dr. J. Robert Oppenheimer, whose writings are a source of inspiration to all who read them. The author is also greatly indebted to the Military, Naval and Air Correspondents of the leading journals, who do so much to explain the meaning of armaments to the public.

He must also express his gratitude to those who have helped and advised him in his work; to Professor A. C. Pigou, to whom he owes a life-long debt; to Dr. Peter Hodgson, without whose guidance the nuclear section could never have been attempted, and whose kindness has been unfailing; to Mr. Leonard Woolf, who gave much time to reading the manuscript in its early stages, and who made invaluable suggestions; to Mr. F. P. Walters and Mr. Francis Noel-Baker, who both spent many days on the final version, and did much to remove its blemishes; to Miss Elizabeth Furlong, whose wide knowledge and great skill in finding, arranging, collating and indexing the material, and whose devoted assistance over a period of years have alone made possible the completion of the work; to Miss Helen Armstrong; and to many more. For the manifold shortcomings of the book the author is alone responsible; they would have been much graver, but for the help he has received.

As this book is the result of personal experiences which began at the Peace Conference in Paris in 1919, the author cannot end this Foreword without giving expression to the debt which he has always owed to Lord Cecil of Chelwood, to Dr. Fridtjof Nansen, and to the late Mr. Arthur Henderson, for whom he worked during the first fifteen years of the international discussion of disarmament. History has proved that they were right.

# *Abbreviations*

A-bomb
: Atomic or fission bomb, in which the explosive is U235, U233 or plutonium 239.

Assembly
: League of Nations Assembly from 1920 to 1939; United Nations General Assembly from 1946.

C.D.
: Civil Defence.

CEA
: United Kingdom Central Electricity Authority.

Disarmament Commission
: UN Disarmament Commission, established January 11, 1952.

ENEA
: European Nuclear Energy Agency, which came into legal existence on February 1, 1958. It was set up by OEEC.

H-bomb
: Hydrogen bomb, *i.e.*, a bomb with a fission core (U235 or plutonium) and a sheath of hydrogen isotopes (tritium mixed with deuterium) and lithium 6.

H.C.P.
: High Contracting Parties.

IADA
: International Atomic Development Authority (proposed in Lilienthal Report).

IAEA
: International Atomic Energy Agency (established in Vienna, October 1957).

ICBM
: Inter-continental Ballistic Missile.

IRBM
: Intermediate range Ballistic Missile.

kg.
: Kilogramme = 2·205 lb.

kil.
: Kiloton, the equivalent of the explosive power of 1,000 tons of TNT.

KW.
: Kilowatt: 1,000 watts capacity.

M.G.
: *Manchester Guardian.*

MW.
: Megawatt: 1,000 kilowatts.

m.
: Million.

meg.
: Megaton, the equivalent of the explosive power of m. tons of TNT.

NATO
: North Atlantic Treaty Organisation.

N.C.
: *News Chronicle.*

N.Y.T.
: *New York Times* (European Edition).

N.Y.H.T.
: *New York Herald Tribune* (European Edition).

P.D.C.            Preparatory Disarmament Commission of the League of Nations, 1926–30; also Permanent Disarmament Commission proposed in British Draft Convention for Disarmament, March 1933.

Sub-Committee     Sub-Committee of UN Disarmament Commission, 1954–57.

3-Decker bomb     Fission-fusion-fission bomb, *i.e.*, H-bomb as above, with an outer sheath of U238.

UKAEA             United Kingdom Atomic Energy Authority.

UN                United Nations.

UNAEC             United Nations Atomic Energy Commission, 1946–52.

UNCCA             United Nations Commission for Conventional Armaments, 1946–52.

UNEF              United Nations Emergency Force.

U.S.              United States.

# PART ONE

# THE ARMS RACE AND THE CASE FOR DISARMAMENT

# 1

## " *The Greatest Challenge* "

In the autumn of 1957, Sir John Cockcroft wrote:

" the military consequences of fission and fusion have
led to a revolution in military thinking and practice
which has still a good way to go. It is clear enough
already, however, that our civilisation can be destroyed
in a night if ever these great forces are released for our
destruction. This presents the human race with the
greatest challenge it has ever had: *to co-operate in
disarmament and so to banish the threat which now
hangs over the whole world.*" [1]

On the last day of 1957, one of Sir John's fellow
physicists in the United States, Professor Rabi,[2] said:

" The combining of military techniques and science
makes it easy to apply scientific principles to kill people
—who are not strong structures. . . . When we look
at what has been accomplished in seventeen years, we
must remember that we have no reason to believe that
development will be slower in the future. . . . We have
to solve the problem of living together on this planet or
we won't live." [3]

Dr. J. Robert Oppenheimer, who led the team which
made the first atomic bomb, wrote in 1953:

" I have never discussed these prospects candidly
with any responsible group, whether of scientists or

---

[1] " The Nuclear Revolution," *Sunday Times* Atomic Energy Issue, October 6,
1957.

[2] Prof. Isidor Rabi has been Chairman, President Eisenhower's Science Advisory
Committee and Consultant Military Research and Development Board since
1946; Nobel Prize for Physics, 1944; member of the Gaither Committee, 1957.

[3] N.Y.T., January 1, 1958.

3

statesmen, whether citizens or officers of the government, with any group that could steadily look at the facts, that did not come away with a great sense of anxiety and sombreness at what they saw." [4]

These men are all physicists; they are thinking of the dangers that nuclear weapons combined with missiles now involve. But these are not the only dangers that modern armaments have brought; let the reader turn on to the explanation of why the Nazis' " nerve-gases " were not used in 1945 [5]; or the account of what might have happened if Hitler's V 1s had carried " biologicals " instead of high explosive [6]; or how 83,000 men, women and children were burnt to death in Tokyo in a single night.[7] He will see that the major military powers already have the means to destroy humanity in many different ways. And in ten or fifteen years from now, if the arms race goes on, there may be half a dozen major military powers, as there always were in times gone by.

The men who have been quoted are scientists; they are entitled to be heard, for they, not the soldiers or the politicians, have made the modern weapons. They are entitled to be heard about the effects which the weapons will produce; and they are entitled to be heard—far more than anyone else—about disarmament. When they say that the greatest challenge the human race has ever faced is to co-operate in disarmament; that we must solve the problem of living together or we won't live, they are not thinking of " partial " measures which will leave an immense stock of modern weapons intact in the hands of many nations, making them dependent for their national safety on instant readiness to *annihilate* each other—the word annihilate is always used. They are not talking of an indefinite future in which " limited " wars will be expected and allowed. They are thinking of disarmament, in the literal meaning of the word; the abolition of the " modern " weapons; a

---

[4] *Foreign Affairs*, July 1953, p. 527.    [5] See pp. 324 *et seq.*
[6] See pp. 352-353.    [7] See p. 340.

reduction of national forces so drastic that no nation will be able to wage aggressive war; the substitution of the rule of law for the arbitrament of force. That is why Professor Otto Hahn, who first split the uranium atom in 1939, led the eighteen foremost German physicists in 1957 in declaring that they would never " take part in any way in the production, testing, or use of atomic weapons." That is why in 1958 nine thousand leading scientists from more than forty countries, including thirty-six Nobel Prize winners, and thirty-five Fellows of the Royal Society, presented a petition to the Secretary-General of the UN; they demanded an international agreement to stop nuclear tests, because that " could serve as a first step towards a more general disarmament and the ultimate effective abolition of nuclear weapons, averting the possibility of a nuclear war that would be a catastrophe to all humanity." [8] Let it be noted; they say that the abolition of nuclear weapons —of *all* nuclear weapons—is required to avert the final catastrophe of nuclear war.

How have the nations reached this dire dilemma, in which their " civilisation can be destroyed in a night "; in which, at last, in literal and urgent truth, they must " disarm or perish "? The answer is: the arms race; the arms race providing the dynamic force that secures the immense allocation of money, men, machines and brains; with two other major factors, euphemism and legend, helping to win acceptance of burdens that are as onerous as they are hateful to those who pay.

The arms race has become, perhaps it has been for seventy years, the most important fact in men's affairs. It is itself the strangest paradox in history.

The armaments, the modern weapons, have been developed for national defence. But every scientist, general, Minister and military commentator is agreed that they have destroyed the hope of national defence; there is, quite literally, no present or prospective hope of defence

[8] N.Y.T., January 14, 1958.

against them; the very employment of the word defence to describe modern military preparation is an extreme example of how language can deceive.

The armaments have been developed for use in war; but "war," says President Eisenhower, and every government agrees, "war in our time has become an anachronism. Whatever the case in the past, war in the future can serve no useful purpose." [9] Yet every government, great and small alike, is training more men to arms, spending more on weapons, devoting incomparably more to military research, than ever in time of peace before. Why? If the armaments give no defence, if war can serve no useful purpose, why does any government impose such sacrifices on its people? The answer is simple: because other governments are doing the same. Each nation strains its resources to the uttermost, rather than risk finding itself at the mercy of a hostile or a predatory power. Thus no one will stop the arms race, unless all others stop it, too.

But why have the nations not perceived the mortal dangers of the arms race? Why has disarmament not succeeded long ago? Because, as Professor Rabi says, "the facts about modern warfare have just not penetrated; and that goes," he added, "for the heads of governments, for otherwise they would ponder these facts every day as the daily number one problem." The governments, the general staffs, the peoples, simply have not grasped what the modern armaments mean.

Here euphemism has played a deadly part. The weapon which destroyed Hiroshima is called a "nominal" bomb; a weapon with more explosive power than all the bombs dropped on Germany in the 1939 War is called "a low-yield thermo-nuclear device"; staffs give the name of "tactical" to weapons that would mean four Hiroshimas in one; governments describe as "disarmament plans" proposals that would leave them with double the number of troops, and fifty times the striking power that Hitler had in 1939.

[9] Address to United States Society of Newspaper Editors, April 21, 1956.

The constant repetition of these disingenuous phrases has led to a kind of self-induced hypnosis among those who ought to understand, while with the general public it has simply blanketed the facts.

Legend, too, has played a major part. It is generally believed that the arms race has always been as great a burden, relatively, as it is today; that the little wars, and the World Wars, of the last half-century were disastrous, but inevitable; that disarmament, whenever it has been adopted or attempted, has always broken down; that the attempts between the wars to stop the general arms race by a disarmament treaty were a total failure, doomed to futility from the start, leaving no lessons that can help us now.[10]

All this is legend. The arms race, in its modern form of constantly increasing preparation and counter-preparation, with ever new and more potent weapons, began only about three-quarters of a century ago. But with each decade it gathered momentum, and the pace since 1945 has been incomparably swifter than ever before.[11]

Nor were the wars of the last half-century inevitable: Sir Winston Churchill told President Roosevelt that the Second World War should be called " The Unnecessary War "[12]; he wrote in 1944 that it " could easily have been prevented if the League of Nations had been used with courage and loyalty by the associated nations."[13]

Nor has disarmament always broken down when it has been tried; the disarmament of the United States-Canadian, and the Swedish-Norwegian, frontiers was a total and a permanent success, with results from which the whole world benefits today.[14] The League Disarmament Conference was not doomed to futility from the start. It failed, indeed; but if Sir John (Lord) Simon had succeeded in persuading the

---

[10] Mr. Dulles: " The Washington Conference for Naval Limitation (1921) established Naval equations as between the five principal Naval Powers. But that relatively simple effort produced an unhappy end. Throughout the period of 1926 to 1933 the Allies of World War One earnestly, but vainly, sought formulas for the limitation of land armaments." Radio/TV Address, July 22, 1957.                                    [11] See pp. 46 *et seq.*

[12] Preface to *The Second World War*, p. x.

[13] Letter to Lord Cecil, September 1, 1944.          [14] See pp. 511 *et seq.*

British Cabinet to accept President Hoover's proposals of June 1932 [15]; if Mr. Stanley (Lord) Baldwin had beaten Lord Londonderry more swiftly and decisively in the long-drawn Cabinet struggle about the abolition of the bomber [16]; if Sir Anthony Eden's belated Draft Convention of March 1933 had been put forward a year earlier,[17] it might have had a rapid and notable success.[18]

But the greatest of the errors about the past is that the disarmament debates between the wars failed to solve the technical problems which the reduction and limitation of armaments involve; that the Washington Naval Treaty did not succeed; that "formulas for the limitation of land armaments" could not be found. The Washington Naval Treaty of 1922 was an outstanding success [19]; its weakness was that it was "partial" in that it dealt with naval armaments alone; it lapsed in 1937 because—and only because—no general disarmament treaty had been made. By 1932 every technical problem of land disarmament had been solved; on every point, "formulas" had been found [20]; all that was needed was a political decision by the leading governments,[21] and most of all by Britain, that, on terms that were fair and equitable to all, they would disarm. It was the failure to make that decision in time which brought Hitler to power, frustrated the constructive work which had been accomplished, and in a short period of years led to Hitler's war.

This is the vitally important lesson from the past, for it is a similar failure to face big political decisions that has brought the present deadlock in the UN. The nature of the deadlock, and the way it has been reached, are explained in Chapter 2. The facts there recorded show that until May 1955 the Russians were overwhelmingly to blame—not only for their general foreign policy of cold war, Communist *coups d'état*, and "sponsored" aggression, but for

[15] See pp. 397–398 and 450.    [16] See pp. 406 *et seq.*
[17] See pp. 398 and 479 *et seq.*    [18] See p. 481.
[19] See pp. 446–447.    [20] See pp. 473–480.
[21] Sir J. Simon, L.N. Assembly, *Records of the 14th Assembly,* 1933, p. 39.

the cynical nihilism of their approach to disarmament in the Commissions and Sub-Committees of the UN.

But a careful study of the record shows that since May 1955 the Russians have made considerable efforts to reach agreement, including the acceptance, in principle, of a large measure of international inspection and control; while the Western Governments have withdrawn the reasonable " comprehensive " proposal for a first-stage disarmament agreement which they had previously urged.

The reason given for the Western change of front is the technical difficulty of nuclear disarmament. " It is not practicable to assure the abolition of nuclear weapons," says Mr. Dulles. " The scientists tell us that there is no known method of detecting and surely accounting for the fission-able material already produced. Therefore we must make our plans on the assumption that the nations which now have nuclear weapons would use them in war." [22]

This is a genuine technical difficulty—long known to the Western Governments before 1955, but not less formid-able for that. It is the only serious technical difficulty in the whole programme of disarmament measures that are required. It is the crux of the present deadlock—the point on which the Russians have withdrawn. It is, therefore, to borrow a metaphor from Dr. Oppenheimer, the tiger that must be looked resolutely in the eye.

Mr. Dulles' proposition has been accepted and expounded by his Western colleagues. When examined, it means this: we cannot be sure of tracing secret stocks of nuclear weapons; we do not trust the Russians not to keep and use them; there is nothing we can do about this danger; therefore we will keep our own stocks, and we will use them to repel aggression, since they enable us to offset Russian preponderance in " conventional " power. But Mr. Dulles' " assumption " is a *non sequitur*. The secret nuclear stock is a genuine technical difficulty; there is no geiger-counter, no " divining rod " that will find it out.[23] But there are many

[22] *Loc. cit.*                    [23] See pp. 288 *et seq.*

things that can be done about it; a whole range of technical solutions which would make an agreement to abolish nuclear stocks incomparably safer than the retention for " decades ahead " of nuclear stocks in the hands of individual governments.[24]

These technical solutions would involve a more drastic measure of disarmament, a wider pooling of national sovereignty, than the " partial " plan on which the Western Governments stood in 1957. No one in his senses would oppose a " partial " plan for armament reduction, provided it was genuine, capable of being internationally controlled, and calculated to lead to further measures of reduction in an early future. But " partial " disarmament has difficulties of its own. It is harder to solve the technical problems, to get what Mr. Dulles calls " dependable equations " of military strength between the Powers, when the level of armaments is very high. Control is more difficult, if not impossible. Small-scale reductions do not restore the governments' " confidence," or arouse the popular support without which no real disarmament will be accepted or endure. And " partial " disarmament is very fragile. There was much more of it between the wars than is now proposed; it collapsed because no " comprehensive," more drastic, general disarmament was carried through.

Unless the governments can make such a general treaty now, the arms race will go on, with the dire consequences of which Professor Rabi gives us warning. Already the race is leading to incredible results. Military chiefs predict, as the basis of strategic planning, that battles in space will be decisive several decades from now.[25] Liberal-minded Senators declare that space-supremacy will make control of tides and climate the foundation of democratic freedom— you will dry up an enemy's country, or threaten him with an ice-age.[26] A Governor of a state loads his official cars with iron rations and first-aid sets, in case the nuclear

---

[24] See Chaps. 24 and 25.
[25] See p. 360.                                    [26] See p. 382.

onslaught should take him unawares.[27] Everybody knows
it is a race without a finish. In the struggle for the " lead "
in weapons, first one side, then another, gets ahead. With
every " advance," the tension mounts. With every year of
arms-race thinking, the moral basis of society is further
eroded. The Nazi leaders were hanged at Nuremburg for
crimes of " genocide." [28] The dropping of an H-bomb
against an enemy city would be an act of " genocide " more
terrible even than theirs. Yet *every* government declares
that it would not hesitate to drop the bomb.

The arms race was a major factor in the causation of
the 1914 War.[29] The failure of the Disarmament Conference in 1933 was the turning-point at which Hitler's war
began. Every year the race goes on, the danger that it will
bring the final catastrophe to pass grows more acute. The
only way to stop it is to make a multilateral, " comprehensive," world-wide disarmament treaty, by which all the
" modern " weapons are totally abolished, and the armed
forces and " conventional " armaments drastically cut down.
This immense reform will only be effected by gradual
stages, perhaps over a period of many years. But the final
goals must be established from the start; the first steps
forward must bring great reductions; UN controls must
guarantee that it is a reality and not a sham.

There is nothing difficult in making such a treaty.
There are no technical difficulties, as this book will show,
which cannot easily be overcome. The further disarmament
is carried, the simpler it becomes, and the easier to control.
Such a treaty is several decades overdue; if war is an
anachronism, then armaments are, too. When a leading
government works it out and puts it forward, it will evoke,
in all the continents, a responsive tide of popular support.
The tradition of the British Commonwealth, founded on
freedom and the rule of law, makes it right and timely that
Britain should now perform this task.

[27] N.Y.H.T., January 27, 1958.          [28] See p. 245.
[29] See pp. 80–82.

# 2

## The Moment of Hope:
### May 10, 1955

In January 1952 the UN Assembly set up a new Disarmament Commission to deal with both nuclear and conventional armaments, and " to prepare proposals to be embodied in a Draft Treaty . . . for the regulation, limitation and balanced reduction of all armed forces and armaments, for the elimination of all major weapons adaptable to mass destruction, and for effective international control of atomic energy to ensure the prohibition of atomic weapons and the use of atomic energy for peaceful purposes only." [1] Mr. Vyshinsky at first said that the proposal for this new Commission, which was put forward by Mr. Acheson for the United States of America, had made him " laugh all night." The world reaction to this speech made the Kremlin change its mind, and the decision to set up the Commission was unanimously agreed.

## Western Proposals in the Disarmament Commission, 1952

### The Six Principles

On April 24, 1952, the United States delegate laid before the Commission a paper entitled " Essential Principles for a Disarmament Programme." It read as follows:

> " 1. The goal of disarmament is not to regulate but to prevent war . . . by making war inherently, as it is constitutionally under the Charter, impossible as a means of settling disputes between nations.

[1] Resolution of January 11, 1952. Cmd. 8589, p. 5.

12

" 2. To achieve this goal, all States must co-operate to establish an open and substantially disarmed world,

(a) in which armed forces and armaments will be reduced to such a point and in such a thorough fashion that no State will be in a condition of armed prepared-ness to start a war, and

(b) in which no State will be in a position to under-take preparations for war without other States having knowledge of such preparations long before an offend-ing State could start a war.

" 3. To reach and keep this goal, international agreements must be entered into by which all States would reduce their armed forces to levels, and restrict their armaments to types and quantities, necessary for

(a) the maintenance of internal security,

(b) fulfilment of obligations of States to maintain peace and security in accordance with the United Nations Charter.

" 4. Such international agreements must ensure by a comprehensive and co-ordinated programme both :

(a) the progressive reduction of armed forces and permitted armaments to fixed maximum levels, radic-ally less than present levels and balanced throughout the process of reduction, thereby eliminating mass armies and preventing any disequilibrium of power dangerous to peace, and .

(b) the elimination of all instruments adaptable to mass destruction.

" 5. Such international agreements must provide effective safeguards to ensure that all phases of the dis-armament programme are carried out. In particular, the elimination of atomic weapons must be accom-plished by an effective system of international control of atomic energy to ensure that atomic energy is used for peaceful purposes only.

" 6. Such international agreements must provide an effective system of progressive and continuing disclosure and verification of all armed forces and armaments, including atomic, to achieve the open world in which alone there can be effective disarmament." [2]

This paper (hereafter called " the Six Principles ") was warmly endorsed by all the members of the Commission except Russia, and by the great majority of the Assembly at its next session.

## Manpower Ceilings

On May 28, Britain, United States and France submitted to the Commission their " Proposals for Fixing Numerical Limitation of all Armed Forces." They suggested the following manpower " ceilings " for the armed forces of the signatory nations:

| Nation | Total Manpower for Army, Navy, Air Force, Security or other Armed Police, and all Para-military formations. |
|--------|------------------------------------------------------------------------------|
| U.S.A. | Between 1 and 1·5 million |
| Russia | ,,   ,,  ,,   ,,   ,, |
| China | ,,   ,,  ,,   ,,   ,, |
| France | ,,   700 and 800,000 |
| Britain | ,,   ,,   ,,   ,, |

The ceilings for other nations " would normally be less than 1 per cent. of the population." [3]    In putting the proposal forward, the British delegate said that the " ceiling " for the United States, Russia and China should be " 1 million or *at the most* 1·5 million." [4] It was explained in debate that conventional armaments should be reduced in proportion to the reductions of manpower which were made. [5]

## The UN Sub-Committee 1954

In 1954, the so-called Disarmament Sub-Committee, consisting of Britain, the United States, France, Canada and Russia (the " atomic Powers "), met in London. This

[2] Cmd. 8589, pp. 14–15.    [3] Cmd. 8589, pp. 12, 13.
[4] Disarmament Commission, May 28, 1952, p. 11.
[5] *e.g.,* by M. Moch, Disarmament Commission, May 28, 1952, p. 41.

Sub-Committee had been set up to try to break the deadlock which Russian obstruction had caused in the Commission. On June 11, Britain and France laid " the Anglo-French Memorandum " before the Sub-Committee. This was endorsed by all Members except Russia; later in the year, and again under the pressure of world opinion shown in the Assembly debates, the Kremlin once more changed its mind, and Mr. Vyshinsky, in the last speech he made before his sudden death, said that Russia would accept the Memorandum as the basis of the Commission's and Sub-Committee's future work. The essential passage of this Anglo-French Memorandum read as follows:

" The Draft Disarmament Treaty prepared by the Disarmament Commission . . . should include provisions covering the following:

(a) The total prohibition of the use and manufacture of nuclear weapons and weapons of mass destruction of every type, together with the conversion of existing stocks of nuclear weapons for peaceful purposes.

(b) Major reductions in all armed forces and conventional armaments.

(c) The establishment of a control organ with rights and powers and functions adequate to guarantee the effective observance of the agreed prohibitions and reductions."

The words in paragraph (b) " major reductions, etc." meant the Western Governments' 1952 proposals for " manpower ceilings," and proportionate reductions of conventional weapons.

This was the programme of Disarmament which was to be carried out by the *first* Disarmament Treaty; the Memorandum had another paragraph which read:

" It is to be hoped that when all the measures enumerated above have been carried out, the armaments and armed forces of the Powers will be further

reduced to the levels strictly necessary for the maintenance of internal security and the fulfilment of the
obligations of signatory states under the terms of the
UN Charter." [6]

The Western Governments thus still adhered in 1954 to
the Six Principles, and, as the first step towards the realisation of these principles, they put forward a programme of
large reductions to be carried through in an early future.

## The UN Sub-Committee
## February 25 to May 18, 1955

This was still their policy when the Sub-Committee met
again on February 25, 1955. From that day (the dates are
important) until May 10, their delegates urged the Russians
to accept this programme. On March 23, the United States
delegate explained that a ceiling of between 1 and 1·5
million men would mean, at the higher level, a reduction
of 53 per cent., or at the lower level, a reduction of 69 per
cent. of the United States Forces, *i.e.*, much more than the
one-third reduction which the Soviets had proposed. He
said: " If we can reach agreement with our friends of the
Soviet Union on a ceiling of between one million and one-
and-a-half million, I believe there will be no difficulty so
far as my instructions are concerned." [7]   He and his
colleagues repeatedly said that, unless these ceilings and the
proportionate cuts in conventional arms were taken as a
basis, it would be no use going on. They affirmed and
reaffirmed that their governments were ready to abolish all
weapons of mass-destruction, including nuclear weapons of
every kind, and all existing nuclear stocks. On April 19
the British delegate said: " It is still a fundamental principle
of United Kingdom policy that the prohibition of nuclear

---

[6] Cmd. 9204, para. 8, p. 32.
[7] Cmd. 9549, p. 189.

weapons must amount to no less than the total prohibition of manufacture, possession and use of nuclear weapons." [8]

The United States delegate said on the same day: " All our proposals include, and have always included, provision for this prohibition and elimination of nuclear weapons." [9]

The Russians professed to think that this was of capital importance. They had constantly expressed their scepticism about the sincerity of what the Western delegates said about nuclear disarmament; the Western delegates had as constantly spoken of the vast Russian preponderance in conventional arms and forces, and had suggested, as a safeguard against disloyal Russian aggression, that the conversion of nuclear stocks should only start when the conventional reductions (*i.e.*, down to the 1 to 1·5 million manpower ceiling, etc.) had been carried through. At length, on this day, April 19, the French and British delegates proposed, as a great concession to the Russians, that the *new production* of " atomic, hydrogen and all other weapons of mass destruction " should cease (*i.e.*, the " cut-off " should begin) when one-half (50 per cent.) of the conventional reductions had been made; and that, when three-quarters (75 per cent.) of these conventional reductions had been effected there should be:

(i) " a complete prohibition on the *use* of atomic, hydrogen and other weapons of mass destruction " (*i.e.*, they accepted the famous " ban the bomb " which from the very start of the UN discussions, the Russians had urged as the first step towards disarmament);

(ii) " *Simultaneously, the elimination of these weapons, and the final quarter of the agreed reductions in armed forces and conventional armaments shall begin; and both processes shall be completed within the limit laid down in the Disarmament Treaty. All atomic materials shall then be used only for peaceful purposes.*" (This was always referred to as " the 75 per cent. arrangement.")

[8] Cmd. 9650, p. 416          [9] *Loc. cit.*, p. 423.

The French and British delegates declared at the same time that they wished "to make it clear" that this proposal was:

"dependent on agreement being reached on two essential elements in the disarmament programme, namely:

"(a) *drastic reductions in the armed forces and conventional armaments of the great Powers, so that an equilibrium is attained as suggested in the Anglo-French Memorandum of March 29, 1955.*" (This had reaffirmed that the manpower ceilings for the United States, Russia, and China should "be fixed at a figure between 1 and 1·5 million," but had proposed the *lower* ceiling of 650,000 for Britain and France) [10];

"(b) the institution of an effective system of control which would operate throughout the whole disarmament programme."

This question of effective control had already been the subject of controversy between the Russian and the Western delegates. The Russians had suggested a preliminary Organ of Control with very limited powers, to be followed at a later stage by another and different organ, with wider powers. The West had urged that the system of Inspection and Control must be established, and that the inspectors must be in position in every country, before any reductions were begun; and that there should only be one organ with gradually expanding rights and powers.

This, then, was what, all through March and April 1955, the Western delegates were appealing to the Russians to accept; reductions of manpower and conventional arms which might amount for the United States to as much as 53 to 69 per cent., together with the total abolition of all weapons of mass destruction, including all existing nuclear stocks, and a single organ of control, set up in advance, and given expanding powers. The United States delegates asked

[10] Cmd. 9636, p. 28.

for a clear answer, Yes or No, to these proposals: " Will it (the Soviet Union) accept the drastic reductions which the United States is prepared to accept, such as a ceiling of from 1 million to 1·5 million men?" [11]

In May they passed from appeals to stronger language; the French delegate said on May 3:

> " It is now for the Soviet Government to say whether it maintains its original position in its entirety, and thereby bears the responsibility for the failure of these talks, or whether, on the contrary, it recognises that we have gone half-way to meet it and consents to follow suit." [12]

And the United States delegate complained that " fifteen days have elapsed since the Franco-British proposal on 75 per cent.—25 per cent.," [13] and he said that if they got no answer to the proposals that were made, he and his Western colleagues could " arrive at no other conclusion than that there is no desire to negotiate."

## Russian Proposals of May 10, 1955

A week later, on May 10, the Russians answered. They laid a paper before the Sub-Committee in which they accepted:

   (i) the manpower ceilings of between 1 and 1·5 million, etc.;

   (ii) " the 5 Powers shall undertake also to reduce their conventional armaments correspondingly ";

   (iii) the 50 per cent. arrangement for the " cut-off ";

   (iv) the 75 per cent. arrangement for the abolition of stocks of nuclear and other mass-destruction weapons;

   (v) " appropriations by States for armed forces and conventional armaments shall be reduced *correspondingly* ";

[11] Cmd. 9650, p. 438.
[12] *Loc. cit.*, p. 526.
[13] *Loc. cit.*, p. 517.

(vi) there should be *one* " International Control Organ," with expanding powers;

(vii) the International Control Organ should:

(a) have " staff . . . selected on an international basis ";

(b) enjoy the right " to require from States any necessary information on the execution of measures for the reduction of armaments and armed forces ";

(c) " have *permanently in all States signatories . . . its own staff of inspectors having, within the bounds of the control functions they exercise, unimpeded access at all times to all objects of control* ";

(d) " have unimpeded access to records relating to the budgetary appropriation of States for military needs ";

(e) have "*rights and powers to exercise control, including inspection on a continuing basis, to the extent necessary to ensure implementation of the above-mentioned Convention by all States* ";

(viii) the further measures envisaged in paragraph 8 of the Anglo-French Memorandum:

" On the completion of all the measures enumerated above, it would be desirable that the Powers should further reduce their armaments and armed forces to the levels strictly necessary for the maintenance of internal security and the fulfilment " of the UN Charter.

Their plan was only the first measure of disarmament; Russia accepted the ultimate objectives of the Six Principles.

The proposals about Inspection and Control left some points obscure [14]; but if they meant anything at all, they would have made an immense breach in the Iron Curtain

[14] See pp. 540–543.

—hundreds, if not thousands, of UN Inspectors, chosen by the UN, " on an international basis," permanently in residence in Russia, with wide powers of access to military and other installations, and with the right to full information about all aspects of Russian military finance—in itself a powerful instrument of control. But for full measure the Russians also put forward their plan for the establishment of ground " Control Posts " at large ports, at railway junctions, on main motor highways and in aerodromes. This was to guard against the danger of surprise attack by modern weapons; it was to start before any measures of armament reduction began; it was a spontaneous Russian suggestion, which made a further great breach in the Iron Curtain; and it was put forward a good two months before President Eisenhower's proposal for preventing surprise attack by aerial photography had seen the light of day.[15]

There were, of course, many other points in the Russian paper on which there was not yet agreement, and on which, perhaps, agreement might have been difficult to secure. It is possible that it was all a bluff—though the language of the paper, and the discussions of the Sub-Committee for the next twenty-six months do not read like that. But, on paper, it was a very notable change of policy; it appeared to be a victory for Khruschev's and Zhukov's view that A and H bombs would destroy *all* civilisation over Molotoff's oft-proclaimed view that they would only destroy *capitalist* civilisation. The proposals would have been the logical result of a decision, if the Kremlin had, indeed, made a decision, that nuclear war was too dangerous to be risked.

In any case, this was the view first taken by the Western delegates. M. Moch's immediate response on May 10 was that " the whole thing looks too good to be true." [16]  On May 12, after forty-eight hours' consultation with his

---

[15] The full text of the Russian Plan of May 10, 1955, can be found in Cmd. 9639, pp. 33–42, and the Plan and the Sub-Committee's discussion on it in Cmd. 9650, pp. 607 *et seq.*
[16] Cmd. 9650, p. 627.

Government, the American delegate, speaking " as representative of the United States," said:

> " We have been gratified to find that the concepts
> which we have put forward over a considerable length
> of time, and which we have repeated many times
> during this past two months, have been accepted in a
> large measure by the Soviet Union." [17]

The British delegate, likewise having had two days to
consult his Government, said that he was glad that the
Western " policy of patience " had

> " now achieved this welcome dividend, and that the
> proposals (of the West) have now been largely, and in
> some cases, entirely, adopted by the Soviet Union and
> made into its own proposals."

He listed seven major points on which there was agreement; said " we have made an advance that I never dreamed
possible on Monday last "; and added that he was " anxious
to continue our search for agreement on . . . a draft
international Disarmament Treaty," which was the Sub-
Committee's task.[18]

## The Western Proposals Withdrawn
## September 1955

But the Sub-Committee did not continue its search for a
draft treaty. The Russians wanted to go straight on with
its work [19]; but their wishes were overruled by the Western
Governments, who insisted on a recess. The Sub-Committee did not meet again for serious business until
August 29. When it did meet, after this long delay, it
did not take up its work again where it had left off. The
Russians tried, politely but persistently, to make it do so;
they completely failed. The United States delegate made

[17] *Loc. cit.*, pp. 640–641.
[18] *Loc. cit.*, pp. 637–638.
[19] *Loc. cit.*, p. 651.

repeated speeches about the proposal for " open skies " as a measure to prevent " surprise attack," which President Eisenhower had put forward in the " Summit meeting " in Geneva in July.  He said that its acceptance would be the " curtain-raiser for " or the " gateway to " disarmament. But, after a week's debate, he said on September 6 that:

> *" the United States does now place a reservation upon all of its pre-Geneva substantive positions taken in this Sub-Committee or in the Disarmament Commission or in the UN on these questions in relationship to levels of armament."*

In other words, the Six Principles, the manpower ceilings, the disarmament programme of the Anglo-French Memorandum of 1954, the 50 per cent. arrangement about the " cut-off," the 75 per cent. arrangement about the elimination of nuclear stocks, the detailed plan for Inspection and Control, all the other proposals urged with such vigour and persistence only three months before—all were withdrawn.

The reason given for the withdrawal was as unpredictable as the withdrawal itself.  It was argued in a hundred speeches that the Western Governments could not adhere to their previous proposals because the Russians had pointed out in the paper of May 10 that a secret stock of nuclear weapons, which the UN Inspectors might not be able to detect, might be retained by a disloyal Power.  This was the argument the Russians had used to justify to the satellites, and to the outside world, their acceptance of Ground Control Posts and their UN Inspection system, and the great breach in the Iron Curtain policy which these measures involved.  Of course, it was true that there was a special difficulty about secret nuclear stocks.  But this difficulty did not come as a sudden, blinding revelation to the Western Governments when the Russians mentioned it on May 10. Dr. Oppenheimer had warned them about it in 1946; M. Moch had spoken of it in UN discussions every year since 1952; as late as May 5—five days before the Russian paper

—he had urged that, for the very reason that there was the difficulty about a secret stock, it was better to have an imperfect plan of nuclear disarmament and control than to have no plan at all. Yet this was used—and it was the *only argument* adduced—to justify the withdrawal of the disarmament proposals which had been pressed for years upon the Russians, and to which they had, at long last, agreed.

## Russian Proposals 1956 and 1957

The proposals were withdrawn, and they have remained withdrawn until today. In 1956 the Russians made further efforts to meet the West, which will be described hereafter [20]; on every point they were rebuffed. In 1957 they put forward again their programme of May 10, 1955, having clarified and improved their stand on Inspection and Control, and having added—a notable addition in March 1957—the total abolition of all missiles, both intercontinental missiles and intermediate- and short-range missiles as well.[21] The Western Governments said—some of them with genuine reluctance—that they had come to the conclusion that no " comprehensive " disarmament could be reached and that agreement should be sought on measures of " partial " disarmament instead. The measures suggested were very " partial " indeed; they are set out in the following table, side by side with what the Russians proposed:

[20] See pp. 228–230.
[21] Mr. Zorin's words were these: " Recent technical developments have also given prominence to the problem of rocket missiles. In our view this question should be considered in close relation to the prohibition of atomic and hydrogen weapons as a whole, for the danger to mankind lies less in the missiles themselves than in the atomic and hydrogen warheads which may be fitted to them. In our view, again, we cannot confine ourselves to the adoption of measures concerning intercontinental missiles alone, without regard to short- and medium-range rockets or atomic artillery, which are no less dangerous to the security of States, especially in Europe with its comparatively short distances and dense population. The Soviet Union considers necessary a complete prohibition of atomic and hydrogen weapons, including the use of all types of rocket missiles and artillery which are suitable for employment as atomic and hydrogen weapons." Sub-Committee, March 18, 1957, pp. 25–26.

### Table of Proposals Made in 1957 by the Four Western Governments and by Russia

| The Four Western Governments | Russia |
|---|---|
| Proposals for Partial Measures of Disarmament : August 29, 1957 | Proposal on the Reduction of Armaments and Armed Forces and the Prohibition of Atomic and Hydrogen Weapons : March 18, 1957 |

#### I. Total Manpower for All Armed Forces, Security Police and Para-Military Formations

| | |
|---|---|
| *1st Stage :* | *1st Stage :* |
| Reduction within one year to: | Reduction by December 31, 1958, to : |
| U.S.    2·5m. | U.S.    2·5m. |
| Russia    2·5m. | Russia    2·5m. |
| France    750,000 | China    2·5m. |
| U.K.    750,000 | France    750,000 |
| | Britain    750,000 |
| | *Note* : Russia said this total should include all civilians working full-time for the Forces; the Western Governments made no such proposal. |

Willing to negotiate two further reductions to:

| | *2nd Stage :* | *3rd Stage :* |
|---|---|---|
| U.S. | 2·1m. | 1·7m. |
| Russia | 2·1m. | 1·7m. |
| France | 700,000 | 650,000 |
| U.K. | 700,000 | 650,000 |

provided " there has been progress toward the solution of political issues." No definition of this " progress " or of what political issues were envisaged.

*2nd Stage :*
Reduction by December 31, 1959, to :

| | |
|---|---|
| U.S. | 1–1·5m. |
| Russia | 1–1·5m. |
| China | 1–1·5m. |
| France | 650,000 |
| U.K. | 650,000 |

#### II. Manpower to be Permitted to Other Nations

| The Four Western Governments | Russia |
|---|---|
| " Levels with other essential States would be specified through negotiation with them." | " The levels . . . shall not exceed 150,000–200,000 men." |

#### III. Conventional Armaments

| The Four Western Governments | Russia |
|---|---|
| The five States " will place in storage depots, within their own territories, and under the supervision of an International Control Organisation, specific quantities of designated types of armaments to be agreed upon and set forth in lists annexed to the Conventions." No indication was given about the types to be designated or about the quantities envisaged and no model list was provided. | The five States " shall reduce their appropriations for armed forces and conventional armaments correspondingly " (*i.e.*, in proportion to the manpower cuts). |

*Table of Proposals Made in 1957 by
the Four Western Governments and by Russia—continued*

| The Four Western Governments | Russia |
| --- | --- |

### IV. Nuclear Disarmament

| The Four Western Governments | Russia |
| --- | --- |
| 1. "Cut-off" of new production of new weapons to begin one month after the ICO has certified that an effective inspection system has been installed. <br> 2. A "group of technical experts" to design the inspection system. <br> 3. "Equitable transfers, in successive increments, of fissionable materials from previous production to non-weapons purposes." <br> (*i.e.*, reduction of nuclear stocks.) <br> No proposals about quantities and dates of transfers were proposed. <br> See comments below on the Western Governments' intentions about the substantial stocks of nuclear weapons they proposed to retain. | 1. "The total prohibition of the use and manufacture of nuclear weapons and weapons of mass destruction of every type, together with the conversion of existing stocks of nuclear weapons for peaceful purposes." <br> 2. "Cut-off" of new production of nuclear weapons at end of 1st stage (manpower reduced to 2·5 million, etc.). <br> 3. Conversion of nuclear stocks to begin when half of the 2nd stage conventional reductions has been made. <br> (*i.e.*, the Western Governments' 75 per cent. arrangement.) |

### V. Missiles

| The Four Western Governments | Russia |
| --- | --- |
| Parties to agree that within three months after the Treaty enters into force they will establish a "technical committee to study the design of an inspection system which would make it possible to assure that the sending of objects through outer space will be exclusively for peaceful and scientific purposes." | Total abolition under international control of all missiles for warlike purposes, including inter-continental, intermediate-range and short-range missiles. |

### VI. Military Expenditure

| The Four Western Governments | Russia |
| --- | --- |
| Parties to make available to ICO information about budgets and expenditures. The categories of information to be "agreed in advance"; no proposals were made. | 1. As above: appropriations to be reduced proportionately to manpower cuts. <br> 2. Alternatively: a reduction in expenditure of 15 per cent.[22] |

### VII. Inspection and Control

| The Four Western Governments | Russia |
| --- | --- |
| 1. An International Control Organ with a Board of Control in which the five Powers and "other parties" would have a veto. <br> 2. The Parties to supply information to the ICO. <br> 3. Its functions would expand as the treaty was carried out. <br> 4. Its duties, composition, rights and functioning to be determined later. <br> No proposals were made. | An "effective International Control Organ, possessing all the rights and functions necessary" to supervision of the fulfilment of the Treaty. <br> (Details as on p. 20.) |

[22] Cmd. 333, p. 46. Russian proposals of April 20, 1957. This was only a "partial" plan, which would have meant a much smaller budgetary reduction than a reduction proportionate to a man-power ceiling of 1 to 1·5 million men proposed on March 18.

*Table of Proposals Made in 1957 by*
*the Four Western Governments and by Russia—continued*

| The Four Western Governments | Russia |
|---|---|
| **VIII. *Measures against Surprise Attack*** | |
| 1. Aerial photography: "A working group of experts to examine the technical problems and to report their conclusions."  2. Ground Observation Posts as proposed by Russia.  3. Mobile ground teams with defined authority.  No definitions suggested. | 1. Ground Control Posts at large ports, railway junctions, main motor highways, and aerodromes.  2. Aerial photography in a zone extending to 500 miles on each side of the line dividing NATO and Warsaw Treaty forces. |

*Note*: The proposals and counter-proposals made about nuclear tests have been omitted, as they are too complicated to be shown in a Table. The question of Tests is dealt with in Chap. 22.

## The Russian Case, September 1957

This juxtaposition of the proposals made by Russia and the Western Governments in 1957 shows that, *on paper*, the Russians were offering to accept *much more disarmament*, and *much more inspection and control*, than the West. It must be added that the Russians considered the Western "package plan" extremely unfair to them in various ways:

1. The 2·5 million ceiling for manpower meant a large reduction for them, and virtually *none* for the United States or any other Western Power.

2. Soon after the "cut-off" of the new production of nuclear weapons was proposed, together with retention of a "substantial part of existing nuclear stocks," President Eisenhower explained to the American people that

> "In numbers, our stock of nuclear weapons is so large and so rapidly growing that we are able safely to disperse it to positions assuring its instant availability against attack and still keep strong reserves. Our scientists assure me that we are well ahead of the Soviets in the nuclear field, both in quantity and in quality. We intend to stay ahead." [23]

[23] Broadcast on "Science and National Security," November 7, 1957.

Russia was thus asked to accept a large and permanent inferiority in nuclear weapons *vis-à-vis* the United States, without counting in the British stocks, which they knew to be considerable.

3. They professed to be particularly alarmed by Mr. Stassen's explanations in the Sub-Committee of how the United States proposed to use the " substantial nuclear weapon capability " (*i.e.*, the much larger nuclear stock) which it would, under the Western " partial " plan, retain.[24] He stated that the United States would be free:

(i) to make new nuclear weapons from fissile material " on hand on that date " (the date of the first disarmament treaty);

(ii) to " refabricate " existing weapons into new and more efficient weapons;

(iii) to introduce and maintain nuclear weapons on the territory of its allies;

(iv) to train the forces of its allies " in the use of nuclear weapons ";

(v) to equip its allies' forces " with the means of delivering such weapons." [25]

The Russians held that preparation for nuclear warfare by a large number of new countries (the United States has military agreements with over thirty) was not a good way of making progress towards disarmament.

## Why Did the Western Governments Change?

The Russian proposals may all be bluff; there are many points on which their policy is still obscure. The only way to find out is to take them up on what they say, and to try to negotiate a treaty.

But the purpose of this chapter is to ask what caused the Western *volte face* of 1955. Why did the Governments

[24] April 12, 1957, p. 12.
[25] July 5, 1957, pp. 7–9.

repudiate in September 1955 what they had urged in 1952, 1953, 1954 and up to May 10, 1955? Not because Russian policy gave them greater reason for distrust; in 1952 the Korea and Indo-China Wars were going on; by 1955 these wars had ceased, Austria had been freed, the Russian bases at Port Arthur and Porkkala had been given back to China and Finland, and many other proofs of a change of policy had been seen.

Is it possible that the real cause is revealed by other statements made by Mr. Stassen in the Sub-Committee, and by Mr. Dulles outside? Mr. Stassen strove valiantly in 1957 to keep the disarmament talks alive; but, no doubt speaking under State Department instructions, he was led to say:

> " It is our view that if an effort is made to reduce armaments, armed forces, and military expenditures to a level that is too low, to a level that reflects weakness, it would not be conducive to stability in the world, and to the best interests of peace. . . . It is our view that if armaments, armed forces and military expenditures are brought down to too low a level, then . . . instead of the prospects of peace being improved, the danger of war is increased." [26]

Again:

> " There was a time when there was in my country considerable thought of a very extreme form of control and inspection, and a very low level of armaments, armed forces, and military expenditure. We have concluded that that extreme form of control and inspection is not practical, feasible or attainable." [27]

Mr. Dulles:

> " Past efforts have usually proceeded from the assumption that it is possible to establish and maintain certain defined levels of military strength, and to equate these dependably as between the nations.

[26] April 11, 1957, pp. 15–16.
[27] *Loc. cit.*, p. 17.

*Actually, military potentials are so imponderable that this has always been and always will be a futile pursuit.*" [28]

This is to throw over the policy of disarmament altogether, now and for the future. Taken with Mr. Stassen's statements, they compel the question: Has the thinking that inspired the United States policy of 1952–55 been eroded by the arms race? Have the United States Government reached the point reached by the British, French and Germans in 1914—do they now believe that only armaments can make them safe, and that " keeping a lead " in weapons and in forces is the only way to safeguard the national interest and uphold the peace? Are they ready to let the arms race go on, year after year, with mounting cost, and new inventions which force all other nations to follow suit? Can they believe that, under the pressure of this competitive preparation for total war, national safety, now or ever, can be found?

[28] *Foreign Affairs*, October, 1957.

# 3

# *How the Arms Race Works:*
# *"Keeping a Lead"*

MOST people in most countries accept their present burden
of armament as the peoples of the under-developed countries
used to accept their poverty: with unquestioning, even
unresentful, resignation. It seems to them quite normal;
part of the heritage of the past; and they hardly question
that it will be needed still for many years.

In fact, no earlier generation has ever borne in peace time
the burden of armament which almost every nation bears
today. As said in Chapter 1, the growth of modern
armaments had hardly begun seventy years ago. It is only
since then that the arms race, the constant, competitive
expansion of national armaments, has been the dominating
factor in international life.

There were many and diverse political forces and events
which helped, in the last quarter of the nineteenth century,
to stimulate the arms race. Of special importance was the
success of Bismarck's conscript army in 1866 and 1870
against the professional armies of Austria and France.
Almost overnight the rest of Europe adopted the system of
universal short-term service, which enormously increased
the numbers trained to arms. There were technological
advances which made it possible for governments to raise
and train much larger forces, and to equip them with more
powerful, complex, and costly weapons. Any progress in
metallurgy and engineering was immediately applied to
"improving" the quality, and increasing the quantity,
of arms. The engineers developed railways; then, with improved mechanical equipment, more and better roads; then
motorised road transport: each was quickly seized on by

31

General Staffs to increase their military strength. Before 1914, strategic railways had become the basis of their plans for war. Oil displaced coal in warship propulsion. When war came in 1914, petrol engines took tracked mobile guns, tanks and ammunition wagons on to the field of battle, aircraft into the sky, and submarines beneath the sea. From then on, technical and scientific development of many kinds facilitated the increase of standing military and naval forces, and the equipment of these forces with more and better arms.

But the real cause of the unbroken expansion of national armaments since 1870 has been the arms race itself. When one nation kept more divisions under arms, raised the period of national service, or introduced more powerful weapons, its neighbours, or its potential enemies, felt that they must do the same. They dared not lag behind, or refuse any sacrifice which they believed might discourage an enemy assault or avert defeat. By a chain reaction which Lord Grey vividly described after the 1914 War,[1] armaments produced fear, and fear produced more armaments, with disastrous results for the national security of all the peoples concerned. Three examples may be given of how this chain-reaction process works: one drawn from " conventional " weapons half a century ago; the others from " modern " weapons, developed during and since the last World War.

In 1884 France and Britain began building warships against each other. In 1899 Tirpitz persuaded the Kaiser that Germany must do the same; a reluctant Reichstag passed a first, modest Navy Law. In 1900, during the Boer War, the British Navy, in pursuance of its belligerent rights, arrested a German vessel, the *Bundesrath*. This aroused a storm of indignation in the German Press; Tirpitz took his chance, and carried a second Naval Law, which almost doubled his Fleet. Both the Kaiser and Tirpitz constantly asserted that they were not building

1 See pp. 80–81.

against Britain; they simply needed ships to guard their coasts and colonies. But the British Admiralty were alarmed. In 1907 they produced the Dreadnought, which was faster, had guns of greater power and range, and heavier armour than any previous warship. In 1908, the Kaiser wrote to the First Lord of the Admiralty, Lord Tweedmouth, as follows:

> " It was in England that the first Dreadnought had been built, in the greatest secrecy, and on its completion Admiral Fisher and the Press had at once announced that she was capable of sinking the whole of the German Navy. These statements had forced the German Government to begin building ships of a similar type, to satisfy public opinion in Germany." [2]

Within two years Britain and Germany were engaged in the frenzied construction of Dreadnoughts, and later super-Dreadnoughts, which continued until the war began. By then German Dreadnoughts had, in effect, done to seventy-five pre-Dreadnought British battleships and armoured cruisers just what Lord Fisher said the first Dreadnought would do to the German Fleet. They had rendered obsolescent incomparably the most powerful line of battle the world had ever known. Germany, with the type of ship which, till 1907, Tirpitz had been laying down, could not have come for many years within measurable distance of challenging the supremacy of the British fleet. But, with Dreadnoughts on both sides, the margin of battleship strength at Jutland was narrower than the British Navy had known since Drake destroyed the Spanish Armada in 1588.

As a move in the arms race, the construction of the Dreadnought was a brilliant achievement, putting Britain for the moment far in the lead. But from the point of view of the national interest, it turned out to be a serious, almost a catastrophic, mistake. Britain's naval security, on which

---

[2] Quoted by G. Lowes Dickinson, *The International Anarchy, 1904–14*, p. 386.

the whole Empire and Commonwealth then depended, was gravely compromised.[3]

But in the second, " modern," example of how the arms race works, the men who introduced a new and revolutionary weapon were clearly right. In the long run, this weapon has undermined the national security of their countries and made them liable to total annihilation; in the short run, they judged, and rightly, that it might save their countries, and all mankind, from an imminent and measureless disaster. The story may best be given in the words of one of the scientists concerned, exactly as he told it in 1954:

" The scale of the damage of Nagasaki drained the blood from my heart then (*i.e.*, in autumn, 1945), and does so now when I speak of it. For three miles my road lay through a desert which man had made in a second. Now, nine years later, the hydrogen bomb is ready to dwarf this scale, and to turn each mile of destruction into ten miles, and citizens and scientists stare at one another and ask: ' How did we blunder into this nightmare?'

" I put this first as a question of history, because the history of this is known to few people. The fission of uranium was discovered by two German scientists a year before the war. Within a few months, it was reported that Germany had forbidden the export of uranium from the mines of Czechoslovakia, which she had just annexed. Scientists on the continent, in England and America, asked themselves whether the secret weapon on which the Germans were said to be

---

[3] " He (Lord Fisher) hoped to render the German fleet obsolete at a single stroke by building a type of battleship so superior to all existing types that Germany, as he supposed, could not imitate it for lack of the requisite resources, financial if not technical. . . . The Dreadnought was so superior in fighting power to earlier battleships that her appearance automatically rendered obsolete, not only the German battle fleet, but all other battle fleets, including the British. . . . By adopting the Dreadnought policy we had simply forfeited our enormous preponderance over the prospective enemy without gaining anything in return. . . . By 1914 the strength of the British Navy as against the German had declined by 40 to 50 per cent. Such were the immediate fruits of the Dreadnought policy ": H. C. Bywater, *Navies and Nations*, 1927, pp. 26–29.

working was an atomic bomb. If the fission of uranium could be used explosively (and this already seemed possible in 1939) it might in theory make an explosion a million times larger than hitherto. The monopoly of such an atomic bomb would give Hitler instant victory, and make him master of Europe and the world. The scientists knew the scale of what they feared very well: they feared first desolation and then slavery. With heavy hearts, they told Albert Einstein what they knew of atomic fission. Einstein had been a pacifist all his life, and he did not easily put his conscience on one side. But it seemed clear to him that no scientist was free to keep this knowledge to himself. . . . On August 2, 1939, a month before Hitler invaded Poland, Einstein wrote to President Roosevelt to tell him that he thought an atomic bomb might be made, and he feared that the Germans were trying to make one.

" This is how it came about that, later in the war, scientists worked together in England, in Canada and America, to make the atomic bomb. They hated war no less than the layman does—no less than the soldier does; they, too, had wrestled with their consciences; and they had decided that their duty was to let the nation use their skill, just as it uses the skill of the soldier or the expert in camouflage. The atomic scientists believed that they were in a race against Germany whose outcome might decide the war even in its last weeks." [4]

Looking back to August 1939, and remembering Hitler's previous aggressions, the atrocities he had already committed against the Jews, the Social-Democrats, the Austrians, and the Czechs; remembering the ghastly nature of his despotism, and the certainty that he was planning

[4] J. Bronowski, *The Listener*, July 1, 1954. See also Gordon Dean, ex-Chairman of U.S. Atomic Energy Commission, *Report on the Atom*, 1954, pp. 216–251. The text of Einstein's letter to President Roosevelt is on pp. 220–221.

the conquest of the world, who would say that Einstein and the other scientists were not right?

The third example of the working of the arms race may seem to some people to have offered a less obvious choice; it is President Truman's decision in 1950 to make the H-bomb. President Truman had amply proved that he was a loyal supporter of the UN and that he ardently desired a general and genuine disarmament. Admiral Strauss has thus described the situation which the President faced:

"We detected the test of an atomic weapon or device by the Russians in August of 1949. Realising that our leadership was therefore challenged and that our sole possession of the weapon which had been a major deterrent to aggression had been cancelled, it became clear that our superiority would thereafter be only relative and dependent upon a quantitative lead— that is to say, upon our possession of greater numbers of atomic weapons so long as that could be maintained.

"There was the alternative of a qualitative lead if we could make a weapon of greater force—greater than the fission weapons by a degree of magnitude comparable to the difference between fission bombs and conventional bombs. A theoretical method of accomplishing this was known to our scientists. In January 1950 the President directed the Atomic Energy Commission to undertake the necessary steps to see if this weapon, variously called the hydrogen bomb, the fusion bomb, and the thermonuclear bomb, could in fact be made.

"As you know, thanks to the ingenuity of those scientists and engineers who devoted themselves to the project the feasibility of the fusion reaction was demonstrated and a prototype was tested at Eniwetok in November 1952."

And the Admiral added:

"In August of last year (1953) the Russians also

tested a weapon or device of a yield well beyond the range of regular fission weapons and which derived a part of its force from the fusion of light elements. There is good reason to believe that they had begun work on this weapon substantially before we did." [5]

President Truman gave the Commission his approval, and ordered them to go ahead. In the light of Stalin's post-war policy, with the Czechoslovak *coup d'état*, the Berlin blockade, and the Korean aggression still fresh in his mind, he could not face the prospect of allowing Russia to have the sole possession of a weapon a thousand times more powerful than the Hiroshima bomb. He felt he could not risk the blackmail the free world might have had to face. When he made his decision, the Russians had already started the research for an H-bomb which ended in 1953 with their success.

But the choice which confronted Einstein and President Truman is the choice which, in one shape or another, confronts governments at every new development of the arms race. They dare not leave their nation at the mercy of some better-armed and, as they think, ruthless foe.[6] So, in the quest for national safety, they increase their armaments to the limit of their power. And while the general level of armaments goes on increasing, no government dares to stand aside. Even Sweden is now contemplating nuclear bombs. This ceaseless competition, and the fear which it creates, explain the constant growth, over two generations, of military expenditure and preparation with which the next two chapters deal.

---

[5] M.G., April 1, 1954.

[6] A more recent example is given in the following extract from the N.Y.T. *Economic Review,* January 6, 1958: " Stocks of companies in the missile field have been stand-outs in recent weeks. Chief beneficiaries, of course, will be some major aircraft companies. They were hurt last year when defence contracts were cut back or cancelled. Then came the Soviet earth satellites, and whoosh! Missiles became the prime weapon in military planning and procurement. . . . It is now apparent that the Federal Government will step up spending for missiles, perhaps by $2,000m. or more."

# 4

# *The Growth of Armaments:*
## *Men and Money*

THIS chapter and the next set out some of the forgotten facts about the growth of warlike preparation since the modern arms race began, They show what it has meant in increased manpower under arms, in increased taxation, and in the increased destructive power of weapons. They give a preliminary picture of this swift development of military might; of the kinds of warfare it produced in two world wars; and of the greater perils which threaten now.

The subject falls naturally into three periods, divided by the two world wars.

## *1884 to 1914*

The first period may be said to have begun with the " naval panic " in Britain directed against France. This " panic "—it was the word in common use before 1914— led the British Government to increase its programme of battleship construction in 1884 and in the following years. France replied by doing the same.

There was another naval panic against France in 1889, and yet another in 1892; in 1893 Gladstone resigned the post of Prime Minister for the last time, because he opposed the increase of the annual expenditure on new warships from £3m. to £7m., on which his Cabinet, against his advice, agreed. France again replied by building extra ships. This started what was then called " the Navy fashion "; it led to the Tirpitz Naval Laws in Germany which have been described.

Meanwhile, the Japanese, with an army created by a German military mission, a navy created by a British naval mission, and an arms industry created by British private firms, had made war on China, and won swift victories. Imbued by the militarist and imperialist doctrines they had learnt from Europe, they annexed Formosa by the Treaty of Peace in 1895. Nine years later they went to war against Czarist Russia; again they were victorious; by the Treaty of Peace Korea virtually became a Japanese Protectorate, and they acquired a naval base at Port Arthur. Japan had become a " Great Power," and from then on her army and her navy continued to increase, and her General Staffs exercised a growing influence in State affairs.

For many years before 1914 Europe had been divided by rival alliances, which gradually grew closer: Germany, Austria-Hungary and Italy on one side; France and Russia on the other. In 1904 anxiety about the German navy led the British Government to make the Entente Cordiale with France. In effect, Britain was now the ally of both France and Russia, and people talked of the Triple Entente. Within each of the alliances the Governments encouraged each other to increase their warlike preparations, both by land and sea.[1]

But up to 1914 this expansion of armaments was mainly confined, apart from Japan, to the Great Powers of Europe. The Balkan nations had good armies, as their victories against Turkey proved; but their numbers were relatively small. The other smaller nations were largely unaffected by the arms race, as were the Latin-American Republics, the self-governing members of the British Commonwealth, the nations of Africa and the Middle East, and most of Asia. The United States had made some increase in her navy, as the result of anxiety about Japan.

In 1913–14, on the eve of the First World War, British defence expenditure had risen in twenty years from £32m., which it had been when Mr. Gladstone resigned, to £77m. The taxation this involved was regarded as an intolerable burden; the tension created by the naval race, and the

[1] See p. 75.

increase in land armies on the Continent, became more and more acute; there was widespread foreboding; people used to say " it would be better to have the war and get it over."

The broad picture of the increase in armaments during the three decades before the 1914 war is shown in the following tables:

TABLE I

*Men Under Arms—Army and Navy* (thousands)

|  | 1884 | 1900 | 1908 | 1914 |
|---|---|---|---|---|
| Britain | 281 | 327 | 375 | 397 |
| France | 556 | 659 | 657 | 834 |
| Russia | 806 | 938 | 1,260 | 1,253 |
| Germany | 458 | 629 | 653 | 864 |
| Austria-Hungary | 300 | 383 | 389 | 443 |
| Italy |  |  | 270 | 345 |
| U.S.A. | 37 | 126 | 128 | 165 |
| Japan | 43 | 273 | 256 | 301 [2] |

TABLE II

*Defence Expenditure in £ Sterling* (millions)

|  | 1883 | 1900 | 1908 | 1913 |
|---|---|---|---|---|
| Britain | 28 | 89 [3] | 59 | 77 |
| France | 31 | 39·1 | 44 | 82 |
| Russia | 36 | 44·6 | 60 | 92 |
| Germany | 20 | 40 | 59 | 100 |
| Austria-Hungary | 13 | 13·8 | 21 | 24 |
| Italy | 12 | 15·4 | 18 | 29 |
| U.S.A. | 11 | 40·1 | 53 | 64 |
| Japan | ·5 | 5 | 4·5 | 12 |
| *Total* | 151·5 | 227 | 318·5 | 480 |
| Average Price Level (1913: 100) | 95 |  | 90 | 100 |

It is noticeable, moreover, and important to the argument of this book, that while the expansion was continuous throughout this period of thirty years, the pace greatly quickened towards the end; in the last five years before the war there was little resistance in any Parliament to the

[2] The sources of information from which these figures are drawn do not on all points agree, and some of the figures are, therefore, an approximation. But they give a general picture of the growth of armaments which is sufficiently accurate for the purposes of this chapter.

[3] Boer War.

increased taxation demanded by governments for defence. In those years the cost of British armaments went up by more than 30 per cent., of Russian armaments by 53 per cent., of German armaments by 69 per cent., and of French armaments by 86 per cent. In the year 1913–14 Germany raised a capital levy of £50m. for expenditure on arms, and Russia spent £50m. of a fund that had been " earmarked for war." [4]

The competition in land armaments was so keen that all observers were agreed that the tension could not go on increasing for very long without a smash. The term of national service was raised in France, and in turn by Germany, first to two years and then to three. By 1914 the first-line war strength of the rival armies was estimated to be: France and Russia, 4,570,000 plus 500,000 troops from outside Europe; Germany and Austria-Hungary, 3,358,000.[5]

First- and second-line strength of the six Great Powers was reckoned at 18 million; their full mobilised strength in all the services at 37·8 million.[6] These figures give some picture of the stupendous military preparation which Europe had made.

But, if the competition was keen on land, it was keener still at sea. Here are figures of naval expenditure from 1908 onwards:

TABLE III

*Total Naval Expenditure, Voted or Estimated*
*£ million*

|  | 1908 | 1909 | 1910 | 1911 | 1912 | 1913 | 1914 |
|---|---|---|---|---|---|---|---|
| Britain | 32·2 | 35·7 | 40·4 | 42·4 | 45·1 | 46·3 | 51·5 |
| Germany | 16·5 | 19·7 | 20·8 | 22 | 22·6 | 23 | 23·4 |
| Italy | 6·2 | 6·5 | 8·3 | 8·4 | 8·5 | 10·2 | 10·4 |
| France | 12·7 | 13·3 | 15 | 17·3 | 18 | 20·8 | 19·8 |
| Russia | 10 | 9·6 | 9·7 | 11·6 | 17·6 | 25·3 | 26·7 |
| Austria-Hungary | 2·4 | 4 | 3·5 | 5·1 | 5·8 | 5·9 | 3·8 [7] |

[4] G. P. Gooch, *History of Modern Europe, 1871–1919*, p. 532.
[5] G. Lowes Dickinson, *The International Anarchy*, p. 369.
[6] Official figures discussed under the heading " Army," *Encyclopaedia Britannica*, 11th ed., 1910–11, Vol. II, p. 610.
[7] Brassey's *Naval Annual*, 1914, p. 83.

This was an increase in naval expenditure for the six Powers together from approximately £80m. to £136m. in five years. It was when the arms race had reached this climax on land and sea that the 1914 War broke out.

## *1919 to 1939*

The 1914 War caused casualties and devastation on a scale unknown in history before. When it ended, it had become, in the minds of the troops on both sides, " the war to end war."

There is no doubt that the leaders of the victorious governments intended that the pledge embodied in this phrase should be fulfilled. They disarmed Germany and her allies,[8] and gave the Germans a formal undertaking that this would be followed by a general limitation of the armaments of all nations. They set up the League of Nations and for a dozen years they made it work; the League stopped four wars within a week of the day when they began, settled numerous international disputes, built up effective international co-operation in economic, social, transport and other fields; created the International Labour Office, and the Permanent Court of International Justice. The ILO brought about great improvements in the working conditions of hundreds of millions of people throughout the world; the International Court dealt with more than forty cases in such a way that its authority stood very high.

In short, the League system worked even better than the authors of the Covenant had hoped. Only on disarmament did it fail. The Assembly set up Commissions to draft a treaty; the Commissions produced technical solutions for all the technical problems of reducing and limiting man-power, weapons and other war material, and military budgets.[9] The Washington Naval Conference showed how

[8] See pp. 394–397.
[9] See Parts VI and VII.

agreement could be obtained, when a Great Power gave a lead, and what beneficent results a measure of actual disarmament could bring.[10] Public opinion in every country was strongly in favour of disarmament, and grew in vehemence as the years went by. But the governments, and in particular the Governments of Britain and France, delayed too long in putting forward proposals on which a general disarmament could certainly have been made. The Geneva Disarmament Conference ultimately met in February 1932; it was not till March 1933 that the British Government laid before it a comprehensive Draft Convention which Sir Anthony Eden had prepared. There was a general consensus of opinion at the time that, if this had come at the beginning instead of at the end, the Conference could hardly have failed; " had only this laudable desire for action and contribution found earlier expression," says Mr. Wheeler-Bennett, " the history of the Disarmament Conference might have been very different." [11] But the British Government, like the French, took too long to make up its mind that disarming itself was better than allowing Germany to rearm; by the time it had done so, Hitler was in power, and the Conference was dead.

The causes for this fatal hesitation have not yet been fully sifted by historians.[12] But one factor is clear. In spite of the terrible losses of the 1914 War, in spite of their pledges to disarm, in spite of all the favourable developments discussed above, the arms race still went on. The German, Austro-Hungarian and Turkish Empires had been broken up; Russia was no menace—she was left prostrate by war, revolution, civil war, famine and disease; but the victorious Allies went on with competitive warlike preparations—against each other. The numbers of their men under arms, and their military budgets reckoned at 1914 prices, never fell below the level they had reached in 1914,

[10] See pp. 446–447.
[11] *The Disarmament Deadlock*, p. 104.
[12] For a discussion written by an eye-witness soon after the conference ended, see Noel-Baker, *Private Manufacture of Armaments*, 1937, pp. 511 *et seq.*

at the climax of the pre-war competition. They went on "improving" the quality of their arms. If budget appropriations were ever questioned in the British Parliament, Ministers (of all parties), incredible as it now seems, answered by saying that France and the United States were spending more; the French and United States legislators accepted similar replies as final. After the "Coolidge Conference" on Naval Disarmament had failed in 1927, Lord (Robert) Cecil resigned from the British Government, because he thought the United States had been treated as a rival and potential enemy.[13]

People sometimes talked as though by 1929 Britain and France had disarmed to the bone. But in December of that year—three years before Hitler came to power, and when he had only a dozen members in the Reichstag—Mr. Lloyd George, who had been a great war Prime Minister, and who understood armaments extremely well, said in the House of Commons:

> "You have, according to President Hoover, 10,000,000 more men trained to war than you had at the beginning of the late war, and you have weapons of destruction which, in number and in power, are five times more shattering than those which the whole of the armies had when they went into battle on August 4, 1914. . . . One is ashamed to be constantly reading Article 8 of the Covenant of the League of Nations— an Article drafted by the Conference. . . . Are 30,000,000 trained men the lowest figure compatible with national safety? Are scores of thousands of cannon necessary for national safety?"[14]

But, in spite of these tremendous figures, the competitive arming of the Allies was relatively restrained until 1933 by the pressure for "economy," and by the popular demand that the Disarmament Conference should succeed. After

---

[13] "It was quite wrong to treat the question as if we and the Americans were enemies, if not actual, at least possible." Lord Cecil, *All the Way*, p. 191.
[14] *Hansard*, December 4, 1929, col. 2423.

the Conference had failed, and Hitler began to set the pace, armaments in all countries expanded as never before.

TABLE IV

*Men under Arms : Army, Navy and Air Force* (thousands)

|         | 1914  | 1924   | 1932   | 1939       |
|---------|-------|--------|--------|------------|
| Britain | 397   | 349    | 316    | 460        |
| France  | 834   | 835    | 690    | 864        |
| Russia  | 1,254 | 678    | 562    | 2,269      |
| Germany | 864   | 114 [15] | 114 [15] | 1,182 [16] |
| Italy   | 345   | 359    | 324    | 1,077      |
| U.S.A.  | 165   | 251    | 237    | 551        |
| Japan   | 301   | 407    | 354    | over 900 [17] |

TABLE V

*Defence Expenditure : £ million*

|         | 1913 | 1924     | 1932 | 1939    |
|---------|------|----------|------|---------|
| Britain | 77   | 121·2    | 106  | 382·5   |
| France  | 82   | 64·2 [18] | 110  | 164     |
| Russia  | 92   | 49       | 198  | 1,575   |
| Germany | 100  | 26       | 43   | 1,000   |
| Italy   | 29   | 40·4     | 79   | 170     |
| Japan   | 12   | 40       | 54   | 107     |
| U.S.A.  | 64   | 118      | 132  | 267 [19] |

It will be noted that the total expenditure for these seven Powers was nearly £3,700m. in 1939, *i.e.*, more than eight times the total for 1913.

This time the expansion of armaments was not confined to the Great Powers. The nations of the " Little Entente " —Jugoslavia, Czechoslovakia and Rumania, all allies of France—made great increases. So did Poland, Finland,

[15] The German Forces were limited by the Treaty of Versailles.

[16] This is an estimate derived from various sources; the total for 1938 was given as 1,006,000 by the *Encyclopaedia Britannica Book of the Year*, pp. 69 and 458.

[17] 860,000 for Army and Air Force, plus the Navy.

[18] This figure is much affected by the exchange rate of the franc in 1924.

[19] No attempt has been made to relate the figures of expenditure in this and subsequent Tables to the movements of prices. For the British figures, some guidance is given by the following Treasury estimate of the value of the £ at different dates, taking the 1958 value as 20s.

|                 |                 |                 |
|-----------------|-----------------|-----------------|
| 1919: 9s. 9d.   | 1929: 7s. 6d.   | 1949: 14s. 2d.  |
| 1924: 7s. 11d.  | 1939: 7s. 4d.   | 1954: 17s. 5d.  |

the Balkan countries, and other small nations.   Switzerland, in spite of her neutrality, built up her forces; Sweden's defence expenditure went up from 125m. kronor in 1932 to 292m. in 1939—an increase of 230 per cent.   Latin America was not immune.   Chile doubled her expenditure between 1929 and 1939; Brazil and the Argentine increased theirs by two-and-a-half times.   After 1933 some self-governing members of the British Commonwealth did the same; Australia, with her eyes on Japan, trebled her expenditure between 1932 and 1939; Canada increased from $14·1m. to $34·4m.; New Zealand and South Africa quadrupled theirs.   Even so, the armaments of the Latin American and Commonwealth countries were still, by European standards, relatively low; so were those of the United States.   Most of Asia and the Middle East were still unaffected.

But this did not save them from the effects of the 1939 War, in which hostilities involved or ravaged not only the whole of Europe except Sweden, Switzerland and Portugal,[20] but also much of the Middle East, great parts of Russia, Africa and Australasia, and almost all of Asia except Siam.

## 1945 to 1958

Hitler's blitzkrieg lasted for six years, and caused casualties, devastation and atrocities far more terrible than those of the 1914 War.   Nevertheless, it has been followed by an expansion of the peacetime level of armaments incomparably more formidable, more rapid and more world-wide.   This was not the fault of the Western Governments; they sought to demobilise their forces as quickly as they could, and in the UN made very bold proposals for world disarmament. Britain reduced from over 5 million with the Colours in 1945 to 770,000 in 1949; the United States from 12

---

[20] Spain was ravaged before 1939 by the civil war, in which Hitler and Mussolini played a major part.

million in 1945 to 1·4 million in 1947. Even so, the numbers retained were nearly twice and nearly three times those which Britain and the United States had had in their forces on the eve of Hitler's war. From 1948 onwards their manpower and their armaments swiftly rose. Russia had never demobilised as the West had done. She kept 5 to 6 million men in her forces; 50,000 tanks; 20,000 aircraft; and she began the construction of a navy which, in the number of its submarines, far exceeded the combined navies of the world.

Moreover, Russia did not confine herself to maintaining a high level of armed forces. From 1946 till 1955 she frustrated the disarmament discussions of the UN. During the war she had annexed Latvia, Esthonia, Lithuania, Bessarabia, Ruthenia and part of Poland. In 1945 she occupied, and established a Communist régime in, six European countries—Poland, Eastern Germany, Hungary, Bulgaria, Rumania and Albania. She engineered a Communist *coup d'état* which added a seventh, Czechoslovakia, in 1948. She encouraged and armed the forces which made the prolonged Communist attack on Greece from 1946 to 1950. She attempted to occupy Persia, and was only prevented from doing so by the Security Council of the UN. She blockaded Berlin, hoping to drive the Western Allies out. She promoted Communist revolts in Burma, the Philippines, Indo-China, Indonesia and Malaya. Finally she launched the North Korean Communist Army in 1950 against the Republic of Korea, which the UN Assembly had set up.

Russia, therefore, bears in full measure responsibility for the armament expansion of the last twelve years. The Western Governments' programmes were a reply to her long-continued policy of open aggression and " sponsored " civil war. But this should not blind us to the immense scale of these programmes, nor to what they mean in the militarisation of the world. In the year before the 1914 War the six Great Powers of Europe spent £404m. on armaments; in a single year the United States alone is now spending nearly thirty-five times that amount.

The intensity of the arms race today is illustrated in the following tables. But, grim as these are, they show nothing of what are by far the most important, and the most sinister, changes from pre-war days, namely, the immense increase in expenditure on military research,[21] and the development of new weapons of mass destruction. These will be dealt with in the next and later chapters.

TABLE VI

*Men under Arms: Army, Navy and Air Force* (thousands)

|         | 1939  | 1949     | 1955     |
|---------|-------|----------|----------|
| Britain | 460   | 770      | 803      |
| France  | 864   | 589      | 950      |
| Russia  | 2,269 | 4,000 [22] | 4,500 [22] |
| U.S.A.  | 334   | 1,616    | 2,935    |

TABLE VII

*Defence Expenditure: £ million*

|         | 1939  | 1949      | 1955       |
|---------|-------|-----------|------------|
| Britain | 382   | 779       | 1,569      |
| France  | 164   | 380       | 1,125      |
| Russia  | 1,575 | 3,900 [23] | 9,900 [23] |
| U.S.A.  | 267   | 2,302     | 13,749     |

It will be noted that the total expenditure of the four Powers was £2,388m. in 1939, and £26,343m. in 1955. Even allowing for the change in price levels, these figures are very striking. British expenditure, in 1955, in terms of real resources, was nearly twice what it had been in 1939, on the eve of war.

TABLE VIII

*Men under Arms: Army, Navy and Air Force* (thousands)

|           | 1939  | 1949    | 1955 |
|-----------|-------|---------|------|
| Canada    | 7     | 42      | 118  |
| Australia | 12    | 34      | 51   |
| Belgium   | 125   | 74      | 140  |
| Denmark   | 15    | 16      | 41   |
| Holland   | 92·6  | 166 [24] | 135  |
| Sweden    | 54    | 99      | 115  |

[21] See Chap. 39.
[22] NATO estimate.
[23] NATO estimate.
[24] 38,000 in Dutch East Indies.

TABLE IX

*Defence Expenditure : £ million*

|         | 1939 | 1949 | 1955 |
|---------|------|------|------|
| Canada    | 8  | 92 | 676 |
| Australia | 11 | 49 | 152 |
| Belgium   | 63 | 43 | 122 |
| Norway    | 3  | 16 | 48  |
| Denmark   | 3  | 17 | 48  |
| Holland   | 25 | 64 | 160 |
| Sweden    | 16 | 63 | 149 |

## ASIA

Asia may become a new and vital factor in the arms race. Until 1939, apart from those of India and Japan, there were in that continent no armed forces of any account. That is no longer true, and the numbers of trained men and the quantity and quality of their armaments have, since 1945, rapidly increased.

There are no figures available that make it possible to draw up tables for Asia like those above. But certain facts are known. Japan has much smaller forces than she had before the war, and her people seem reluctant to rearm. But China, which was militarily negligible before 1939, now has an efficient army estimated at 5 million men, armed by Russia, and is creating an arms industry of her own.

In 1939, when India included the territories that now constitute Pakistan, her peacetime forces numbered 206,000. Today India has about 400,000 and Pakistan 250,000—a combined total of 650,000. They are well equipped with warships, aircraft, tanks and guns.

In 1939 Thailand (Siam) had forces that numbered 29,000. Today her forces number 45,000; they are trained by a United States mission, and well equipped. In 1939 Korea had no forces except the Japanese. Today the Republic of Korea (South Korea) has forces that total 700,000; they are well equipped and have been trained by a United States mission. North Korea likewise has forces of 700,000, trained and equipped by Russia. The total population of Korea, North and South, is 28 million.

In 1939 Indo-China had a few levies raised and officered by the French. Today South Viet-Nam has an army and air force that number 400,000, trained and equipped by the United States. North Viet-Nam has forces that number about 600,000, equipped by Russia, and trained and organised by the Chinese. In addition, there are smaller forces in Laos and Cambodia.

In 1939 Indonesia, the Philippines and Burma had virtually no armed forces at all. They now all have considerable armies; Indonesia has a population as numerous as Japan.

These facts show the great growth of armaments in Asia since 1945. Defence expenditure is now a heavy burden on most Asian peoples, whose standard of living is very low; but it is the large-scale training of these peoples in the methods of modern war that should concern us most. Asia has more than half the population of the world; and we should do well to remember the results of the pre-war growth of militarism, under Western stimulus and example, in Japan.

## GERMANY, ITALY AND JAPAN

In 1939, Germany, Italy and Japan were, in proportion to their populations, the most heavily armed nations in the world. Today, they are not even in the second rank of military powers. Italy has begun to play a part in NATO, but her contribution is still relatively small. Germany may have forces of 500,000 in two or three years' time. Japan's future policy remains obscure.

But nothing can be more certain than that, if the arms race continues for a few more years, these nations will re-establish their position among the leading military Powers. They will not continue to accept restrictions on their forces which other neighbouring nations do not accept. They will not consent to remain secondary Powers, without nuclear weapons, missiles and the other modern means of war.

In any estimate of the future armament situation, this inevitable development must be taken into account. And it must be remembered that the Germans and the Japanese are second to none in the large-scale administrative and organising capacity, the technical skills, and the other qualities required for modern war.

This fragmentary outline of the growth of armaments in terms of men and money is sufficiently alarming in itself. It shows how, over two generations, competitive warlike preparation, by nations great and small, has grown constantly more intense. It must be completed by a brief review of the development of the weapons and material with which the men have been equipped. This is much the most important aspect of the arms race, and much the strongest reason why it should now be stopped.

# 5

## *The Development of Weapons*

THIS chapter explains how, over two generations, weapons and equipment have become progressively more important than manpower as factors of military strength; it shows what amazing ingenuity and skill is devoted to perfecting both " modern " and " conventional " weapons; and it suggests that no disarmament treaty can be effective, unless it deals drastically, by abolition, reduction and limitation, with weapons and " war material " of every kind, and prevents their subsequent " improvement." But many important related matters are dealt with in later chapters: the power and effect of air bombing; guided and ballistic missiles; incendiary, chemical and biological weapons; and the still developing methods of nuclear war. These must necessarily be discussed with the proposals for disarmament that will be made: only a few brief preliminary remarks about them are appropriate here.

## *1884 to 1919*

The Old Testament speaks of " engines invented by cunning men to shoot arrows and great stones." [1] In New Testament days, the Romans had catapults, chariots, swords, spears, shields and helmets. Gunpowder, invented by the Chinese, but never used by them in war, was first known in Europe in the early fourteenth century. After 500 years, it had much improved the catapult artillery of the Romans. There were more guns than the Romans had; they had larger charges and longer range; they were used, not in sieges only, but in the open field. Gunpowder gave infantry the rifle, cavalry the carbine and the pistol.

[1] II Chronicles, 26, 15.

Daggers were turned into bayonets in the seventeenth century. But these were only minor changes; infantry were still deployed in the open, cavalry still charged with spears; battles and campaigns remained, till Bismarck's day, remarkably like what they had been 2,000 years before.

The success of Krupp's steel guns in the Franco-Prussian War started a revolution in the armament of land forces. In the 1880s Sir Hiram Maxim took out the patent for his machine-gun. There followed a period of intense competitive improvement of revolvers, rifles, machine-guns, guns and howitzers; a competition to increase the speed of fire, the accuracy of aim, the range, the weight, and the explosive force of the projectile. This continued without intermission until the outbreak of the 1914 War. By then land troops were much more heavily armed, especially with mobile artillery, including 8-inch and even 12-inch howitzers and guns.

During this period there was an equally active competition in naval armaments. Beginning from 1884, not only was the number of warships much increased, but also their size and speed, the calibre and range of their guns, their protective belts of armour plate. The submarine was introduced, and was sold by Sir Basil Zaharoff in quick succession, first to Greece and then to Turkey; the larger navies soon took it up. In the years immediately preceding the 1914 War, both the Triple Alliance and the Triple Entente expanded their fleets as swiftly as they could; dreadnoughts, super-dreadnoughts, cruisers, destroyers and submarines increased in power and numbers.

The 1914 War brought further big improvements in the weapons with which it began. But it also led to new weapons and methods of war: fighter aircraft, which did artillery spotting, reconnaissance, and close support for the infantry; embryo bombers; tanks; many varieties of poison gas; flame-throwers; trench mortars; the artillery barrage; and many more. It enormously multiplied the number of machine-guns, mortars, light and heavy field artillery (up to 15 inch) with which each division was equipped. Mechanical transport increased both the fire-power and the mobility of land forces. Large independent air forces were created. Warships of every class constructed during the war surpassed their predecessors in tonnage, speed and armament.

These weapons greatly added to the terrors and hardships of the fighting men, and, at sea and in the land-battle zones, of civilians as well.

## *1919 to 1945*

After the First World War, the competitive improvement in the quality of weapons continued without a break. The tonnage and gun-power of capital ships, aircraft carriers and submarines were limited, and their numbers were much reduced, by the Washington Convention of 1922[2]; but cruisers and destroyers were increased in size and were more powerfully armed. Tanks increased in weight, in capacity to travel over rough country, and in the calibre of the guns they carried; by 1932, when the Disarmament Conference met, France had two tanks of seventy tons. Aircraft, under the impulse of Lord Trenchard's principle that the " performance " of machines and pilots must be improved every year, increased in speed, range, useful load, and defensive armament.

But although they had been improved, it was still with the weapons of the 1914 War that the 1939 War began. But it was a very different kind of warfare from the start. Hitler's conception of the " blitzkrieg " was founded on the large-scale use on and behind the field of battle of bombing aircraft and great numbers of tanks. He understood this use of aircraft, and the role of tanks, better than his adversaries. Britain, for example, which produced the first tanks in 1917, had not a single armoured division in 1939; the French had 2,000 tanks, which, in spite of

2 See pp. 446–447.

General De Gaulle's appeals, they never used. It was only after Hitler had overrun the whole of Europe with his armour that Britain, Russia and the United States all produced tanks that were superior to his.

But the British and, later, the Americans, understood the general strategic conception and use of air power better than Hitler and his staff. The R.A.F. soon came to play a major part in every battle, whether by land or sea, while its strategic bombing became a most powerful factor in the general conduct of the war. The power and the performance of both fighters and bombers grew very rapidly. Aircraft virtually drove the larger naval vessels off the sea; they became the chief menace to merchant shipping, and to enemy submarines. In the later stages of the war the Nazi ground troops were greatly handicapped by being without air-cover and the German and Italian transport systems were largely destroyed or paralysed. The weight of the largest bomb used by the Allies increased to ten tons—the " Berlin block-buster."

But besides the development of the 1914–19 weapons, the 1939 War also brought the introduction of new weapons of many kinds. The scientists were called in to help in great numbers. They were given great resources [3]; and they produced astonishing results. Incendiary bombs were used on towns and cities; the new Tabun gases were discovered, and produced in large quantities, although not used; radar and electronics were put to many uses; magnetic mines, rockets and guided missiles were employed. With his pilotless aircraft, the V 1, and his ballistic missile, the V 2, Hitler made the first beginning in a new kind of war. Finally, in 1945, came the first atomic bombs.

Some of these new weapons were plainly inconsistent with what had been till 1939 the accepted principles of the laws of war. But even more striking was the unbridled ferocity with which the older " conventional " weapons were employed, first by Hitler and Mussolini, and then by

[3] See Chap. 39.

the Western Allies in reply.  The British Draft Disarmament Convention of 1933 had embodied the "established rules of International Law" described in Chapter 12, which forbade the indiscriminate sinking of merchant ships by submarines, the use of all incendiary weapons, and of all bombing from the air.[4]  Exactly ten years later, in reprisal for Hitler's bombing of Coventry, London and other towns, the R.A.F. burnt Hamburg to the ground; and thereafter the destruction of towns and cities by aerial bombardment, and in particular by fire, remained a normal method of warfare on both sides.  40,000 British seamen lost their lives from submarine attack (12,000 in the 1914 War); almost the whole of the German, Italian and Japanese commercial fleets were sunk by submarines or aircraft.

## *1945 to 1958*

No less striking was the fact that when the war was over these methods of warfare were accepted as normal and conventional by all governments and staffs.  Aerial bombardment and the use of fire marked the operations in Korea and Indo-China from the first day to the last.  Everyone assumes that submarines would now be used as Hitler used them.  The "established rules of International Law" have perished in the flames of war.

All governments and General Staffs have also assumed that, if world war broke out again, the most dangerous new weapons of the 1939 War, missiles and nuclear bombs, would be used as they were used by Hitler and at Hiroshima and Nagasaki in 1945.  This, together with the development and recognition as "conventional" of poison gas, incendiary and biological weapons,[5] has been the main feature of the arms race since 1945.

Since 1945 the scientists have been given far greater resources than they had ever had, even during the 1939

[4] *Conference Documents*, Vol. II, pp. 476 *et seq.*
[5] See pp. 316–319.

War. In consequence, there has been a development of weapons which makes the achievements even of that war pale into insignificance. It has not been confined to Russia and the United States, as is sometimes believed. Britain has made major advances in aircraft carriers, field artillery, anti-submarine weapons, H-bombs, and other things. Belgium has produced a new and much improved rifle. France has developed a new machine-gun; high-grade supersonic aircraft; missiles; and what *The Times* Correspondent called " an impressive range of new equipment," by which she " staked a bold claim for export markets." [6] Canada has produced an anti-tank weapon which fires a projectile generating such heat that it burns its way through heavy armour, and a hit almost anywhere on a tank destroys it.

Other nations, too, have been striving to develop new weapons and to improve the weapons that exist. A few examples will serve to show what astonishing achievements, in every branch of armament, have been made since 1945.[7]

## ARMY WEAPONS AND EQUIPMENT

*Rifles*

Constant research and development since 1945 produced the Belgian F.N. It weighs 9·2 lbs.; it fires a ·300 inch round; it can fire sixty single-aimed shots per minute from 20-round magazines, and has an automatic fire rate of 700 rounds a minute. In all these regards it is much superior to any rifle used in the 1939 War. After extended trials against the British E.M.2 rifle, it was adopted as the standard weapon for the ground forces of the fourteen NATO Powers. It costs approximately £30.[8] To re-equip their forces with this rifle, the NATO governments would have to spend scores of millions of pounds in the next few

---

[6] *The Times*, June 18, 1956.
[7] Almost all these examples relate to advances made by the Western Powers. Those made on the Russian side receive much less publicity but it may be assumed that they are no less far-reaching.
[8] M.G., January 20, 1954. *Hansard*, February 1, 1954, cols. 39–108.

years. Since it was adopted, a United States firm has produced another weapon, the T 44, which is 1 lb. lighter, has a higher rate of fire, and the bullets from which " will penetrate a steel helmet at 1,200 yards." [9]   The United States have adopted this rifle instead of the F.N.

## Mobile Guns

The most remarkable new gun produced since 1945 was probably the United States Army anti-aircraft weapon, the " Skysweeper." It fired a 75 mm. 12 lb. shell at the rate of forty-five a minute; it was " in effect an artillery machine-gun." [10]   It could pick up, and follow, a target fifteen miles away; it could destroy an aircraft at a distance of four miles. It was " equipped to fire both proximity and percussion fuses; the former detonate electronically when they get within lethal distance of the target, the latter on impact." [11] The Skysweeper, for the first time, combined in one unit the gun, radar and predictor; previously they were three cumbersome entities. It was claimed in 1954 that the Skysweeper could " certainly cope with any existing jet aircraft." It was a marvel of ingenuity, and it rendered obsolete the previous AA weapons of its class. Each gun cost £112,000. It is now obsolete itself.

## Tanks

The tank has had a curious history. A British inventor designed a tank in 1907; the War Office filed his drawings away with the simple minute: " The man's mad." Sir Winston Churchill forced the Army to accept it in the 1914 War; it was used with success in the 1918 campaign. Between the wars British arms firms made big improvements in its mobility, armour and gun-power. During the 1939 War more powerful types were evolved; and further

---

[9] N.Y.T., May 2, 1957.
[10] *The Times* Military Correspondent, August 14, 1954.
[11] M.G., June 30, 1954.

big improvements have been made since then. Nevertheless, it is a matter of dispute whether tanks are not already
out of date. Brigadier C. N. Barclay wrote in 1953:

> " Anti-tank weapons and devices have improved to
> a considerably greater extent than the tank's ability to
> counter them. . . . The tank is in much the same
> position as the cavalry man was in 1914 . . . and the
> battleship in 1939 . . . (it) remains a major weapon
> of war, but its position is seriously challenged and its
> future in dispute." [12]

Its future is also menaced by napalm and by the so-called
" tactical " atomic missile or shell. But it is still in large
demand. In 1954 there were more than five times as many
tanks in infantry divisions as during the 1939 War.[13] In
1957 the Dutch Army, for example, decided to form eleven
tank battalions equipped with 600 heavy tanks.[14] In the
case of tanks, as of other weapons, competition leads to a
continuous growth in power, as in cost. In May 1954 the
United States Army " took the wraps off " the long-secret
T 43 Heavy Tank. It weighs sixty tons; mounts a 120 mm.
(4·8 inch) high velocity gun, said to be " the greatest firepower ever placed on a United States tank." It is officially
described as the United States Army's " answer to Russia's
57-ton heavy." [15]

In 1955 the British Royal Armoured Corps demonstrated the Centurion's successor, the Conqueror, which, it
is claimed,

> " outguns any other fighting vehicle in the world. . . .
> The agility tests, in which all the types of vehicles are
> driven up and down the steepest imaginable gradients,
> over a knife-edged obstacle, and in and out of ditches,
> are always an exciting feature of the day's displays.

[12] *British Army Quarterly*, October 1953.
[13] Mr. Robert Stevens, U.S. Secretary of the Army, N.Y.T., September 22,
1954.
[14] N.Y.H.T., May 3, 1957.
[15] N.Y.T., May 13, 1954.

. . . The Conqueror showed itself most remarkably agile, for all its immense bulk; even more so than the smaller Centurion which won such renown in the Korean War." [16]

As early as 1952 the United States Army were testing robot tanks which are "remote-controlled," manoeuvre, aim and fire with no human crew inside; new track and wheel vehicles with bullet-proof plastic turrets which "go many places a mountain goat cannot "; and heavy armoured vehicles which can be taken apart and transported in sections by air. These new vehicles "have only the most casual resemblance to comparable equipment used in World War II." [17]

### Anti-Tank Weapons

*The Times* Correspondent reports in 1955 that the French guided anti-tank rockets, the " SS 10 " and " Entac," " seemed like a glimpse into a somewhat disquieting future." At the press of a button, the bomb-shaped projectile leaped

"horizontally from a simple metal container and skimmed, driven by a small buzzing blue flame in its rear, across fields and hedgerows like a giant hornet until, apparently infallibly, it reached and demolished its target. It took only three projectiles to knock out a line of three moving tanks a mile away." [18]

### Army Transport

The prospect of attack by nuclear weapons has led the General Staffs to consider new plans for mobilisation, troop-transport and supply. It is thought that the old system of large-scale depots, railway and road transport convoys might be useless; helicopters and transport aircraft must play a much greater part. [19] The French have a jet

16 *The Times*, May 12, 1955.
17 Ansel Talbert, N.Y.H.T., March 8, 1952.
18 *The Times*, June 18, 1955.
19 Press Conference by Secretary of State for War, Rt. Hon. A. Head, August 4, 1954.

helicopter, the " Djinn "—a two-seater machine, which moves by "spouting compressed air from the tips of its twin rotor blades."

> "It gave a breathless display of manoeuvrability, leaping as though released by a spring vertically into the air, and skimming at a high speed behind trees and bushes a few feet only from the ground." [20]

This machine went into quantity production in April 1956.

Mr. Stevens, the Secretary of the United States Army, said in 1954 that the helicopter is perhaps already "the greatest single advance in military equipment since World War II." [21]

## Radar

The United States Army have developed a method of using radar to detect the source of enemy mortar-fire during ground combat.

> "An electronic locator known as ' counter-mortar radar' gives front line Army troops the capability of discovering the path of enemy mortar shells, automatically tracking their trajectory and obtaining range data on the enemy unit firing the mortar. The exact position of the enemy is relayed to an ' artillery fire direction centre,' which immediately responds with accurately aimed fire destroying the enemy position." [22]

Early models of the radar locator helped to halt a major enemy offensive in Korea, during the closing stages of the war.

## Television

In a United States Army exercise in 1955, television was employed to enable the commander of the attacking forces to direct the operations of an amphibious assault.

[20] *The Times*, June 18, 1955.
[21] N.Y.H.T., September 22, 1954.
[22] N.Y.H.T., December 13, 1954.

" An L20 Beaver observation plane with two television cameras aboard patrolled over the beach-head.
The views it picked up were relayed by radio to half
a dozen receiving stations on the ground and to the
invasion command ship, the *Mount Olympus*. The
idea is to give the nerve centres of a military operation
a quicker and broader view of developments than they
could get from verbal reports. . . . Observers in the
command centres kept in constant radio contact with
the camera units, telling them what they wanted to
see." [23]

## NAVAL ARMAMENTS

### Aircraft Carriers

It is the accepted doctrine of the British and United
States Navies that the aircraft carrier has replaced the battleship and battle-cruiser as the " capital ship " of the Fleet.
The British Admiralty favour carriers of medium size.   In
1953 a new *Hermes* was launched—the third carrier of that
name, and the first to include " the three British inventions,
the angled deck, the steam catapult and the landing mirror
device." [24]   She is 18,300 tons; has a speed of 30 knots; a
complement of 1,400 men.   At her launching, the First
Lord said:

" Her flight deck is larger than a football field; her
distillery plant is sufficient for most small towns; her
generators could supply 10,000 homes without fear of
power-cuts, and two games of badminton could be
played on the after-lift." [25]

The United States Navy believe in bigger carriers.   The
first " modern " carrier in the United States Fleet was the
*Forrestal*, commissioned in 1956.   When fully loaded with
oil, aviation spirit, water, etc., the *Forrestal* displaces 75 to
80,000 tons—that is, she may be the biggest ship, naval or

23 Gladwin Hill, N.Y.T., March 22, 1955.
24 First Lord's Memorandum 1955–56.   Cmd. 9396, para. 9, p. 4.
25 *The Times*, February 17, 1953.

commercial, in the world. Her flight deck is so big that the Atlantic liners, the *Queen Mary* and the *Queen Elizabeth*, could be placed side by side on it, with room to spare. Her engines deliver more than 200,000 h.p.; they could supply enough electricity for a city of 1·5 million population. She has a greatly strengthened under-water hull, and 1,240 watertight compartments. The height from her keel to her masthead is 187 feet—higher than Niagara Falls. The masts are hinged, to enable her to pass under bridges. She has eight 5-inch AA radar controlled guns; an armoured and angled flight deck [26]; 100 aircraft of the latest jet design; she can launch thirty-two fighter-planes in four minutes. Her crew will vary from 3,500 to 3,800. She cost $220 million. The United States Navy plan to build ten aircraft carriers of this class.

## Guided Weapon Vessels

It is now generally agreed that the old type of cruiser will be replaced by vessels designed or adapted for launching guided missiles. The First Lord said in his Memorandum on the Estimates for 1955–56:

" . . . The guided weapon ship is revolutionary, and will, we believe, effect changes in certain types of naval warfare comparable to that once brought about by the introduction of the Dreadnought." [27]

The first United States " Missile Warship," the heavy cruiser *Boston*, was completed in November 1955. Her missiles have a range of twenty miles, travel at a speed of 1,700 m.p.h., and " home " on to their target. Four missiles can be fired in 8/10ths of a second; the launchers can be reloaded twice a minute.[28]

Guided weapon ships will be much more expensive than the old type of cruiser.

[26] Hanson Baldwin, N.Y.T., December 15, 1954.
[27] Cmd. 9396, p. 5.
[28] N.Y.H.T., November 2, 1955.

## Other Surface Vessels

Naval authorities are agreed that besides large numbers of conventional destroyers, minesweepers and frigates, various other surface vessels are required. They will include radar-warning and sonar-warning ships, to form a " picket-line " across the oceans; Tactical Command ships, like the *U.S.S. Northampton*, a transformed heavy cruiser, which, instead of 8-inch guns, carries an immense radio and radar installation to enable her commander to control the operations of a naval force at sea [29]; " drone launchers "; radio-controlled robot assault vessels; and " submersibles," capable of travelling at high speed both on the surface, and when submerged. These submersibles will be equipped to launch guided missiles and to carry fighter-planes. [30]

## Submarines

But most naval authorities are agreed that the most important single naval ship may be the submarine. Mr. Hanson Baldwin says that it " may be the capital ship of tomorrow's navy." [31] It has the supreme advantage that it can travel unseen by hostile aircraft; and modern developments have greatly increased its power. The United States *Nautilus* (3,400 tons) was the first warship to be propelled by atomic power. She carries heavy shielding to protect her crew from radiation; her speed, when submerged, is over twenty knots; she has cruised 60,000 miles without refuelling and 12,000 miles without surfacing; and she can cruise under the polar ice caps. She is armed with the Regulus guided missile, a surface-to-surface weapon which is 32 feet long, weighs seven tons and is in the high subsonic range of speed, [32] and with torpedoes. When she was launched in 1954, *The Times* Special Correspondent reported

---

[29] Brassey's *Annual*, 1953, p. 142.
[30] Hanson Baldwin, *The Price of Power*, pp. 97–98 and 197.
[31] *Loc. cit.*, p. 97.
[32] Announced by Mr. Smith, Assistant Secretary of the Navy for Air, N.Y.T., June 13, 1954.

that "many United States Navy men believe that the *Nautilus* at once makes all other warships obsolescent." [33]

Atomic power has three immense advantages for submarines; 1 lb. of nuclear fuel produces the energy of 5,900 barrels of oil; this nuclear fuel requires no oxygen; the deeper the submarine goes, the faster it can travel. [34]

Atomic-powered submarines will be used in various ways: to attack enemy surface shipping; as a "radar picket" ship [35]; to tow a train of submersibles, perhaps carrying troops for an amphibious landing, under the sea [36]; above all, to launch nuclear missiles, and this without having to come to the surface themselves. [37]

The development of the *Nautilus* cost the United States Government about $150 million [38]; the vessel itself cost $55 million. It is three times as expensive as an ordinary submarine and it costs three times as much to maintain.

A flying submarine has been designed by the United States aircraft designer, Mr. Northrop, who built the U.S.A.F.'s Scorpion jet interceptor. It is to travel under the sea, come to the surface, take off from water-skis, and fly in the air until its pilot desires to go under water again. [39]

## Anti-Submarine Weapons

A British anti-submarine weapon is the "Limbo." Electronic machines calculate the angle at which its big barrels should fire its bombs, and the depth at which the bombs should explode. It is said to be extremely accurate. [40]

## AIR ARMAMENTS

General Prentiss has shown in graphic form how military aircraft had improved between 1920 and 1948. The

[33] *The Times,* January 22, 1954.
[34] Hanson Baldwin, N.Y.T., July 21, 1955.
[35] Wm. Conklin, N.Y.T., August 24, 1955.
[36] N.Y.H.T., October 30, 1955.
[37] Senator Clinton Anderson, reported in *The Times,* March 25, 1955.
[38] Peter Kihss, N.Y.T., March 31, 1955.
[39] Ansel Talbert, N.Y.H.T., November 8, 1955.
[40] *The Times* Naval Correspondent, July 27, 1956.

maximum speed of an aircraft had increased by twelve
times since 1920; the maximum range by fifty times since
1925; the maximum bomb load by seventy times since
1928.[41]

They have gone on improving since 1948; the specifica-
tions issued for each " next generation " by the Air Staffs
are more and more severe. " Armament research is
developing so rapidly," said an important manufacturer in
1955, " that aircraft are obsolescent before they can come
off the assembly line." [42]

A few details of recent types will give a rough idea of
present aircraft, and of changes still to come. Most of them
are taken from United States sources; the United States
authorities release information more freely than do air
authorities elsewhere.

### Bombers

The best known bombers used in the latter stages of
the 1939 War were the British Lancaster, the United States
B.17 Flying Fortress and B.29. The Lancaster, with a
speed of 250 m.p.h. and a range of over a thousand miles,
could carry the 10-ton " block-buster." This was a big step
forward from the end of the 1914 War, when the extreme
range was 170 miles, and the bomb load less than half a
ton.

The B.52, the present United States heavy bomber,
weighs 185 tons, has a maximum speed of over 600
m.p.h.,[43] and can carry eleven tons for 6,000 miles. Refuelled in the air, it can deliver a load of nuclear bombs to
any target in the world and return to its base in the United
States. It costs $8 million.[44] The B.52's successor, the
B.58, called the " Hustler," reverses the trend to bigger
and bigger bombers; its weight is only 80 tons. But its

---

[41] Gen. Augustin M. Prentiss, *Civil Defence in Modern War*, p. 21. This most
valuable book was published in 1951.

[42] Vice-President of the Ford Instrument Co., N.Y.T., March 30, 1955.

[43] *Jane's All the World's Aircraft*, 1954–55, p. 215.

[44] See note on next page.

speed is almost twice the speed of sound, and " its naviga-
tion and bombing controls are centred in an electronic
brain," which is said to have " ten times the accuracy of
previous equipment with about two-thirds the weight." [45]

## Fighters

The present operational jet fighter aircraft, like the
British Hunter, " are pushing up against the sound
barrier "; that is, they travel at over 600 m.p.h.  To
penetrate the sound barrier they must employ a horse-
power several times greater than the Hunter can carry.
Hitherto this has given an advantage to a modern bomber
like the B.52, which is also " pushing up against the sound
barrier."  Both fighter and bomber have been therefore

> " restricted to virtually the same speed, with some slight
> advantage in favour of the fighter, but not enough to
> make it practical to indulge in a long, stern chase." [46]

But the fighters are forging ahead.  The United States
Navy have a supersonic jet fighter designed to operate from
aircraft carriers—the XF.8U.1.  It is largely made of
titanium, a strong light-weight metal; its speed will much
exceed 700 miles an hour.  Although an interceptor plane,
" *it will be able to carry atomic weapons.*"  It has undergone a series of successful tests.[47]  A prototype French
fighter, the So.9000 Trident, " burst through the sound
barrier . . . with rocket assistance, *in the course of a climb,*
from which it levelled out at a speed well above that of

[44] President Eisenhower said in 1953:
　　"The cost of one modern heavy bomber is this: a modern brick school
in more than thirty cities.
　　"It is: two electric power plants, each serving a town of 60,000
population.
　　"It is two fine fully equipped hospitals.
　　"It is some fifty miles of concrete highway.
　　"We pay for a single fighter plane with half a million bushels of wheat.
　　"We pay for a single destroyer with new homes that could have housed
more than 8,000 people."  Address to the American Society of Newspaper
Editors, April 16, 1953.
[45] N.Y.T., July 11, 1957.
[46] Air Chief Marshal Sir Ralph Cochrane, *The Listener,* September 16, 1954.
[47] N.Y.T., June 21, 1955.

sound." It has a single Viper jet engine, assisted by rocket propulsion, and is made by the French nationalised company, S.N.C.A.S.O.[48] The improved version of the Russian fighter, the Yak 25, known to Western military men as the " Farmer," is believed to be capable of 900 m.p.h.[49]

In 1956 the U.S.A.F. gave the F.104 Starfighter its first public demonstration. General Weyland, Commander of the Tactical Air Force, told the reporters that it was " envisaged as giving the United States a commanding lead in air power." It is " A tube of metal wrapped around a powerful new jet engine, with hardly more than a suggestion of wings and a snug cockpit far out on its pointed nose." Its engine develops 60,000 horse-power. It only weighs 6½ tons, less than half the weight of most fighters. It is built for a top speed of 1,320 to 1,400 m.p.h.; it can cruise at 50,000 feet; " it climbs at a rate of something like 40,000 feet a minute." It was scheduled for service " in the near future." It was " designed to attack invading bombers and fighters over battle areas, as the Sabre jet did in eight-mile high combat with MIG planes in Korea." [50]

## Supersonic Fighter Techniques

For some years the U.S.A.F. have practised a technique for fighters that do more than 1,000 feet a second, *i.e.*, over 600 m.p.h. It is called " thunderbolt geometry," because " at such speeds the rate of closure is so fast that the aircraft must be lined up on the objective and combat action started as much as thirty miles off." This manoeuvre, said General Chidlaw, " is much faster than a pistol shot." It is made possible by airborne and ground radar and electrical computers.[51]

[48] *The Times*, May 3, 1955.
[49] *The Times*, June 25, 1956.
[50] N.Y.H.T., April 17, 1956.
[51] *The Times*, April 21, 1955.

*Fighter-Bombers*

The fighter-bomber is thought of as a small single-seater aircraft, of light " unladen weight " and short range, used as a tactical weapon close to a battle on the ground.

The United States single-seater F.84.F. Thunderstreak weighs twelve tons; its maximum speed is " more than 650 m.p.h."—in an air display in Norfolk it did 720 m.p.h.; its combat radius is more than 1,000 miles, but it can also be transported " under the belly " of a B.36, and so add indefinitely to its range; it can also be refuelled in the air; its operational ceiling is " over 45,000 feet." It carries six ·50 machine guns for self-defence. Its " useful load " is three tons of bombs, rockets or tanks of napalm—*more than the load of the B.17 Flying Fortress* of the last war. Further, it can, and does, " carry atomic weapons that have much greater explosive power than the bombs that wrecked Hiroshima and Nagasaki." [52]

The U.S.A.F. F.84 Thunderjet has been modernised so that it can now be launched by rocket propulsion from a lorry-vehicle about as large as that which hauls the United States atomic cannon. The launching platform is only 39 feet long. The Thunderjet is a fighter, but it can carry two half-ton bombs or thirty-two 5-inch rockets.

*" Mother " Aircraft and Fighters*

In 1955 the U.S.A.F. announced the formation of the first unit of fighters capable of being carried, launched and recovered in flight by heavy bombers.

*Flying L.S.T.*

There is now a flying L.S.T. to help in amphibious operations. The Convair R.3Y2 lands on the water, unfolds a ramp, and unloads guns, trucks, supplies and an assault force.[53]

[52] Mr. Hanson Baldwin, N.Y.T., February 11, 1955.
[53] N.Y.T., June 12, 1954, published a photograph of this aircraft.

## Transport Aircraft

The transport plane. C.130A Hercules, is a turbine-propeller aircraft, which flies at nearly 400 m.p.h. It can carry ninety infantrymen to the front, convert to a hospital plane in a few minutes, and fly back with seventy stretcher cases. It can drop a load of twenty tons of arms. It can carry a 5,000-gallon petrol trailer; a 29-passenger omnibus; or a six-ton 6·1 inch howitzer with its 13-ton tractor.[54] The United States staff were not satisfied with this performance; they wanted a plane with a load of fifty tons, a speed of 500 m.p.h., and a range of 1,500 to 3,000 miles. Nine such aircraft could do the work of fifty-eight C.124 Globemasters, which were still in use as late as 1955; and they could do it at one-third the cost, and in less than half the time.[55]

## DEVELOPMENT OF WEAPONS OF MASS DESTRUCTION SINCE 1945

The above examples of weapon development since 1945 have been deliberately chosen from the ordinary conventional armaments, which most people take for granted. They are only a small selection from a great number that could have been given. They are intended to impress on the reader the fact that, even in conventional weapons, there has never been, in any similar period of years, either in peace-time *or in war*, anything approaching the present scale or rapidity of progress. The progress, moreover, has

[54] N.Y.T., June 11, 1955.
[55] N.Y.T., December 17, 1954.

The general rise in the standard of aircraft and in the complication of the equipment they now require is illustrated by the following Table of the cost of British aircraft since the 1914 war.

| *Fighters* | | £ | *Bombers* | | £ |
|---|---|---|---|---|---|
| 1917 | Sopwith Camel | 1,650 | 1918 | D.H. Day bomber | 3,845 |
| 1935 | Gladiator | 8,400 | 1939 | Wellington IA | 21,900 |
| 1945 | Spitfire VIII | 12,000 | 1945 | Lancaster | 42,000 |
| 1954 | Hunter | 70,000 | 1952 | Canberra (Light B'er) | 100,000 |
| 1957 | Javelin | 120,000 | 1955 | Valiant (Medium ,, ) | 600,000 |

much increased the speed, " agility " and fire-power of conventional weapons; that is to say, it has increased their *offensive* power, and thus tipped the balance of advantage still further to attack against defence. This point is important to the later argument of this book.[56]

But while he considers this astonishing development of conventional weapons since 1945, the reader must also remember that, during the whole of this period, the main effort of all the leading military powers has been devoted, not to this class of armament at all, but to the weapons of mass-destruction: strategic and tactical nuclear weapons of many kinds; poison gas, incendiary bombs and liquids; biological weapons and missiles. The progress made since 1945 with these " modern " methods of warfare completely dwarfs what has been done with conventional arms, and the rate of progress, already terrifying, is still growing *more* rapid and not *less*.[57] Together they have already, since the end of Hitler's War, multiplied the destructive power of the armed forces by a factor of many thousands.

These developments can be more appropriately described in later sections of this book. The present chapter is intended to establish at the outset two main propositions in the reader's mind: first, that no disarmament treaty will be worth while which does not deal drastically with the conventional weapons above described and also prevent competition in their " improvement " after the treaty has been made; secondly, that while the competition in conventional armaments remains as great a danger as it was half a century ago, and while these armaments still absorb a surprisingly high proportion of the resources which governments devote to their warlike preparations, they are nevertheless becoming of less and less importance, and might well be of no use or significance at all, if the weapons of mass-destruction were ever used in war.

[56] See Chap. 33.
[57] See Part II, Chaps. 10–13, and Part V.

The competition in these "modern" weapons has become a mortal peril to mankind, the horror and urgency of which no language can express. There is only one means by which it can be stopped: an all-round disarmament treaty, bringing really drastic reductions and abolitions, under stringent and effective international control.

# 6

# *The Arms Race:*
# *A Cause of War?*

ARMAMENTS now cost the British people, on the average, £150 per annum for each family of five. This is the direct lowering of the standard of living which they involve. Immense sums are spent on military research.[1] If the scientists and technicians engaged on this work could be diverted from "improving" armaments to peaceful industrial, agricultural and medical research, and if they were given the same equipment and resources that they have today, their achievements might quite quickly revolutionise man's individual and social life.

But the economic case for disarmament will not be further argued. In the early stages of the arms race people used to say that armament expansion was "good for trade." Now everybody agrees that that is nonsense, and every reader knows, from his own experience, the cost of the use of armaments in war, and the heavy burden they impose in peace. For this reason, the economic case will be taken as proved.

The political case for disarmament is another matter. It has been highly controversial in the past; there is much wider agreement about it now; but a brief statement of the argument is, none the less, required.

## *The Arms Race as a Contributory Cause of War*

There were many contributory causes which together led to the smaller wars and to the two world wars which happened in the epoch with which this book deals.

[1] See Part VII, Chap. 39.

Before 1914, there were the nationalism of subject peoples in central and southern Europe, and their hope of throwing off the German, Austrian, Russian or Turkish yoke; the French desire to recover Alsace-Lorraine; the scramble for colonies in Africa and Asia; the belief that conquest brought glory, strength and trade; the fatalist acceptance of the view that war was an inevitable fact of human life.

Before 1939, there were the United States withdrawal from the League; the sustained hostility of militarist interests in many countries to the League, to disarmament and to all organised international co-operation; the disastrous treatment of Weimar Germany by the Western Allies before Hitler came to power; the financing and popularising of the Nazi movement by the German arms firms, and their propaganda in the newspapers and other media which they bribed or bought; the misery caused by the world economic slump of 1929, and the consequent collapse of democratic governments in Germany and elsewhere; the attempt of the Japanese militarists, beginning in Manchuria in 1931, to carve out an Empire on the mainland of Asia; Mussolini's war in Abyssinia; the advent of a madman to supreme power in Germany; and many other contributory influences and events too numerous to mention.

But throughout the whole period there was also the arms race. The arms race was not the *sole* cause of war; but it was a powerful and constant contributory cause. In many ways, direct and indirect, it stimulated or fostered militarist, Fascist and Nazi movements, and made their appeal effective. It influenced governments both in their general policy, and at moments of crisis. Above all, it kept alive the anachronistic idea that wars were inevitable.

Innumerable examples could be given of how, as the result of the arms race, General Staffs came to exercise an undue influence on general policy in normal times, and on great decisions at moments of crisis; of how rival alliances, which were the concomitant of the arms race, militated against the maintenance of a stable peace; of how competitive military advantage became the dominating consideration in almost every issue of international affairs; of how the pressure of armaments and the principle of " my ally right or wrong " undermined the new system of the Rule of Law, to which, after 1919, all governments were committed, and on which the hope of an ordered international society depended, then, as now. A few illustrations, out of many, must suffice.

As the arms race grew keener before 1914, each Power hoped that its allies would increase their military preparations; and strange devices were sometimes adopted to accomplish this result. The French General Staff insisted on the making of a large loan to Russia, and then insisted that the loan should be used by Russia to re-equip the Russian Army, and to build strategic railways to the German frontier.[2] This was an unfortunate enterprise for all concerned. The French investors lost everything they had lent. The re-equipment of the Russian Army and the building of the railways had not been completed when war broke out in 1914; but the very fact that these measures had been begun gave the German General Staff a powerful argument for striking then. While the Russian loan was being raised in France, the Russians bribed the Paris Press to support the passage of the French Government's Three-Year National Service Bill.[3] In such ways, the existence of the alliances increased the pressure and the pace of the arms race, while gradually the arms race came to dominate the whole character of the alliances. In the end, the alliances became a contributory factor which made it harder to prevent the war, and ensured that, if war broke out, most of Europe would be involved.

This was proved disastrously in 1914. As the result of the arms race, all the major governments of Europe had come to think that, sooner or later, war was certain. But so far as the political leaders were concerned, few or none

[2] G. Lowes Dickinson, *The International Anarchy*, p. 44.      [3] *Ibid.*

of them *wanted* it to happen. They " stumbled and staggered into war," as Mr. Lloyd George said when it was over. But the General Staffs, in Austria and Germany, had other ideas.

" The Russian General Staff was not indeed ready to fight and would have preferred to put off war as long as possible. The German, on the other hand, was convinced that delay would add to the strength of Russia " (the railways and equipment referred to above) " so that in 1914 it was a case of ' now or never.' The practice of Frederick and Napoleon, the theory of Clausewitz, urged them to strike. *And the Kaiser and the political governors of Germany found it impossible to resist the General Staff*. When Austria-Hungary determined to strike against Serbia, there was no hope left. *Politicians might talk and protest, but the General Staffs, alike in Russia, in Germany and in Austria-Hungary, were in the saddle. They clapped in their spurs and thus Europe found itself at war in 1914.*" [4]

Between the wars, both the French and German General Staffs had great influence, often openly exercised, and often clandestine, through their connections with the powerful private arms interests and the organs of the Press, radio and cinema which these interests controlled.[5] The French Staff consistently opposed all policies favourable to the League; sent officers to Geneva to obstruct disarmament; during the Manchurian and Abyssinian crises exercised their influence to the utmost against the policy of upholding the Covenant; and on Hitler's and Mussolini's aggressions in Spain, Czechoslovakia, Austria and Albania, gave the worst possible advice. If France had followed a strong League policy from 1919 onwards, history might have been different.

But the German Staff were still more clearly responsible for some of the developments that led to the 1939 War.

[4] Grant and Temperley, *Europe in the 19th Century*, p. 538.
[5] See P. J. Noel-Baker, *Private Manufacture of Armaments, passim*.

For nearly fourteen years after the Peace Treaty, the demo-
cratically elected governments of Germany adhered, though
with ever-growing reluctance, to the policy of " fulfilment,"
*i.e.*, of carrying out the Treaty of Versailles, including its
provisions for German disarmament.   For most of those
years it was quite plain that the great mass of working-
class Germans accepted this policy.   But the German
General Staff never accepted it at all.   Disbelieving in,
and detesting, general disarmament, they sought to
" strengthen " Germany by every practicable evasion of the
treaty.[6]   They encouraged, and with the help of the armament magnates, they *financed* the para-military organisa-
tions—the Stahlhelm and the Nazi Storm Troops—who in
the end brought Hitler into power.   Hitler himself they
paid and used,[7] until he made himself their master, to their
ruin and his.   As before 1914, they gained such power and
used it so ill, that the fear of the military caste is still very
much alive in Germany today.   In August 1956, Mr. Jäger,
the Chairman of the Bundestag Defence Committee, found
it necessary to explain in public that " great efforts were
being made to prevent the Army from again asserting itself
as a State within a State." [8]

The most striking single example between the Wars of
the effect of competitive armament preparation was the
policy of the French and British Governments over Mussolini's aggression in Abyssinia in 1935.   Both were deeply
pledged to their peoples to uphold the Covenant, and the
British Foreign Secretary, Sir S. Hoare (Lord Templewood),
made a speech in the League Assembly in which he said:

> " The League stands, and my country stands with
> it, for the collective maintenance of the Covenant in
> its entirety, and particularly for steady and collective
> resistance to all acts of unprovoked aggression." [9]

[6] See Chap. 43.
[7] See Thyssen, *I Paid Hitler, passim.*   P. J. Noel-Baker, *Private Manufacture of Armaments, passim.*
[8] *The Times*, August 30, 1956.
[9] September 11, 1935, L.N. *Official Journal*, Supplement 138, p. 46.

As a result certain economic sanctions were imposed by League Members against Italy; just when they were producing their effect, Britain and France proposed that they should be removed. The " real reason " for this action, says Dr. G. P. Gooch, " was our fear that opposition would drive him [Mussolini] into Hitler's arms." [10] The two Governments wanted Mussolini as an ally against Germany. In that hope, they betrayed their pledges under the Covenant, and thus sounded the death-knell of the League. The folly of their action in abandoning the instrument they had created to stop aggression has been frequently denounced by Sir Winston Churchill.[11] As an exercise in power politics it reaped the reward it deserved. Mussolini knew very well that Britain and France could have united the League against him, and could thus have defeated his aggression; by their surrender to him, and their disruption of the League, they convinced him that he could safely join Hitler, with hopes of expanding his " empire," at the expense of Britain and France. This is, perhaps, the supreme example of how competitive armament preparation undermines the policy of establishing the Rule of Law in international affairs.

But it is also an example of what has been throughout two generations the most dangerous result of the arms race —the mounting fear or " tension " which it creates. The remainder of this chapter will be given to statements by eminent authorities, made before and after the two World Wars, showing how the arms race helped to make people believe that war was inevitable, and thus ultimately helped to cause its outbreak.

## WARNINGS BEFORE 1914

In the " Rescript " in which the Czar of Russia proposed the first Hague Conference in 1898, he said:

[10] *Studies in Diplomacy and Statecraft*, p. 199.
[11] *e.g.*, *Hansard*, October 5, 1938, cols. 359 *et seq*.

*" In proportion as the armaments of each Power increase, so do they less and less fulfil the object which the Governments have set before themselves. . . . It appears evident that if this state of things were prolonged, it would inevitably lead to the very cataclysm which it is desired to avert, and the horrors of which make every thinking man shudder in advance."* [12]

In 1909, when the competition between Britain and Germany had seriously begun, the British Foreign Secretary, Sir Edward (Lord) Grey, told the House of Commons that " the naval rivalry was the only obstacle to confidence " between Britain and Germany.

*" If I were asked,"* he said, *" to name the one thing which would reassure Europe with regard to the prospects of peace, I think it would be that the naval expenditure in Germany would be diminished, and that ours was following suit."* [13]

Unfortunately Tirpitz had become too powerful by now; he was constantly supported by the " robust agitation " of the German Navy League, of which the Chancellor, Bethmann-Hollweg, bitterly complained.[14]   In 1912 he won the Kaiser over to a further Navy Law, against Bethmann-Hollweg, who warned him that " it would lead to war with England." [15]   After vigorous efforts by the British Government to reach a compromise, the Law went through, and the naval race went on.   Later in 1912 Sir Winston Churchill predicted that it was likely to lead " to war within the next two years." [16]   On the German side, Count Metternich and Bethmann-Hollweg foretold war by 1915, if not before.[17]

The rivalry between the armies of France, Germany, Austria-Hungary and Russia was no less keen, and no less

[12] Holls, *The Peace Conference at The Hague*, pp. 8–10.
[13] *Hansard*, March 29, 1909.
[14] Bethmann-Hollweg, *Reflections*, Vol. 1, Chap. 1.
[15] Cited by Gooch, *History of Modern Europe*, p. 490.
[16] G. Lowes Dickinson, *op. cit.*, p. 397.
[17] *Ibid.*

potent in arousing the conviction that nothing could avert the impending disaster. Thus Europe drifted from crisis to crisis, until the nerves of the governments were frayed, the passions of their peoples aroused, and their judgments distracted by the conviction that war was bound to come.

The Kaiser wrote in June 1914: " Any German who still disbelieves that Russia and France are working full steam for an early war against us . . . is fit for a mad-house." [18]

A Russian military organ wrote: " We all know we are preparing . . . for a war of annihilation against the Germans." [19]

M. Poincaré, the French President, said early in 1914: " In two years the war will take place. All my efforts will be devoted to preparing for it." [20]

## Verdicts after 1919

Seven years after the war was ended, Lord Grey of Fallodon published the results of his long reflections on the events in which he had had a central part to play. Discussing the origins of the " cataclysm " of 1914, he wrote:

> " The moral is obvious; it is that great armaments lead inevitably to war. If there are armaments on one side, there must be armaments on other sides. . . . While one nation arms, other nations cannot tempt it to aggression by remaining defenceless. Armaments must have equipment; armies cannot be of use without strategic railways. Each measure taken by one nation is noted, and leads to counter-measures by others.
>
> " The increase of armaments that is intended in each nation to produce consciousness of strength, and a sense of security, does not produce these effects. On the contrary, it produces a consciousness of the strength of other nations and a sense of fear. Fear begets

[18] Cited by Gooch, *op. cit.*, p. 524.
[19] *Ibid.*, p. 519.
[20] G. Lowes Dickinson, *op. cit.*, p. 355.

suspicion and distrust and evil imaginings of all sorts, till each government feels it would be criminal and a betrayal of its own country not to take every precaution, while every government regards every precaution of every other government as evidence of hostile intent. . . ."

(Here follows a reference to the diplomatic negotiations between Lord Grey and the Germans for the prevention of war in 1914.)

" But, although all this be true, it is not in my opinion the real and final account of the origin of the Great War. *The enormous growth of armaments in Europe, the sense of insecurity and fear caused by them —it was these that made war inevitable. This, it seems to me, is the truest reading of history, and the lesson that the present should be learning from the past in the interests of future peace, the warning to be handed on to those who come after us."* [21]

Mr. Lloyd George was Lord Grey's colleague. He was Chancellor of the Exchequer when the war began; Minister of Munitions from 1915 to 1916; Prime Minister from 1916 to 1922. In March 1919 he wrote a memorandum for the " Big Four " in the Paris Peace Conference, entitled: " Some considerations for the Peace Conference before they finally draft their terms."

In this memorandum he " *put in the forefront of the programme the importance of making provision in the Treaty for the setting up of machinery which would secure a general reduction of the huge armaments responsible for precipitating the Great War."* [22]

He thus sums up the discussion in the Imperial War Cabinet in December 1918 on the creation of a League of Nations:

[21] *Twenty Five Years*, Vol. 1, pp. 91–92.
[22] *The Truth about the Peace Treaties*, p. 601.

" Any Government that dared to set up a League of
Nations that was not real would be sternly dealt with
by the people.  If the League of Nations did not include
some provision for Disarmament it would be regarded
as a sham. . . .  Disarmament would be regarded as the
real test of whether the League of Nations was a farce
or whether business was meant." [23]

After the murder of the Austrian Archduke at Serajevo
in 1914, the German Government gave Austria a blank
cheque to send to Serbia whatever ultimatum she desired.
Writing of that decision, Professor G. M. Trevelyan says:

" It is probable that neither he [the Kaiser] nor
Bethmann-Hollweg, on that fatal day, knew that they
were unchaining universal war; they hoped that Russia
would not dare to fight. . . .

" The authorities in Berlin and Vienna knew that
Russian railways and Serbian reorganisation would be
more formidable in 1917 than in 1914.  Russia, they
thought, was less likely to march now than she might
be in a few years' time.  Better crush Serbia at once.
*Thus the armament race and the fear-struck calcula-
tions it everywhere engendered, helped to cause the
actual outbreak of the war.*" [24]

## WARNINGS BEFORE 1939

There were many authoritative warnings before 1939 that a
failure to make a general disarmament treaty, and a renewal
of the arms race, might lead to war.  At the Disarmament
Conference in 1933, President Roosevelt's delegate, Mr.
Norman Davis, said:

" The States of the world must either go forward
in good faith to carry out in all its implications the
disarmament policy which they adopted in 1919, or we

[23] *Op. cit.*, p. 631.
[24] *Grey of Fallodon*, p. 244.

must recognise frankly that this policy has been abandoned, and *reconcile ourselves to reverting to a race in competitive armament. If the latter course is taken, the consequences are inevitable; sooner or later there will be a break-down of the peace-machinery which has been so elaborately built up since 1918, and the world will be swept into another war.*" [25]

In 1936 Sir Winston Churchill repeated the warning he had given in 1912: " I cannot believe," he said in the House of Commons,

" *that after armaments of all countries have reached a towering height, they will settle down and continue at a hideous level far above the present level—already crushing—and that that will be for many years a normal feature of the world routine.*

" Whatever happens, I do not believe that. Europe is approaching a climax. I believe that climax will be reached during the lifetime of the present Parliament. *Either there will be a melting of hearts, and a joining of hands between great nations—*which will set out to realise the glorious age of prosperity now within the reach of millions of toiling people—*or there will be an explosion and a catastrophe, the course of which no imagination can measure and no human eye can see.*" [26]

### Verdict after 1939

The war came, as Sir Winston had foretold. Before it was over, he wrote a letter to Lord Cecil, which may be again recalled:

" This war could easily have been prevented, if the League of Nations had been used with courage and loyalty by the associated nations." [27]

---

[25] *Minutes of the General Commission*, Vol. II, p. 474.
[26] *Hansard*, April 23, 1936, col. 339.
[27] *All The Way*, p. 234.

It is not a waste of time to recall these warnings from the past. It is necessary to remember that the arms race was an important contributory cause of the 1914 War, and that the failure to end the arms race by a disarmament treaty was the turning point away from the Rule of Law back to the international anarchy that ended in the war of 1939. The present international situation differs in many ways from any that the governments had to face in earlier days. But the arms race goes on; and it is still the part of wisdom to remember the mistakes the governments made, and the price their peoples paid.

# 7

## *Must Disputes be Settled First?*

It is often said that disarmament should follow, but cannot precede, the settlement of international disputes. The Western Governments' " package plan " of 1957 included a " ceiling " for manpower for the United States and Russia of 2·5 million, and of 750,000 for France and Britain; it said that they would be prepared to " negotiate a further limitation of their armed forces and armaments upon condition that . . . there has been progress toward the solution of political issues." [1]

Everyone will agree with what President Eisenhower has said so often: that it is desirable to work both for disarmament and for the settlement of political disputes; that the work on both should go forward simultaneously; and that any progress on one will improve the hope of progress on the other.[2] It would, of course, help to create the conditions in which disarmament will be agreed to, if East and West Germany, North and South Korea, and North and South Viet Nam were re-united, under governments freely elected by their peoples; and if the question of Formosa were settled, and the Peking Government allowed to occupy China's seat in the UN. Those who desire disarmament will desire also that the utmost efforts should be made to get political settlements of this kind.

But to say in the crude terms often used that disarmament is dependent on political conditions, and that reductions of national armaments cannot be made until agreed solutions have been reached in certain disputes, is as though the British working classes had said a century ago that they would not have a parliament, law courts and a police

[1] Cmd. 333, p. 96.
[2] *e.g.*, in a Presidential Press Conference, N.Y.T., March 31, 1955.

force until the gulf between rich and poor had been done away with, and social equality for all had been obtained. It is one of the glories of Britain that the Chartists said the exact opposite; because they did so Britain has been the leader of political thought, and British institutions the model for democratic government, throughout the world. The argument that political settlements must be made before armaments can be reduced inevitably implies that the armaments are wanted to secure settlements by the use or threat of force; it cannot mean anything else. The Russians have not failed to point this out.

The argument is sometimes stated another way: " Disarmament can only be a consequence, and never a cause, of an improvement in international relations." [3]   Many historical examples could be given to prove the falsity of this assumption; two will suffice, one from the early nineteenth century, the other from the early twentieth. The Rush-Bagot Agreement of 1817, made against the wishes of the generals in both Britain and the United States, totally disarmed the Canadian frontier. The Washington Naval Disarmament Convention of 1922 made very big reductions in the navies of Britain, the United States and Japan. Both produced the most remarkable " improvements in international relations." [4]   Since, as experience shows and as present conditions only too clearly confirm, competition in armaments embitters international relations, producing mutual fear, suspicion and tension, it necessarily follows that the ending of an arms race by a disarmament treaty would improve international relations, reduce the tension, and facilitate the settlement of outstanding political disputes.

Indeed, there is much more substance in the counterargument used by those who favour disarmament, namely, that political disputes are much less likely to be settled while an arms race is going on, and that, if you want settlements, the arms race must first be stopped. The delegate

[3] *Spectator*, September 27, 1957.
[4] See pp. 511–515 and pp. 446–447.

of France gave powerful expression to this view in the UN Assembly:

> " The Sub-Committee had no right to wait, before resuming its progress on the path of disarmament, for a settlement of the most serious political disputes. Indeed, M. Moch was convinced that they were practically insoluble in an atmosphere of distrust, whereas they would constitute no major problem once included in the general framework of agreement on disarmament." [5]

A specific example will serve to show how strong the case is for this view. Russia's control of Poland and East Germany gives her a buffer zone 300 miles wide between her frontier and the NATO forces; this is of special importance against bomber attack, which requires " defence in depth." Her control of these territories and of Czechoslovakia gives her the rich coal and industrial resources which all three possess; it gives her the Skoda Works—one of the most famous arms factories in the world; and the Czech uranium mines. It is clear that her General Staff will produce strong arguments against " sacrificing " all this while they are engaged in competitive preparation for aerial and nuclear war. But if armaments had been reduced to the level which Russia, under Western pressure, accepted in principle in 1955—the " manpower ceiling " of 1 to 1·5 million men for U.S.A., Russia and China, the total abolition of all nuclear weapons and other weapons of mass destruction, etc. (see p. 19)—the chances for a German settlement and for the freedom of the satellites could only have been improved. Indeed, if manpower had been fixed at the lower level of one million, which Russia apparently professed herself as willing to accept, it may be doubted whether she would have had the forces to spare to hold the satellites down.

[5] First Committee, December 6, 1955, pp. 240–241.

Nothing could be more impolitic, or indeed improper, than for the UN Disarmament Commission or Sub-Committee to hold up its work, while it discusses what political problems must be settled and how it should be done. The task entrusted to the Commission by the Assembly in 1952 was to prepare a Draft Disarmament Treaty, showing in the form of detailed articles and schedules how the weapons of mass destruction could be abolished, and how all other armed forces and armaments could be drastically reduced and limited under international control. After three years' fruitless discussion, Mr. Paul Martin, of Canada, said to his colleagues in the Sub-Committee that he thought it would be worth while for them

> " to become platonist in the sense of formulating for some ideal purpose, if for no other purpose, the kind of plan for disarmament which we believe to be practical, and which could be put into effect if other considerations were met." [6]

This is precisely the task which the Sub-Committee was set up to accomplish. If such a Treaty were prepared, with detailed solutions for the technical problems which now seem baffling, and with figures setting out the large reductions which ought to be made, it is extremely probable that public opinion would insist on its being signed and carried out, whether the outstanding political problems had been settled or not. But it is also probable in a high degree that the mere preparation and publication of the treaty would do more than all else to advance the settlement of the political disputes. In any case, what is now wanted is the Draft Treaty, and it is the urgent duty of the Western Governments not to delay matters by posing hypothetical and undefined political conditions, but to put forward the proposals for large-scale reductions, and the detailed clauses for carrying them out, which are the first and indispensable step to a more peaceful world.

[6] September 19, 1955.   Cmd. 9652, p. 878.

# PART TWO

# NUCLEAR ARMAMENTS

# 8

## *Facts and Special Difficulties*

On July 1, 1945, two weeks before the first atomic bomb had been tested in the Nevada desert, the United States War Department printed a Report [1] which said:

"A weapon has been developed that is potentially destructive beyond the wildest nightmares of the imagination: a weapon so ideally suited to sudden unannounced attack that a country's major cities might be destroyed overnight by an ostensibly friendly Power. This weapon has been created not by the devilish inspiration of some warped genius, but by the arduous labour of thousands of normal men and women working for the safety of their country."

"Initially," the Report went on, "many scientists could and did hope that some principle would emerge which would prove that atomic bombs were inherently impossible."

But this hope faded; the danger that Hitler might make atomic bombs remained; so Einstein and Oppenheimer inspired and led the effort by which the bombs were made.

"Many of the principles that have been used," said the Report, "were well known to the international scientific world in 1940." From the beginning of the century fundamental research in nuclear physics had been going on in many countries, not with any thought of practical application, but simply to increase men's understanding of the structure of matter. Except for radium, soon used in medicine, the new knowledge seemed, up to 1939, to have

---

[1] *Atomic Energy : A General Account of the Development of Methods of Using Atomic Energy for Military Purposes under the Auspices of the United States Government.* Published in August 1945 after the bombs had been dropped on Hiroshima and Nagasaki.

no more than academic interest. Two decades later it has given results which may end the human race, or which, if governments are wiser, may bring true civilisation to all the nations of the world.

This chapter is not an essay in popular science; there are many admirable books about the atom.[2] It is an attempt to do two things: first, to bring home to people who do not read these books what a fantastic achievement the release of nuclear energy is; second, to show the special and formidable difficulties of nuclear disarmament which result from the scientific and engineering facts which it describes.

## *Fission*

Descriptions of the fission process have become familiar to many non-scientists. But they have not conveyed to most people a true idea of what the scientists have done. In brief outline, the scientists' main relevant discoveries are these:

### RADIUM

In 1896 Becquerel discovered radio-activity [3]; this gave the first evidence of a source of energy within the atom that far exceeded its *chemical* energy. This led directly to the work of the Curies through which they found the new chemical element radium. Radium is an " unstable " element; it emits radio-activity by gradual disintegration; its " half-life " is 1,600 years, which means that half the atoms in a gramme of radium will have disintegrated in 1,600 years; this rate of decay means that in one gramme there are 37,000 million disintegrations per second. This " activity "

---

[2] *e.g.*, J. L. Michiels, *Finding Out about Atomic Energy*; A. Asimov, *Inside the Atom*; J. L. Crammer and R. E. Peierls (Editors), *Atomic Energy*; J. Rotblat (Editor), *Atomic Energy : A Survey*; Gordon Dean (Ex-Chairman of the United States Atomic Energy Commission), *Report on the Atom*; K. E. B. Jay, *Britain's Atomic Factories*; A. Angelopoulos, *Will the Atom Unite the World ?* and many more.

[3] Radio-activity is defined as " the property possessed by certain atoms of breaking down spontaneously, emitting charged particles or electro-magnetic waves, or both, in the process, and transmuting themselves into different chemical elements ": K. E. B. Jay, *Britain's Atomic Factories*, 1954, p. 87.

of one gramme of radium is taken as the unit of activity of radio-active substance, and is called a " Curie."

## THE ATOM AND ITS NUCLEUS

The chemical elements which constitute the matter of the universe are made up of " ultimate particles " called atoms; an atom is " the smallest recognisable particle of any element." The atom is so small that ten million (10,000,000) atoms could be placed side by side in a row across the head of an ordinary pin. But although it is so unimaginably small, the atom is in itself a complicated structure of much smaller particles called electrons, with a central particle called the " nucleus." Electrons are extremely light, and carry a negative electric charge. The nucleus is much smaller than the atom; if the atom were magnified 1,000 million times it would be as large as a small ball; the nucleus would still be a tiny speck, barely visible to the naked eye.

The nucleus is made up of elementary particles called nucleons, of which there are two principal kinds: protons and neutrons. Protons are about 1,800 times as heavy as electrons; they have a positive electric charge. Neutrons are slightly heavier than protons, but have no electric charge—a very important fact, since it enables neutrons to penetrate the nuclei of atoms more easily than protons.

## TRANSMUTATION OF ATOMS

The element iodine consists of atoms; each nucleus of an atom of iodine contains fifty-three protons and seventy-four neutrons—what is called its " mass number " (protons and neutrons together) is, therefore, 127. If one *neutron* were removed the atom would be chemically unchanged—it would still be an atom of iodine, with mass number 126; but instead of being stable it would become radio-active— it would be called a " radio-active isotope " of iodine. But if one *proton* were removed the electrical charge of the nucleus, as well as its mass, would be reduced; its chemical nature would be changed; it would become an isotope, not of iodine, but of a different element, tellurium; it would be radio-active instead of stable.

In 1919 Rutherford showed that transmutation was more than a theoretical possibility; he transmuted atoms of nitrogen into atoms of an isotope of oxygen by bombarding them with alpha particles. In 1933 Joliot-Curie showed that, by bombarding normally stable elements with charged particles, radio-active isotopes of many elements could be manufactured artificially.

### Fission of the Nuclei of Uranium Atoms

In 1939 two Germans, Hahn and Strassmann, found that when the heavy, rather rare metal uranium was bombarded by neutrons, its nuclei sometimes underwent a process called " fission," during which they broke into two nuclei of about the same size. Other features of fission were soon established; the secondary nuclei, or " fission fragments," are intensely radio-active; they fly apart with a great deal of energy, which ultimately takes the form of heat; a few more neutrons are also emitted, and these neutrons can cause further fissions in neighbouring uranium nuclei. These characteristics are of vital importance, and together they make possible the use of the fission process as a source of energy.

Further work showed that natural uranium—the pure metal refined from uranium ore—consists of two different kinds of atom, chemically identical, but of slightly different mass—Uranium 235 and Uranium 238. There are about 140 atoms of U238 for each atom of U235; *i.e.*, U235 is only 0·7 per cent. of natural uranium. It was the atoms of U235—the rare and very costly isotope of uranium—which underwent fission when struck by neutrons released by fission. If these neutrons entered atoms of U238, something quite different, though no less important, was likely to happen—see below. It was further discovered that each fission of a nucleus of U235 released two or more neutrons; experiments showed that the average number—it is an important number—was 2·5.

Investigation of the neutron showed that the speed with which it left the nucleus when fission occurred was 6,000 miles a second—360,000 miles a minute; but if released in natural uranium at that speed, the neutron was much more likely to enter an atom of U238 than an atom of U235. This would, *a priori*, have seemed likely, since there are 140 times as many atoms of U238; but, in addition, it was firmly established that atoms of U238 absorb " fast " neutrons (*i.e.*, neutrons travelling at their original speed of 6,000 miles a second) much more easily than do atoms of U235. It followed that if the U235 could be separated from the U238, and a metal of pure, or almost pure, U235 produced, then the neutrons would have nowhere to be absorbed except the U235; they would " bounce about " until ultimately, and perhaps at a reduced speed, they entered an atom of U235; then fission would occur. As each fission, on the average, emitted 2·5 neutrons, a " chain reaction " would follow, with the number of fissions more than doubling with every " generation," and consequently with a rapidly cumulative release of energy. The energy of each neutron was relatively small; but in every ounce of U235 there are 72,000 million million million atoms; if *complete* fission of one ounce of U235 could be obtained, it would release three million times as much energy as the same weight of coal. It was clear that a chain-reaction in quite a small quantity of U235—a few kilograms, perhaps —would release an amount of energy which, if it could be released all together, would make the most powerful weapon ever known. This chain-reaction, with millions of millions of nuclear fissions, would run its course in a few millionths of a second.

After this fission chain-reaction had been obtained in U235 it was discovered that the atoms of a new man-made element, plutonium (Pu239), could also be split,[4] and that when they are split they emit, on the average, not 2·5 but 2·9 neutrons per fission. This means that plutonium can sustain a chain reaction of even greater intensity than U235; it is even more effective for use in weapons; can be used for controlled reactions to produce electric power; and may be even better than U235 for the " breeder reactors " described below. Yet another man-made element, Uranium 233, can be made to undergo fission and can be used for bombs and power; it is derived from thorium, which is a much more abundant raw material than uranium. How plutonium and U233 are made will be described a little later.

## *Fusion*

It was proved in 1945 that the fission of the " heavy " atoms of U235 would release great amounts of energy; it was known that still greater energy could be obtained if atoms of " light " elements, especially hydrogen, could be made to fuse together, and could be converted by fusion into helium.

It was shown by experiments that this could only be done by exposing these atoms to extremely high temperatures; at 50,000 degrees centigrade the reaction is so slow that it cannot even be observed; at one million degrees centigrade it costs more energy than it releases; at some millions of degrees the energy production begins to grow much faster than the loss, the reaction then runs its course in a very short time, converting most of the material into energy and raising the temperature to the fantastic level of 1,000 million degrees centigrade.[5]

This " thermo-nuclear burning " is produced most readily with the isotopes of hydrogen, deuterium and tritium.[6] Tritium requires only one million degrees; it does

---

[4] See p. 103.
[5] Prof. O. R. Frisch, *Atomic Energy : A Survey* (Rotblat), p. 15.
[6] Sometimes popularly called " double-weight " and " triple-weight " hydrogen.

not occur in nature, but can be made in reactors. But it is very costly, and a small amount of it, to start the thermo-nuclear reaction, is therefore mixed with deuterium, which requires 50 million degrees. Further improvements made it possible to raise the temperature of a fission-fusion bomb towards 1,000 million degrees centigrade.

> "In these conditions," says Mr. Maddox, "both lithium 6 and lithium 7 react with deuterium at com-paratively high efficiency. Weight for weight, the reactions would yield respectively four and three times the explosive power of fissile uranium." [7]

Lithium is comparatively cheap, and so, compared to other forms of fuel, is deuterium; and deuterium is very plentiful. In fact, there is one nucleus of deuterium for every 6,400 nuclei of ordinary hydrogen in water; in consequence the total amount of deuterium available in the oceans is so enormous that, if its energy could be released under control, as that of uranium has been, it would provide many times the present rate of world energy consumption for more than a thousand million years.[8]

But so far only one way has been found by which the necessary temperature can be produced to start the thermo-nuclear burning, and that is by the explosion of an A (fission) bomb.[9] That is why every H-bomb must have a fission " core " of plutonium or U235. The advantage of hydrogen as a weapon is that there is no limit to the amount that can be assembled in a bomb; unlike plutonium, U235, and U233, there is no " critical mass," which, if it is assembled, will automatically cause the chain-reaction to start.

With U235, plutonium and U233 there is a " critical mass " of the material, and when this " critical mass " is assembled a chain-reaction automatically starts, and an

[7] John Maddox in *The New Scientist*, June 6, 1957, p. 28.
[8] Prof. Spitzer of Princeton, M.G., October 4, 1955.
[9] The Zeta experiments at Harwell, and parallel United States experiments at Princeton, are developing methods of *controlled* production of these tempera-tures and of thermo-nuclear reactions.

explosion occurs. The "critical mass" is not simply a given weight of the material—it depends partly on the shape in which the material is assembled—a smaller weight in the form of a sphere will constitute a "critical mass," when a larger weight in the form of an oblong or a "rod" will not, because the greater external surface of the oblong or the "rod" allows more neutrons to "escape" without causing fissions of the nuclei of U235, plutonium or U233.[10]  In the production of these fissile materials, therefore, care must be taken that at no point is a sufficient quantity of the material assembled in a single lump to constitute a "critical mass."  And when the materials are made into weapons, the "critical mass" must not be formed until the moment when it is desired that the weapon shall explode.

But with the isotopes of hydrogen, and with lithium 6 and 7, there is no "critical mass" at which the chain-reaction automatically starts.  There is, therefore, no limit to the amount that can be safely assembled in a weapon and the power of an H-bomb can be indefinitely increased.

## Fission—Fusion—Fission

The scientists have further shown that the fusion process releases neutrons of such immense energy that they will penetrate and cause fission in the inert and otherwise non-explosive U238.  In the ordinary A-bomb, this U238 would be non-fissionable; at the immense temperatures created by the H-bomb, it explodes with colossal power.  It is also highly poisonous, and causes radio-active "fall-out" on a very heavy scale.  The "super-bomb" exploded at Bikini in March 1954 had an inner core of U235, a casing of hydrogen, and an outer sheath of U238.  The U238 was

---

[10] An admirably clear exposition of the scientific theory of the "critical mass" is given in the United States Government Handbook, *Effects of Nuclear Weapons*, 1957, pp. 11 *et seq*.

responsible for approximately 13/15ths of its explosive power, and for nearly all of its " fall-out." [11]

## *The Scientists' Instrumentation*

The physicists have developed an " instrumentation " of research that surpasses by far in its ingenuity, its complexity and its precision anything that human beings have ever conceived before. Machines for accelerating atomic particles are of great importance. The California Institute of Technology have an atom-disintegrating " synchrotron " which has accelerated electrons to a speed of 186,000 miles a second—only 324 miles per second less than the speed of light. When the machine is working, the electrons go round the circular vacuum chamber two million times—a distance of more than 3,700 miles—in one-fifth of a second. They are then ejected, having acquired energies of up to 1,200 million electron volts, and directed at a target. The results, it is hoped, will throw light on the forces which bind the different parts of the nucleus together—forces which are still only partially understood. [12]

" As an example of nuclear instrument technology," says Sir John Cockcroft, " time intervals between events as short as a thousand millionth of a second can now be measured." [13]

This short selection of some of the basic facts about atomic energy reveals a realm of discovery and achievement which still means little to the untrained mind. Most people cannot really grasp the size of something that is only one-ten-millionth of a pin's head across. They cannot imagine how the 235 smaller particles of which that something's nucleus is composed can be weighed and counted, and their charge of electric energy measured. They cannot take in the nature of a chain-reaction that is accomplished, with

[11] Indian Government Report, *Nuclear Explosions and Their Effects*, p. 26.
[12] N.Y.T., September 30, 1956.
[13] *Atomic Energy : A Survey* (Rotblat), p. 11.

millions of millions of successive explosions, within a few millionths of a second. But the physicists have proved the validity of their almost incredible hypotheses and calculations by producing bombs and power. By so doing, they have revolutionised, not only military strategy, but, for good or ill, the social and economic future of mankind.

## Nuclear Engineering

The physicists have only produced bombs and power with the help of engineers, chemists, metallurgists and other technicians whose work has reached a level of achievement only less remarkable than their own.

### RAW MATERIALS

The world has been scoured for uranium. Before the war a tiny quantity was used to colour pottery and glass a brilliant yellow. Now it is mined in every quarter of the globe; it has been found to be a thousand times as plentiful as gold. Yet it is so precious that some deposits are worked that give only 2 lb. of uranium from a ton of ore. Even from the " rich " deposits of Canada and the Congo scores of truck-loads are needed for one atomic bomb. When the ore is crushed, the uranium must be separated from the clay and rock; it is in microscopic particles the size of a pin's point; particles so small that the naked eye of the mining engineer cannot see them.

### SEPARATION OF U235

When the natural uranium has been purified, and cast in ingots, the 0·7 per cent. of U235 must be separated from the U238. This is done by " gaseous diffusion "; the metal is transformed by heat into gas; combined, one part of uranium to six, with fluorine; then passed through thousands of metal barriers like sieves, the holes in which are less than two-millionths of an inch across. This process of " sieving " individual molecules of matter so small that they cannot be seen even with the most powerful micro-scope lasts for months; it gradually segregates and concen-trates the slightly lighter atoms of U235 from the U238; in the end, they are separated from the fluorine, and recast into ingots of pure U235. The process is immensely costly; the plant at Oak Ridge uses more water per day than a city with a million inhabitants; two new plants were con-structed in the United States in 1953 which consume more than half the total electricity production of the United Kingdom.[14] The amount of U235 obtained is only a fraction of an ounce from the original ton of ore.

The U235 must be far purer in quality than is required for any similar material used in ordinary industry. There are very few elements that can be tolerated in amounts greater than one part in 10,000; boron [15] is so " greedy for neutrons " that one part in one million is too much, *i.e.*, in every ton of uranium there must be less boron than would cover a sixpence. The same is true of the natural uranium used as the fuel of Calder Hall. Every ingot is tested chemically to ensure that the necessary quality has been attained; the ingot is then stamped with its number, and sent on to be prepared for use in weapons or in reactors for producing plutonium and/or power.

### PREPARATION OF URANIUM " RODS "

This preparation is, in itself, a major engineering job. When natural uranium is prepared for a reactor it must be machined into a cylindrical " rod " with great preci-sion [16]; the rod must be " canned," *i.e.*, enclosed in an aluminium container to prevent the radio-active fission products from escaping, and the uranium from being oxidised when the chain-reaction has begun. " Canning "

---

[14] Sir F. Simon, *Atomic Energy : A Survey* (Rotblat), p. 23.

[15] Boron is a non-metallic element, occurring in nature in the form of boric acid, borax and other " borates."

[16] The rods used at Calder Hall and Windscale are forty inches long and one inch in diameter.

is such a complicated business that more than fifty separate operations are required.

## PRODUCTION OF POWER IN A NUCLEAR REACTOR

The next problem was to devise a reactor in which the energy could be released safely and efficiently from the uranium in the rods. The danger of radiation, and of possible explosions, makes the whole construction of an atomic plant a matter of great complexity. Work on the neutrons released by the fission of U235 showed that their speed could be reduced by making them pass through " moderators "—other substances which did not absorb them, but slowed them down.

The best moderator is " heavy water," but it is very costly—£75,000 a ton. The next best, and that in use at Windscale and Calder Hall, is graphite (heavy carbon). When the neutron leaves the nucleus of U235 and enters the graphite it " bounces about " among the atoms of the graphite and, after some hundreds of collisions, its speed is reduced from 6,000 miles to one mile a second. At this speed it is not so readily absorbed by atoms of U238, but, on the contrary, has the greatest chance of causing the fission of another atom of U235.

Thus it was found possible to use natural uranium (*i.e.,* uranium metal with 99·3 per cent. of U238 and 0·7 per cent. of U235) as the fuel for a *controlled* chain-reaction to produce moderate temperatures of heat for making electricity. A large amount of natural uranium is required; at Calder Hall the rods in each reactor weigh 110 tons; they are disposed in channels which run, at eight-inch intervals, through a cube made up of graphite blocks. The weight of the graphite is 1,200 tons. There are also *control* rods passed through other channels in the graphite, which consist of steel with boron; when the control rods are inserted the boron absorbs the neutrons, and no chain-reaction can begin. When they are withdrawn, however, the fission of the U235 can start, and the majority of the neutrons thus released end up by causing further fissions in other atoms of U235. The number of these fissions, and thus the heat generated in the reactor, can be very accurately and speedily controlled. This heat is then transferred by " heat-exchangers," using a stream of gas,[17] to conventional boilers, which make steam for the conventional turbines and alternators which generate the electricity.

## The Production of Plutonium 239

But in this process something else of great importance also occurs. Some of the neutrons released by the fission of the U235 strike atoms of U238 before they ever reach the graphite, that is, before they have been slowed down; others are absorbed by U238 even after their speed has been reduced. When this happens, the neutron transmutes the U238 into another element, called neptunium; the neptunium is highly radio-active, and rapidly disintegrates until it becomes the new, artificial element, plutonium. Plutonium is fissionable by either fast or slow neutrons, and it can be used both for weapons and for power. It has to be separated from the irradiated or " burnt " rods of natural uranium by a chemical process [18]; the quantity so obtained is very small—only two to three kg. per ton of natural uranium.[19] But it is of the highest value, both for military and peaceful use.

## The Production of Uranium 233

U233 is another artificial " nuclear fuel." By a nuclear transformation similar to that which produces plutonium from U238, thorium 232 absorbs a neutron, becomes the radio-active isotope thorium 233, and then decays to form U233. U233 is even more readily fissionable than plutonium or U235; for that reason it has a smaller

[17] See p. 105.
[18] See pp. 105 and 276.
[19] Sir J. Cockcroft, *Atomic Energy : A Survey* (Rotblat), p. 6.

" critical mass," and thus has special uses as a weapon. It can also be used for producing power.

### OTHER REACTORS

Many types of nuclear reactors have been, and are being, designed. The most important may be the " fast breeder " reactor, which is designed to produce more nuclear fuel—U235, U233 or plutonium—than it consumes; of course, new supplies of natural uranium are required. A " fast breeder " reactor has been built at Dounreay in Scotland, and is due to start producing power in 1958. It has no moderator, since it is designed to work with fast neutrons. The core is to be of pure U235, surrounded by a " blanket " of natural uranium. It will generate much greater heat than the Calder Hall type of slow neutron reactor; the heat will be carried away, not by gas, but by a liquid metal—an alloy of sodium and potassium—which permits a higher temperature to be transferred. The reactor is housed in an immense steel sphere, weighing 1,500 tons. The heat it generates will produce 150MW of power; the neutrons it releases will transmute some of the U238 atoms in the " blanket " into plutonium. It is expected that the Dounreay reactor will produce 1·1 lb. of plutonium for every 1 lb. of U235 that is consumed; it will thus breed nuclear fuel faster than it uses it up. When such a reactor can be given a core of plutonium, which emits an average of 2·9 neutrons per nuclear fission, instead of the 2·5 from U235, it is expected that 1 lb. of the plutonium consumed will breed 1·7 lb. of new plutonium. If this succeeds, it might be a better economic proposition than the slow neutron type of reactor at Calder Hall.

### OTHER PROBLEMS OF NUCLEAR PLANT CONSTRUCTION

The reactor in the plant at Windscale for the making of plutonium was built on the foundation of a concrete " mat." The mat had to carry a weight of 57,000 tons;

its dimensional accuracy had to be such that there was no deviation from the vertical of more than a quarter inch in ninety feet; some items of the equipment had to be set in the concrete with an accuracy of 1/100th of an inch. The whole reactor—graphite blocks and channels for the uranium rods—had to be enclosed in a steel pressure container, six inches thick, in which there were 50,000 welds, each of which was X-rayed to ensure that there was no fault or weakness; around this there had to be a " biological shield " of eight feet of concrete, to prevent the escape of nuclear radiation.

The graphite block in the reactor is made up of 57,000 separate bricks; graphite is very hard to work, but each brick had to be machined to 1/1000th of an inch, and numbered, to ensure that it fitted exactly with the next; for this cutting process a British firm developed a special tungsten steel, harder than any known before. During the " stacking " of these graphite bricks it was necessary to maintain surgical cleanliness, to prevent neutron absorbing materials from getting into the reactor.

The operator at Windscale must be able to adjust the position of the steel and boron control rods in their channels to within a few 1000ths of an inch.

The heat generated in the reactor has to be conveyed to the boilers by a stream of gas; the gas chosen is carbon dioxide; to increase its capacity it is pressurised to 128 lb. to the square inch; immense fans drive it through at hurricane force; one ton of carbon dioxide passes through every second.

The chemical plant at Windscale for separating the plutonium from the " burnt " uranium rods deals with materials so radio-active that the whole place has to be hermetically sealed. This means that it must perform its functions throughout its working life without repairs or maintenance of any kind. It has already worked for seven years without being opened, or anyone going inside. No such thing has ever been attempted in industry before.

All these extraordinary refinements of the work in concrete, steel, graphite, boron and the rest are essential to make the reactor work, and for safety against radiation. The construction of reactors, and, indeed, the whole of nuclear engineering, is in its infancy; and there is no likelihood that it will grow less complex in times to come. But the significance of this fact, and of the other scientific and engineering facts set out above, lies in the difficulties to which they give rise in the preparation of schemes for nuclear disarmament. These difficulties must be clearly grasped before an intelligent discussion of the matter can be begun.

## *Special Difficulties of Nuclear Disarmament*

The special difficulties of nuclear disarmament are real, and they grow greater with every extension of national atomic industry and research, and with every increase in the quantities of fissionable or fusionable material that exist in national stocks. They may be summarized:

### THE SAME PROCESSES PRODUCE WEAPONS AND PEACEFUL PRODUCTS

Dr. Oppenheimer wrote in 1948: " The development of atomic power (for peaceful use) could not be separated from technological development essential for, and largely sufficient for, the manufacture of atomic weapons." [20]

Research into the peaceful uses of atomic energy may help the development of warlike uses; reactors for power production produce plutonium; U235 and plutonium can both be used in weapons or for power. Nuclear research and factories cannot be separated into two classes, civilian and military; they are inseparable; atomic energy used for

---

[20] *Foreign Affairs*, January 1948, p. 243.

peaceful purposes produces materials for deadly weapons. Thus, if there is to be nuclear disarmament at all, all nuclear research and all nuclear plants of every kind must be subject to control.

## THE NATURE OF NUCLEAR PLANTS

Owing to the nature of nuclear materials (*i.e.*, their mortally dangerous radio-activity) they cannot be directly handled or measured. Every process inside a nuclear plant in which U235 or plutonium is made is carried on inside a sealed and shielded container, and is conducted from outside by remote control. To know how much potential weapon material is being made you must know *precisely* what goes in, what happens to it, and what eventually comes out. This is a very different matter from inspecting an engineering works to ensure, for instance, that guided missiles are not being made; and a very different system of inspection and control would be required.

## THE SMALL WEIGHT AND VOLUME OF FISSILE AND FUSIONABLE MATERIAL REQUIRED FOR WEAPONS

" It is now the fact," said Sir Winston Churchill in the House of Commons in 1955, " that a quantity of plutonium, probably less than would fill this Box on the Table . . . would suffice to produce weapons which would give indisputable world domination to any great Power which was the only one to have it." [21]

This may have been a picturesque exaggeration; but if so, it was only a slight exaggeration; the point it conveys is of fundamental importance in nuclear disarmament. A weapon of relatively small weight will produce an immense explosion. The explosive power which destroyed Hiroshima, the equivalent of 20,000 tons of TNT, could now, by improved techniques, be obtained from seven or

[21] *Hansard*, March 1, 1955, col. 1899.

eight kg. of U235 or four kg. of U233.[22]   Sir John
Cockcroft has written:

> " Today we are in the early stages of another revolu-
> tionary change—the harnessing of the energy of the
> atomic nucleus to serve man's need or to destroy him.
> This revolution may transcend all earlier ones because
> of the enormous increase in the forces now available to
> man. *The magnitude of this force was displayed in a
> devastating way by the destruction of the cities of
> Hiroshima and Nagasaki from a ball of uranium or
> plutonium little bigger than a cricket ball.*" [23]

The same point applies to H-bombs in no less degree.
" The explosion of a fission bomb of 25 kg. (55 lb.) and
200 kg. of a tritium-deuterium mixture would yield an
explosive force of $16\frac{1}{2}$ megatons." [24]

It was of such H-bombs that Mr. Stassen said in the
Sub-Committee:

> " A comparatively small basketful of this refined
> nuclear material, properly fabricated, can make a
> bomb which alone can substantially destroy any major
> city in the world.  Furthermore, such a bomb is not
> of extreme weight.  It does not require a very massive
> powerful aeroplane to carry it; it is not simple to carry,
> but neither is it of such complexity that the delivery is
> too difficult to control." [25]

It follows from these facts that the " diversion " of very
small quantities of fissile, or of relatively small quantities
of fusionable, material from peaceful to warlike use might
mean a grave and dangerous violation of a nuclear disarmament agreement.  The system of Inspection and
Control must, therefore, be adequate to prevent such
diversions from taking place.

---

[22] John Maddox in *The New Scientist*, June 6, 1957.
[23] Cockcroft, " The Nuclear Revolution," *Sunday Times*, Atomic Energy Issue,
     October 6, 1957.
[24] Wm. L. Laurence, N.Y.T., May 22, 1956.
[25] Sub-Committee, April 12, 1957, p. 6.

## Fissile Material can be made into Weapons in Small Plants

While the plants required for producing fissile material are very large, and cannot easily be hidden, the fissile material, when produced, can be made into weapons in very small establishments which it might be hard to find.[26] This makes effective Inspection of the nuclear plants, and the prevention of " diversion," all the more important.

## Clandestine Stocks of Nuclear Weapons

It may be possible by Inspection to prevent " diversion " of fissile material from the current production of nuclear plants; it is much more difficult to make an accurate reckoning of the total past production of a plant since its reactors first began to " burn." This means that a government which contemplated aggression might be able to violate an agreement for the abolition of nuclear weapons by retaining part of its past production as a clandestine stock. Nuclear weapons are only slightly radio-active, and if shielded by lead or concrete could not be found by any geiger-counter or other instrument that now exists.[27] This, as has been said, is by far the greatest technical difficulty of all in nuclear disarmament; it is increased by the fact that so much potentially aggressive power can be packed into so small a quantity of material.

These special technical difficulties of nuclear disarmament result from the scientific and engineering facts set out above. They have been baldly stated here so that no one should think that they are being shirked. In later chapters it will be shown that technical solutions can be found for all the technical problems which they present. But it must always be remembered that these technical solutions, if they are to hold the least hope of success, will mean a measure of general disarmament, and will require a more rigid system of Inspection and Control, and a

[26] See p. 196.
[27] For Mr. Stassen's explanation of this point, see pp. 292-294.

greater sacrifice of national sovereignty, than is needed for armaments of other kinds. Unless the nations are prepared for that sacrifice, the problem will remain unsolved, and the nuclear arms race will go on. It would be a tragic paradox if they were to hesitate. The harnessing of atomic energy has been achieved by the pooling of knowledge and discoveries, and by constant and intimate co-operation, between men of genius belonging to many nations. It is itself a symbol of both a technical and a sociological revolution in the affairs of man. In the new world which it is creating, no policy but that of international co-operation now makes sense.[28]

[28] See A. Angelopoulos, *op. cit.*, Chap. 2. Gordon Dean, *Report on the Atom*, pp 216 *et passim*.

# 9

# *Peaceful Uses: "Can the Atomic Age be Repealed?"*

## *The Cost of Atomic Energy*

THE achievements of scientific discovery, and of metallurgical, chemical and industrial technique described in previous chapters would have been impossible, if the men in charge had not been given the resources they required. In fact, almost every request they made was at once agreed to. In the U.S.A., in Britain, and no doubt in Russia, the investment in research, in mining, and in plant has been immense. In the United States it had amounted to $9,000m. by 1953—much more than the combined capital investment of General Motors, U.S. Steel, du Pont, Bethlehem Steel, Alcoa and Goodyear. Allowing for the depreciation of the dollar, it was ten times the cost of the Panama Canal.[1] Such sums could only be found by governments; at the present stage in human history, governments would never have approved them, and legislatures would never have voted them, unless they had been judged necessary for national defence. They have given a return in weapons the magnitude of which will be described in the following chapters. But they have given a great return for the peaceful progress of mankind as well.

## *The Peaceful Application of Nuclear Science*

The scientists had always hoped that this might be true. They envisaged

"two classes of peaceful applications. . . . One is the

---

[1] Gordon Dean, *Report on the Atom*, pp. 66–67.

111

development of a new source of power; the other is a family of new instruments of research, investigation, technology and therapy." [2]

In recent decades, the need for some new source of power has become painfully plain. Mankind has a recorded history of about 6,000 years. Some nations began to use a little coal 600 years ago. So much is used today that the known reserves may last 300, or, at most, 400 years. Oil has been used on an increasing scale since 1900. It is now the motive power of almost all road transport, many locomotives, ocean-going ships, tractors and other agricultural machines, of all aircraft, and of many industries. If consumption expands as now expected, the world reserves, including what lies beneath the sea, may last, say some authorities, for seventy years. Without coal and oil, how could civilisation survive and the world be fed? As a source of power, nuclear energy has become available just when it is urgently required.

Both for power and for research and therapy, it is being harnessed to peaceful uses more swiftly than most scientists expected. Writing in 1947, Dr. Oppenheimer spoke of "many years, perhaps many decades, of development, largely engineering development," that would be needed to provide new sources of power, and to develop the "new arsenal of instruments for the exploration of the physical and biological world, and in time, for their future control." [3] In both fields progress has been more rapid than those words suggested.

## *Atomic Energy as a Source of Power*

Calder Hall was the first nuclear plant in any country to produce electric power on a *commercial* scale. It was planned to make plutonium; power is a by-product. When

[2] J. Robert Oppenheimer, *Foreign Affairs*, January 1948, p. 241.
[3] *Loc. cit.*, pp. 242–243.

its two stations and four reactors are complete, it will feed 150 MW of electricity into the national grid—enough to serve a town of 100,000 people. The capital cost of the plant was extremely high, but the cost per unit of electricity is about the same as that of a power station run on coal.

Calder Hall was experimental; and it is already producing more power per ton of uranium than was expected —the equivalent of the power from 10,000 tons of coal. The uranium costs £20,000; 10,000 tons of coal cost £40,000. In addition, there is the plutonium it produces—two to three kg. per ton of uranium. When this is used for power production, it will raise the output to the equivalent of 30,000 tons of coal—£120,000. Furthermore, the used uranium, depleted of the small proportion of atoms of U235 which have been " burnt," can be reprocessed, " enriched " to its original proportion of U235, and used again. Thus the Calder Hall reactors, in spite of their high capital cost, are already a sound economic proposition.

But Sir John Cockcroft has predicted that reactors of this general design can be much improved. They can be made to take, perhaps, double the quantity of uranium; if the metallurgists can make " cans " of beryllium, heat can be developed at which the present aluminium " cans " would melt, and the power per reactor may be multiplied by four. Sir John has forecast the possibility of nuclear stations with a capacity of 1,000 MW; twice the electricity produced by Battersea Power Station.[4] The longer term perspectives are even better. Basing himself on the assumption that metallurgical and other advances can be made, and higher temperatures and pressures thus achieved, Sir Christopher Hinton has made the following forecast about the cost of electricity produced respectively by coal and nuclear power:

[4] M.G., March 13, 1957. The British Government have authorised nineteen new nuclear plants, which are expected to produce 6,000 MW by 1965, thus saving eighteen million tons of coal.

COST OF POWER FROM CONVENTIONAL COAL AND NUCLEAR STATIONS
IN PENCE PER UNIT SENT OUT

| Commissioning Date | Coal | Nuclear |
|---|---|---|
| 1960 | 0·60 | 0·66 |
| 1970 | 0·67 | 0·47 |
| 1980 | 0·73 | 0·38 |
| 1990 | 0·84 | 0·32 [5] |

The rapid and very large scale development of nuclear power thus seems assured. It is estimated that the world reserves of raw materials for the types of nuclear stations now envisaged—uranium and thorium—are sufficient to meet the world demand for power for some hundreds of thousands of years.

## Fusion as a Source of Power

If the heat generated by the hydrogen bomb could be " tamed " and put to peaceful use, it would, as said above,[6] solve the problem of power for good and all. If deuterium could be used, the energy obtained from one gallon of sea-water would be equal to the energy from 100 gallons of high grade petrol. But the difficulties are formidable.

" Thermo-nuclear burning," says Professor Spitzer, " occurs only at enormous temperatures—above 100 million degrees Fahrenheit. . . . To convert the inexhaustible supply of energy in the earth's deuterium into useful power, we must achieve such temperatures in a gas confined within walls that remain relatively cool. We must control the thermo-nuclear reaction when it occurs. We must extract the energy released and use it to generate electricity. The scientific and technical difficulties to be surmounted are obviously formidable." [7]

---

[5] Axel Axson Johnson Lecture delivered March 15, 1957, at the Royal Swedish Academy of Engineering Sciences, Stockholm, and printed by the Guardian Press, Tables 3 and 4.

[6] See p. 97.

[7] Prof. Spitzer, who is directing the research work into the subject at Princeton University, M.G., October 4, 1955.

But both Harwell and USAEC are doing large-scale research, and confidently believe that it will succeed. In 1955 Admiral Strauss announced that " the task of taming the hydrogen bomb " had achieved " the status of a major project." [8]

> " I am convinced that it will come about," he said, " but I can't reduce my optimism to a number of years . . . twenty years seems a fair guess. It won't astonish me if it comes sooner, or if it takes longer." [9]

Sir John Cockcroft has virtually been given *carte blanche* for this research at Harwell.

## New Uses for Nuclear Power

Nuclear power has already been used for submarine propulsion.[10] The United States are now building an atomic merchant ship of 21,000 tons displacement, the cost of which will be $42m. This ship will be able to travel 350,000 miles, or 3½ years, on one charge of nuclear fuel.[11] There are safety risks in nuclear power at sea, if the ships are wrecked; but there is no doubt that nuclear power has a great future in marine propulsion.

Since nuclear fuel is so light and easy to transport, it may bring power to remote and underdeveloped territories which have no coal or oil. " Very often," said Professor Sir Francis Simon, " mineral deposits cannot be worked because there is no power either for the mines or for transport."

> " Another application would be for irrigation. . . . In Africa . . . vast tracts of land could be made fertile if power were available for pumping water from wells. Also in places where no fresh water is available, sea-

---

[8] M.G., October 4, 1955.
[9] N.Y.T., October 4, 1955.
[10] See pp. 64–65.
[11] N.Y.T., July 31, 1957.

water could be distilled with the off-steam of power stations situated on the coast." [12]

Mr. Walter Busbridge, the head of the Isotopes School at Harwell, has said that sea-water could be distilled to irrigate Australia at a cost of 5s. per million gallons.[13]   An American geophysicist, Dr. Lloyd Berkner, Vice-President of the International Geophysical Year Committee, endorsed this idea, said that with water Australia could have more arable land than the United States, and predicted that Australia's population might thus increase to 200 million.[14]

## " *A Family of New Instruments of Research, Investigation, Technology and Therapy* "

This application of atomic energy is the result of the unique properties of the radio-active substances or " isotopes " that are produced.   These substances emit radiations which can penetrate considerable thicknesses of solid matter, although in doing so their intensity is gradually reduced.   The radiations " ionise," *i.e.*, break up, the atoms or molecules of the matter they traverse, and this makes it possible to detect their presence, by special instruments, with great sensitivity.

These properties of radio-active substances have already received a multitude of applications.[15]   Atomic radiations are used to detect hidden flaws in welds or castings.   A small quantity of a radio-isotope floated on the surface of a liquid will indicate to someone outside the level of that liquid in a storage tank.   It can be similarly used to study " flow processes," *e.g.*, the velocity of the gas in a blast furnace, or the flow of blood in the human body.   The reduction in the intensity of radiation as it passes through matter can be used as a thickness gauge.   In many industrial

[12] *Atomic Energy : A Survey* (Rotblat), p. 32.
[13] M.G., March 17, 1957.
[14] *Ibid*.
[15] See p. 266.

processes, where the final product is a continuous sheet of material, *e.g.*, paper, linoleum or thin sheet metal, this method of detecting variations of thickness is much better than any previously known.

An exceedingly small quantity of a radio-isotope can be detected. This makes it possible to use it to study the wear and tear in the metal parts of an engine. It can be used by doctors to help in diagnosis, and by those engaged in medical research, to study the chemical and physical processes inside the human body, *e.g.*, a tiny quantity of radio-sodium mixed with food will enable the researcher to detect by his instruments exactly where the sodium has gone. Many of the processes that go on in men, in animals and in plants are being studied in this way. Radio-isotopes are also used in clinical treatment, *e.g.*, to destroy the tumour cells of cancer.

Sir John Cockcroft said in September 1956 that Britain was distributing each year about 22,000 consignments of radio-active products, and output was increasing by 25 per cent. per year. She was now " the world's greatest distributor of radio-active isotopes." [16] In 1957 Dr. Libby, also a member of the USAEC, said that radio-isotopes (he called them the " clinkers " of the atoms " burned " in nuclear furnaces) were already saving United States industry $400m. a year. He predicted that by *1960* the savings to industry and agriculture would reach $5,000m. annually, and the isotopes " would be paying the whole way for the atom, and the American people and the Western world will get their atomic armament and their atomic power development costs all free." Physicians were using the isotopes, he said, to diagnose or treat a million patients a year; agricultural researchers were using them to study the application of fertilisers, the better knowledge of animal nutrition and animal diseases, and insect disinfestation; oil companies were using them for " oil-well stimulation—more oil out of the same piece of ground "—this had given savings of

[16] M.G., September 8, 1956.

$180m. a year, which would soon rise to more than
$1,000m.[17]

These facts answer those who say that it would have
been better for mankind if the secrets of nuclear energy had
never been unlocked. It is impossible to "repeal the
nuclear age," even if it were desirable. But it is not
desirable. Nuclear energy presents mankind with great
benefits from its peaceful uses, and with great dangers from
the weapons in which it can be used. Some way must be
found to keep the benefits, and end the dangers. The first
step to finding it is to understand just what the dangers
are. The next four chapters will be devoted to this task.

17 Prof. W. F. Libby, N.Y.T. *Weekly Review*, August 4, 1957.

# 10

## *Atomic Weapons:*
## *Hiroshima and Since*

On September 5, 1945, the first Allied reporter who reached Hiroshima after the end of the 1939 War wrote:

"Thirty days after the first atomic bomb destroyed the city and shook the world, people are still dying, mysteriously and horribly—people who were uninjured in the cataclysm—from an unknown something which I can only describe as the atomic plague.

"Hiroshima does not look like a bombed city. . . . I write these facts as dispassionately as I can, in the hope that they will act as a warning to the world. In this first testing ground of the atomic bomb . . . it gives you an empty feeling in the stomach to see such man-made devastation. . . . I could see about three miles of reddish rubble. That is all the atomic bomb left. . . . The Police Chief of Hiroshima . . . took me to hospitals where the victims of the bombs are still being treated. In these hospitals I found people who, when the bomb fell, suffered absolutely no injuries, but now are dying from the uncanny after-effects. For no apparent reason their health began to fail. They lost appetite. Their hair fell out. Bluish spots appeared on their bodies. And then bleeding began from the ears, nose and mouth.

"At first, the doctors told me, they thought these were the symptoms of general debility. They gave their patients Vitamin A injections. The results were horrible. The flesh started rotting away from the hole caused by the injection of the needle. And in every case the victim dies."

The reporter wrote of other after-effects of the first atomic bomb: " a peculiar odour . . . given off by the poisonous gas still issuing from the earth soaked with radio-activity," against which the inhabitants all wore gauze masks over their mouths and noses; the many thousands of people who had simply vanished—" the atomic heat was so great that they burned instantly to ashes—except that there were no ashes "—they were " vaporised "; and then he wrote:

> " From the moment that this devastation was loosed upon Hiroshima, the people who survived have hated the white man. It is a hate the intensity of which is almost as frightening as the bomb itself." [1]

This first report from a Western observer forms an appropriate introduction to the discussion of the nuclear weapons developed in the last twelve years.

## The Hiroshima Bomb

The weapon used against Hiroshima was a 20-kiloton (kil.) fission bomb, *i.e.*, it had an explosive power equivalent to 20,000 tons of TNT; that means that it was equal in explosive power to 2,000 of the ten-ton " block busters " used by the R.A.F. against Berlin; it was in itself nearly forty times as powerful as the heaviest raid carried out by Hitler against London (590 tons, May 10, 1941). The bomb was dropped from a height of 7,000 feet by a Flying Fortress, operating alone; it was detonated at a height of 1,850 feet on August 6, 1945.

## A-Bomb: Four Weapons in One

An A-bomb is four weapons in one: (1) Its blast can be " many thousands of times more powerful than the largest TNT bombs." [2] (2) Its " heat-flash " is " a potent fire-

---

[1] Peter Burchett, *Daily Express*, September 5, 1945.
[2] *U.S. Handbook*, 1957, p. 1.

raiser." [3]   (3) " The explosion is accompanied by highly
penetrating and harmful, but invisible, rays called ' gamma
radiation,' gamma rays being similar to X-rays."   (4) " The
substances remaining after a nuclear explosion are radio-
active, emitting similar radiations over an extended period
of time.   This is known as the . . . ' residual radio-
activity.' " [4]

The first three of these effects of an atomic bomb
happen simultaneously, and are, for practical purposes,
instantaneous.

## Air, Ground and Under-Water Bursts

The casualties caused and the damage done by an A-bomb
vary according to where it is burst.   An air-burst at the
appropriate height produces the maximum effect from blast
and heat-flash—there are no obstacles between the bomb
and the target area to intercept or weaken the shock-wave
or the heat which it creates; but gamma radiation may be
rather less than with a ground-burst, and residual radiation
is much reduced.

A ground-burst reduces the effect of blast and heat-flash;
the areas of destruction and of fire are less.   But the residual
radio-activity may be much greater, for the blast will
pulverise buildings, earth and other objects, and the result-
ing dust and rubble will be very highly radio-active, and
may remain so for a considerable period of time.

This is still more true of bombs burst under the ground
(*e.g.*, after they have penetrated perhaps fifty feet through
soft sand), and under the water. [5]   In both cases the area
of destruction will be less, but the radio-activity and, in
particular, the residual radio-activity will be even greater
than from a ground-burst.   Deaths from this cause may not
happen for some days, or even weeks, after the explosion.

[3] *Select Committee Report on Civil Defence*, 1954, p. 193.
[4] *U.S. Handbook*, 1957, p. 1.
[5] On under-water bursts, see p. 125.

The number and type of casualties caused, and the damage done, by any given bomb will also depend on the nature of the terrain (Hiroshima was flat, Nagasaki hilly, and therefore, of the two, Nagasaki suffered proportionately rather less); on the " disposition of the populace " (whether they have shelters, etc.); and even on the weather.

## The Hiroshima Yardstick

But, in spite of these facts, the United States experts who wrote the 1957 Handbook use the Hiroshima bomb as their yardstick in estimating the effects of nuclear weapons. They say:

" The only information concerning the casualties to be expected from the use of nuclear weapons is that to be obtained in connection with the air-bursts over Japan, and so these will be used largely as the basis for the subsequent discussion." [6]

It is, indeed, impossible intelligently to discuss the subsequent development of nuclear weapons without bearing in mind what happened at Hiroshima in 1945.

The Japanese authorities estimate the immediate casualties and other results of the bomb as follows:

| | |
|---|---|
| Total population, including troops .. .. .. .. | 300,000 |
| Killed and missing .. .. .. .. .. .. | 100,000 |
| Injured .. .. .. .. .. .. .. .. | 100,000 |
| Still requiring regular clinical examination .. .. .. | 98,000 [7] |
| Still requiring treatment .. .. .. .. .. | 6,000 [7] |
| Dead during the year 1956–57 .. .. .. .. | 185 [8] |

Destruction of property:
 the barracks, the port facilities, all the factories, all the office accommodation, 50,000 houses.[7]

We cannot assume that the casualties would be less in a Western city. " Contrary to popular belief," says the United States Handbook, " the resistance to blast of American residences in general would not be markedly

[6] p. 456.
[7] *The Times*, August 6, 1956.
[8] *The Times*, August 7, 1957.

different from that of the houses in Hiroshima." [9] Most
of the dead were in the buildings destroyed. More
optimistic estimates were made for British towns in 1947,[10]
but they should be treated with reserve.

The ways in which these casualties and this damage
were caused by the Hiroshima bomb have been discussed
in detail by various authorities:

## BLAST

An Indian Government Report says that at Hiroshima
" damage was complete (including collapse of earthquake-
resistant reinforced concrete buildings) within half a mile
from ground zero "—*i.e.*, within a circle one mile across;
" most of the houses within 1½ miles " (*i.e.*, within a circle
three miles across) " were destroyed. Houses up to two
miles were badly damaged." [11]

The British Home Office Memorandum, speaking of
what would be expected in a British town, says:

" There is an area of some three or four square
miles of severe devastation and a total damaged area
which may be ten or twenty square miles. Within the
area of severe devastation, streets would be blocked
with debris." [12]

It was estimated that at Hiroshima 20 per cent. of the
casualties, dead and wounded, were due to blast, *i.e.*, to
injuries caused by falling structures and flying debris.[13]

## FIRE

The temperature generated by a 20-kil. bomb is several
million degrees centigrade; " thermal radiation " travels

[9] p. 123.
[10] *e.g.*, the Home Office calculated that the number killed in an average British
town would be 50,000. (*The Effects of the Atomic Bombs at Hiroshima and
Nagasaki*, p. 19.) In 1954 the Home Office estimated that 30,000 would be
killed in *Central* London *at night*; they made no allowance for flash-burn
casualties or casualties from fires in burning buildings.
[11] *Indian Government Report*, p. 51.
[12] *Select Committee Report on Civil Defence*, p. 193.
[13] *Indian Government Report*, p. 52.

with the speed of light. At Hiroshima it ignited so many fires (started by newspapers, dried leaves, shop awnings, etc.) that it swept across the entire area of devastation, and caused a " fire-storm." The Home Office Memorandum says: " It has been estimated that a [20-kil.] bomb bursting over London would produce some 1,200 developing fires, that is, fires that need the attention of a fire brigade." It points out again that the streets would be blocked with debris, and adds: " Heat-flash also produces burns on people in the open, varying from burns of the greatest severity within half a mile of the explosion."

It is believed that about 60 per cent. of the deaths at Hiroshima and 75 per cent. of the total casualties were due to burning, including direct burns from the heat-flash, and burns from the subsequent conflagration. In other words, 60,000 people, men, women and children, were burnt to death.

### INITIAL NUCLEAR RADIATION

Gamma radiation has a range of only two miles. It is estimated that " about 30 per cent. of those who died at Hiroshima had received lethal doses of nuclear radiation." [14] But most of them had been already crushed or burnt to death. With A-bombs in the kiloton range, this will generally be true.

### RESIDUAL RADIO-ACTIVITY

This is not an instantaneous, but a lingering, effect. In the case of an air-burst, as at Hiroshima, the number of casualties is small. Thus at Hiroshima there were relatively very few. " It is in the case of surface, or below surface, bursts," say the Home Office,

> " that the dangers of residual radio-activity assume greater proportions. Our knowledge is incomplete, but from published information about the American atomic

[14] *U.S. Handbook*, 1957, p. 457.

test at Bikini (in 1946) it can be calculated that if a burst of this type occurred inshore, and the radio-active mist and spray drifted onto the land, *an area of several square miles would be so heavily contaminated that the chance of survival of people in that area would be very small indeed.* A water-burst of this kind, in or adjacent to a port with an onshore wind, might therefore produce casualties on a scale comparable with those from an air-burst. This type of attack on ports cannot be ruled out. . . . *Any general decontamination of the area is out of the question, and indeed the free use of the area by personnel might not be possible for weeks or even months.*" [15]

In this test at Bikini, the Americans exploded a 20-kil. bomb some fifty feet below the level of the sea; a column of water with a straight stem and a mushroom head rushed upwards; in fifteen seconds it was a mile high; the mushroom head was 1½ miles across; the column contained a million tons of radio-active water. From the base of the column there rolled out a white ring of mist, named the "base surge," travelling at fifty miles an hour, and covering ultimately an area of more than five square miles.

These facts show that the Home Office alarm is more than justified; to a nation that depends on its ports, 20-kil. bombs used in this way might be a mortal danger.

## Larger and Smaller Atomic (Fission) Bombs

It was at first believed that an atomic bomb could be neither much larger nor much smaller than the 20-kil. weapon used at Hiroshima. This is because there is a "critical mass" of U235 or plutonium below which so many neutrons escape that a chain-reaction cannot start; but once the critical mass is assembled, the chain-reaction "will be set off by some stray neutron, of which there are always some

---

[15] *Select Committee Report on Civil Defence*, p. 194.

about." [16]   It is conjectured that, to overcome this difficulty, the Hiroshima bomb had two pieces of U235, each less than a critical mass; and that they were brought together by a gun-barrel device, in which a high-explosive was used to blow one piece from the breach end of the gun into another sub-critical piece firmly held in the muzzle end.

But mechanisms were subsequently devised by which a larger number of pieces of U235 or plutonium could be assembled when the explosion was wanted; and this gave larger bombs.   But there was a limit to the number of pieces that could be used—" the mechanism . . . becomes prohibitively complicated when the total mass is more than a few times the critical mass." [17]

Another discovery raised the limit again.   The critical mass depends on various factors, and among them, on the density of the material (U235, U233, plutonium).   It turned out that in all cases the critical *radius* of a bomb is inversely proportional to its density; the greater the density, the smaller the sphere required for an explosion.   For U235 of normal density the critical radius is six centimetres, which means that the critical mass must be eighteen kilograms. But the density can be increased above normal by compression; this was achieved by a spherical arrangement of specially fabricated shapes of conventional high explosive. In a hole in the centre a sphere of U235 of less than critical size was placed; when the high explosive was detonated, " an inwardly directed ' implosion wave ' " was produced. This compressed the U235, raised its density, made the sphere become critical, and the explosion occurred. [18]   " A 10 per cent. increase of density, which should be easily practicable, would allow a reduction of 30 per cent. in the amount of fissile material needed to create an explosion." [19]

---

[16] Prof. O. R. Frisch, *Atomic Energy : A Survey* (Rotblat), p. 17.   The " critical mass " is not a matter of weight only; the *shape* of the U235 or plutonium is also a vital factor.   A sphere is the shape which retains most neutrons. See *U.S. Handbook*, 1957, pp. 11–13.

[17] Prof. O. R. Frisch, *Atomic Energy : A Survey* (Rotblat), p. 17.

[18] *U.S. Handbook*, 1957, p. 13.

[19] J. Maddox in *The New Scientist*, June 6, 1957, p. 28.

Another device was the use on the inner lining of the bomb of " tampers " or " neutron reflectors," to cut down the escape of neutrons and to hold the U235 together until more generations of fissions had occurred.

" By means of such techniques," says Mr. Maddox, " it is probably now possible to create a 20-kil. explosion out of less than seven or eight kgs. of U235 (costing say $200,000) or four kgs. of U233." [20]

These technical details are very relevant to nuclear disarmament. They show that weapons as powerful as the Hiroshima bomb can be made with quantities of fissile material much less than were required in 1945; they show that existing stocks of weapons could be " re-fabricated " to make a more formidable armament; and that, if nuclear disarmament were agreed to, the disloyal diversion of very small amounts could lead to serious results.

By the techniques above described, and others, the efficiency of the use of fissile material in weapons has much increased, and is still increasing.[21] This has made it possible to produce atomic (fission) weapons both much *less* and much *more* powerful than the Hiroshima bomb. The Indian Government say that the weapons range from half-kil. (500 tons of TNT) to 500-kil. (half a million tons of TNT).[22] The British Government say that " they could range all the way down to something less than the equivalent of 1,000 tons of TNT." [23] The Indian Government say that the less powerful weapons are probably made of U233, which has a substantially smaller " critical mass " than U235 or plutonium. They also say that below five kils., the use of fissile material is not very efficient; the quantity required is the same, but the weapon is so devised that its energy is released when fewer " generations of fissions " have occurred.

[20] *Ibid*.
[21] See p. 258 for a statement by Mr. D. Sandys on July 23, 1957.
[22] *Loc. cit.*, p. 53.
[23] Lord Mancroft, *Hansard*, House of Lords, May 8, 1957, col. 432.

## *The Decision of the U.S. to make " Tactical" Nuclear Weapons*

These developments led the United States Government to make a decision of vital importance. When Mr. Gordon Dean, then the Chairman of the United States Atomic Energy Commission, asked Congress for funds in 1953, he said that the whole concept of how atomic weapons can be utilised in warfare had been radically revised.

" No longer are they looked upon only as devices to be used in an ' Hiroshima-type ' way against cities and industrial areas. It is now possible to have a complete ' family ' of atomic weapons, for use not only by strategic bombers, but also by ground-support aircraft, armies and navies. The Department of Defence is very much aware of this change in concept, and atomic weapons are being incorporated into the operational plans for all three of the armed services. This, quite naturally, has greatly increased the demand for atomic weapons—to an entirely different order of magnitude than obtained a few years ago." [24]

This was a most terrible development in the preparation for war. The United States example was quickly followed by Russia and Britain. The tactical weapons were designed and manufactured with amazing speed. By March 1955, Mr. Hanson Baldwin could give this summary of the types of weapons then available in the U.S.A.:

" nuclear depth charges for use at sea; atomic shells for use with 280mm. (11 inch) gun with a range of about eighteen miles; atomic shells for use with 5- or 7-inch guns; atomic warheads for the 762mm. ' Honest John ' free flight artillery rocket with a range of about eighteen miles; atomic warheads for the Army's ' Corporal ' guided missile with a range of about seventy-five miles; atomic warheads for anti-aircraft and air-to-air

24 Gordon Dean, *Report on the Atom*, p. 71.

missiles; atomic warheads for the Army's ' Redstone ' guided missile; warheads for the ' Matador ' and ' Regulus ' pilotless bombers; and bombs to be dropped from planes." [25]

This list could be extended today; it would include nuclear warheads for missiles to replace guns on all types of naval vessels; nuclear warheads for IRBM (800–1,500 miles) and ICBM missiles, and many more.

In March 1957, Mr. Dulles said that American Forces " almost everywhere " are equipped with atomic weapons. " It is almost a normal part of their equipment," he told a news conference.[26]

In November of the same year, Mr. Sandys said: " Practically every modern weapon of importance now carries a nuclear warhead." [27]   A small proportion of these weapons may have less explosive power than the Hiroshima bomb; but, if Mr. Thomas Murray is to be believed, the number is relatively very small.[28]   Many of them, as will be shown, are much more powerful.   Some of them *may* be the equivalent of half a million tons of TNT; let readers look back to the beginning of this chapter, and realise that that means twenty-five Hiroshimas in one.

[25] N.Y.T., March 20, 1955.
[26] N.Y.T., March 14, 1957.
[27] *Hansard*, November 7, 1957, col 346.
[28] Mr. Murray was a member of the USAEC, who resigned because large, rather than small, nuclear weapons were being made.   He said he had " recommended tens of thousands of small weapons," but so far the United States had only " a development program." *Life*, May 6, 1957.

# 11

# *Hydrogen Weapons,*
## *" Dirty " and " Clean "*

THE United States Handbook of 1945 said that the Hiroshima bomb released only a very small part of the potential energy of the U235 employed [1]; the complete fission of 1 lb. of U235 or plutonium would produce as much energy as 9,000 tons of TNT. The 1957 Handbook said that the fusion of all the nuclei in 1 lb. of the hydrogen isotope deuterium would release as much energy as 26,000 tons of TNT.[2] This is the first reason why the advance from A- to H-bombs was as great a step as the advance from TNT to A-bombs.

The second has already been explained; the hydrogen isotopes have no " critical mass " at which an explosion automatically occurs, and therefore there is no difficulty in making H-bombs as large as is desired.

The third has also been explained; a fission-fusion bomb (U235 or plutonium surrounded by the hydrogen isotopes above described) generates such temperatures, and releases neutrons of such tremendous energy, that they cause the fission of the atoms of the cheap and plentiful U238. Thus U238 can be used as the outer sheath of a fusion bomb, and it gives, at very low cost, a tremendous added explosive power and an immense and very poisonous " fall-out." This discovery was used in the making of the early United States H-bombs; they were known as " 3-deckers ": an inner core of U235 to act as " trigger "; then the hydrogen isotopes, tritium and deuterium, and lithium 6; and finally the outer covering of U238, perhaps in the first experiment

---

[1] *Atomic Energy*, July 1, 1945, pp. 134–135.
[2] pp. 4–5.

a little enriched with U235. The second of these " 3-decker " bombs, exploded at Bikini on March 1, 1954, showed what this new weapon might be made to do. It was a 15-meg. " device," the equivalent in explosive power of ten times all the high explosive dropped by Allied aircraft on Hitler's Germany; 750 Hiroshimas in one. The fission core of U235 was probably equal to 20 to 50,000 tons of TNT in power; the deuterium and lithium to 2m. tons; the U238 to 13m. Its power " was about double that of the calculated estimate," so Admiral Strauss declared, and provided " a stupendous blast in the megaton range " [3]; its residual radio-activity, or " fall-out," contaminated an " area of over 7,000 square miles . . . to such an extent that survival might have depended upon evacuation of the area or taking protective measures." [4] Everyone remembers the Japanese fishermen who got radiation sickness eighty miles away.

It is not clear how *small* an H-bomb can be made; one estimate is 50 kilotons. But it is certain that H-bombs can be made much larger even than the 15-meg. bomb exploded in 1954. It is reported that " the current [United States] Air Force requirement is for a deliverable bomb of *50* [*fifty*] megatons." [5]

## Making Nuclear Weapons
## " Purely Military "

It is doubtful whether there is much future for such super-bombs. Writing before the Bikini test in 1954, Professor Frisch said of the H-bomb:

> " The same amount of destruction can be obtained more economically by several smaller bombs; *indeed, it has been questioned whether the H-bomb has any real advantage in practical warfare.*" [6]

[3] N.Y.T., April 1, 1954.
[4] *U.S. Handbook*, 1957, p. 423.
[5] S. Alsop, N.Y.H.T., June 21, 1957.
[6] *Loc. cit.*, p. 18.

The United States Government have not gone as far as that; like the Russians and the British, they are still testing H-bombs " in the megaton range." But they have had second thoughts since the days of the early H-bomb experiments, when their policy was founded on " massive retaliation." " The Western Powers," said Mr. Dulles in August 1957, " hold that . . . the atomic weapon *should be as nearly as possible a purely military instrument*." [7] President Eisenhower has often said that the purpose of the United States tests is to make the nuclear weapons as " purely military " as may be; to develop *smaller* A-bombs which can strike at military targets, without damaging civilian lives or property; to make the weapons *defensive*, *e.g.*, against submarines or enemy bombers; and to make the H-bombs " clean," *i.e.*, without the massive " fall-out " of the 15-meg. Bikini bomb.

In some degree they have succeeded. There are alleged to be atomic bombs as small as 1-kil.; there are defensive nuclear weapons for use against submarines, and defensive nuclear missiles to be launched against enemy bombers, either from the ground or by fighters in the air; both the United States and the United Kingdom have megaton H-bombs which cause little more " fall-out " than the Hiroshima bomb of 1945—bombs which are, in President Eisenhower's phrase, " 95 per cent. clean." Admiral Strauss has claimed that considerable progress has been made toward development of a " humanised " thermo-nuclear weapon [8]—a memorable adjective indeed.

But it is difficult to understand how any of these weapons can be called " purely military." The 1-kil. A-bomb is the equivalent of more than 1,000 of the 12-inch shells used in the 1914 War. No one who saw a 12-inch shell explode will believe that a thousand of them could strike a military target without doing indiscriminate damage to civilians and their property as well. Experts may call it

[7] M.G., August 3, 1957.
[8] N.Y.T. *Weekly Review*, June 23, 1957.

" conventional "; it is a mass-destruction weapon all the same.[9] Most of the " defensive " nuclear weapons are far more powerful than 1 kil.; they could be used to launch a devastating attack. The " clean " H-bombs are clean, because the outer sheath of U238 has been left off, and bismuth, which is heavy and will neither fuse nor fission, used instead. Since the tritium, deuterium and lithium have no radio-active products, the only " fall-out " is from the " triggering " core of plutonium or U235.

But these " clean " H-bombs can be made with a " yield," *i.e.*, an explosive power, equivalent to that of 10m. tons of TNT. It is on the use of such weapons as a " deterrent " that British defence policy is based. It is on the expectation that 10-meg. bombs, " clean " or " dirty," will be used against us, that British Civil Defence is being planned. It is worth considering, therefore, just what a " clean " 10-meg. bomb would do.

## The Home Office Manual on the 10 Meg. Bomb

A " clean " 10-meg. H-bomb would have the same blast and heat-flash as a " dirty " bomb of the same " yield." The effects of this blast and heat-flash have been carefully assessed in two Government Manuals on Civil Defence.[10] This, in summary, is what they say:

### BLAST

The " shock-wave," which moves through the air with the speed of sound, behaves " like a moving wall of highly compressed air." For a 10-meg. bomb, it lasts five seconds

---

[9] Dr. Libby, one of the USAEC's leading scientists, told the Senate Foreign Relations Committee that a 1·7-kil. bomb had been fired experimentally underground; " its yield was about as small as has been fired "—*i.e.*, so far there are *no* 1-kil. bombs; " this little fellow," he said, " broke 400,000 tons of rock, crushing it up " : M.G., March 15, 1958.

[10] *Home Office Manual of C.D.*, Vol. 1, Pamphlet No. 1, *Nuclear Weapons*, 1956; Fire Research Bulletin No. 1, *Fire and the Atomic Bomb*, Department of Scientific and Industrial Research, 1954.

or more. " Clean " H-bombs would probably be burst in the air, at 8,000 feet.[11] A 10-meg. bomb, so burst, would cause total destruction for four miles from " ground zero " (the point immediately below where the bomb is burst). That is to say, there would be a circle of *total destruction eight miles across*; the area of " moderate to severe damage " would be a circle thirty-two miles across. As the Manual says: " In London, if a 10-meg. bomb dropped centrally, there would be irreparable damage over most of the L.C.C. area, with minor damage over the whole of the Metropolitan area. *In most other British cities*, however, a good deal of the area of potential damage would consist of open country."

The " overground installations " of public utilities (gas holders, electricity generating stations, water-pumping stations, telegraph and telephone cables, buses, etc.) would be damaged " more or less severely " up to eight miles (*i.e.*, a circle sixteen miles across). A ground burst would destroy underground installations up to a distance of " a few miles."

Most of the blast casualties would be caused by falling masonry, flying debris and glass, and by people being trapped under buildings that collapsed all over the circle of " moderate to severe damage," which is thirty-two miles across.

The inner circle of " total destruction," eight miles across, would have " a complete covering of very heavy debris." In other words, no movement would be possible. " Debris is going to be one of the outstanding problems." [12]

## FIRE

Fire, however, would be more terrible than the blast. " People directly exposed to the heat-flash " would receive " severe third degree burns [charring] " up to a distance of eight miles from ground zero. If they were in shelter,

[11] The effects of H-bombs vary as do those of A-bombs, according to whether they are burst in the air, on the ground, underground or underwater. See pp. 121–125.

[12] The quotations are from *Nuclear Weapons*, paras. 123 to 152.

they would be safe; but not for long, because the heat-flash would ignite innumerable fires, and there would almost certainly be a " fire-storm," as there was at Hiroshima, and when the R.A.F. bombed Hamburg with incendiaries in 1943. " In such circumstances, it seems that nothing can prevent all the fires from joining together into one mass fire engulfing the whole area."

A 10-meg. bomb would radiate 500 times as much heat as the 20-kil. Hiroshima bomb. For a ground burst, " this will mean a fire ring extending from about $3\frac{1}{2}$ miles to ten miles "; *i.e.*, within the inner circle, seven miles across, there will *not* be fire, because everything is smashed into " debris " so pulverised that it will not ignite; outside that circle, there will be a ring of fire twenty miles across. " Isolated fires may occur at greater distances." [13] For an air-burst, the outer ring of all " engulfing " conflagration would be from four miles to twelve (*i.e.*, twenty-four miles across).

These propositions are all elaborated, with a wealth of tables, diagrams, higher mathematics and medical learning in the Government publication *Fire and the Atomic Bomb*. They all add up to the simple conclusion that, if a 10-meg. H-bomb, " clean " or " dirty," should be dropped, everything would be destroyed by blast or burnt, and few human beings would survive, within a circle of more than twenty miles across.

Both these invaluable Government publications deserve the closest study. In the light of what they say it is difficult to accept Admiral Strauss's conception of a " humanised " thermo-nuclear weapon; indeed it is difficult not to agree with the man who said: " To call an H-bomb . . . ' clean ' is to make an obscene farce out of words."

## RESIDUAL RADIO-ACTIVITY

The devastation wrought by a few " clean " 10-meg. bombs in Britain would no doubt bring our military resistance to

[13] The quotations are from *Nuclear Weapons*, paras. 24 to 45.

an end.  But there is no present reason to hope that any 10-meg. bombs that might be used against us would, in fact, be " clean."  The Russians have been making " dirty " bombs.  The United States have not yet begun to clean up the " dirty " bombs they have in stock.[14]  No doubt there is considerable resistance to the proposal to clean them up; the U238, which makes the " fall-out," also provides a very high proportion of the explosive power.  And it is the cheapest of all nuclear bomb materials: besides the " fall-out," it gives a *megaton* of blast and fire for £5,000.[15]

What will the residual radio-activity of a " dirty " 10-meg. bomb be like?  The Home Office say it will contaminate a cigar-shaped area extending 200 miles downwind, plus twenty miles up-wind, and varying in width up to forty miles.  They estimate this area as the result of a " dirty " H-bomb burst on the ground.  They believe the enemy *would* burst his H-bombs on the ground; it would mean a reduction of 20 per cent. in the area destroyed by blast and fire; but, they say, " this reduction might well be accepted because the potential area of damage would still be far greater than the size of most target areas " (in plain English, any city would be completely destroyed); thus a ground-burst would give an " enormous additional residual radiation hazard from ' fall-out ' . . . without any important reduction in actual blast damage." [16]

They say that people who were in the open for thirty-six hours after the bomb exploded would receive the following doses of radio-activity, and that the following percentages of them would die:

| Distance from Bomb Explosion | Dose of Radio-activity in Roentgens | Percentage who would die |
|---|---|---|
| 190 miles | 300 r. | 5–10 |
| 160 ,, | 500 r. | 50 |
| 140 ,, | 800 r. | 100 [17] |

[14] President Eisenhower at his Press Conference, N.Y.T., August 8, 1957.
[15] Indian Government Report, pp. 23–24.
[16] *Nuclear Weapons*, p. 17.
[17] *Loc. cit.*, pp. 18 and 35.

The Home Office add this reassuring comment: " People do not usually spend thirty-six consecutive hours in the open." Quite true. *Usually* they do not. But if H-bombs had been falling, would not every city and town have been evacuated by everyone who survived? Would the country be able to give shelter to more than a tiny proportion of the refugees? If proper air-raid shelters had been prepared, of course the dose of radiation would be proportionately reduced. But, for the foreseeable future, a high proportion of those within *140 miles* would die.

What kind of death would these victims suffer? The United States Department of Defence gives the following tabular description of what happens to people who have received a dose of 550 r. to 300 r., and who therefore have a chance of living:

SUMMARY OF CLINICAL SYMPTOMS OF RADIATION SICKNESS

| *Time after exposure* | *Survival possible* (550 r. to 300 r.) |
| --- | --- |
| 1st week | Nausea, vomiting, and diarrhoea in first few hours. |
| | No definite symptoms (Latent period) |
| 2nd week | |
| 3rd week | Epilation (loss of hair) Loss of appetite and general malaise Fever Haemorrhage Purpura Petechiae Nosebleeds Pallor Inflammation of mouth and throat Diarrhoea Emaciation |
| 4th week | |
| | Death in most serious cases (Mortality 50 per cent. for 450 r.) [18] |

[18] *U.S. Handbook*, 1957, Table 11.72, p. 477.

People who receive a dose of 700 r. are more fortunate; they die, but their agony is shorter; in the second week they suffer rapid emaciation, and then, for *all* of them, death brings release.[19]

People who receive less than mortal doses do not emerge unscathed [20]; they may contract leukemia (cancer of the blood), or cancer of the bone; or they may suffer " mutations," which make them sterile, or cause their children to be born defective.   Slight " mutations " may only make them generally a little less fitted to survive; but these slight " mutations " may in reality be worse than severe ones, for the severe " mutations " cause death, while slight " mutations " may be transmitted to descendants, generation after generation, for thousands of years.

These facts explain why the British Medical Research Council say in their Report of June 1956 that " atomic warfare on a large scale could not fail to increase for many generations the load of distress and suffering that all human societies would be called upon to support." [21]

[19] *Ibid*.
[20] *Loc. cit*., pp. 496–498.
[21] Cmd. 9780, p. 69.

# 12

## *Can War be "Limited"?*

"ATOMIC weapons of the power of the Hiroshima bomb," said the British Minister of Defence in February 1957, "are now regarded as primarily suitable for tactical use by troops in the field." [1] Let the reader look back to page 119 and contrast these words with the eyewitness report from Hiroshima in 1945. He can measure the swift advance in weapons, and the swift change in ministerial and military thinking, in the last twelve years.

For the view expressed by the Minister of Defence is now generally accepted by the governments and the Staffs of the major military Powers. As early as December 1953 President Eisenhower said that "atomic weapons have virtually achieved conventional status within our armed services." [2] Mr. Gordon Dean wrote in 1954:

> "It is our objective to have on hand sufficient strategic weapons to destroy completely an aggressor's industrial capability to make war, plus enough for tactical use to stop in the field any aggressive move he might make." [3]

And in August 1957 Mr. Sandys said that if Britain reduces the number of her troops in *Malaya*, "those who remain will have their fire-power increased by the availability of nuclear weapons." [4]

There have been, moreover, very firm declarations that, if war should happen, the nuclear weapons would be used. In 1955 Mr. Dulles said that "small tactical atomic weapons probably would be used if the United States became involved in any major military action anywhere."

[1] *Hansard*, February 13, 1957, col. 1311.
[2] Address to UN Assembly.
[3] *Report on the Atom*, p. 117.
[4] *Cambridge Daily News*, August 20, 1957.

He added that there was " rather general agreement at the NATO meeting last December on atomic missiles *as conventional weapons for European defence* "; and that his statement, therefore, was " simply an application of this NATO principle." [5]   In 1957 Mr. Quarles, Secretary of the United States Air Force, rejected any idea that the United States could engage in war against Communist aggression without using atomic weapons. " I cannot believe," he said, " that any atomic power would accept defeat while withholding *its best weapons.*" Even in little wars, the United States should act " with all necessary strength, using our best weapons, if required." The report adds: " The remarks by Mr. Quarles were cleared by his superiors in the Defence Department." [6]   General Twining, Chairman of the United States Chiefs of Staff, said that it should be

> " clearly understood by our possible adversaries that the United States is prepared, in the event of aggression, to employ its best weapons whenever it is in our essential interests to do so. . . . This strategy should apply to the kind of situation that some call ' little wars,' no less than to a wider conflict." [7]

Mr. Sandys has said the same: " aggression will meet with the instant resistance of the combined forces of the Western Alliance, if need be, by the full power of nuclear retaliation." [8]

The Russians are quite as clear. " Atomic weapons," said Marshal Zhukov, " will be widely introduced into the armed forces as an established weapon " (" established " is no doubt the equivalent of Mr. Dulles' " conventional ") " . . . and, in the event of a serious military conflict, *atomic weapons will inevitably be employed as the basic means of inflicting defeat.*" [9]

[5] N.Y.H.T., March 16, 1955.
[6] N.Y.H.T., February 3, 1957.
[7] N.Y.H.T., May 5, 1957.
[8] *Hansard*, February 13, 1957, col. 1313.
[9] *The Times*, March 20, 1957.

The sinister significance of these statements requires attention. In 1940 there was world-wide horror at Hitler's concept of "total" war; but by 1942 the Western Allies were using the same methods of "total" war themselves. In 1945, after Hiroshima and Nagasaki, the world recoiled at the thought that nuclear weapons might be used again. But by 1957 the Ministers and generals of the leading nations not only took it for granted that nuclear weapons would be used on a "total" scale in any future world war, but they also believed that they could be used "tactically" in smaller wars. And they began to think of "weapons of the power of the Hiroshima bomb" not only as "tactical" but even as "conventional" weapons.

This is so astonishing a change that it is worth considering how it has come about. There appear to have been two main factors.

The first was the success of the A-bombs on Japan. There were many men in the United States Government who did not want to use them. But after a decade of debate and historians' research into what really happened, most authorities agree that, before the A-bombs were used, the Japanese were *not* definitely defeated; that their militarist generals could still control the government, and were resolved to fight on, if need be, till all Japan was in ruins, and millions more were killed. It was the A-bombs that brought them to surrender.

> "In the terrible evil of war," wrote Dr. Arthur Compton, "this was the lesser evil. When the boys who had been poised for the invasion of Japan began to come home, I could not help feeling that our choice was justified. As I look over the record, I hear again the voice of the Japanese reporter: 'Had it not been for the bomb, I would not be here.'"[10]

Mr. Henry Stimson, who was ultimately responsible for the decision, wrote:

[10] *Atomic Quest*, 1956, p. 284. See also pp. 219–255, and V. Bush, *Modern Arms and Free Men*, 1950, pp. 163 *et passim*.

" This deliberate, premeditated destruction was our least abhorrent choice. The destruction of Hiroshima and Nagasaki put an end to the Japanese war. It stopped the fire raids, and the strangling blockade; it ended the ghastly spectre of a clash of great land armies." [11]

There can be no doubt that this experience had a profound influence on military thinking; reinforced the sincere conviction of all military men that their troops deserved, and must have, the " best weapons " that can be made; and so reconciled them to acceptance of the nuclear arms. But in fact it lost all relevance when the prospective " enemy " got nuclear weapons too; once that happened, these weapons were simply a particularly cruel addition to the sufferings that all the troops, and civilians, on both sides, would endure. Nevertheless, the Japanese experience still influences thought.

The second factor was the use of the word " tactical," now applied by Mr. Sandys to the Hiroshima bomb. No one thought that bomb was " tactical " in 1945. It caused casualties three or four times the number of the British Army of the Rhine. It was the substitute for an Allied campaign, by land and sea and air, expected to last for eighteen months, to which several million troops had been assigned; and it caused immediate, unconditional surrender. This was the most astonishing *strategic* result the world had ever seen. The Lilienthal Committee,[12] writing in March 1946, while the impact of these events was still quite fresh, spoke of

" the really revolutionary character of these [atomic] weapons, *particularly as weapons of strategic bombardment* aimed at the destruction of enemy cities and the eradication of their populations."

11 " The Decision to Use the A-Bomb," *Harper's Magazine*, February 1947, pp. 106–107.
12 *Lilienthal Report*, p. 1. See pp. 183 *et seq.*

And this view was universally accepted until the first H-bomb was exploded in 1952. Only then did general staffs begin to say that A-bombs were "tactical." And they called them "tactical" because something much bigger and more devastating had been found. Having these bigger weapons, the staffs have made plans for war in which A-bombs are regarded as artillery, and, by the evolution of thought, it came to be assumed that nuclear missiles, equivalent to the Hiroshima bomb in power, and with a range of twenty, ninety or 200 miles,[13] would do what conventional artillery did till 1945. That is really the explanation of what Mr. Sandys said about Malaya; his words do not seem to rest on an appreciation of whether any nuclear weapon could, in fact, be usefully employed in Malaya, or, indeed, in other parts of Asia. It is the explanation why Marshal of the Royal Air Force Sir John Slessor wrote:

> "We may use nuclear power in a bomb or shell . . . tactically, for 'conventional' purposes. That is merely to employ one projectile to do what we had to use thousands to do in Korea."[14]

But, in fact, no nuclear weapon, not even the 1-kil. fission bomb, if, in fact, it yet exists, bears any relation to what artillery used to do. It is something entirely different in kind; that is why, year by year, nuclear armament is revolutionising the organisation and training of all armed forces by land, sea and air, and why the staffs find it so difficult to draw up combat plans that seem to other people practicable and sound.

As these plans place more and more emphasis on nuclear weapons, so more and more people, including scientists and military experts, have begun to ask the question whether these weapons can, in fact, be used in war without irreparable disaster to all concerned.

[13] See p. 128.
[14] *Strategy for the West*, p. 155.

## *Are A-Bombs "Tactical" Weapons?*

Is there any validity at all in the concept of the "tactical nuclear weapon"? If so, can it include, as Mr. Sandys made it include, the Hiroshima bomb?

So far as can be judged from Ministers' and generals' statements,[15] and from the details of the nuclear "Exercises" they carry out, the staffs' thinking about A-bombs is far from clear. The exercises are, perhaps, more important, and certainly more revealing, than the statements.

In the late autumn of 1955, the United States Army and Air Force carried out a joint exercise called "Sage Brush" in the state of Louisiana and in neighbouring states. Its purpose was to try out in practice what Mr. Sandys described: the use of "atomic weapons of the power of the Hiroshima bomb" in "tactical support of troops in the field." It was explained to the Press that these "20-kil. atomic weapons" were "*toward the low end of the destructive scale*," and that, as Mr. Sandys said, "they are at present standard Air Force tactical weapons for use in and around the battlefield and against enemy airfields." [16] General Weyland, the Chief of the Tactical Air Command, said *before* the exercise began:

> "The atomic weapons we are using are not weapons of mass destruction that obliterate great areas of the world's surface. These tactical weapons are just as selective as the older weapons. *There is no reason to believe any more innocent people would be killed than in any other kind of war*." [17]

The "tactical" targets to be attacked were carefully selected, and the simulated bombs were dropped. Here are two accounts of the results: Mr. Hadley, who has been quoted, wrote:

[15] *e.g.*, F. M. Lord Montgomery, "The Panorama of Warfare in a Nuclear Age," NATO *Civil Defence Bulletin*, December 1956.
[16] A. T. Hadley, "Low Yield Atomic Weapons," *The Reporter*, April 19, 1956.
[17] N.Y.T., November 5, 1955.

" About seventy of these [20-kil.] ' bombs ' were
dropped on Louisiana in one day. The umpires ruled
that all life ' had ceased to exist ' in Louisiana."

Mr. Hanson Baldwin said that in all " a theoretical total
of 275 nuclear weapons," ranging in power from 2 kils. to
more than 40 kils. had been expended. He wrote :

" The biggest lesson of Exercise Sage Brush is that
there *probably can be no such thing as a limited or
purely tactical nuclear war. . . . The almost frightening
experience of the joint Air Force-Army manoeuvre
that ends this week indicates that even a so-called
tactical nuclear war would cause vast devastation. It
probably could not be limited at least in any heavily
populated or industrialised areas. . . .* If Sage Brush
had been actual instead of simulated, it is safe to say
that much of the twelve-state area would have been
devastated. Cities would have been partially destroyed
and their surviving inhabitants menaced by radio-
activity.

" Western Louisiana, the area of ground fighting,
would be desolate. Its pine forests would have been
blown by nuclear blasts into tangled impassable dead-
falls. Huge forest fires would have swept the area,
trapping the scattered survivors of the ground fighting.
The Red River and much of the area would have been
contaminated with radio-activity and clinging mustard
and nerve gas.

" This," he concludes, " is a seemingly apocalyptic
vision. But it is not overdrawn." [18]

Compared to this most NATO exercises have an air of
unreality or make-believe. In 1955 there was one exercise
in North Germany called " Full House "; *eleven* A-bombs
were fired into an area twelve miles long by six miles wide;
all were 20 kil. in power [19]; yet most of the troops engaged

[18] N.Y.T., December 5, 1955.
[19] *The Times*, September 26, 1955.

were supposed to have survived. In Exercise "Carte Blanche" 335 A-missiles, shells and bombs were used; it covered the whole of Western Germany, the area of which is less than that covered by "Sage Brush"; when an airfield was "atomised," it was declared to be "out of action for a representative time of a few hours only" [20]; "radioactivity was not being taken into account." [21]   In 1957 Exercise "Lion Noir," according to German press accounts, began with a bombardment of 100 H- and A-weapons; in the course of the operations, the enemy arrived at the gates of Hamburg and Frankfurt, only to find them both engulfed in flames. All the NATO troops were withdrawn to the west of the Rhine. After a month Germany was "liberated" by a counter-attack, made under a screen of nuclear weapons—which fell on German soil.[22] No official appreciation of what happened to Germany and the Germans has been published. But writing of the earlier exercises in the United States *Bulletin of Atomic Scientists*, Mr. Hanson Baldwin said:

"NATO's basic strategy for the defence of Western Europe is based upon a nuclear concept; we will use, it is said, tactical A-weapons to bomb the enemy's airfields, troops, supply dumps, and other 'military' targets. In a thickly settled area like Western Europe this is a stultifying and self-defeating strategy, for no such large-scale tactical nuclear war in this heavily industrialised, heavily populated region could be limited. Contact bursts are the best means of knocking out airfields; 40- to 80-kiloton bombs—one, two, or three of them to an airfield—would be certain to cause widespread havoc, and radio-activity would poison the adjacent areas for months or years. Since most of Europe's airfields are situated near cities or towns, and

[20] *Aeroplane*, July 15, 1955, p. 83.
[21] *Aeroplane*, July 22, 1955, p. 133.
[22] *Vorwärts*, April 19, 1957.

since it is virtually impossible, in any case, to distinguish clearly between military and non-military targets in an area where troops and civilians are co-mingled, the result seems obvious. A nuclear war in Western Europe would almost certainly spread into a ' no-holds-barred' conflict, and Western Europe, *in any case*, would emerge a desert—a consummation not likely to win friends or influence people." [23]

Note the significance of Mr. Baldwin's words: " *in any case.*" *They mean : whether the H-bombs are used or not.* And when Mr. Baldwin speaks of 40- to 80-kil. A-bombs being used, two or three per airfield, he is not romancing; no doubt he is speaking with knowledge of what is planned. An 80-kil. bomb is four Hiroshimas in one.

Even in the United States, an A-bomb attack might produce a grave disaster. A contributor to the United States *Bulletin of Atomic Scientists*, Mr. Hart, concluded, on the basis of detailed estimates, that in 1954 the total area of vital strategic targets in the United States, including the United States strategic bombing bases; the big centres of population, business and industry; the coal and oil fields; and the crucial transportation centres, was *somewhat less than 2,000 square miles. Destruction of this vital area,* he said, *would lead to complete national disruption and paralysis.*[24] Mr. Hart's estimate of the area of vital United States strategic targets may seem astonishingly small. But suppose he was in error by 100 per cent., and that the true total should be 4,000 square miles. On Professor Blackett's basis of calculation [25]—fifty A-bombs for the *total* destruction of 400 square miles—only 500 A-bombs would be required to bring about the complete disruption of the United States of America. The Russians must have many thousands of such bombs.

[23] United States *Bulletin of Atomic Scientists*, May 1956, p. 157.
[24] *Bulletin*, June 1954, pp. 197–205.
[25] See p. 162.

It is true that, in all these calculations, the A-bombs are assumed to be of 20-kil. power or more, and that smaller A-bombs can be made. But Mr. Murray says that very few of these smaller bombs have yet been made; Ministers and generals still talk in terms of " A-weapons of the power of the Hiroshima bomb "; it is said that "current military thinking in Paris " (*i.e.*, at NATO) was that anything up to a 50-kil. weapon (2½ times Hiroshima) was a " tactical battlefield bomb " [26]; in their exercises simulated weapons of this power are used; not even Mr. Murray suggests that the enormous stocks which now exist should be destroyed; it seems unlikely that the Staffs will agree to use their scarce and costly U235, plutonium and U233 with the very low " efficiency " achieved by the 1- or 2- or 4-kil. bomb. In any case, the weapons that now exist, and that will for years constitute the backbone of the nuclear armoury of the Powers, are " of the power of the Hiroshima bomb," or larger. Consideration of what happened at Hiroshima in 1945 shows that it is a dangerous distortion of language to call them " tactical." [27] Their use in the ways envisaged in the exercises discussed above would bring irreparable disaster to all concerned.

## A-Bombs Might Lead to All-Out War

But there is another danger which their use would inevitably involve: if one side began by using 20-kil. weapons, the other might reply with 40-kil. weapons, until,

[26] Rt. Hon. G. Brown, *Hansard*, December 20, 1957, cols. 841–842.
[27] Liddell Hart, in *Brighton Conference Paper No. 26*, pp. 7–9, writes: " Confusion in the planning has been increased . . . by the introduction of what are called ' tactical atomic weapons.' This is a general term for weapons of this tremendously destructive kind that are intended for use in the fighting zone of the armies, or against their immediate lines of supply and reinforcement. A new and very dangerous complication has arisen from the decision in 1954 to equip the NATO ground forces and their supporting ' tactical' air forces, with such weapons." He arrives at the conclusion that it would be far safer to resist small Communist aggressions by using mustard gas, and then says: " The safest course of all would be to rely on conventional forces using purely conventional weapons."

maddened by the chaos and passion that resulted, one of them sought to end it by using the " heavy stuff " as well. It is one thing to theorise in time of peace about the use of weapons; it is quite another to decide on their employment under the pressure of actual war. General Norstad has said:

> " It would be extremely difficult to limit the use of atomic weapons. There would be a very rapid tendency for things to get bigger rapidly. . . . I believe that if you have an incident, the assumption must be that great power will be used." [28]

Lord Tedder knows what it is to carry the responsibility of supreme command in desperate battle, with the odds all on the other side.

> " To believe," he says, " that there will be tactical atomic weapons which could be used without leading to the use of the ultimate so-called strategic weapon . . . would be to live in a fool's paradise." [29]

These are warnings that no one can afford to disregard.

### CAN NUCLEAR WAR BE LIMITED?

But so many able people have urged the doctrine of " limited " nuclear war, and there are so many books about it,[30] that a brief consideration of their thesis is required.

They argue that " total " nuclear war, with the use of H-bombs, is mutual suicide, and must, therefore, *at all costs,* be avoided. But disputes between nations are sure to happen, and they are sure to lead to war; the Communists, if they know that total nuclear war is regarded by the West

---

[28] *Newsweek*, July 15, 1957, pp. 28–29.
[29] *Hansard*, House of Lords, May 9, 1957, col. 586.
[30] The leading books are: H. A. Kissinger, *Nuclear Weapons and Foreign Policy*; R. E. Osgood, *Limited War*; Carl Berger, *The Korea Knot*. The Brighton Conference Association have collected a large number of articles and other documents on the subject. Also R.I.I.A. study, *On Limiting Atomic War*, by Rear-Admiral Sir Anthony Buzzard and others.

as too dangerous to be risked, will " nibble " at the free world by such limited aggressions as those in Korea, Indo-China or Greece; unless the West is ready to use small " tactical " nuclear weapons the more numerous man-power of the Communists will prevail, and bit by bit the cause of freedom will be lost.  To meet this danger, the West must agree on a doctrine of " limited war," setting out clearly the way in which they will resist aggressions, and must ensure that the potential enemy understands this doctrine in advance, in order that he, too, may follow the accepted code in any operations he may undertake.

" Limited " war must mean, if possible: (i) the limitation of the geographical area of the war; (ii) the limitation of the political objectives of the war; (iii) the limitation of the weapons used; (iv) the limitation of the targets attacked.

These points may be considered in turn.

## Geographical Limitation

This suggestion is founded on experience in Korea, where, by tacit agreement of the belligerent forces, geographical limitation was successfully achieved.  If war happens, this is certainly a desirable objective; but it must not be allowed to hamper measures of wider application, *e.g.*, economic sanctions, which might bring the aggression to an end.[31] In any case, it is unlikely that the decision about the area of the war will be made by the nations which resist aggression; the aggressor, embarked on a criminal adventure, will do what he thinks will pay him best.

## Political Limitation

This proposal is put forward in reaction against the lament-able demand for " unconditional surrender " which did so much to prolong the 1939 War.  No doubt it would be a

31 See pp. 551–552.

good thing if all belligerents would decide that their purpose was not " total victory," that they did not intend to " annihilate " their enemies, or to destroy their states, and would declare this purpose when hostilities began. It does not seem likely at present that this will be done; the word " annihilation " is in frequent use among the General Staffs. Nor would it create much confidence, if it were done; " war aims," however clearly declared, change swiftly with the course of military events; it rarely happens that a peace settlement bears much relation to the issues about which the war began.

## LIMITATION OF WEAPONS

Rear-Admiral Buzzard says:

> " We would, in such a (' limited ') war, only use the smaller and cleaner, discriminate bombs, and weapons, and if anybody wants to know the sort of size, I would say down to the bottom end of the kiloton range, somewhere down there." [32]

Other particulars have been suggested: an arbitrary upper limit of so many kilotons; restrictions on the height of an air-burst, or on the locality of an underwater-burst; special rules for use of nuclear bombs at sea, etc. Usually the limitations proposed are wrapped in ambiguous phrases, no doubt because the details would show how unrealistic they are. A Swedish admiral wrote a book in 1955 to propose that large A- and H-bombs should be abolished. He suggested that a treaty should be made by which " a maximum explosive power—much lower than that of the Hiroshima bomb—heat radiation and radio-activity must be fixed by agreement." [33] A treaty to limit the maximum temperature which an A-bomb would be permitted to attain! This egregious sentence is simply the *reductio ad absurdum* of much thinking which, though honest, is inherently unreal.

[32] B.B.C. broadcast, July 2, 1957.
[33] Admiral Elis Biorkland, *International Atomic Policy*, 1955, p. 127.

But, even if the Swedish admiral's treaty could be made, or even if, without a treaty, there was an informal understanding about the power of the weapons that would be used, it is difficult to understand how anybody can hope that such limitations would be observed in war. Recent experience holds out no hope that they would be. Until 1939 it was agreed that " the established rules of international law " forbade bombardment from the air; the use of fire, either from the air or on the field of battle; indiscriminate air or submarine attack on merchant vessels.[34] The Western Allies began by observing these " established rules "; by 1942 they had been swept away, and not even the exponents of " limited war " propose to restore them now.

## LIMITATION OF TARGETS

The same argument applies to the limitation of the targets to be attacked. Rear-Admiral Buzzard explains this plan as follows :

> " Generally speaking, we shall keep off centres of population, with very few exceptions . . . unless those centres of population are being used as a safe sanctuary for direct attacks against us."

The immense difficulties of codifying or applying such a formula, allowing for railway centres, airfields, ports and so on, speak for themselves. One " exception " by one side, one mistaken intelligence report that a centre of population is being used as a " sanctuary " for attack, even one accidental use of a bomb or missile, and the whole system of limitation might collapse. Again experience encourages no hope. In 1939, it was an " established rule " that civilians, and " open " towns and cities, must not be attacked. For almost a year, the Western Allies scrupulously observed it; by 1940, Hitler had destroyed it, and in Korea it remained destroyed.

[34] See Sir Anthony Eden's Draft Disarmament Convention, pp. 56 and 244.

## LIMITED WAR AND THE PRECEDENT OF POISON GAS

It is true that the exponents of " limited war " do not rely on the moral power of legal rules to uphold their system; they believe it would be the mutual interest of all belligerents to observe the limitations they propose; they rely on the kind of " self-imposed restraint " that prevented the use of poison gas in the 1939 War. It is, of course, possible that this may happen; it is *possible* that a " major " war, even a third World War, might be fought without any nuclear weapons being employed. But it would be unwise to rely on what happened about poison gas,[35] for that in no way helps the case for " limited war." There was *no* use of poison gas by any party to the 1939 War. And nothing can be more certain than that, if Hitler had tried to make a " limited " use of his deadly gases, the Western Allies would have replied in kind, and the full horror of chemical warfare would have been unleashed.[36] The passions aroused by the 1939 War swept away the " established rules of international law." It is difficult to believe that amid the passions aroused by the " limited " use of " small," but terrible, nuclear weapons, any new limitations would long survive.

## OTHER DISPUTABLE ASSUMPTIONS

There are two further points about the doctrine of " limited war " that deserve attention.

First, it assumes that, while total H-bomb war *must* be avoided, smaller wars *cannot* be avoided. Sometimes it is said that they will happen on what is called the " periphery "[37]; a phrase which usually turns out to mean someone else's country, and not one's own. The Middle East is often chosen as the place where wars will be

[35] See pp. 324 *et seq.*
[36] See p. 326.
[37] or outside the " Tacit Bomb Line." Cockburn, see p. 161, below. Mr. D. Healey, M.P., in *Encounter*, December 1957, writes: " There is only a small number of specific theatres around the Sino-Soviet periphery where it might be to the West's advantage to use nuclear weapons." See Mr. Osgood's work, *passim*

inevitable in years to come [38]; yet recent experience suggests
that, if the Western nations united to uphold the UN
Charter against aggression, no such war need ever occur.
Many of the exponents of " limited war " simply ignore
the Charter; Mr. Murray even says: " Limited war is the
legal institution available as a last resort " [39] for the settlement of international disputes. But the Charter, like the
Kellogg Pact, made *all* wars, *all* resort to force *illegal*; if
that basic law is upheld by the democratic governments,
they can make it prevail; if it is not upheld, then great
wars, as well as small ones, will surely come. The way to
avoid both is to make a Disarmament Treaty and to establish the rule of law through the UN. By far the easiest
part of that task, especially after the Disarmament Treaty
has been made, is to stop the little wars.[40]

Second, the exponents of " limited war " usually assume
that disarmament is impracticable. Thus Mr. Kissinger,
after a perfunctory exposition of the standard arguments
about the difficulties of disarmament, concludes: " A
meaningful agreement is, therefore, almost impossible." [41]
But whatever the difficulties, political and technical, and
whatever the risks, of disarmament, they are certainly far
less than those of Mr. Kissinger's system of " limited war."
Faced by the fact that war with nuclear weapons will
destroy mankind, he, and those who think like him,
devise ways of " limiting " wars that are infinitely more
difficult, infinitely more unrealistic, and infinitely more
hazardous than the disarmament which is still the declared
objective of all their governments, but which they
implicitly, or like Mr. Kissinger, explicitly, reject.

---

[38] *e.g.*, Mr. George Kennan, Reith Lectures. Mr. Sandys, however, says:
" The areas in which limited war seems most likely to occur, if it does, are
in the Far East and the Persian Gulf ": *Hansard*, November 7, 1957, col. 337.
[39] *Loc. cit.*
[40] Mr. D. Healey, M.P., B.B.C. broadcast on " Limited War," July 5, 1957:
" It is almost certain that the Russians would not have started the war in
Korea if they had known for sure that the Americans were going to react
even with conventional force."
[41] *Op. cit.*, p. 208.

## CAN H-BOMBS BE USED IN WAR?

It has been shown above that the use of the word
" tactical " to describe " atomic weapons of the power of
the Hiroshima bomb " cannot be justified; that the use of
such weapons would bring irreparable disaster to all concerned; and that there are no solid grounds for hoping
that, if nuclear war began, it could be " limited," either
in the power of the nuclear weapons used, or in other
ways. In fact, if war began, the use of any nuclear
weapon, however " small," might all too easily lead to
total H-bomb war.

The effects which H-bombs would produce were
described in Chapter 11. Remembering the official accounts
there reproduced of what the blast, fire and fall-out from
an H-bomb would accomplish, is it rational to think that
such a weapon can be used? Doubt about the answer is
spreading far and wide. The British White Paper on
Defence appeared in April 1957 to reassert Mr. Dulles'
doctrine of " deterrence " by " massive retaliation "; but
Mr. Dulles' well-known article of October 1957 [42] appeared
to abandon this doctrine in favour of " limited " war by
tactical A-weapons. In any case, Mr. Murray, who, let it
be repeated, resigned from the USAEC on the H-bomb
issue, has made an unanswerable case for thinking that an
all-out H-bomb war would be so great a catastrophe that
" we are hurled into the midst of absurdity." " The
multi-megaton H-bomb," he says, " was born in a vacuum
of military strategy. No one had antecedently determined
its uses. After the event the vacuum was filled with confusion. The confusion is not surprising. The multi-
megaton bomb fits badly, if at all, the standards of military
usefulness hitherto accepted. . . . It will be altogether
efficient in annihilating beyond repair the industrial and
human potential of great cities. But this terrible

[42] *Foreign Affairs*, October 1957.

'efficiency' is linked to no reasonable military usefulness "; for an H-bomb war will be " a war of sudden
catastrophe, not of slow attrition."

Besides the destruction of the cities, there will be the
fall-out; and Mr. Murray gives the most illuminating
quantitative estimate of the strontium 90 risk which has
yet been made. Quoting Mr. Khruschev's aphorism: " We
will bury you," Mr. Murray says:

> " I presume that he has no wish to spoil his own
> pleasure on the occasion by finding himself in the same
> grave. It is a fair conclusion that he does not intend
> to dig the grave with several thousand megatons of
> fission energy."

He calculates that in a Russian–United States H-bomb
war " ground-bursts releasing 3,500 megatons of fission
energy would sufficiently fill out the concept of ' destruction ' that would be the shared aim of both belligerents."
This would give the inhabitants of the two countries a
strontium 90 level in their bones " of the order of fifty
times the maximum considered acceptable." [43]   In other
words, if they escaped the blast and heat-flash of the
H-bomb and radiation sickness, they would still die of
cancer of the bone; and so would many people in all the
other countries of the world.   Mr. Murray insists that his
figures are " not unreasonable "; and when they are used,
he says, the concept of the " war of survival . . . blows
apart into patent absurdity." [44]

Rear-Admiral Buzzard has pointed out two other
aspects of H-bomb war which are equally absurd.  A total
global war, he said, would be " such a disaster that it could
never be in proportion to any issue at stake "; and it
" could never be the lesser of two evils." [45]   Captain Liddell
Hart supports this view, denounces the " confusion " in

[43] See pp. 253–254.
[44] Mr. Murray's article was published in *Life* on May 6, 1957.  Copies can be
obtained from the Brighton Conference Association.
[45] Address to the British Council of Churches, M.G., October 23, 1957.

NATO planning and in the thinking of the General Staffs, and says that if the H-bomb were used " it would merely result in mutual suicide. That would be the inevitable outcome of war with H-bombs." [46]

Unfortunately, although Mr. Dulles' attitude has changed, no " nuclear " government has yet acknowledged the truth of the arguments set forth above. The United States Government have allowed Mr. Murray to resign from the AEC. The Russians still use language that implies that H-bombs can be used. In one of his letters to Dr. Adenauer, Mr. Bulganin said that, if nuclear war should happen,

> " the territory of the Federal Republic would inevitably suffer the heaviest and most concentrated attack and be reduced ' entirely to a graveyard.' . . . The vital centres of so thickly populated a country, with its concentrations of industry, ' could be paralysed by the effects of a single hydrogen bomb.' " [47]

What Mr. Bulganin ignored was that, if this were to happen in Germany, it would infallibly be happening in Russia, too. There is still great scope for Mr. Murray and Rear-Admiral Buzzard to convince the governments that Professor Frisch was right to ask " whether the hydrogen bomb has any real advantage in practical warfare." [48]

## WILL NUCLEAR WEAPONS BE USED IN WAR?

But will any A- or H-bombs actually be used in war? Knowing the facts set out above, will any Prime Minister, President, dictator or general, in his senses, give the order to use even the smallest nuclear weapon that exists?

There is a danger—very real, if their public statements are a guide—that both Ministers and Staffs have been " conditioned," by the constant repetition of the language which they habitually use, into thinking that the so-called

[46] *Brighton Conference Paper 26*, September 1957.
[47] *The Times*, April 29, 1957.
[48] See p. 131.

" tactical " weapons, including the 50-kil. bomb, *could* be employed without leading to the most terrible results. One more Hiroshima, if it happened, would shock them back to a sense of reality. But, with the speed of modern armaments, and " instant readiness," it might then be too late; one Hiroshima would have provoked a hundred, or a thousand, more.

But, apart from this, there are three other ways in which, while nuclear weapons continue to exist, their use in war might be begun.

First, there might come to power a megalomaniac obsessed by dreams of empire, and resolved by all means to make these dreams come true. This is not an imaginary danger. In the last two decades there have been Hitler, Mussolini and the Japanese generals, all of whom had absolute personal power over the nations whom they ruled. All of them, if they had had the H-bomb, would have given the order for it to be used; and the order would have been obeyed.

Second, there is the danger of the " accidental " bomb. With great numbers of air force and aircraft carrier crews —and soon submarine and missile crews as well—under the strain of " instant readiness," doing unbroken air patrols with A- and H-bombs, with standing orders to obliterate specific enemy targets immediately a given code signal is received by radio from their base, there is a danger that a signal might be garbled or misunderstood, and that thus, by accident, a nuclear war might start. Captain Liddell Hart gives specific examples from modern military history of cases where signals have gone wrong, with grave results.[49]

[49] Captain B. H. Liddell Hart, *Reynolds News*, January 12, 1958. There is also the danger, much emphasised by Russian propaganda, that an aircraft pilot, under the severe physical and mental strain of his Service duties, might go mad : it has, of course, happened that pilots have gone mad while in the air; but this danger is less serious than the others, because bombing aircraft carry a crew of three or more and it is unlikely that more than one would go mad at once.

Third, the use of nuclear weapons might begin in quite a different way. " No war of tomorrow," says Mr. Hanson Baldwin, " is likely to start with a planned and deliberate nuclear blitz, unless a megalomaniac comes to political power." It may well begin with conventional armaments alone; " the atomic danger will come, not as war starts, but when one side or the other starts losing." [50] It is when defeat or disaster looms that the urge to use " the best weapons " available may seem impossible to resist.

Captain Liddell Hart says that

" commanders will always tend to use every weapon they possess rather than risk their troops being over-run. . . . Once doctrine and organisation are estab-lished on a particular weapon basis, an almost irresistible pressure is generated. Such pressure becomes all the more certain, now that medium field artillery can be provided with atomic ammunition." [51]

While nuclear weapons not only exist in great quantities, but are regarded as a legitimate and necessary means to national security, these dangers will threaten mankind. They show how urgent is the warning given by Mr. Gordon Dean:

" Whereas, before, the problem was simply one of war or peace, it is now one of oblivion or peace. . . . Yet man, even in the atomic age, has not chosen peace. He also has not chosen oblivion, and he seems to think he can go on for ever without deciding upon one or the other. Maybe he can, but the risks are enormous. . . . In flirting with world war in the atomic age, man . . . is playing with the means by which mortal life on earth can be ended." [52]

[50] N.Y.T. *Weekly Review*, August 18, 1957.
[51] *Loc. cit.*, p. 8.
[52] *Report on the Atom*, p. 278.

# 13

## *Is There Any Defence?*

Is there any defence against the weapons which the preceding chapters have described? Is there any *military* defence which can meet a major nuclear attack? And is there any *civil* defence that will preserve the structure of civilised society and ensure the survival of enough people to maintain it when the nuclear war is over?

For the purpose of considering these questions, it will be assumed that the next war, if it starts, will be a war of the kind for which NATO, according to its official publications,[1] is preparing; a war in which H-weapons in limited numbers will be used, together with much larger numbers of A-weapons of various kinds.

## *Military Defence*

"We must take account," said the British Minister of Defence in February 1957, " of the realities of today. . . . However efficient our defences, it is inconceivable that they could provide 100 per cent. immunity against attack, and if only half a dozen nuclear bombers got through, they might, in a single raid, cause incalculable death and devastation over immense areas. I am referring to attacks by manned bombers. . . . But we are now entering a new phase in which we may quite soon be open to attack by ballistic rockets. . . . It would be absurd to pretend that we shall be quick to evolve an effective defence against this form of attack." [2]

---

[1] *e.g.*, *Facts about NATO,* September 1957, Section B.I, p. 3, and Section B. V, on " Survival Requirements."

[2] *Hansard*, February 13, 1957, cols. 1311–1312. On defence against missiles, see pp. 374–375.

Two months later, Mr. Sandys said: "In present circumstances it is impossible effectively to defend this country against an attack with hydrogen bombs."

That summer he said:

> "We have taken a very bold step in deciding not to do the impossible. We decided not to defend the whole country, but to defend only our bomber bases. I must pay tribute to the people of Britain for the readiness with which they have accepted these harsh but inescapable facts." [3]

Dr. Cockburn, Chief Scientist to the Ministry of Supply, explained in 1956, in a lecture to which reference will be made again,[4] why defence is so difficult. There are two main factors. The first is the enormous explosive power of nuclear bombs; the second is "the increasing speed of flight."

Thanks to the power of nuclear bombs, there is now no need for a long-sustained offensive; "one concerted raid can annihilate an entire target system"; "the offence can decide the time and place of attack"; switch from target to target; while the defence must be effective at every point, and never surprised or overwhelmed.

The increase in speed of flight also helps attack. Air defence depends on radar, and is fully effective only within the radar horizon. Even if the defending aircraft gain in speed as much as the attacking bombers, "the time available for implementing the defensive system is becoming steadily smaller." The missile will make it much less still. "These two factors between them," says Dr. Cockburn, "provide an immense advantage to the offence, the ability to surprise and overwhelm the defence." [5]

## THE DEFENCE OF BRITAIN

In the 1939 War, when the most powerful bomb that could be dropped contained ten tons of TNT, a bombing offensive

---

[3] *The Times*, August 21, 1957.
[4] See p. 393.
[5] *Journal of the Royal United Service Institution*, February 1956, pp. 25–26.

became prohibitively expensive, if an average of 5 per cent. of the attacking aircraft were brought down per raid. Professor P. M. S. Blackett, a physicist and adviser to the Government on operational research during the 1939 War, has given a quantitative application of Dr. Cockburn's principles which shows how radically things have changed:

"Let us compare the number of successful aircraft sorties required to destroy an area of 400 square miles [6] when three types of bombs are carried. The relative number of sorties are:

1 for H-bombs
50 for A-bombs
10,000 for chemical (conventional HE) bombs carried by bombers with a 10-ton load.

"These figures are alone sufficient to show why the problem of effective defence against H-bombs is almost insoluble—so few bombers can be permitted to get through." [7]

Professor Blackett applied this proposition to the air defence of Britain:

"Suppose Britain expected, during the first month of an atomic war, to have launched against her some 1,000 sorties of A-bombers. . . . Let us take 100 as the maximum number of A-bombs Britain could take and survive as a fighting unit. This would mean that not more than 10 per cent. of the attacking A-bombers can be allowed to penetrate the defence, that is, 90 per cent. must be shot down. This would be extremely difficult to achieve with our present or our projected defence system. If some of the attacking bombers carried H-bombs—one would not know which—more than 99 per cent. would have to be shot down to achieve an effective defence; this is certainly impossible." [8]

[6] Rather larger than the area of Greater London.
[7] Prof. P. M. S. Blackett, F.R.S., President of the British Association 1957, Lees Knowles Lectures on Military Science, *Atomic Weapons and East-West Relations*, 1957, pp. 47–48.
[8] *Op. cit.*, p. 49.

In this analysis, Professor Blackett is dealing with air attack alone; the fact that Russia has large numbers of missiles with a range sufficient to reach most of Britain presents a different, and a more difficult, problem. Professor Blackett says there is " no defence in sight against them." [9]

## THE DEFENCE OF THE U.S.A.

The United States have a much more favourable geographical position than Britain. They have spent immense sums on warning systems, on anti-aircraft weapons, and on fighter aircraft. Their Distant Early Warning system, a line of radar posts stretching across the Arctic Circle from Alaska through Canada to Baffin Island, is now in full operation; it cost $600m. There is another line of radar posts in the Atlantic, and aircraft patrol it every day. All large centres of population are ringed by batteries of Nikes and other missiles which will " home " on enemy bombers before they come too near. The United States Air Force has many wings of fighters, now equipped with air-to-air nuclear missiles.[10] But it is officially expected that in case of war a considerable number of Russian bombers could still get through. It is also believed that the Russian Navy, launching missiles from submarines, could make a heavy nuclear attack on many of the industrial cities of the United States. It has been suggested that such attacks could reach more than thirty of the forty-eight states. If this is an over-estimate of what the Russian Navy could do in 1958, there is every reason to expect that it will soon be true.

The Russians certainly believe that they could pierce the United States defences. In an important article, published in 1957 in the Russian Army paper *Krasnaya Zviezda*, Marshal Vassilevsky claimed that their forces could inflict immense damage on the United States. No one has claimed

[9] *Op. cit.*, p. 54. The United States Air Defence Command has openly admitted that even " a 90 per cent. effective defence might not be good enough to guarantee national survival."
[10] President Eisenhower Address on " Science and National Security," November 7, 1957.

that NATO could strike at Russia with sufficient speed to prevent this happening.

## The Defence of Russia

Russia has a more favourable geographical position even than the United States. It has a vast territory, with great open spaces for the dispersal of population, industry, air bases and other defence. The Russian Government have spent immense sums on their air force. They have nuclear weapons in great numbers. It has been known for some years that they were ahead of other nations in many types of short-range and medium-range missiles. But General Norstad, Supreme Commander of NATO, testifying in 1957 to the United States Senate Committee on Foreign Relations, said that the Western Powers could launch atomic attacks on Russia from a perimeter of 360 degrees, manned by more than 250 separate bases—with " relative impunity," and were capable of the " absolute " destruction of Russia's ability to make war. When asked: " Did you say that NATO has the capacity of destroying everything of significance in Russia? " the General replied: " I meant of military significance. Yes, I believe that to be true." [11]

This means that even the two most powerfully defended nations in the world are in the same position as Britain; against nuclear weapons, transported by modern aircraft and guided or ballistic missiles, there is no military defence.

## Civil Defence

Is there better hope in passive, or civil, defence? Some people of great authority think there is. Dr. E. Teller of the USAEC had a share in the production of the A-bomb; he is said to have been " widely acclaimed as the ' father ' of the H-bomb " [12]; in 1957 he led the opposition to the abolition of nuclear tests, on the ground that five more

[11] *The Times*, June 14, 1957.
[12] *The Times*, November 26, 1957.

years of research and experiment might enable the USAEC to make " clean " H-bombs. The official NATO *Civil Defence Bulletin* for December 1957 reported Dr. Teller's five-point programme to " ensure survival in the nuclear age " :

> " I believe we must train our civilians to defend themselves, and we must build a vast system of underground shelters to save our population and our industrial plant. Civilians, organised as Home Reserves, should be trained to defend limited areas against enemy troops that would try to take over after an atomic attack on the United States. . . .
>
> " In densely populated areas, where psychological bombing would have its greatest effect, I believe we should build deep underground shelters for our civilian population. In out of the way places we should build other shelters to protect food supplies and our industrial resources. This is vital to our defence. . . . Even if our people, safe in civilian shelters, survived a nuclear attack, we could be licked to starvation if our food supplies and industrial plant were totally destroyed. We have food surpluses. We could store enough of these to feed our entire population for two years. During the two years after a nuclear attack we would have time to find where food could be grown. . . .
>
> " We could store road-repair equipment and large numbers of trucks so a nuclear attack would not seriously interrupt our transportation system. We could store nuclear power plants and intricate machine tools for our factories. We could store weapons for our armed forces." [13]

Dr. Teller, in evidence to a Senate Sub-Committee, said that his programme would mean that " a great majority of our people will survive an attack, though American industries would most likely be knocked out." [14] He estimated

[13] *Loc. cit.*, p. 10.
[14] *The Times*, November 26, 1957.

that his programme would cost about $24,000m.; other authorities said that it would cost much more.[15]

NATO's official policy does not go all the way with Dr. Teller. Under the heading " Survival of the Population," a 1957 document says:

> " The cost of building shelters to resist the effect of thermo-nuclear explosion within about ten miles of the point of burst is so stupendous that it is not being entered into anywhere. On the other hand, the building of shelters outside that particular radius, although costly, is of more manageable proportions. The answer to the problem of the survival of the population is a combination of evacuation and shelters." [16]

The ten-mile radius is here applied to the effects of a *1*-meg. *not* a 10-meg. bomb. This is a very different proposition from Dr. Teller's; and if defence of the civil population is the purpose, it is much less realistic. But NATO appears to share Dr. Teller's generally optimistic approach. In the NATO *Civil Defence Bulletin* which has been quoted, a leading article was entitled: " Civil Defence Can Do the Job." It argued that, even if large areas are destroyed by H-bombs, there will remain much larger areas where civil defence " can and must operate." " Much hard thinking is required. . . . For the moment " (for the moment!)

> " the power of the offensive has outstripped the power of defence. But the balance will be righted, and the contribution of civil defence in helping to restore the balance is not only vital, but can, and must be, highly effective." [17]

This reflects precisely the outlook of the British Home Office. The Manual already quoted,[18] having given a

---

[15] N.C., November 5, 1957. The Gaither Committee said there ought to be radiation shelters at a cost of $22,000m. They rejected Dr. Teller's plan for deep shelters " to ride out the fire storm that follows nuclear bombing " because it would be much more expensive.

[16] *Facts about NATO*, September 1957, Section B. V, p. III.2.

[17] April 1957, pp. 2–3.   [18] See pp. 133 *et seq*.

faithful account of what A- and H-bombs would do, and having declared that blast, fire and radiation would cause " widespread casualties and damage . . . on a scale never before experienced," goes on to say:

> " Nevertheless an immense amount can be done by proper planning and organisation, and by the determined effort of trained men and women to save life, to minimise fire damage, and to lessen the hazard from all forms of radio-activity." [19]

Few people would dispute that, while the arms race goes on, it may be wise to build up some civil defence. If £1,500m. a year are to be spent on preparation for war, it is not unreasonable that a small percentage should be devoted to mitigating the disaster that would befall the general population if war should come; it may well be argued that this is an essential part of a balanced defence programme. The NATO countries have nine million volunteers in their Civil Defence Services; if another war were fought with conventional weapons—which is always possible—these nine million could render great service to their nations and to NATO. But is it true, in any significant sense, that in nuclear war " civil defence can do the job "? Is it true that " an *immense amount* can be done to save life, minimise fire damage, and lessen the hazard from radio-activity "? Do the Governments which belong to NATO really believe that that is true? If they do, they have not translated their belief into action.

Civil defence was developed on a very large scale in the 1939 War, especially in Germany; yet it could not cope with the weapons which existed then. The Home Office Manual of 1956 says that in the raids on German cities

> " half the buildings in the target area were set on fire in about half an hour. In such circumstances, it seems that nothing can prevent all the fires from joining together into one mass fire engulfing the whole area." [20]

[19] *Nuclear Weapons*, p. 1.
[20] *Nuclear Weapons*, para. 38, p. 8.

In other words, civil defence was helpless, except to clear up when the fire was over. Services on a far greater scale are needed to cope with the effects of nuclear weapons; and nothing is more certain than that they do not now exist.

Three countries have done more than the rest—one of them not in NATO.

### Swedish Civil Defence

The Swedes have done most of all. Their measures include (i) planned evacuation of the population from the cities and towns; (ii) private shelters for protection of people against near-hits of conventional bombs, and against poison gas; (iii) public shelters capable of resisting direct hits, perhaps even from nuclear bombs; (iv) rescue and relief after the attack is over.

The Swedes have great advantages. They have much open country, with scattered villages and dwellings, to which evacuees could go; plans are ready for the evacuation of three million people: 40 per cent. of the nation. Most of their cities and towns are built on granite, which is ideal for blast- and fire-proof shelters. Under Stockholm they have built huge three-storey public shelters, blasted out of the rock; the programme is for twenty shelters, to house 300,000. In Gothenburg and other places they are doing the same—in all 150 rock shelters will be made. By law, every new block of flats in an urban area must be built with a standard shelter in the basement big enough to house the occupants; the walls and roof are of eight-inch reinforced concrete; there is plant to purify the air, and so on. In peace-time they are used as garages or for storing bicycles and prams. By the beginning of 1955 there were already shelters of this kind for $1\frac{1}{4}$ million people; their total cost will be £80m.

Of the forty control centres of the Swedish Civil Defence Service, thirty-seven are built deep down in granite; the other twelve are under six feet or more of reinforced concrete. Service in civil defence is compulsory for all men

and women between sixteen and sixty-five years of age;
they do sixty hours' training a year.

This is the most comprehensive programme in the
world. It would be of the utmost value in a war fought
with conventional weapons, or if only a few small atomic
bombs were used by Sweden's enemy. But if H-bombs
were used, the shelters might be death-traps from which
no one would escape. If the H-bombs were " dirty," how
would the evacuees avoid a lethal radio-active dose?
Sweden is a very large country for its population; yet
twenty-five " dirty " 10-meg. H-bombs would cover it all
with a " fall-out " that would give everyone in the open a
radiation dose of 500 r., and half of them would die.[21]

## BRITISH CIVIL DEFENCE

The British Home Departments (the Home Office and
Scottish Office) spent £64m. on civil defence in the five
years 1952–53 to 1956–57 inclusive. The service departments spent additional small sums as well. A civil defence
service has been organised numbering 2,750 full-time
employees and 634,000 volunteers.[22] The Territorial Army
and R.A.F. reservists have been trained to assist in rescue,
fire-fighting, and other work. A number of strong control
centres, and an admirable system of communications,
have been established. Much new equipment has been
developed: instruments for measuring radio-activity; protective clothing for civil defence workers; vans that could
lay six-inch hosepipes at 30 m.p.h.; light plastic piping and
featherweight pumps that one man could carry over debris,
and much more. Plans have been made for evacuating
twelve million people from the urban areas,[23] though it has
not been revealed where they will go.

In a conventional, or a *very* " limited " nuclear, war,
these plans for large-scale evacuation, and the organisation

[21] See p. 136.
[22] *Daily Telegraph*, October 16, 1957.
[23] See pp. 135–138.

of control and rescue, might save many lives that would otherwise be lost. But if the Government are seriously preparing for an H-bomb attack, something more like the Swedish programme is evidently required. But, in fact, an air of make-believe hangs over the whole subject: in 1957 a NATO " Senior Civil Defence Emergency Planning Committee " worked on the " basic assumption " that a hydrogen attack on Britain would kill one million people; they said this figure is " staggering," but " insist it is not exaggerated." [24]   The 1956 Home Office Manual shows that one H-bomb on London alone would kill many times that number.

The 1956 White Paper on Defence frankly admitted that " full protection " for the British people against radio-activity and the other " hazards of a thermo-nuclear attack " would place a " crippling burden on the national resources "; but it said that " the Government's aim will be to take the precautions without which, should the worst happen, ordered society could not survive." Professor Blackett comments on this that the Government's present measures would certainly not enable ordered society to survive; the expenditure of £500m. over several years " might possibly, but not by any means certainly, achieve this objective." [25]

He adds:

> " Some five to ten hydrogen bombs would suffice to knock her (Britain), at least for a time, out of a war, however well-prepared with passive and civil defence organisation, and however high the morale. Fewer would be needed in the present condition of almost non-existent Civil Defence." [26]

## UNITED STATES CIVIL DEFENCE

The United States Government have obtained from Congress fantastic sums for national defence. They have

[24] *Sunday Times*, January 20, 1957.
[25] Prof. P. M. S. Blackett, *op. cit.*, pp. 24–25.
[26] *Loc. cit.*, pp. 48–49.

taken civil defence very seriously. It has been organised by a large body of able and public-spirited people, who have obtained the services of millions of volunteers. They have had a long series of local and national exercises to test their plans; in one of these exercises *everybody* in the nation took part, including President Eisenhower and his staff, who went by helicopter to emergency headquarters in the country. The work was for five years under the direction of Mr. Val Peterson, an administrator of great ability. What Mr. Peterson came to think of the power of civil defence to protect the American people against nuclear attack may best be shown by the following extracts from his speeches year by year:

*1953*: Mr. Peterson refused to recommend a project costing $15m. to use part of the New York subway as a shelter; he said that, in the event of an atomic attack in the canyons of New York, there would be from 75 to 100 feet of rubble piled up in the streets; " It may be that you would suffocate those people down in those proposed shelters simply by the rubble and debris that would be piled on top of them." [27]

*1954*: Mr. Peterson said one study " showed that we could have 22,000,000 casualties, of which I think 7,000,000 would be dead." [28]

*1955*: Mr. Peterson said " the studies would be aimed at developing plans for evacuating, feeding and sheltering *100 million* persons living in ninety-two ' critical ' target areas." [29]

*1956*: Mr. Peterson said that " if thermo-nuclear bombs ever fell on the United States, ' no one in the world ' would be able to ' meet the situation.' The ' casualties ' of last year's exercises were put at 23 million. This year, one-third of the population (*i.e.*, 56 million people) are expected to become casualties." [30]

[27] N.Y.T., August 21, 1953.      [28] N.Y.T., July 16, 1954.
[29] N.Y.T., March 26, 1955.      [30] *The Times,* July 23, 1956.

*1957* : Mr. Peterson proposed a shelter programme that would have cost nearly £12,000m.—Britain's defence budget for eight years. And then he said:

" If the whole 170 million Americans had air-raid shelters, at least 50 per cent. of them would die in a surprise enemy attack. In the final analysis," he said, " there is no such thing as a nation being prepared for a thermo-nuclear war." [31]

The conclusion to be drawn from these facts about the efficacy of military and civil defence against nuclear attack is well expressed in the words of General Gavin, the Chief of the United States Army Research and Development. Testifying to a Senate Sub-Committee about the probable results of a full-scale nuclear attack on Russia, he said:

" Current planning estimates run on the order of several hundred million deaths; that would be either way, depending upon which way the wind blew. If the wind blew to the south-east, they would be mostly in the USSR, although they would extend into the Japanese, and perhaps into the Philippine area. If the wind blew the other way, they would extend well back up into Western Europe." [32]

This is the only quantitative official estimate of the effects of nuclear warfare which has yet been made. It is a modern application of the truth which Mr. Stanley Baldwin stated in 1932:

" I think it is well for the man in the street . . . to realise that there is no power on earth that can prevent him from being bombed. . . . *The only defence is in offence, which means that you have to kill more women and children more quickly than the enemy, if you want to save yourselves.*" [33]

[31] M.G., February 20, 1956.
[32] N.Y.T., June 29, 1956.
[33] *Hansard*, November 10, 1932, col. 631.

# 14

## *Stocks and Distribution*

DR. ARTHUR COMPTON, one of the leaders, with Oppenheimer, of the team which made the first A-bomb, wrote
after the Bikini H-bomb test of 1954 that " a level of
radiation above that considered safe by those who work
with radio-active materials . . . might be produced by the
explosion of fewer than a thousand super-bombs." [1]   Are
there 1,000 super-bombs in the armouries of the nuclear
Powers?  No one except Ministers and General Staffs can
say.  What can be said with assurance is that the nuclear
Powers have now in stock fissile and fusionable material
enough to make many more than 1,000 super-bombs.
And, as Mr. Acheson pointed out to the UN Assembly in
1951, it is not the number of weapons that really matters;
it is the stock of material from which they can be
made.[2]

There is the highest authority for saying that these
stocks are now immense.  Writing in 1953, Mr. Gordon
Dean, who had been Chairman of the USAEC since 1950,
said : " After the current expansions are completed and the
new plants have been in operation for several years, we will,
figuratively, have atomic bomb material running out of
our ears." [3]

In 1955 Dr. Lapp, a former consultant to the USAEC,
said that the United States stockpile of " atomic bombs "
then amounted " to several tons of TNT for every

[1] A. H. Compton, *Atomic Quest*, 1956, p. 308.
[2] UN Assembly, Committee I, November 19, 1951.
[3] *Report on the Atom*, p. 87.

173

inhabitant of our planet." [4]    Since then the United States
plants have been running at full pressure for three more
years.

What is the Russian nuclear stock?    United States
guesses, which may have their origin in Intelligence
reports, suggest that they are quite substantial, but far
behind the U.S.A.    Thus Congressman Van Zandt said in
1957 that the " United States stockpile of materials for
atomic weapons had been estimated at 3 ½ times that of
the Soviet Union." [5]    President Eisenhower later made the
statement quoted on p. 27 above.    Nevertheless, Admiral
Burke, the United States Chief of Naval Operations, said
in 1957 that " the United States now has the nuclear
weapons for ' complete destruction ' of the Soviet Union,
and the Soviet Union either now has or will soon have the
' capability of doing the same thing to us.' " [6]

Britain has been producing A-bombs for a number of
years; she was reported to have " at least a thousand " in
1956 [7]; in 1957 Mr. Sandys said: " Britain, building up
quite a stock of atomic weapons, was now in a position
to manufacture quantities of hydrogen weapons." [8]    Thus
we are already making a considerable contribution to the
total world stock.    There can be little doubt that the
nuclear Powers already have among them many more
bombs than would be required to poison the atmosphere
of all the continents, and to obliterate mankind.    Note the
final words from the following report from Washington :

> " In testimony made public this week-end, leading
> atomic scientists . . . argued before the [Senate] sub-
> committee that even in a world war *such clean bombs
> would not wipe out humanity, as the present bombs
> would.*" [9]

[4] N.Y.H.T., September 22, 1955.
[5] N.Y.T., April 17, 1957.
[6] *The Times*, July 27, 1957.
[7] Scientific Correspondent, M.G., February 27, 1956.
[8] *Cambridge Daily News*, August 20, 1957.
[9] Report from Washington by Mr. P. Deane, *Observer*, June 23, 1957.

# The Distribution of Nuclear Weapons Throughout the World

Official United States and British information has established that nuclear weapons have already been distributed in the following way:

(i) A United States Air Force Division (the 49th) based in Britain is assigned the major mission of tactical atomic retaliation against any Soviet thrust into Europe.[10]

(ii) There are six United States A-gun battalions in Europe, with a total of thirty-six guns. Their shells are each equivalent in power to the Hiroshima bomb.[11]

(iii) A United States Navy spokesman said that the United States Pacific Fleet is " as ready as can be. . . . Every aircraft carrier has nuclear weapons." [12]

(iv) United States fighter aircraft now carry nuclear rockets for use against enemy bombers.[13]

(v) The United States has stockpiled atomic warheads for guided missiles at its NATO bases in Europe.[14]

(vi) There are United States " Army and Air Force units with atomic capability already stationed in West Germany." [15]

(vii) Admiral Wright, Supreme Allied Commander, Atlantic, said he had drawn up plans for " the Allied Atlantic Command projecting its atomic nuclear capabilities against the enemy airfields and naval bases." His NATO Fleet, he said, was " in essence a mobile, elusive airfield complex at sea, and it is geared for atomic war." [16]

(viii) There are A-weapons in Okinawa.[17]

(ix) British nuclear weapons will be " available for the defence of the SEATO area." [18]

[10] N.Y.H.T., December 6, 1954.
[11] N.Y.H.T., December 18, 1956.
[12] N.Y.H.T., November 21, 1956.
[13] N.Y.H.T., February 21, 1957.
[14] N.Y.H.T., March 14, 1957.
[15] Gen. Norstad, *The Times*, March 21, 1957.
[16] *The Times*, April 16, 1957.
[17] N.Y.H.T., July 11, 1957.
[18] Mr. D. Sandys, British Minister of Defence, *The Times*, August 21, 1957.

(x) Nuclear weapons are to be stocked in Malaya.[19]

(xi) If the Russian General Staff are like other soldiers, it may be assumed that they have scattered their nuclear bases as widely as they can, throughout the satellite countries, and, no doubt, in China, too; and it is known that they have atomic cannon and other " tactical " weapons, like those of the United States.

The forces which have these nuclear weapons are kept in a state of readiness for war never known in time of peace before. " Instant retaliation " is the watchword for them all. A garbled signal might start " delivery " at any moment. A sober contemplation of the facts related in this chapter and the last—and they are *all* taken from official British and United States Government publications —recalls the warning given by the Pope in 1955:

" This is the spectacle offered to the terrified gaze as the result of such use: entire cities, even the largest and richest in art and history, wiped out; a pall of death over pulverised ruins, covering countless victims with limbs burnt, twisted, and scattered while others groan in their death agony.

" Meanwhile the spectre of a radio-active cloud hinders survivors from giving any help and inexorably advances to snuff out any remaining life. There will be no song of victors, only the inconsolable weeping of humanity, which in desolation will gaze upon a catastrophe brought on by its own folly." [20]

[19] Mr. D. Sandys, *Cambridge Daily News*, August 20, 1957.
[20] Pope Pius XII, Christmas Message, 1955.

# 15

## " *No Legitimate Place* "

THE only valid conclusion to be drawn from the facts given in the preceding chapters about nuclear weapons and their use in war was that expressed by three members of the British Government which signed the UN Charter in 1945.

Sir Anthony Eden:

" Science has placed us several laps ahead of the present phase of international political development, and unless we catch up politically . . . we are all going to be blown to smithereens." [1]

Sir John Anderson (the late Lord Waverley), then Chairman of the United Kingdom Advisory Committee on Atomic Energy:

" A world peopled by men who have atomic energy at their disposal is bound to be quite a different place from the old world with which we are so familiar. The development calls for nothing less than a complete readjustment of all international relations, and for the framing of a new order of society." [2]

Lord Attlee:

" No one of these weapons has any legitimate place in the armaments which are necessary for ordinary purposes of internal security, or for the protection of a government against lawlessness. . . . They are weapons of total war designed for mass destruction, and we must banish total war from the world, if civilisation is to continue." [3]

[1] *Hansard*, November 22, 1945, col. 611.
[2] *Sunday Times*, September 30, 1945.
[3] *Hansard*, November 22, 1945, col. 608.

This view was reaffirmed by the democratic governments in the early UN disarmament debates, in the Six Principles of 1952, and in the Anglo-French Memorandum of 1954. They proposed, as the foundation of a disarmament system, the total abolition of all nuclear weapons, including all existing nuclear stocks. Attention must now be turned to the practical proposals which were made for carrying these pledges out.

PART THREE

THE HISTORY OF NEGOTIATIONS FOR
NUCLEAR DISARMAMENT

# 16

## The United Nations Plan: International Management, 1946—1950

### The UN Assembly Resolution

In 1945 nobody had any doubt about the right policy for atomic bombs. Hiroshima was destroyed on August 6; on November 15 the President of the United States and the Prime Ministers of Britain and Canada met in Washington and issued a declaration, which began:

> "We recognise that the application of recent scientific discoveries to the methods and practice of war has placed at the disposal of mankind *means of destruction hitherto unknown, against which there can be no adequate military defence and in the employment of which no single nation can, in fact, have a monopoly.*" [1]

They therefore urged that it was the responsibility of " the whole civilised world " to ensure that atomic energy should be used not for destruction, but to promote the common prosperity and happiness of all peoples, and they proposed that the UN should establish a Commission to " make specific proposals ":

> " (a) for extending between all nations the exchange of basic scientific information for peaceful ends;
>
> " (b) for control of atomic energy to the extent necessary to ensure its use only for peaceful purposes;
>
> " (c) for the elimination from national armaments of atomic weapons and of all other major weapons adaptable to mass destruction;

[1] United States *Green Book*, p. 80.

181
60
241

" (d) for effective safeguards by way of inspection and other means to protect complying States against the hazards of violations and evasions." [2]

Until this scheme had been drawn up and accepted, they thought it would not serve the cause of peace to publish to the world the atomic secrets which their governments possessed.

On December 27 Stalin agreed with Mr. Bevin and Mr. Byrnes in Moscow that a UN Commission should be set up, and the proposal was placed on the agenda of the first meeting of the UN Assembly in the name of the four nations. On January 24, 1946, the Assembly adopted a Resolution setting up a Commission, to consist of " one representative from each of those States represented on the Security Council, and Canada, when that State is not a member of the Security Council." Its terms of reference were textually the same as the Washington Declaration; it was instructed to " proceed with the utmost dispatch and inquire into all phases of the problem," and to make " recommendations " as soon as it could.[3]

During all this time, while the impression made by the Hiroshima bomb was fresh, not a single voice was raised in any country against the proposal that atomic weapons should be " eliminated from national armaments "; the Press of every shade of opinion was unanimous; in governments, Ministries, Parliaments, even General Staffs, there was one universally accepted view—somehow the bomb must be abolished. In all democratic countries another proposition was also accepted: whatever " sacrifice " of national sovereignty was needed, it must certainly be made.

## The United States Government's Proposals

On January 7, 1946, three days before the UN Assembly met, the United States State Department set up its own

---

[2] The United Nations Atomic Energy Commission, hereafter referred to as UNAEC.

[3] General Assembly Resolution No. 1 (I), January 24, 1946.

committee to consider how the Washington Declaration could be carried out. Its chairman was Mr. Dean Acheson; among its members were Dr. Vannevar Bush, the leader of the 35,000 scientists who had worked for the United States Government on weapon research during the war; Major-General L. R. Groves, military commander of the United States Army organisation concerned with the bomb; Dr. J. B. Conant, a well-known scientist, President of Harvard, and Mr. J. J. McCloy. This eminent body at once appointed a Board of Consultants, which included Mr. David Lilienthal, the chairman of the Tennessee Valley Authority; Dr. Oppenheimer, the leader of the team at Los Alamos who had made the bomb; and three leading men from private chemical, electrical, and engineering firms.

These were all able men, but the moving spirit among them was Dr. Oppenheimer. The Report which he drafted for the Board of Consultants became the foundation of the UN Plan for the Control of Atomic Energy. In its final form, after prolonged and detailed consideration by the highest living authorities, the UN plan hardly differed in principle from Dr. Oppenheimer's first proposals; but it had become a most audacious, authoritative, and carefully considered international proposal. It has been constantly misrepresented and many people have subconsciously accepted the designation the Russians gave it: " the notorious Baruch Plan." It is important to remember that it was, in fact, chiefly the work of Dr. Oppenheimer's bold and generous heart and brain.

In the Introduction to their Report, the Board of Consultants said:

"For more than seven weeks . . . we devoted virtually our entire time and energies to the problem. Our absorption in this task . . . is relevant as a measure of *how important and urgent we feel it to be that the Government and people of the United States develop a rational and workable plan, before the already launched atomic armament race attains such momentum that it cannot be stopped.* . . . As we steeped ourselves in the facts and caught a feeling of the nature of the problem, we became more hopeful. That hopefulness grew, not out of any pre-conceived solution, but out of a patient and time-consuming analysis and understanding of the facts. . . . Five men of widely differing backgrounds and experiences, who were far apart at the outset, found themselves . . . in agreement on the essentials of a plan. We believe others would have a similar experience, if a similar process is followed." [4]

Later in their Report they say :

" The programme we propose will undoubtedly arouse scepticism when it is first considered. It did so among us, but thought and discussion have converted us. *It may seem too idealistic. It seems time we endeavour to bring some of our expressed ideals into being. It may seem too radical, too advanced, too much beyond human experience. All these terms apply with peculiar fitness to the atomic bomb.*

" In considering the plan, as inevitable doubts arise as to its acceptability, *one should ask oneself : ' What are the alternatives ? ' We have, and we find no tolerable answer.*" [5]

## THE PRINCIPLES OF THE LILIENTHAL REPORT

The principles of the Board's Plan may be briefly summarised :

1. The A-bomb is a frightful new danger to mankind; " its uncontrolled development would not only intensify the ferocity of warfare, but might " (by helping surprise aggression) " directly contribute to the outbreak of war."

2. The UN could not fulfil its functions unless it solved this problem; the solution, by setting a pattern of international co-operation, might greatly strengthen the UN.

[4] *Loc. cit.*, p. vii.
[5] *Loc cit.*, p. 27.

3. There are special difficulties in any attempt to prevent individual nations from making atomic bombs by a system of outlawry and " police inspection," if they have the knowledge and the plant required for developing atomic energy—*i.e.*, the special difficulties of nuclear disarmament set out above.[6]

4. It follows from these special difficulties that, if the diversion of very small quantities of fissile material to military use is to be prevented,

> " every stage in the activity, leading from raw materials to weapon, needs some sort of control and . . . this must be exercised on all the various paths that lead from one to the other," [7] and " at no single point can *external* control " (*i.e.*, Inspection) " of an operation be sufficiently reliable to be an adequate sole safeguard." [8]
> The Report gave a concrete example: " Take the case of a controlled reactor, a power pile, producing plutonium " (like Calder Hall). "Assume an international agreement barring use of the plutonium in a bomb, but permitting use of the pile for heat or power. No system of inspection . . . could afford any reasonable security against the diversion of such materials to the purposes of war." [9]

5. Atomic energy is a new and rapidly developing science; the controlling organisation must be as well informed about the operations as the operators themselves; *this cannot be so " in any organisational arrangements in which the only instrument of control is Inspection."* [10]

6. The " human factors " in a system of control by simple " police inspection " would make it difficult and unsatisfactory to work; the numbers of inspectors would be large—perhaps 300 for a gaseous diffusion plant like that at Oak Ridge; people of high scientific competence would

[6] See pp. 106–110.
[7] *Loc. cit.*, p. 6.
[8] *Ibid.*
[9] *Loc. cit.*, p. 19.
[10] *Loc. cit.*, p. 6.

be required; they would be difficult to recruit; the inspectors would be "foreigners" in the country where their controlling functions were carried on. "They would have to check not merely accounts and instruments, but also individuals personally. Inquiries would have to be made of individuals, without regard to rank or general status." This would mean "a persistent challenge of the good faith of the nations inspected." The Inspectors would be in an invidious position, especially

> "when a government (or its officials or employees) interferes with the functions of Inspectors or molests or threatens them personally, or bribes or coerces them, or is accused of doing any of these things. Such incidents could not be avoided." [11]

In short, a system based on Inspection alone would not only be inefficacious; it might be positively pernicious, because of the frictions which it might create.

7. These difficulties appear insuperable when they are "viewed against a background of national rivalry."

> "So long as intrinsically dangerous activities may be carried on by nations, rivalries are inevitable, and fears are engendered that place so great a pressure upon a system of international enforcement by police methods that no degree of ingenuity or technical competence could possibly hope to cope with them." [12]

For example, rivalry in securing deposits of uranium or thorium "might easily produce intolerable tensions in international relations." [13]   The words were prophetic; two years later Russia engineered the *coup d'etat* in Czechoslovakia, and, without doubt, one of the reasons was to secure the rich Czechoslovak uranium mines. [14] This *coup d'etat* did more than anything else, except the Communist

[11] *Loc. cit.*, p. 7.
[12] *Loc. cit.*, p. 5.
[13] *Loc. cit.*, p. 18.
[14] Dame Kathleen Lonsdale, *Is Peace Possible?* p. 14.

aggression in Korea, to create the bitter suspicion that still exists.

8. The best way to remove national rivalry in " dangerous activities " is to entrust these activities to an International Atomic Development Authority to be established by the UN. All nations should participate in this Authority on " a fair and equitable basis "; " fair and equitable financial policies " would ensure that " the contributions of nations to, and their receipt of benefits from, the organisation will be justly apportioned "; the staff must consist of properly qualified persons, but, subject to that, must be internationally recruited, must have the same freedom from government interference and the same international loyalty as the Secretariat of the UN.

9. The " dangerous activities " to be undertaken by the IADA would include the following:

geographical surveys for uranium and thorium;

the mining of these raw materials;

the ownership and management of refineries for the reduction of the ores to metal;

the manufacture of reactor " rods ";

the ownership of the materials;

the sale of the refined metals and of by-products, such as vanadium and radium;

the construction and operation of atomic reactors and separation plants, like those at Hanford, Oak Ridge, Capenhurst and Windscale;

research on mining methods, power development, nuclear explosives, etc.

Research into nuclear explosives was of special importance. " Those in whose hands lies the prevention of atomic warfare must be the first to know and to exploit technical advances in this field." But in all these " dangerous activities " the IADA was to have an absolute monopoly; if an individual nation began mining uranium, building a refinery or a separation plant, its action would be a warning signal to the world that aggression was being prepared.

10. But there would remain a wide range of " safe activities " in which national Atomic Energy Authorities, universities, private firms, and individuals would be encouraged, and perhaps assisted, to take part. These " safe activities " would include:

(i) " The construction and operation of research reactors not exceeding a prescribed power level." [15] The IADA would grant the licence for these reactors, approve the design, and lease them the plutonium or U235 which they required. They would only need " a minimal inspection " to ensure that all was well.

(ii) " The construction and operation of reactors for making radio-active materials."

(iii) The construction and operation of reactors for producing electric power from nuclear fuel which the IADA would lease. In such reactors " there should be no provision . . . for the introduction of (natural) uranium or thorium "—for if there were, the dangerous plutonium or U233 would be produced. This would still have permitted, as the Report pointed out, the large-scale production of electric power, which would be safe, since the rods, being " leased," would be returned to the Authority to be reprocessed, after they had been " burnt." But it would have meant that power stations such as Calder Hall, or breeder reactors like Dounreay (which produces plutonium), could only have been constructed by the IADA.

11. The power stations and reactors owned and managed by IADA would produce electric power, which it would have to sell to the consumers of the country in which the plant was placed; they would produce the fissile material from which weapons could be made. Both products would face the Authority with difficult problems. The plants should be put in places where power was needed; and no country must be favoured in this regard. But they must

[15] *Loc. cit.*, p. 34.

be so distributed that a " strategic balance among the nations " would be preserved; a disloyal government might seize a plant; the UN might collapse; the IADA might fail; if these things happened, the " strategic balance " would ensure that no one country or group of countries could dominate the rest.

12. Auxiliary devices to prevent diversion of fissile material to illegal uses would be required: UN guards to protect the IADA plants and to supervise the transport of dangerous materials; " the design of primary production plants should make them as little dangerous as possible "; the stockpiles of materials suitable for bombs should be kept as small as possible; stockpiles, so far as possible, should be denatured. These and other measures would ensure that, if a disloyal government seized an IADA plant it would require at least a year to produce atomic weapons in quantities sufficient for a war; while its seizure would be " an instantaneous dramatic danger signal " to the other nations of the world.

13. If a disloyal government committed the international crime of seeking to make atomic weapons, sanctions would clearly be required; it must not be protected by a veto in the Security Council of the UN.

## THE ATTITUDE OF THE UNITED STATES GOVERNMENT AND PEOPLE

This was the ambitious scheme which Dr. Oppenheimer and his colleagues laid before Mr. Acheson's State Department Committee in the Lilienthal Report. They said that it was " not a final plan, but a place to begin, a foundation on which to build." It was, as they said, as revolutionary as atomic energy itself. If it had succeeded, it would have ensured total nuclear disarmament before the nuclear arms race had effectively begun; it would have created an international administration, owning immense capital assets; employing a numerous scientific, commercial and industrial staff; and conducting business operations on an enormous scale. This administration would have played a rapidly increasing part in the economic life of mankind, and its creation would have given the UN great authority and prestige.

But was it so ambitious that the " realists," the " practical men," of the United States government departments, General Staff, capitalist business world and individualist American public, would incontinently turn it down? Many people thought so, when it was published in the middle of March. The Secretary of State said in his foreword that " informed public opinion " was " one of the essential factors in developing sound policy," and that the document was " being made public, *not as a statement of policy, but solely as a basis for such discussion.*" The discussion immediately began; it is a notable fact that its outcome was the full endorsement of the plan by Mr. Acheson's Committee, by the United States Government, and by the United States people.

## Mr. Baruch's Speech in the UNAEC

On June 14 Mr. Bernard Baruch, the United States delegate, laid the plan before the UNAEC. He put great stress on the urgent dangers which the world confronted; emphasised the fact that the IADA would have wide positive functions for the development of atomic energy for peaceful uses, as well as the duty to ensure that no nuclear weapons should be made; proposed that at the proper moment the use, manufacture and possession of nuclear weapons should be forbidden; and urged that violations of this ban should be treated as matters of extreme gravity. In the opening paragraphs of his speech he said:

> " We must provide the mechanism to assure that atomic energy is used for peaceful purposes, and preclude its use for war. To that end we must provide immediate, swift, and sure punishment to those who violate the agreements that are reached by the nations. Penalisation is essential. . . ."

He went on to say that the UN should " prescribe individual responsibility and punishment on the principles applied at Nuremburg " by the victorious Allies.

" The matter of punishment lies at the very heart of our present security system. It might as well be admitted, here and now, that the subject goes straight to the veto power contained in the Charter." And he said in terms : " There must be no veto to protect those who violate their solemn agreements not to develop atomic energy for destructive purposes." [16]

There was nothing in this to which anybody could reasonably object, if he accepted the proposition that nuclear disarmament was of supreme importance to mankind. Nor was it surprising that Mr. Baruch should use such un-varnished language about the veto power; Russia had amply shown by June 1946 that the veto could be a menace to peace and justice. But his words were not calculated to evoke a favourable Soviet response. Nor was his assertion that " the peoples of the democracies . . . are unwilling to be fobbed off by mouthings about narrow sovereignty "; arguments based on " national sovereignty " were often heard on Russian lips in 1946. Probably no presentation of the Oppenheimer plan would have induced the Kremlin to accept it; but this opening speech gave them the chance to denounce it as a plot to amend the Charter, conceived in hostility to Russia; and they proceeded, with their vast machinery of propaganda, to distort and to discredit the " Baruch plan."

## The Russian Attitude

To make their propaganda more effective, they put forward counter-proposals of their own. On June 19, Mr. Gromyko proposed : (i) prohibition of the production or use of nuclear weapons—" ban the bomb "; (ii) destruction of all existing

[16] United States *Green Book*, pp. 189–193.

nuclear weapons within three months; (iii) a Committee to supervise the international exchange of scientific information; (iv) another Committee to ensure the prevention of the use of atomic energy to the detriment of mankind. In his speech, he spoke roughly about attempts to undermine the Charter, and about the difficulty of reconciling the proposed powers of the IADA with the sovereignty of States. " Such sovereignty," he said, " was the base of the UN." [17]

It was thus evident from the start that Russia was bitterly opposed to the whole proposal for an IADA. They betrayed the fact that they never gave it serious consideration by the extravagance of their attacks. Two years later Mr. Gromyko still found it possible to say that " the notorious Baruch Plan " provided for " a sort of international trust . . . in which American financial and industrial monopolies would exercise command as they think fit." Again: " An elaborate scheme for making the U.S.A. or, to be more exact, the United States monopolistic combines, the masters of the atomic industry of the whole world." And again: " The United States industrial and financial magnates would lay their hands on the raw materials in other countries." [18] A second line of attack accused the United States of refusing to abolish atomic weapons, of seeking to " legalise " them, and of preparing an aggressive nuclear war. " The United States," said a Ukrainian delegate, " relying on an obedient majority in the atomic control organ, might attempt to provoke a third world war." [19]

It would be hard to guess from these and from the other Communist speeches that what the United States had actually proposed was that the source of power in a new, world-wide industrial revolution should be handed over to a publicly owned International Authority, in which all nations should have fair and equal rights and shares; to which the United States would give, for nothing, the most

[17] 1st UNAEC Report to the Security Council, 1946, p. 118.
[18] Security Council, June 16, 1948.
[19] Tarasenko, UNAEC, March 22, 1949.

valuable industrial secret ever known; to which it would
hand over capital assets worth at least $4,000m.  It would
be just as hard to guess that the United States had proposed
to give up the A-bomb, which it alone possessed; to distribute the vitally important strategic industry of atomic
energy on an agreed and equitable basis around the world;
and to dedicate all the knowledge and experience at its
command to ensuring that no more nuclear weapons should
ever again be made.  The greatest capitalist nation had
proposed the international socialist control of the source of
world prosperity for centuries to come; the greatest military
power had proposed a total nuclear disarmament, in order
that the rule of law through the United Nations should
prevail.

The extravagance of the Russians' language, and the
open hostility it showed, made it difficult for their Western
colleagues to appreciate their point of view.  It was not
unnatural that in 1946 the Russians should feel nervous
about allowing the world atomic energy industry to be controlled by an International Authority in which the Communist nations would be in a small minority.  The essence
of their objection to international ownership was their
desire to develop the use of atomic energy in Russia without
outside interference.  The conduct of the Western Governments in the League of Nations before 1939 had left them
intensely suspicious of Western good faith; they were a
power-hungry country, and in 1946 most of their power
stations had been destroyed by Hitler; they needed atomic
energy far more than the United States with its cheap
water-power, oil and coal; they were violently repelled by
the idea that a body, which the United States would effectively dominate, should obtain control over what was
potentially a most important sector of Russian industry.  It
is necessary to understand this point of view.

But it must be added that, if they had, in 1946, been
seriously interested in disarmament and peace, they would
have sought, not to destroy the United States plan, but to

amend it by inserting even more specific guarantees than it contained that Russia and her allies would be fairly treated, and that peaceful nuclear development in their countries would not be hampered in any way. The Western delegates had made it plain that the plan was only an outline draft proposal, in which they were ready to make any reasonable change. In the UNAEC the Russians had every opportunity for making such proposals. In the technical committees which the Commission set up, the Western nations were represented by their leading scientists and experts: Dr. Oppenheimer, Dr. Charles Thomas, Dr. Robert Bacher, Dr. J. B. Conant, for the United States; Sir James Chadwick, Sir Charles Darwin, Sir George Thomson, Sir William Penney, for Britain; Professors Joliot-Curie and Perrin for France. These eminent men ardently desired to reach agreement [20]; they held hundreds of meetings in which every detail of the plan was sincerely and meticulously discussed, and in which, under Dr. Oppenheimer's lead, they sought to meet the Russian view.

## The Reports of the UNAEC

The results of these discussions must be briefly outlined. On September 26, 1946, the Scientific and Technical Committee issued their first considered statement. Having examined the whole problem of producing atomic weapons, from the mining of uranium and thorium to the manufacture of bombs, in the light of the United States proposals, they decided that for many of the operations " very close and careful safeguards " were required to prevent diversion of fissile material being disguised as " process losses "; but their broad conclusion was: " We do not find any basis in the available scientific facts for supposing that effective control (of atomic energy) is not technologically feasible." [21]

[20] An interesting account of these debates was given by Sir George Thomson in a paper on International Control published in *Atomic Challenge : A Symposium*, 1947, by Sir J. Cockcroft and others, pp. 123 *et seq*.
[21] 1st UNAEC Report to Security Council, p. 37.

On this basis, the Committee on Control Problems proceeded to examine " the types of safeguards necessary to prevent diversion at the various stages of atomic production," the problem of " clandestine activities," and the question of " direct seizure of atomic installations " by a disloyal government. As a result, the Committee proposed one important change in the United States plan : diversion of uranium and thorium from " declared mines and mills " and from " declared refineries and chemical and metallurgical plants " could be adequately prevented by

> " a system of Inspection, including guards, similar to normal managerial operating controls, provided that the Inspectorate has unrestricted access to all equipment and operations, and has facilities for independent weighing, assay, and analysis, and provided that it has the right to require the plant to be shut down for purposes of clean up and accounting," etc.[22]

In other words, since Inspection was a sufficient guarantee against " diversion," the IADA need not undertake these very large-scale mining, industrial and commercial operations itself.

But in " declared isotope separation plants,"[23] it is at present " *not possible to place reliance on the method of obtaining a material balance of uranium isotopes* " (*i.e.*, on determining how much natural uranium goes into a gaseous diffusion plant and how much U235 and U238 comes out).

> " This is one of the important reasons why . . . the management must be established by, and be responsible to, the international control agency. Even if the material balance could be greatly improved, the inherent dangers of the operation would still require management by the international control agency."

[22] *Loc. cit.*, pp. 12–13.
[23] " Declared " here means mines, mills, etc., the existence of which is reported to the UN, as distinct from *clandestine* mines, etc. In fact, " declared " mines and mills and plants are all that matter; they are such large-scale installations that they could not be kept hidden.

The same applies to the production of plutonium in large reactors and the associated chemical separation plants. For smaller reactors " the safeguards . . . should include licensing and inspection "; " close supervision of the design and construction of reactors is essential in all cases."

" Periodic inspection " is adequate for small research reactors; but

" adequate safeguards for chemical extraction plants . . . and for the preparation of high grade or pure nuclear fuels . . . and during the storage and shipment of such fuels, are only possible through management by the international control agency."

The detection of " clandestine activities " would require " broad privileges of inspection, including rights to conduct surveys by ground and air "; only the final manufacture of bombs from fissile material would be difficult to detect; to prevent that, " it is vital that any unauthorised accumulation of essential nuclear fuels be prevented."

On the " seizure of plants " by a disloyal government preparing an aggression, the Committee said that " technical measures could reduce the military advantages,[24] and therefore, the dangers of seizure."

Their broad conclusion was that scientifically, technologically, and practically, it was feasible to carry out the UN Assembly's Resolution,[25] if " appropriate mechanisms of control . . . including one or more of the following types of safeguard: accounting, inspection, supervision, management, and licensing," were applied to every stage from the mining of uranium and thorium " until they became nuclear fuel and are used." This would require " an international organ or agency within the UN, possessing adequate powers and properly organised, staffed and equipped for the purpose." [26] In other words, they broadly adopted the United States plan.

[24] See p. 269.
[25] See pp. 181–182.
[26] *Loc. cit.*, p. 16.

These two statements by the Scientific and Control Committees made up the UNAEC's First Report to the Security Council; it was approved by the Council by nine votes to none: Poland and Russia abstained. But it was recognised as being only a preliminary Report, and the discussions went on throughout 1947, and until May 1948.

The Russians continued to urge that the UNAEC proposals (as they had now become) meant an unwarranted interference in the economic development, national sovereignty, and security of States; they refused to commit themselves to the proposition that Inspection should be conducted by an exclusively international personnel [27]; they said that Russia " could not accept any proposal which would undermine in any degree " the principle of the veto [28]; they even said that " any violation of this principle would have far-reaching and negative consequences . . . maybe for its [the UN's] very existence " [29]—a serious threat. They ridiculed the whole idea that any international body should be given the powers proposed for the IADA.

## RUSSIAN PROPOSALS, 1947

In June 1947 they submitted detailed control proposals of their own, based on the principle that an International Control Commission should *periodically* carry out inspection of the " dangerous " processes.[30] This was, perhaps, a real advance; but in the light of the scientific facts, it gave no hope of satisfactory control. The scientists and other experts in the UNAEC spent many more months arguing it out with their Russian colleagues, until in April 1948 they definitely decided that the Russian proposals ignored " the existing technical knowledge of the problem " :

" The Soviet Union proposals," they said, " are not an acceptable basis for the international control of atomic energy. The UNAEC cannot endorse any

[27] Gromyko, Committee 2, April 1947.
[28] Gromyko, 1st UNAEC Report, p. 118.
[29] *Ibid*.
[30] 3rd UNAEC Report, May 17, 1948, p. 2.

scheme which would not prevent the diversion of atomic material; which provides no effective means for the detection of clandestine activities; and which has no provision for prompt and effective enforcement action. The Soviet Union Government has not only proposed a scheme that is fundamentally inadequate for the control of atomic energy, but at the same time has made the overriding stipulation that they will not agree to establish even such a feeble scheme of control until all atomic weapons have been prohibited and destroyed. It is completely unrealistic to expect any nation to renounce atomic weapons without any assurance that all nations will be prevented from producing them." [31]

In 1947, the Commission drew up detailed proposals in a Second Report, which showed how control could in practice be carried out; and in May 1948 they adopted a Third and Final Report, in which they gave a summarised history of their work, of their failure to reach agreement with the Russians, and of the arguments which still seemed to all the Commission, except the Russians, to be conclusive in favour of the IADA plan. Their plan, they said, was based on the principle that

" atomic energy must not be developed on the basis of national interests and needs, means and resources; but that its planning and operation should be made a common enterprise in all its phases. . . . *Traditional conceptions of the economic exploitation of the resources of nature for private or national advantage would then be replaced in this field by a new pattern of co-operation in international relations.*"

The Commission fully understood

" the impact of its plan on the traditional prerogatives of national sovereignty. But in the face of the realities of the problem it sees no alternative to the voluntary

[31] *Loc. cit.*, p. 39.

sharing by nations of their sovereignty in this field to the extent required by its proposals." [32]

The Commission concluded that it had reached absolute deadlock with the Russians, and that the deadlock could only be broken by political action at a different level. The Security Council, therefore, submitted their Report to the Assembly, and on November 4, 1948, the Assembly, after full debate, approved it

" as constituting the necessary basis for establishing an effective system of international control of atomic energy to ensure its use only for peaceful purposes and for the elimination from national armaments of atomic weapons."

Only the Communist delegations voted against.

But the Russian opposition was decisive; without their co-operation, nothing could be done. The Assembly called for further consultations, which went on for two more years. But they led to nothing; finally on December 13, 1950, the Assembly once more endorsed the UNAEC plan, and set up a body of twelve members to consider how further disarmament discussions should be carried on. Again, only the Communists voted against.

## The UN Plan in Perspective

No one's view of this long struggle is of greater value than Dr. Oppenheimer's. In July 1947 he wrote an article expounding the functions of the IADA in research and development, and pleading with passion for complete openness between the laboratories of the Agency and all private, university, national and other institutional laboratories.[33] In January 1948 he wrote:

" The UNAEC has established one point: through many months of discussion, under the circumstances of

---

[32] *Loc. cit.*, pp. 4–5.
[33] United States *Bulletin of Atomic Scientists.*

often dispiriting frustration, and by delegates not originally committed to it, the basic idea of security through international co-operative development has proven its extraordinary and profound vitality."

He concluded this article by saying:

> "The aim of those who would work for the establishment of peace, and who would wish to see atomic energy play whatever useful part it can in bringing this to pass, must be to *maintain what was sound in the early hopes, and by all means in their power to look to their eventual realisation.*" [34]

He had no doubt who had been to blame: "to answer simply that we have failed because of non-co-operation on the part of the Soviet Government is certainly to give a most essential part of a true answer." [35] Five years later he wrote:

> "The Government of the United States put forward some modest suggestions" (note the word "modest") "for dealing with the atom in a friendly, open, co-operative way. We need not argue as to whether those proposals were still-born. They have been dead for a long, long time. . . . Openness, friendliness and co-operation did not seem to be what the Soviet Government most prized on this earth." [36]

Perhaps the UN Plan was too ambitious for the world which it was intended to pacify. In 1945 most Americans had believed, with General Eisenhower, that the United States Government would find it easy to work with Russia, because Russia was free of the old colonialism. [37] By 1948

---

[34] *Foreign Affairs*, January 1948, p. 250.
[35] *Loc. cit.*, p. 239.
[36] *Foreign Affairs*, July 1953, p. 522.
[37] President Eisenhower said in his book: "The United States and Russia emerged from the War the two most powerful nations of the globe. . . . What permanence the new-won peace might have; what stature the United Nations could attain; even what the future course of civilisation would be— the answers to these questions now clearly involved, as an important factor, the ability of the East and West to work together in one world. In the past

this trustful hope had given way to bitter distrust of Russian
motives and lively fears of Communist imperialism through-
out the world. |The Russians had become infected with the
dangerous desire to develop nuclear weapons for themselves.
Perhaps they had also persuaded themselves that the United
States desired to destroy their experiment in Communism;
they remembered the betrayal of the League of Nations by
the governments of the capitalist countries between the
wars; and they did not forget that Hiroshima and Nagasaki
were destroyed by American bombs. |

But nothing can obscure the fact that, in their own, as
in other peoples', interests, the Russians were tragically
wrong. The United States had put forward a bold,
imaginative and generous plan, fitted in concept to the new
atomic age that had begun; the rest of the world, after the
most exhaustive examination by the most authoritative
experts of every objection that was made, had endorsed this
plan with astonishing unanimity; the Russians destroyed it
with harsh words, and with appeals to an anachronistic
conception of national sovereignty. Dr. Oppenheimer did
not believe that this failure could be the end. Some day
the time would come again for " serious discussion of the
regulation of armaments."

> " There will have been by then," he said, " a vast
> accumulation of materials for atomic weapons, and a
> troublesome margin " (a prophetic phrase) " of un-
> certainty with regard to its accounting—very trouble-
> some indeed if we still live with vestiges of the
> suspicion, hostility and secretiveness of the world
> today." [38]

relations of America and Russia there was no cause to regard the future with
pessimism. Historically, the two peoples had maintained an unbroken friendship. . . . Both were free from the stigma of colonial empire-building by
force. Twice they had been allies in war. Since 1944 they had been
dependent each on the other for ultimate victory over the European Axis ":
*Crusade in Europe*, p. 499.

[38] *Loc. cit.*, pp. 534–535. See pp. 288 *et seq.*

# 17

# *The Switch to Inspection,*
## *1952–1955*

As said on p. 199, the Assembly in December 1950 set up a Committee of twelve members to consider how the deadlock in the two Disarmament Commissions [1] could be broken, and how future discussions should be carried on. This Committee recommended to the next session of the Assembly that the two Commissions should be dissolved and should be replaced by a single body, to be called the UN Disarmament Commission. This new body would deal with all armaments—nuclear, mass destruction, and conventional—and all armed forces of every kind. Mr. Vyshinsky at first scoffed at this proposal; but later he withdrew his opposition, and in January 1952 the Assembly unanimously set up the new Commission, to consist of delegates named by the Members of the Security Council and by Canada,[2] and with the mandate quoted on p. 12:

> " to prepare proposals *to be embodied in a draft Treaty* . . . for the . . . reduction of all armed forces and all armaments, for the *elimination* of all major weapons adaptable to mass destruction, and for effective international control of atomic energy to ensure the prohibition of atomic weapons, and the use of atomic energy for peaceful purposes only."

There is a widespread belief that the UN disarmament negotiations have been vigorously and continuously conducted ever since this important decision was made. In fact, the new Commission only had one session in which work of any significance was done; then, at the suggestion

---

[1] UNAEC and UN Commission on Conventional Armaments (UNCCA), set up in 1946.
[2] Resolution 502 (VI), dated January 11, 1952.

of the Assembly, it handed over its task to a Sub-Committee of Britain, the United States, France, Canada and Russia; starting in 1954, this Sub-Committee has had five sessions, separated by intervals of many months.

## UN Meetings on Disarmament

| Disarmament Commission | Disarmament Sub-Committee |
|---|---|
| 1952 March 14 to August 29 | |
| 1954 July 20 to 29 | 1954 May 13 to June 22 |
| | 1955 February 25 to May 18 |
| | 1955 August 29 to October 7 |
| | 1956 March 19 to May 4 |
| 1956 July 3 to 16 | |
| | 1957 March 18 to September 6 |

In this table a few meetings of a purely formal or procedural nature have been left out. It shows that there was an interval of twenty-one months of total inaction after the first session of the Commission, and before the Sub-Committee met. The intervals between the sessions of the Sub-Committee were eight months, three and a half months, six months, nine months. In these intervals there were, of course, debates in the Assembly; but they were post-mortems on the Sub-Committee's failures; in the nature of things, they could not advance the preparation of a Draft Treaty. This was a very different record of industry from that of UNAEC. ∮ And the character of the work of the Commission and the Sub-Committee likewise differed from that of UNAEC; there were only headline proposals; no detailed schemes were considered, or—except on Inspection—even proposed; after six years not a single clause of the Draft Treaty had been drawn up, nor the substance of any section of it agreed. ∮

This was the more disappointing, in that the Commission had begun quite well in 1952. It agreed, except for Russia, to the Six Principles and to the scheme for manpower ceilings which the Western Governments proposed.[3] It is particularly regrettable that the Western Governments

[3] See pp. 12–14.

did not work out their 1952 proposals about manpower and conventional arms in a comprehensive and detailed plan, like that prepared on atomic disarmament by the eleven members of the UNAEC. Had they done so, this might have been of great importance, both for conventional and for *nuclear* disarmament, later on. It would have helped to convince the Russians more speedily, and would certainly have convinced the rest of the world, that they meant business when they talked of drastic reductions in armaments of every kind. But instead of doing this, they tamely surrendered to Russia's "Noes," and adjourned their session.

Both in the Commission and the Sub-Committee the discussion of nuclear and conventional armaments continually, and perhaps inevitably, overlapped. The general course of the discussion, and its unfortunate result, have been described in Chapter 2. It would be wearisome to repeat the story of how the Western Governments pressed the Russians to accept the programme of the Six Principles and the Anglo-French Memorandum of 1954; of how, on May 10, 1955, the Russians went very far towards accepting; of how the Western Governments then suspended their proposals, and in 1957 produced their much less adequate " partial disarmament " plan. On most parts of the subject, closer examination would be both wearisome and useless, for nothing that advanced the prospect of disarmament was said. But on nuclear disarmament there were important developments, which must be described.

## UN DISARMAMENT COMMISSION, 1952

In their Third Report the UNAEC said:

> "*Whether the functions of the International Control Agency, as elaborated by the majority*" (*i.e.*, all the Commission except Russia), "*are politically acceptable or not, they provide the technically necessary basis for an effective control of atomic energy. The*

*question is not whether these measures are now
acceptable, but whether governments now want
effective international control.*"

This view was endorsed by the Assembly in 1948, 1949, and
1950. The Assembly Resolution of January 1952 brought
a change:

"*Unless a better or no less effective system is
devised*, the United Nations Plan for the international
control of atomic weapons should continue to serve as
the basis for the international control of atomic energy,"
etc.

Only the Communists voted against this new formula. It
was an invitation to Russia to make a new proposal, coupled
with a Declaration that, until they did so, the Assembly
would stick to the UN Plan. In the Commission's session
in 1952, Russia made no new proposal. M. Moch urged
strongly that a fresh start must be made, in order to find a
system " better or no less effective " than the UN Plan.
" The moment might be coming," he said, " when no
control system would be effective, if only because of the
increased amount of fissionable material in existence." [4]
(Dr. Oppenheimer's " troublesome margin of uncertainty
with regard to its accounting.") The Russians gave their
routine answer; the Soviet plan of 1947 was " real, concrete
and practical and the United States plan unreal, false and
hypocritical." In vain the United States delegate urged that
the Russians had " failed to realise " that the UN Plan
provided for international ownership and management " not
as an end in itself, but as the most effective means of
control." [5] The Russians replied that—

" the U.S.S.R. was opposed to the establishment of an
international atomic supermonopoly on a commercial
basis. As long as the United States did not give up

[4] Disarmament Commission, Second Report, pp. 49–53.
[5] *Loc. cit.*, p. 60.

that proposal, there was no basis on which to speak of inspection on a permanent basis." [6]

During the Commission's session in 1952, the debate on nuclear disarmament never passed that sterile point.

## THE UN SUB-COMMITTEE, 1954

The UN Sub-Committee met on May 13, 1954, six months after the Assembly had urged that it should meet " as soon as possible " in order to prepare and report " an acceptable solution." [7]   In the twenty-one months which had elapsed since the last discussions in the Disarmament Commission, the United States, Russian and British stocks of A-bombs had much increased; the large-scale production of " tactical " A-weapons had begun; and the first three H-bombs had been exploded.

The British delegate to the Sub-Committee, Mr. Selwyn Lloyd, tried to make up for lost time.  He made repeated efforts to get the discussions going on practical lines.  In particular, he sought to explore the Russian attitude to nuclear disarmament and atomic energy control.  He made it plain that he was ready to modify the UN Plan, if something " not less effective " could be found; and he had constructive proposals to put forward.  He said that " the Soviet Union fear about the Control Organisation might be . . . removed if we were to discuss in detail what kind of a control organ we do envisage being set up " and " what we regard as going to be its functions."   He analysed, and showed the weakness of, the Soviet proposals for control by periodical inspection; he explained why there must be *continuous* checking of uranium and thorium ores extracted from the ground, of the processing and purification plants, and " even more strongly " of plants " processing, producing or even utilising nuclear fuels."   " Without that," he said, " the Control Organisation . . . would be in no position

---

[6] *Loc. cit.*, p. 61.
[7] Assembly Resolution of November 28, 1953, Cmd. 9204, p. 12.

to verify any entries appearing in the books." Then he used the key phrase that explained his new idea:

" A system of inspection of a periodic nature as suggested in 1947 by the Soviet Union would not provide any definite knowledge of the rate at which nuclear fuels were produced or consumed between successive inspections. Therefore, *something much more akin to managerial control, operated by the control commission, with personnel constantly resident in the plants,* would seem to be essential."

He added:

" I am leaving on one side whether these plants or these materials have got to be internationally owned and internationally operated. That is one of the principles in the Baruch Plan which I know the Soviet Union do not accept." [8]

This was, at least, the beginning of a shift of attitude. The United States delegate, then Mr. Patterson, carried it a little further.

" I believe," he said, " Mr. Lloyd is pursuing an approach which could lead to some very definite progress in our deliberations. . . . Being here at this meeting is the best earnest that we can offer of the fact that *we have not—and I repeat ' not '—a fixed position on the UN Plan. . . . We are actively seeking new and advanced and up-to-date plans.* We hope that such a plan may appear from Mr. Lloyd's efforts." [9]

Mr. Lloyd explained further what he meant.

" It would not necessarily have to be managerial control to the extent that all managerial functions would be carried out by the control organ, but what I had in mind was that the control organ would have to have the same knowledge of what was going on, of

[8] Cmd. 9205, pp. 122–124.
[9] *Loc. cit.*, pp. 138–139.

every detail of what was going on, in an atomic plant, as would the managers of that plant themselves."

He then drew attention to a " Working Paper " which Mr. Patterson had prepared, and said:

"I should have thought that form of words would be satisfactory even to the most resolute opponent of the Baruch Plan. . . . This paragraph does not say anything about ownership or, indeed, management; it talks of control of atomic energy, and I think this is a very important paragraph indeed."

Mr. Lloyd explained a little later in the House of Commons how this idea might work:

"I mean that in each place dealing with atomic production there should be in parallel with the actual " (national) " management a unit or cell provided by the international organisation. Although they would not actually take the decisions, they would know exactly what decisions were taken. . . . On every decision that is taken by the national management, there has to be also in on these decisions the international control organ representatives." [10]

This was a shift, indeed, for it expressly left each national Government free to decide the development of its own atomic industry.

But it was all in vain. In a later meeting of the Sub-Committee, Mr. Lloyd said bitterly:

"I was excluding ownership . . . and I was excluding actual managerial control. . . . *Apparently, the Soviet Union rejects really even consideration of something akin to managerial control.*" [11]

The Sub-Committee's session of 1954 ended in a wrangle between the Russians and the West. In a last effort at conciliation, M. Moch and Mr. Lloyd proposed the important statement of objectives, and plan of procedural stages,

[10] *Hansard*, July 30, 1954, col. 901.
[11] *Loc. cit.*, p. 168.

which has since been known as the Anglo-French Memorandum of 1954.[12]  The Memorandum was endorsed by
Canada and the United States; the Western Governments
thus formally renewed their pledges to seek early and drastic
disarmament, with the total abolition of nuclear weapons,
including nuclear stocks.  But Mr. Malik laughed it to
scorn.  After harsh exchanges the Sub-Committee, having
held twenty meetings in five and a half weeks, suspended
its labours for eight months.

## THE UN SUB-COMMITTEE, FEBRUARY 25-MAY 18, 1955

In June 1954 Mr. Malik laughed the Anglo-French
Memorandum to scorn.  But three months later, on
September 30, Mr. Vyshinsky formally accepted it in the
Assembly as the basis for the future disarmament work of
the UN.

The Sub-Committee did not meet again, however, until
February 25, 1955.  In spite of this delay there was hope
that Mr. Vyshinsky's declaration would mean that rapid
and satisfactory results could be obtained.  In that hope,
the Western delegates continued to press the objectives of
the Memorandum on the Russians.  But the Russians continued to reply that the Western Governments were not
serious, that they did not want a genuine reduction of conventional armaments and forces, that they only wanted to
" legalise " their nuclear weapons, and, at all costs, to retain
their nuclear stocks.  As the weeks went by, the Western
delegates increased their pressure, as described above.[13]  A
few details may be added to that description.

At the second meeting, on March 1, the British delegate,
Mr. Nutting, said that Her Majesty's Government were
working for a disarmament scheme which would bring the
abolition of the use, *possession* and manufacture of " all
nuclear weapons, be they atomic, thermo-nuclear, or what

---

[12] See pp. 15–16.  This must not be confused with the Anglo-French Memorandum of March 1956, from which all the objectives were dropped.
[13] Chap. 2.

you will "; the similar abolition of "all other weapons of mass destruction "; together with "major reductions in armed forces and conventional armaments to levels to be agreed and to be carried out under an agreed time-table." [14]

On March 12 the four Western delegates proposed a draft Resolution expanding and clarifying what the Anglo-French Memorandum meant by the words "major reductions." The essential words were these: "There shall be an agreed level of armed forces to which all States in excess of it shall reduce, *so that no State shall have armed forces strong enough to be a serious threat to international peace.*" The agreed levels of armed forces were to include not only "armies, navies and air forces, but also . . . all para-military forces, and all internal security forces of a military type." [15] From then on till May 10 the Western pressure on manpower levels and conventional armaments became intense.

There was equal pressure on nuclear arms. The Western delegates constantly assured the Russians that, of course, they meant to forbid the use or manufacture of nuclear weapons and to abolish all their nuclear stocks. On March 3, M. Moch said: "Mr. Nutting has already replied four times that we agree to the destruction of atomic or thermo-nuclear weapons." [16]   On March 29, the United States delegate, Mr. Wadsworth, said: "*Complete prohibition and elimination* of nuclear weapons and other weapons of mass destruction is regarded as *absolutely imperative* all around this table." [17]   On April 19, Mr. Nutting, proposing "the 75 per cent. arrangement," [18] made the statement quoted above: "It is still a fundamental principle of United Kingdom policy that the prohibition of nuclear weapons must amount to no less than the total prohibition of manufacture, *possession* and use of nuclear weapons." [19]

[14] Cmd. 9648, p. 17.
[15] Cmd. 9636, pp. 22–23.
[16] Cmd. 9648, p. 48.
[17] Cmd. 9649, p. 256.
[18] See p. 17.
[19] Cmd. 9650, p. 416. See p. 17.

The day before this 75 per cent. arrangement was proposed, the four Western delegates had put in another paper on nuclear disarmament, in which they said that: " The elimination of nuclear and other weapons of mass destruction must be *supervised* by an effective system of international control." [20]   But what " system " was intended by this phrase?   The UN Plan?   Mr. Lloyd's " something akin to managerial control "?   Inspection only?   The paper of April 18 gave no answer to these questions.   Another paper three days later contained some hints.   It said that

> " The Control Organ shall be accorded powers . . .
> (3) to ensure that installations, facilities, equipment and materials, including stocks of nuclear materials, are disposed of or utilised in accordance with the terms of the Disarmament Treaty; (4) to organise and conduct field and aerial surveys . . . for the purpose of determining whether all installations and facilities have been disclosed; (5) to conduct such research as is necessary to keep itself in the forefront of nuclear knowledge, and to enable it to be fully effective in eliminating the destructive uses of nuclear energy." [21]

Thus the Control Organ was to have a " positive " function : to conduct nuclear research in establishments which, evidently, it was itself to organise and operate.   But for the rest, it was to ensure, *by the method of Inspection*, that fissile material was not disloyally used for making weapons.

There is singularly little in the Verbatim Records of the Sub-Committee about this vitally important change of line. M. Moch spoke most clearly.   On April 20 he said: " In atomic questions (control) officers will have to be empowered to analyse mineral ores." [22]   On May 5 he accused Mr. Malik of trying " to discern from our statements to what extent the Four Power Plan of 1955 is still afflicted with the

[20] Paper dated April 18, 1955, Cmd. 9636, pp. 29–30.
[21] Cmd. 9636, p. 32.
[22] Cmd. 9650, p. 460.

212 The History of Negotiations for Nuclear Disarmament

evils which you impute to the Baruch Plan of 1947 " [23]—
clearly implying that it was *not* so afflicted. Earlier Mr.
Wadsworth had said that the Control Organ must " verify "
detailed information " concerning design, operation and
output of all facilities and installations producing fissionable
and fusionable materials." [24]  This was a strange way of
conveying to the Russian delegate that a major concession
to his point of view was being made. No wonder he was
slow to understand it; no doubt he was genuinely mystified
when he said: " Last year Mr. Lloyd advocated the principle of management. That principle is not apparently
being pressed this year." [25]

The change was made quite clear on May 5, when M.
Moch asked the question: " Would the International Disarmament Control Organ have the right to prohibit a
country from manufacturing a new peaceful reactor whenever it pleased? " and answered " No," provided the reactor
was not producing atomic bombs.[26]  The UN Plan had
been thrown over.

But total nuclear disarmament remained the declared
objective, including the abolition of existing stocks. No one
suggested that this was impracticable; on the contrary, on
May 3, M. Moch urged on Mr. Malik that " the officials of
the Control Organ " must have " the right to ensure that
installations, facilities, equipment and materials, *including
stocks of nuclear materials* . . . are disposed of or utilised
in accordance with the terms of the Disarmament Treaty." [27]
The West were still urging on the Russians the full
programme of the Anglo-French Memorandum of 1954.[28]

Then on May 10 the Russians put in the paper which
has been described.[29]  It consisted of a Draft Declaration
and several Draft Resolutions for the UN Assembly.

The Draft Declaration contained some Soviet propaganda; some of its political propositions and its proposals

[23] *Loc. cit.*, p. 582.     [24] *Loc. cit.*, p. 527.
[25] *Loc. cit.*, p. 464.     [26] *Loc. cit.*, p. 585.
[27] *Loc. cit.*, p. 534.     [28] See pp. 15–16.
[29] See pp. 19 *et seq.*

about bases on foreign soil, were naturally regarded with suspicion by the West. But, broadly, it was a powerful statement of the dangers of the nuclear arms race, and an argument that other political settlements, like the Austrian Peace Treaty, and the truce agreements in Korea and Indo-China, ought to be obtained. ·

The Draft Resolutions on Disarmament and International Control, however, were a far-reaching acceptance of the major policies which the Western delegates had urged.[30] There were still differences and obscurities to be cleared away, and all the detailed drafting had yet to be begun. But, nevertheless, the document of May 10 was a sensational alteration of the Russian line. And Mr. Malik convinced his colleagues that it was a genuine alteration. They asked him a lot of questions; they were particularly anxious about safeguards for the genuine abolition of existing nuclear stocks. Mr. Malik continued to make conciliatory speeches; he gave many answers, especially about manpower levels, that were satisfactory. He claimed that " the new Soviet proposal reflects all the most important and fundamental wishes of the Western Powers." He urged that these drastic armament reductions should be effected without delay; he said that they would

> " render possible prolonged peaceful co-existence between peoples and States regardless of ideology, creed, race or nationality, and regardless of the political and social systems of the individual States." [31]

The Western delegates were cautious on May 10; on May 12, after two days' consultation with their governments, they gave the Russian paper the favourable reception which has been described. They evidently thought that this time the Kremlin was ready to do genuine business. Four weeks later the British Government still seemed to think so; Mr. Nutting told the House of

[30] See pp. 21–22.
[31] *Loc. cit.*, p. 619.

Commons: " This Soviet proposal in fact adopts several of the key proposals which my Western colleagues and I had for many weeks been urging the Soviet delegate to accept." He mentioned the 1 to 1·5 million ceiling for manpower; said Russia agreed that " conventional armaments and military budgets should be limited accordingly "; welcomed the Soviet acceptance of the 75 per cent. arrangement, of a single organ of control, and so on; Russia, he said, " also included a passage on the peaceful uses of nuclear energy, which reflects the Western Powers' own paper on this subject." He said that it was " not clear whether the powers which the Soviet Union proposes for the control organ are yet adequate to guarantee that all States will faithfully carry out the measures of disarmament." But he concluded by saying that Her Majesty's Government " regarded this change of attitude on the part of the Soviet Government as an important step forward in our discussions on disarmament." [32]

32 *Hansard*, June 13, 1955, cols. 271–272.

# 18

## *Retreat and Deadlock, 1955–1957*

### *UN Meetings on Disarmament*

IT was thus clearly established by Mr. Nutting's statement
that, in the British Government's view, there was still, a
month after the Russian plan was launched, no insuperable
difficulty about a secret nuclear stock. The matter had
obviously been considered; it was " not clear " that what
the Soviet said about the Control Organ was " adequate "
—and this sentence meant that it was also " not clear "
that it was *inadequate*. But Russia had accepted the
Western proposals about nuclear disarmament, including
the timing and other arrangements for the total abolition
of all nuclear weapon stocks; and Mr. Nutting expressed
his Government's satisfaction at " this important step
forward."

UN SUB-COMMITTEE, AUGUST 29–OCTOBER 7, 1955

Before Mr. Nutting's statement was made, the Sub-Committee had been adjourned for three and a half months,
till August 29. This decision was made against Russia's
wish; they " would have preferred to continue the Sub-
Committee's work." They wanted to start the long-
delayed task of drafting a treaty, and to do so quickly, on
the basis of what they thought would be the agreed
objectives of their plan. Reluctantly they accepted an
adjournment, " since the Western Powers insist on a
recess." [1]

During the recess the " Summit Conference " had been
held in Geneva. President Eisenhower had put forward
his plan for " Open Skies "—" aerial photography " of the

[1] *Loc. cit.*, p. 651.

215

whole territory of Russia and the United States—to prevent the danger of surprise attack. Mr. Bulganin had restated the proposals of May 10 and he had urged that the drafting of a disarmament treaty should speedily begin. These proposals, and others made by the French and British Prime Ministers, were referred to the Sub-Committee. So far as its public decisions were concerned, the Conference made no progress on disarmament at all.

Nor had the private contacts between the "Heads of Governments" done any good. On the contrary, when the Sub-Committee met again it was clear that the Western delegates' attitude had changed since they had separated in May. They spoke principally about aerial inspection, and constantly repeated that, if President Eisenhower's plan were accepted by the Russians, it would be the "gateway" to armament reduction later on. The Russian delegate constantly inquired what had happened to the Western proposals which were the basis of his Government's plan. At length, on September 6, the United States delegate, now Mr. Stassen, quoted from a speech made by President Eisenhower in Geneva: "We have not as yet been able to discover any scientific or other inspection method which would make certain of the elimination of nuclear weapons. So far as we are aware, no other nation has made such a discovery." [2] Mr. Stassen then went on, in words which have been quoted above [3]:

> "In view of these facts . . . the United States does now place a reservation upon all of its pre-Geneva substantive positions taken in this Sub-Committee or in the Disarmament Commission, or in the United Nations on these questions in relationship to levels of armaments, pending the outcome of our study, jointly or separately, of inspection methods and control arrangements." [4]

[2] Cmd. 9651, p. 745.
[3] See p. 23.
[4] *Loc cit.*, p. 746.

All the " pre-Geneva " proposals of the Western Governments were thus withdrawn. No one could blame the Russians if they drew the conclusion that the Western Governments had only been engaged in " political warfare," like that in which, before May 10, they had themselves indulged. For the reasons given by the Western Governments for their change of front were singularly unimpressive. They said that any progress in armament reduction must be dependent on the settlement of outstanding political disputes—an argument quite irrelevant to the Sub-Committee's treaty-drafting task.[5] They said that a reduction of United States manpower to the 1 to 1·5 million level would mean the break-up of NATO—an argument they should have thought of before May 10, if it was valid; but an argument which was patently *invalid*, since the reduction of the Russian forces to 1 or 1·5 million would have left NATO relatively far stronger *vis-à-vis* the Warsaw allies than ever before.

But, most often and with the greatest emphasis, the Western delegates talked about the dangers of the secret nuclear stock. At frequent intervals they quoted the passage in the Russian plan in which the Kremlin said that a secret stock could not be found. This was a real difficulty in nuclear disarmament, but after what had passed in their meetings in the spring, the Russians could hardly fail to think that the Western delegates were using it as an insincere excuse. Thus the third session dragged on in chaos till October 7. The Sub-Committee then dispersed, no one knowing what was to happen next. The most appropriate comment was made in the Assembly on December 1 by Mr. Sandler, ex-Foreign Minister of Sweden, who had been a Swedish delegate to the Disarmament Conference of 1932. " By placing a reservation on every previously taken position," he said,

> " the United States had caused, if not a certain deterioration, at least a deplorable uncertainty as to the

[5] See Chap. 7.

situation. In many instances there had been good reason to wonder whether that attitude involved a basic change in the manner in which the problem of armaments was to be dealt with." [6]

## UN SUB-COMMITTEE, MARCH 19–MAY 4, 1956

It was clear before the Sub-Committee met in 1956 that there had been " a basic change," and that both the Western proposals for total nuclear disarmament and their plan for the reduction of conventional armaments and forces had been dropped. The general result of this change of policy, and the consequent deadlock in the Sub-Committee in 1957, have been already explained. Here it is only necessary to fill in some details about the evolution of the nuclear proposals put forward in the Western Governments' " package " plan of August 27, 1957.[7]

In the early meetings in 1956 the subject was hardly mentioned, except by Russia. There was a proliferation of new Western papers and proposals about Inspection and Control, including a draft constitution for an " International Disarmament Organisation." [8]    There were numerous suggestions that " general disarmament " was impracticable, but that some measures of " limited " disarmament might do instead. On March 22, Mr. Stassen said that the United States would be prepared to accept a manpower level of 2·5 million men, with " definite reductions " in " all the major types of armaments that are involved in these conventional forces." On March 27, Mr. Gromyko proposed a plan for conventional disarmament only, leaving nuclear armaments and other mass-destruction weapons to be dealt with later on; its significance will be discussed in Chapter 19.

At length Mr. Stassen made some tentative suggestions about nuclear weapons, including the first proposal for a " cut-off " of new production of fissile material for warlike

---

[6] 1st Committee, December 1, 1955, p. 219.
[7] See Table on p. 26.
[8] See p. 538.

use and for " equitable transfers " from existing stocks of nuclear weapons to peaceful use. His paper, dated April 3,[9] also suggested that nuclear tests should be " limited and monitored " under international control.

When he put forward these proposals, Mr. Stassen quoted President Eisenhower's letter of March 1 to Mr. Bulganin, in which the President said that the United States would be willing to " work out with other nations suitable and safeguarded arrangements so that future production of fissionable materials anywhere in the world would no longer be used to increase the stockpile of explosive weapons." [10] But he gave no hint as to what these " arrangements " might be, and the Sub-Committee ended its 1956 session with no progress, either on the conventional or the mass-destruction side.

## UN DISARMAMENT COMMISSION, JULY 3–16, 1956

It was followed by a short session of the full UN Commission in New York. This likewise made no progress, except that the Russians agreed to a first manpower reduction to 2·5 million men, provided it was followed by further reductions at stipulated dates down to the " 1 or at the most 1·5 million " which the West had originally proposed. To this condition the Western Governments did not agree.

The main lesson of the UN work in 1956 was best expressed by M. Moch in the Sub-Committee on April 23 : " A limited agreement seems to me today to be as difficult to reach as a general agreement." [11]

## UN SUB-COMMITTEE, MARCH 18–SEPTEMBER 6, 1957

This truth was again borne out by the meetings of the Sub-Committee in 1957. These meetings were more disjointed than ever before; they were often interrupted in

[9] Cmd. 9770, pp. 35–39.
[10] April 3, 1956, p. 33.
[11] April 23, 1956, p. 30.

order that the Western Governments might have consultations in the NATO Council; it took the Western Governments over five months to formulate their " package " plan. From the beginning of the session they had started from the proposition that " limited " (it was now called " partial ") disarmament was all that they could hope to attain; this was *their* decision, *not* Russia's—Russia put forward the comprehensive and far-reaching proposals shown on pp. 25–27. It would serve no purpose to try to trace the course of the discussions; they will be referred to extensively again. The final upshot was a deadlock over the " package " plan of " partial " measures, put forward after much hesitation by the West, and rejected without any hesitation by the Kremlin.

But on nuclear disarmament the Western Governments made a definite advance from their nebulous position of 1956. In their Working Paper of August 29, 1957 (the " package " plan), they made specific proposals, which will be examined in later chapters, about the *use* of nuclear weapons (" Ban the bomb "); about the cessation of nuclear *tests* under international control; for a definite " *cut-off* " of new production of fissile material for warlike use; for " *equitable transfers,* in successive increments, of fissionable materials from previous production " (*i.e., from stocks*) " *to non-weapons purposes* "; and for " a group of technical experts . . . to design the required Inspection system." [12]  The reasons why the Russians rejected these proposals have been explained above; they wanted the total abolition of nuclear stocks, and they thought that Mr. Stassen had reserved for the United States and its allies the right to make too dangerous an expansion of preparations for nuclear war.[13]  But the proposals, whatever their defects, were more precise, and more like the clauses of a draft disarmament treaty, than anything that the Commission or the Sub-Committee had yet done. Apart from the Russian

---

[12] For the full text see Cmnd. 333, pp. 97–98.
[13] See p. 28.

objections, however, they had another fatal weakness: they threw no light on what kind of Inspection system the " group of experts " would draw up, and they said nothing about how large the " equitable transfers " from stocks of fissile material were to be. M. Moch had made valiant efforts to get his Western colleagues to commit themselves on these vitally important points. He had proposed the abolition of stocks by the conversion to peaceful uses of 20 per cent. per annum for five years; " then in five years all stocks would be de-natured." He had likewise proposed that, when the " cut-off " came into operation, no more weapons should be manufactured from existing stocks of fissile material.[14] Both these proposals were swept aside by Mr. Stassen, who immediately replied that the United States would not " agree to the complete elimination of its nuclear weapon strength " [15]; and Mr. Stassen later insisted that the " first phase agreement " should " leave each affected party with a substantial part of its nuclear weapons capability." [16] The British attitude was no more helpful. Commander Noble said: " We, the Western Powers, in the present state of international tension, regard the possession of these [nuclear] weapons as the best deterrent to aggression." [17] And Mr. Selwyn Lloyd added later: " For geographically small countries such as the United Kingdom, the advent of nuclear weapons has provided greater security and a greater sense of equality." [18]

M. Moch was no more fortunate over nuclear Inspection. On July 5 he expounded the principles, and outlined the organisation, scale, and cost, of a system for the Inspection and Control of nuclear activities [19]; his Western colleagues expressed polite interest, but they gave him no support, and no mention of his scheme appeared in their Working Paper of August 29. It was strange that, after so many years of

14 April 15, 1957, p. 18.
15 p. 22.
16 July 5, 1957, p. 7.
17 March 20, 1957, p. 19.
18 July 2, 1957, p. 2.
19 July 5, 1957, pp. 2–15. See pp. 272–274, below.

labour, the Western Governments, when they proposed a definite " cut-off " and " equitable transfers," could not lay a concrete detailed plan before the world.

## UN ASSEMBLY, OCTOBER–DECEMBER 1957

The Report of the Sub-Committee, and the Western package plan of " partial " measures, were the most important subject of debate in the 1957 session of the Assembly. The rapporteur, Dr. Matsch of Austria, summarised the Russian objections to the Western plan by saying that the Soviet representative had explained that " it would place it [Russia] in an unequal position . . . which would be detrimental to its security." [20]   Mr. Kuznetsov said that Russia stood for

> " a major reduction of armaments and armed forces, and for the complete prohibition of atomic and hydrogen weapons. It favoured the cessation of the production of atomic weapons and their elimination from the arsenals of States." [21]

This was really a declaration against the Western method of seeking a first step in armament reduction by " partial " measures; and this became the main issue of the prolonged debate. In the end the Assembly adopted a Resolution which urged the Disarmament Commission to " give priority to reaching a disarmament agreement " which would achieve six of the " partial " measures which the Western Governments proposed. The Resolution was adopted by fifty-six votes, with nine (Communists) against, and fifteen abstentions.[22]

But this endorsement of the Western plan was qualified in various ways. The vote was only obtained after an amendment was inserted in the Resolution which said: " The Assembly, recalling its Resolution 808 (IX) of November 4, 1954." Resolution 808 had declared for the total

---

[20] *UN Review*, December 1957, p. 5.
[21] *Loc. cit.*, p. 7.
[22] Text of Resolution and votes, *loc. cit.*, pp. 44–45.

abolition of all weapons of mass destruction, and the elimination of all nuclear stocks; thus the Assembly insisted that this should remain the declared objective of the disarmament talks. Some of those who voted for the 1957 Resolution did so apparently believing that it went much further towards total nuclear disarmament than, in fact, it did. Many delegations voted for it, because the Russians' unskilful speeches and their proposal for a new Disarmament Commission of eighty-two nations seemed to them to be unrealistic propaganda. But the decisive factor which influenced the vote was the Western agreement, under heavy pressure, that the Disarmament Commission should be enlarged by fourteen members, including Czechoslovakia, Egypt, India, Mexico, Norway, Poland and Yugoslavia. This seemed to bring in so many influential and impartial Members that the hope of a new start might reasonably be entertained.

But the Kremlin thought they were on strong ground. They rejected this proposal, announced that they would take no further part in this new Commission or in the " bankrupt " Sub-Committee, and thus the Assembly ended, as the Sub-Committee had so often ended, with no one knowing what was going to happen next.

Meanwhile, in Dr. Oppenheimer's phrase, " the atomic clock ticks faster and faster." [23] The stocks and new production of nuclear weapons in the United States, Russia and Britain continually increase. Mr. Selwyn Lloyd said in the Sub-Committee's first meeting in 1957:

> " It is a ludicrous situation that man, through science, can discover the secret of unleashing untold energy, only to find himself in consequence bearing increased economic burdens in the field of defence, instead of enjoying . . . increasing well-being and happiness. . . . How much worse will this situation become, if the possession of nuclear weapons spreads to more and more countries. *Let us make no mistake that*

[23] *Foreign Affairs*, July 1953, p. 529.

*this will inevitably happen unless the countries repre-
sented here can reach some early agreement to end the
arms race in nuclear weapons."* [24]

But now other nations remember his later statement; they
begin to think that if nuclear weapons " are the best
deterrent to aggression," and that these weapons " provide
greater security," then they had better have them, too.
France is about to make her first nuclear tests. Sweden,
according to declarations by Ministers and Generals, may
decide, or is deciding, to manufacture nuclear weapons for
herself.[25] The West German Government may be moving
in the same direction. It is said that Israel has considered
their manufacture, and might succeed by 1961. And as
M. Moch said in the Assembly in 1957: " Soon there would
be an oversupply [of nuclear weapons] which would be
commercialised, or handed over to Allies, as was the case
already with tanks, submarines, and airplanes." [26] This is
not a prospective danger only; it has already begun. It
is a tragic comment on the work of the Disarmament
Commission and the Sub-Committee since 1952.

[24] March 18, 1957, p. 7.
[25] The Swedish Defence Minister, at a Social Democratic Youth Conference,
said: " We neither will nor can enter into competition with the great
Powers as regards atomic weapons or intercontinental missiles. Our resources
are, however, considered adequate for the acquisition of nuclear weapons for
more restricted purposes." *Swedish Press Summary*, November 7, 1957.
   On October 24, 1957, the Swedish C.-in-C. issued a Report on Defence
Problems; a Summary issued by the Ministry of Foreign Affairs said: " In
the preliminary survey it is stated that the atomic weapons are no longer
exclusive weapons . . . as regards nuclear weapons and robots, we also must
further increase our efforts if we are to achieve an effective defence." And
in a lecture on Defence at Lund he said: " Appropriate objects for our
concentration are . . . atomic and ballistic weapons. Atomic weapons could
be manufactured in the country from our own materials for a cost of less
than 100m. Kr. per year, which corresponds to only 4–5 per cent. of the total
Defence expenditure." *Swedish Press Summary*, November 16, 1957.
[26] *UN Review*, December 1957, p. 36.

# 19

# United States and Russian Policy, 1954 to 1957

Two events of overriding importance stand out from the history of the UN work on disarmament since 1952; the Russian acceptance of a great part of the West's proposals on May 10, 1955; and the United States suspension of those proposals four months after Russia had accepted them—a suspension for which the United States received the very reluctant, but in the end complete, support of Britain, France and Canada. Since the agreement of Russia and the United States is an indispensable condition of nuclear disarmament, it may be useful to consider some of the factors that played a part in shaping their policies.

## Russian Policy before and after May 10, 1955

No one who reads the full record of UN Disarmament debates since 1945 can fail to realise that until 1954 the Russian delegates were not making the slightest effort to reach agreement with their colleagues in the UN even when, as over the Six Principles and the manpower ceilings in 1952, the rest of the Commission was unanimously agreed; as Dr. Oppenheimer said, " openness, friendliness and co-operation did not seem to be what the Soviet Government most prized on this earth." The first sign of change came in September 1954 when Mr. Vyshinsky accepted the Anglo-French Memorandum as the basis of the UN's future work. This acceptance came three months after Mr. Selwyn Lloyd and Mr. Patterson had virtually abandoned the UN plan for Atomic Energy Control, and had agreed to accept a system of continuous Inspection instead. Perhaps this may be the key to Russian policy; their unbreakable resolve to keep the development of Russia's nuclear industry in Russian hands. Only when international ownership and management had been abandoned by the West did they begin to consider whether any Disarmament agreement could be reached. It took the Kremlin machine three months to grind out the first favourable decision on the Anglo-French Memorandum; and nearly nine months more to produce the plan of May 10.

If this diagnosis were correct it might mean that, after international ownership and management had been abandoned, the Kremlin came genuinely to desire agreement on the large reductions of conventional armaments and forces, and the total abolition of nuclear and other weapons of mass destruction, which they proposed. To many Western observers this would be a startling, but very welcome, thought; and there is a good deal of other evidence that it may be true.

No one doubts that after Stalin's and Beria's deaths in 1953, and Malenkov's first dismissal, there was a change in Russian foreign policy. Fighting was ended in Korea by a truce; the same thing happened in Indo-China; a Peace Treaty was made with Austria, and all the occupying forces were removed from Austrian soil; the Russian naval bases at Porkkala and Port Arthur were given up. A " change of line " about disarmament would be in keeping with these other important decisions. And Mr. Khruschev once declared that this change of line had taken place. " Dulles once claimed," he said in 1957,

> " that the Soviet had tried for months to torpedo the disarmament talks. Unfortunately this imperialist statesman was practically right. Only it was not the Soviet which tried to torpedo the talks, but Molotoff, Kaganovitch and Shepilov." [1]

This would also fit in with reports that there had been a major difference between Molotoff, on the one side, and

[1] Quoted by Mr. David Price, M.P., *Hansard*, July 23, 1957, col. 307.

Khruschev and Zhukov on the other, about the use of nuclear bombs; Molotoff held that nuclear warfare would destroy capitalism; Khruschev and Zhukov held that nuclear bombs would destroy all civilisation, including that of Soviet Russia. In any case, a Polish delegate made a speech in the Assembly in January 1957 in which he roundly declared that nuclear war *would* destroy both Capitalism *and* Communism [2]; and it may be doubted if, in that month, he would have done so, unless Khruschev had agreed.

The language and the conduct of the Russian delegates in the Sub-Committee since May 10, 1955, also support the view that there was then a genuine change of line. Broadly speaking, at least until August 1957, they avoided hostile phrases; accepted compromise proposals put forward by the West, as a basis for discussion; and often seemed to seek agreement. During and after the Assembly of 1956 the Kremlin did everything they could to make disarmament the most important subject in international affairs. They proposed a " Summit " conference to discuss disarmament alone. They proposed that the Foreign Ministers of the five Powers should make themselves the delegates to the Sub-Committee for its session of 1957. Mr. Bulganin bombarded the heads of the Western Governments with " letters " about disarmament, and immense publicity was given to these letters and to the replies, and to the proceedings of the Sub-Committee, by every agency of Communist propaganda. No doubt this emphasis on disarmament was, in part, intended to make the world forget what happened in Hungary in 1956; but it may also have a real significance of its own. Even the events in Hungary and Poland in 1956 may support the view that the Russian attitude has genuinely changed; the uprising of the two nations must have convinced the Kremlin that their outer defences in the Satellite countries would be worthless to them in a general war; if so, it would be a

[2] General Assembly, First Committee, January 21, 1957.

logical conclusion that disarmament might be a better safe-guard than allies who would desert. Even the Russian General Staff may have felt this to be true.

But there is one other more convincing piece of evidence. On March 27, 1956, before the events in Poland and Hungary, and while the " peaceful co-existence " campaign was still going strong, the Russian delegate in the Sub-Committee—it was Mr. Gromyko himself and he came to London for the purpose—made a proposal that nuclear disarmament should be provisionally shelved, and that a treaty of conventional disarmament should be made. He proposed again the Western manpower ceilings; 1 to 1·5 million for Russia and the United States; and it was clear that the ceiling could be the lower limit of 1 million, if that was what the Western Governments wanted. He further proposed that the governments should " proceed to carry out measures for the reduction of conventional armaments on a scale corresponding to " these manpower cuts, and that budgetary appropriations would be " reduced correspondingly." [3]

This proposal may have been unsound; it might simply have meant, as M. Moch contended, a diversion of resources from conventional armaments to nuclear weapons and to guided missiles. But to judge the Russians' motives fairly, it must be remembered that in March 1956 the Western Governments had " placed a reservation " on all their " pre-Geneva substantive positions," and had done so on the specific ground, constantly repeated, that the abolition of nuclear stocks could not be adequately controlled. Moreover, Western Ministers had suggested that the next step might be conventional disarmament alone. At the Foreign Ministers' Conference in Geneva in October 1955 Mr. Macmillan had said:

> " I find myself asking whether it might not be advisable to turn our attention . . . to some more limited, preliminary agreement. . . . *I think it is clear*

[3] Cmd. 9770, p. 32.

*that any such preliminary agreement would have to concentrate principally, though not exclusively, on reductions in the size of armed forces and conventional armaments.*" [4]

The British Defence White Paper for 1956, published five weeks before the Russians made their proposal, went even further; after speaking of the difficulties of nuclear disarmament, it said:

"The Government have also been giving thought to the possibility of concluding an agreement which would permit a first instalment of disarmament to be carried out without delay. . . . Increased confidence is generally recognised to be an essential pre-condition of any large-scale disarmament. *It follows that the adoption of even a modest degree of disarmament related to conventional weapons, coupled with appropriate measures for control including aerial inspection,* should create an atmosphere in which bolder advances could follow." [5]

Sir Gladwyn Jebb had used this same argument when he moved the manpower proposal in 1952. On March 27, 1956, Mr. Gromyko quoted Sir Gladwyn's words:

"*If we could reach agreement on the levels of all armed forces, which is what we now propose, I am sure that this would in itself restore international confidence to such an extent that the problem of controlling atomic energy so as to make the prohibition of atomic weapons an effective prohibition would present a much less formidable obstacle than it has done in the past.*" [6]

United States Ministers had used similar language in 1956, and the Russians may reasonably have assumed that they meant what they said. Moreover, for nine years, Western spokesmen had been complaining that Russia had

[4] Cmd. 9633, pp. 123–124.
[5] Cmd. 9691, paras. 16, 17.
[6] UN Disarmament Commission, May 28, 1952.

urged nuclear disarmament and the banning of nuclear bombs, although it was obvious that, if this were agreed to, Russian conventional forces and armaments would dominate the world.   They had urged that only Western nuclear power had kept the peace against Russia's great conventional forces.   The Russians must naturally have believed that an offer to reduce their conventional forces to 1 million men—a reduction of 75 or 80 per cent.—without asking in return for any diminution of Western nuclear power, would be taken as a genuine gesture of good will.   And, indeed, if Mr. Gromyko's 1956 proposal had been accepted and carried out, the balance of military power would have been very drastically changed in favour of the West.   This is surely evidence of some importance.

But if the Russians genuinely wanted a beginning of disarmament, why did they turn down the Western " package " plan of 1957? [7]   Some of their reasons have been given above.[8]   One other, relating to the Western nuclear proposals, may be given; Mr. Zorin, arguing that no government could accept the " cut-off," unless it was linked with the abolition of stocks and a ban on the use of nuclear weapons, said:

> " The cessation of atomic and hydrogen bomb production is linked, as everyone recognises, with the institution of a system of control and involves the submission by States of information which is vital to their security.   But can it be seriously believed that any State whatever *will be prepared to admit control officials to its atomic plants when the armed forces of several States have atomic and hydrogen bombs stockpiled for use and there is no ban of any sort on their use ?* " [9]

Then he argued that, so long as the Western Governments insisted on keeping stocks of nuclear weapons, on

[7] See p. 25.
[8] See pp. 27–28.
[9] Sub-Committee, July 8, 1957, p. 9.

supplying them to their Allies, and so on, Russia would naturally be afraid that " information received as a result of the institution of control over a given State's enterprises might be used against that State's interests." [10] Her fears would vanish when the Western Governments were ready to eliminate their stocks and to ban the use of nuclear weapons.[11]

No one can *know* that the Kremlin genuinely desired disarmament on a fair and equitable basis after May 10, 1955. But no one can *know* that they did *not*. It seems certain that they fear the outcome of a nuclear war. They do not fear it enough to make them change their attitude about the international ownership or management of their nuclear industry; but it seems reasonable to assume that they may be prepared to co-operate in working out and in applying whatever other safeguards can be devised. At least, it cannot be assumed that they are insincere in the various proposals for " general," " comprehensive " or " partial " disarmament which they have made.

## *United States Policy before and after May 10, 1955*

Why did the United States, on September 6, 1955, " suspend " the proposals they had been pressing on the Russians up to May 10? There is no doubt that the United States Government, and their General Staff, had definitely accepted the UN Plan. They were genuinely convinced that international ownership and management of " dangerous " activities and plants was the *only* satisfactory plan. Their own Atomic Energy Law of 1946 (which is still in force) gave the USAEC " a monopoly in the field of atomic energy," with " the right to control

---

[10] *Ibid.*

[11] This argument would appear to show that the Kremlin were taking the proposals about the admission " of control inspectors into its atomic plants " very seriously indeed.

all vital activities through direct ownership and management, and all other activities by means of regulations and licences." [12] The Lilienthal Report, said Mr. Gordon Dean, " like the domestic (United States) plan, relied upon direct management as the only really effective means of control." [13] They had all accepted the proposition from the start that Inspection by itself was not enough.

In 1955 they had dropped the UN Plan; they had accepted Inspection, in principle, instead. But no one had even suggested any system by which control by simple Inspection could be made to work. And the United States General Staff had been having bitter experience of how the Communists treated an organ of international control. The UN Truce Commission in Korea consisted of " neutrals "; it had been shamefully hampered, disregarded and deceived in North Korea throughout 1954 and 1955. For ten years the United States had seen Communist Governments, with the guidance and example of the Kremlin, tear up international engagements which they had made. In particular, they had seen the ex-enemy satellites given armaments far in excess of what the Peace Treaties of 1947 laid down. This, naturally and rightly, had induced a great sense of caution, not to say suspicion, in their minds about any proposals which the Soviet Government might make.

Moreover, disarmament, both nuclear and conventional, had been talked about so long in general phrases that it seemed to them to have lost reality as a policy of defence. It was a great disaster that neither the UN Disarmament Commission nor its Sub-Committee had, by 1955, made any progress with their real task of drafting a treaty. If the proposals about nuclear inspection and control, about manpower, conventional armaments, and budgetary limitation had been turned into detailed treaty clauses, the United States Government and General Staff would have seen that a disarmament treaty in itself would be full of guarantees.

[12] Gordon Dean, *Report on the Atom*, p. 29.
[13] *Op. cit.*, p. 31.

But this had not been done; the large-scale reduction of forces and arms which their Government had proposed had remained no more than headline objectives; when, in 1955, the Russians suddenly accepted those reductions, and the United States Staff were thus suddenly called on to face the prospect of carrying them out, it must have seemed to them like a dangerous leap in the dark.

No doubt, too, something else had happened. With part of their minds, the United States leaders, and above all President Eisenhower, were deeply conscious of the perils of the nuclear arms race. But for years they had been saying what Mr. Stassen said to the Sub-Committee in March 1956:

> " We consider that there is now an atomic shield against aggression. It is an important safeguard of peace. It is a powerful deterrent of war. We wish to be very certain of the true worth of any arrangement which we put in its place before we agree to weaken this shield." [14]

Even more significantly, Mr. Stassen said in May:

> " It is the United States view that low force levels and drastic reductions in armaments—even though carried out under an armaments agreement—would not, if they were not accompanied by progress in the settlement of the major political issues, be in the interest of any country represented at this Sub-Committee table. *These reductions would increase the danger of the outbreak of war at some point in the world, and of such a war in turn spreading to involve all nations, particularly major nations.*" [15]

British and United States armaments had helped to keep the peace in many countries in the troubled years after 1945, when Russia would not even discuss disarmament seriously. The United States Staff had carried the main burden in

[14] Sub-Committee, March 19, 1956, p. 27.
[15] May 4, 1956, Cmd. 9770, p. 57.

Korea. It was natural that, in 1955, these experiences should be very vivid in their minds. They had come to rely for national safety and world freedom on very powerful United States armaments, although this meant that Russia, China and other nations kept very powerful armaments, too. They had lost from sight the dangerous momentum of the arms race, and of the tensions it creates.

Time is showing that the United States rejection of the Russian offer of May 10, 1955, may have been a terrible mistake. It may take time before the United States Government comes round again to the belief that equal and balanced armament reductions, under an adequate system of control, do not diminish, but increase, the national security of the signatory States. But at no time has it been open to doubt that the United States Government and people detest war, detest armament competition, and, like their President, are genuinely dedicated to the cause of peace.

# PART FOUR

# PROPOSALS FOR NUCLEAR DISARMAMENT

# 20

## *The Changed Problem of 1958*

TOTAL nuclear disarmament was still declared by the UN Assembly in 1957 to be the ultimate objective to be pursued. Nuclear weapons are so dangerous, and, while they still exist, the risk that they will be used remains so great, that it is the only policy which makes political or military sense.

But the original UN plan is " very, very dead," and cannot be revived. What other measures can be taken to deal with the special difficulties which nuclear disarmament involves? What changes have happened in the technical and political background during the long years of fruitless negotiation since the UN plan was drawn up?

The changes have been great.

## *Unfavourable Changes since 1948*

### RAW MATERIALS

In 1948 it was still believed that Mr. Lilienthal and his colleagues had been right to say that the areas of the world containing significant deposits of uranium and thorium were " relatively limited "; today the deposits are known to be far greater and more widespread than was then believed, very low-grade ores are being or will be worked, and great vested interests have grown up around the mining of them in many countries.

### NATIONAL AND EUROPEAN ATOMIC INDUSTRIES

In 1948 there was no atomic industry in any country except the U.S.A. Today three countries have large-scale industries; and France has important plants at Marcoule. By the end of 1958 the world will have fifty " high-capacity reactors," twenty " large-scale isotope separation or irradiated rod processing installations," and twenty "large plants producing fuel elements." [1] Great expansions are being planned. Britain is constructing nuclear power stations with a capacity of 6,000 mw. of electricity, to be completed by 1965.[2] Euratom is planning nuclear stations with a capacity of 15,000 mw. to be completed in the same year. France alone has a target of 4,000 mw. by 1967. The United States are generously helping this development in Europe. Under bilateral agreements made in 1957 they are supplying 7,000 kg. (over seven tons) of U235 to Italy, 2,500 kg. each to France and West Germany, 500 kg. to the Netherlands.[3] These are large quantities[4]; and under similar bilateral agreements the United States are helping to start industries in other countries. There are research reactors in many countries, some of which (*e.g.*, Sweden and Norway) have begun to build an atomic industry of their own. Plans are being made to furnish nuclear reactors to the under-developed countries of the world, and to countries which are distant from the conventional sources of power—coal, oil, large rivers, waterfalls. Thus a vast industrial development of atomic energy, foreseen, but not begun, in 1948, is now going forward with gathering speed; and every new reactor, or separation plant, in whatever country, is a potential source of the fissile material from which weapons can be made.

## MILITARY CHANGES SINCE 1948

On top of this industrial development there have been the military applications of atomic energy which earlier chapters have described. This is the greatest and most dangerous change of all. In 1948 there were no nuclear weapons in any country but the U.S.A., and the United States stock

---

[1] M. Moch, Sub-Committee, July 5, 1957.
[2] UKAEA, Report for 1956, p. 11.
[3] N.Y.H.T., July 25, 1957.
[4] If the British General Staff asked the UKAEA for an extra ton of U235, it would take three years to produce and would cost many £m. for new plant.

of bombs was small. No "tactical" weapons had been devised, and no military use but that of "strategic" bombing of cities and major targets had been conceived. Russia produced her first A-bomb in 1949; Britain in 1952. The fissile material used for A-bombs was adapted to detonate H-bombs by the United States in 1952, by Russia in 1953, and by Britain in 1957. There are vast stocks of nuclear weapons; there is very large-scale production, and new countries may soon be joining in.

### Special Problems in Under-developed Countries

There will be special problems of Inspection and Control in the under-developed countries. Most of these countries would not, in the measurable future, be able to create an atomic industry of their own; but, if they could divert fissile material from their nuclear power-stations, they might be able, by hiring foreign technicians, to make the smaller plants in which this fissile material could be turned into weapons. And there may be special difficulties in such countries about organising an effective system of control; the experts required may be unwilling to go there, and to cut themselves off from the scientific circles in which they live; the national officials may be susceptible to bribery by the agents of a foreign government seeking fissile material for an aggressive war; and so on.

These industrial and military changes have all made the problem of effectively controlling nuclear disarmament more difficult than it would have been if swift action on the UN Plan, or on some similar system, had been taken in 1948. They have meant that atomic energy has been " developed on the basis of national interests and needs," and " against a background of national rivalry," instead of the " planning and operation " being made, as the UNAEC hoped it would be, " a common (international) enterprise in all its phases."

## *Favourable Changes since 1948*

But there have also been changes which should tend to make control of nuclear disarmament easier in various ways.

### SCIENTIFIC INSTRUMENTS

Instruments have been developed which will make Inspection more reliable, and less costly in skilled manpower, than it would have been in 1948.[5]

### IAEA

The UN has established the International Atomic Energy Agency, with headquarters in Vienna; eighty-two nations have signed its Statute, which came into force in October 1957, and over sixty have already ratified it. One of its tasks, as prescribed in the Statute, is to ensure that nuclear development is not used for military ends.[6] Various problems about the working of this Agency will inevitably arise: its relation with Euratom, with the European Nuclear Energy Agency, and the European Research Centre at Geneva; its control over national atomic industries started under bilateral agreements between various countries and the United States; the part which it will play in the Inspection system to be created by the Disarmament Treaty. These problems will be dealt with in later chapters [7]; in the meantime it must be noted that the establishment of IAEA is a most important and a most favourable change.

### GENEVA CONFERENCES ON PEACEFUL USES

So has been the UN Conference on the peaceful uses of atomic energy, held at Geneva in 1955.[8] It has shown how readily the scientists of different nations would co-operate to use atomic energy for the general benefit of mankind if their governments would give them the necessary mandate. The Secretary General of the first

---

[5] See pp. 277–279.    [6] See p. 267.
[7] See pp. 266 *et seq.*    [8] A similar conference is to be held in September 1958.

Conference, Professor W. G. Whitman, an American by nationality, wrote in 1955:

" The most vital element in our preparation was to recruit a group of younger scientists who could become the planning and operating team for the Conference itself. . . . A team of nineteen men from Argentina, Brazil, Canada, Czechoslovakia, France, India, Japan, the Netherlands, Pakistan, Russia, Britain, the United States, and Yugoslavia, who were assembled in the New York Headquarters of the UN . . . within a week were thinking and acting as Civil Servants of the UN, dedicated to making the Conference a success."

And again:

" To me, and to my twenty associates, the most surprising feature was that arguments were not between the United States and the Russian nationals; they were between the physicists and the chemists, or between the biologists and the metallurgists." [9]

Such words are full of hope.

## The Four Obligations of Total Nuclear Disarmament

How, in the light of these changes since 1948, can a system of total nuclear disarmament be devised, and how can it be controlled? The following chapters will attempt an answer.

The basis of any system of total nuclear disarmament must be the acceptance by governments of four different but complementary obligations. These obligations must be accepted by *all* nations—if even one small and backward State stood out, and, with the help of foreign experts, began to produce nuclear weapons, the whole system might be undermined.

The four obligations are as follows:

(i) Not to *use* nuclear weapons, in any kind of war;

[9] Quoted by James Avery Joyce, *Revolution on East River*, 1957, pp. 148–149.

(ii) Not to *test* new weapons in experimental research;

(iii) Not to *make* new fissile or fusionable material for warlike purposes;

(iv) Not to *stock* nuclear weapons, and to convert existing stocks to peaceful uses at the dates and by the methods which the Disarmament Treaty lays down.

Logically, these four obligations go together; and it seems likely that no one of them will be generally accepted, unless the others are simultaneously accepted too. Since 1946 Russia has urged that the *use* of nuclear weapons should be banned as a separate measure to be taken first; this was vehemently rejected by the West on the ground that, if it were accepted, Russia's conventional armaments would then dominate the world. In 1957 Russia, India and others proposed that all *tests* should be forbidden under a system of international control; M. Moch replied that France could not " accept the idea that the nuclear armaments race should continue between *three* Powers, and that the others should not even be allowed to conduct tests " [10]; stopping tests was impossible without the " *cut-off*." Mr. Zorin replied that the cut-off could never be accepted unless it was simultaneously agreed that existing *stocks* should be abolished.[11]

The conclusion is plain; each part of a programme of nuclear disarmament depends on the rest, even though the different parts may be put into operation at different times. However desirable it may be to separate one or more of them into a " partial " agreement, attempts to do so will probably fail. In any case, no one part would last long without the rest; and what is needed is a complete system of nuclear disarmament that will endure. The four parts of such a system will be considered in turn, taking the simplest and most straightforward of them first.

[10] Sub-Committee, April 1, 1957, p. 8.
[11] See pp. 295–296.

# 21

## *" Ban the Bomb "*

In his first speech in the UNAEC, Mr. Gromyko proposed the following as the first of all disarmament measures, to be accepted without delay:

> *" Article 1.* The High Contracting Parties solemnly declare that they are unanimously resolved to prohibit the production and employment of weapons based on the use of atomic energy, and for this purpose assume the following obligations . . . (a) not to use atomic weapons in any circumstances whatever. . . ." [1]

He argued that

> " the character of this weapon is such that its employment brings untold misery, above all to the peaceful population. The results of its employment are incompatible with the generally accepted standards and ideas riveted in the consciousness of humanity in the course of many centuries to the effect that the rules of warfare must not allow the extermination of innocent civilian populations." [2]

In his last speech in the 1957 session of the Sub-Committee, Mr. Zorin said:

> " Since, moreover, States have at their disposal large stocks of atomic and hydrogen weapons, it is impossible effectively to remove the danger of atomic war unless the use of these is banned." [3]

In the eleven years between these statements, hundreds of thousands of words had been spoken about banning the

---

[1] UNAEC, June 19, 1946, p. 27.
[2] *Ibid.*
[3] Sub-Committee, September 5, 1957, p. 21.

bomb; the Russians had urged it on every suitable and unsuitable occasion; the Western delegates had rejected it with equal vigour; the argument was often acrimonious in the extreme; and at the end, the gulf was as great as when they first began.

Moreover, the Western delegates have often spoken, with indignation, as though it were a proposal that ought never to have been made. In 1947, when the subject had been argued threadbare, Mr. Osborn, a United States delegate in the UNAEC, said that talk about banning the bomb had an " air of unreality "; the real problem was not that at all.

The reasons for this long-continued clash have been given above. The United States genuinely believed that their use of A-bombs had shortened the war against Japan, and had saved great suffering and loss of life; they were making sincere proposals for the total abolition of all nuclear weapons; until nuclear disarmament with effective safe-guards was agreed to, they thought their A-bombs were a guarantee against aggression. The Russians may or may not have believed sincerely what Mr. Gromyko and Mr. Zorin said. But by the way they said it, by their conduct in the early disarmament debates, and by their cold-war policy, they alienated the sympathy of other delegations, and ensured majority support for the Western Governments' view.

## Nuclear Weapons and International Law

On the previously accepted rules of international law, the Russian case was unanswerably strong. Nuclear weapons cannot be reconciled with the principles declared by Hugo Grotius in the seventeenth century, codified by nineteenth-century conventions, and re-stated by Sir Anthony Eden in his Draft Disarmament Convention of 1933.[4] The British Government, with the universal consent of other nations, then declared as " an established rule of international law "

4 See pp. 56 and 152.

that any use of poisonous, incendiary or bacterial weapons " against any State . . . and in any war, whatever its character," was prohibited. The A-bomb was poisonous; it was, by about 100,000 times, the most powerful incendiary weapon ever made; it produced a sickness of the human body not less horrifying than the most terrible of the biological weapons that now exist.[5]

This view cannot be contested [6]; and it is relevant to recall that German Nazi leaders were tried and hanged at Nuremburg, on the charge of " a common plan or conspiracy " which

> " came to embrace the commission of war crimes, in that it contemplated, and the defendants determined upon and carried out, ruthless wars against countries and populations, *in violation of the rules and customs of war, including . . . the indiscriminate destruction of cities, towns, and villages,* and devastation not justified by military necessity."

## The Western Governments' View

The Russian delegates have argued this legal case so unskilfully that the Western Governments have never thought it necessary to reply. Their arguments have been of quite a different kind. They can best be given in the refined form they had achieved in the tenth year of the debate.

" If an international agreement," said Mr. Cabot Lodge, in the Assembly in 1955,

> " makes it impossible for a law-abiding Power to use them (nuclear weapons) first, even in dire extremity of self-defence against a massive aggression, then that

---

[5] In 1957 Captain Liddell-Hart wrote: " Nuclear weapons violate *the lawful code of warfare* on more counts than such a weapon as mustard gas, which is relatively humane." Brighton Conference Paper No. 26, p. 9, September 1957. See also Stone, *Legal Controls of International Conflict*, pp. 342 *et seq.*

[6] See Arts. 9 and 10 of the " Draft Rules for the Limitation of the Dangers Incurred by the Civil Populations in Time of War," laid before a Conference in Delhi in 1957 by the International Committee of the Red Cross.

Power which is strongest in conventional means of warfare would be immediately established as the strongest
military Power on earth."

This argument was used, it may be noted, *after* Russia had
offered to reduce her conventional forces to 1 or 1·5 million
men.  Mr. Cabot Lodge went on:

"The democratic States had always been the first
victims of aggression, with the result that they had
always started with a heavy handicap.  An undertaking
on their part not to use their most powerful weapons in
their own defence after having been attacked would
amount to suicide." [7]

In short, the Western Governments said: " Ban the
Bomb " means " disarm the democracies," and they added:
" No weapon is illegitimate in self-defence against a nation
that commits the crime of Charter-breaking aggression."

They used another argument as well: even if an obligation not to use nuclear weapons were accepted, it would
never be observed.  " Supposing there were another world
war," said Mr. Selwyn Lloyd in 1954, " there would not
even be the probability that such an obligation would be
honoured." [8]  When the Russians answered that the poison
gas agreement of 1925 had been observed in the 1939 War,
the Western delegates replied that it was certainly not a
sense of legal obligation that had restrained Hitler from
using poison gas.

These arguments all boiled down to one: resort to war,
aggression, is the crime which the UN was established to
prevent; our first duty under the Charter is to use all the
means at our disposal to prevent it; Russia has made us all
afraid that she intends aggression; we shall use all the
weapons we possess to stop her from conquering the world;
and we shall retain the right to use them until genuine,
all-round, guaranteed disarmament has been achieved.

[7] 1st Committee, December 9, 1955, p. 275.
[8] Sub-Committee, June 1, 1954, Cmd. 9205, p. 191.

This meant by implication: we have abandoned the nineteenth-century laws of war; Hitler destroyed them, and they cannot be revived. We all burnt towns and cities in the 1939 War by launching incendiary attacks from the air; we did it again in Korea; Hiroshima was no more horrible than Tokyo. If we have all-round disarmament, we shall end the use of nuclear weapons; there is no other way in which it can be done.

There is no real answer to this argument. Modern armaments have become a Frankenstein's monster of which the nations have lost control. Statesmen and international lawyers have given far too much attention in the last hundred years to preparing laws of war, when the only realistic course was to prepare an effective system of law to end war itself; the mistake should not be repeated now. As the Disarmament Commission declared in the Six Principles in 1952: " *The goal of disarmament is not to regulate, but to prevent war.*" [9]

When a system of total nuclear disarmament has been devised and adopted, there will be no difficulty about " Banning the Bomb." The question has always been not *whether*, but *when*, it should be done. The Western Governments in their " 75 per cent. Arrangement " of 1955, suggested that the ban should be effective as soon as three-quarters of the agreed conventional reductions had been carried out.[10] In their proposals of May 10, the Russians, in effect, accepted this proposal. Another possible compromise has been suggested: that the ban should become effective when a large measure of conventional disarmament had been agreed to and carried out. This is defensible in logic, and it might have practical advantages; it is not certain that the United States would agree. The best hope may still lie in a compromise solution on the lines of the " 75 per cent. Arrangement."

[9] Cmd. 8589, p. 14. See p. 12.
[10] See p. 17.

## Can There be a Provisional Prohibition?

But under the 75 per cent. arrangement there was an interval of time, during which three-quarters of the reductions in conventional armaments were to be made, in which the ban would not apply. To deal with this difficulty the Anglo-French Memorandum of 1954 contained the following formula:

> "The States Members . . . regard themselves as prohibited in accordance with the terms of the Charter . . . from the use of nuclear weapons except in defence against aggression." [11]

This was a purely face-saving device, intended to make it easier for the Russians to abandon their demand for the immediate and unconditional banning of the bomb. It was of no substantive importance, since the use of *all* weapons is forbidden by the Charter except in self-defence.

In their plan of May 10 the Russians put up a variant, changed to suit themselves: from the beginning of the conventional armament reductions and until complete prohibition at 75 per cent.,

> "States shall assume a solemn obligation not to use nuclear weapons, which they shall regard as prohibited to them. Exceptions to this rule may be permitted for purposes of defence against aggression, when a decision to that effect is taken by the Security Council." [12]

This would have left Russia with a veto on the use of nuclear weapons, and it was most unlikely that the Western Governments would ever have agreed. It is also unlikely that the Russians would have made this a breaking-point, if negotiations had gone forward on the basis they proposed on May 10. [13]

---

[11] Cmd. 9204, p. 31.

[12] Cmd. 9636, p. 38.

[13] In the Western 1957 "package" plan, yet another formula was proposed, officially summarised thus: "The use of nuclear weapons will be prohibited in circumstances other than of individual or collective self-defence." This was a change of words, with no change of meaning.

## *Russia's Use of " Ban the Bomb "*

If Russia genuinely desires a disarmament agreement, why does she go on saying: " Ban the Bomb," although it only exasperates the West? Obviously because it helps her propaganda, above all in Asia. The Western Governments have never understood how the Asians fear and hate atomic bombs. At Bandung, and in every session of the UN Assembly, they have expressed this fear and hatred with gathering force. To Russia, " Ban the Bomb " is second only in propaganda value to " Ban the Tests." She will certainly continue to declaim it, on every suitable and unsuitable occasion, with all her power. But this clash of views between Russia and the West need not be regarded as a serious obstacle to progress towards agreement on disarmament. If the problems of the tests, of the cut-off, and of nuclear stocks could be successfully solved, it would be an easy matter to find the formula required to ban the bomb.

# 22

## *Tests*

THERE is a large and authoritative literature about the stopping of nuclear tests, and only a brief outline of the case is needed here. A ban on tests is a necessary part of a disarmament programme; but it must be kept in perspective—a century of tests would do less damage to the human race than a few hours of nuclear war. As with the ban on the *use* of nuclear weapons, the question is not *whether*, but *when*, the ban shall be imposed.

## *Why Nuclear Tests Differ from Experiments with Other Weapons*

What makes nuclear tests different from experiments with other weapons is the " fall-out," and the danger to human health which it involves. The general effect of the fall-out (*i.e.*, the residual radio-activity) of A- and H-bombs *used in war* has been explained in Part Two, Chapters 10 and 11. In war, it is generally assumed, fall-out will be one of the weapons which will be employed to subdue the enemy; there will be very heavy doses of radiation over a wide area —heavy enough to kill people who spend thirty-six hours in the open within 140 miles of where a " dirty " H-bomb falls.[1] What must be here assessed is the probable effect of the fall-out of experimental nuclear tests *in time of peace*, when every possible precaution is taken to minimise the harm they do, and when the dose received by human beings, if any, will be relatively small. In spite of these precautions, *some* harm is certain to result; how much is a matter of controversy, on which eminent authorities on both sides will be quoted.

[1] See p. 136.

## THE SCALE OF TESTS

On the basis of the published facts, estimates have been made of the number of tests so far conducted, and of the approximate amount of fall-out they have produced.

## THE NUMBER OF TESTS

Up to the end of 1957, only three nations, Britain, Russia and the United States, had conducted tests. Britain had tested A- and " clean " H-weapons; Russia had tested A- and " dirty " H-weapons; the United States had tested A- and both " clean " and " dirty " H-weapons. The approximate number exploded to the end of that year is estimated to be:

|  | Clean H-bombs | Dirty H-bombs | Atomic bombs | Total |
|---|---|---|---|---|
| Britain | 4 |  | 15 | 19 |
| Russia |  | 6+ | 35+ | 41+ |
| U.S.A. | 2 | 7 | 95 | 104+ |
| Total: | 6 | 13+ | 145+ | 164+ |

The number of tests is not being reduced from year to year; on the contrary, it has tended to increase. Up to 1950 the United States had exploded six experimental A-bombs, besides the two used against Japan. In 1951, when " tactical " nuclear weapons had been thought of, there were sixteen tests in the United States alone.[2] In 1957 there were more than ever before: twenty-four inside the territory of the United States, including one of 80 kil. (four times Hiroshima),[3] and others of 40 kil. and 30 kil. The United States Government also announced the resumption of hydrogen bomb tests for 1958.[4] During 1957 Russia had at least twelve tests, and Britain six—a world total of forty-two.

[2] Gordon Dean, *op. cit.*, pp. 105–106 and 110
[3] N.Y.T., July 6, 1957.
[4] *The Times*, September 20, 1957.

## AMOUNT OF FALL-OUT

As explained in Chapters 10 and 11, the amount of fall-out from a test depends partly on the type of weapon, and on whether it is exploded on the ground, under water or in the air.[5] ~~where~~

But since the great majority of tests are made by air-bursts, it is the *type of weapon* that matters most. Thus Dr. A. H. Compton says:

> " It would require the explosion . . . of ten million of the so-called ' tactical ' atomic bombs over a period of a year to raise the radio-activity of the atmosphere and of the earth's surface so that mankind would be living in a level of radiation above that considered safe by those who work with radio-active materials." [6]

Perhaps Dr. Compton's figure might also be true of " clean " H-bombs. But he goes on: " Such a level of radiation might be produced by the explosion of fewer than 1,000 super bombs " (*i.e.*, " dirty " H-bombs). This view is confirmed by the British Medical Research Council, who said in their Report in 1956: " The most impressive feature of these figures for exposure from fall-out is the very great effect of a very few thermo-nuclear explosions." [7]

The United States Congressional Joint Committee on Atomic Energy took evidence from twelve scientists in 1957 about the amount of fission products which the tests had caused. The scientists, who included Dr. Dunham, head of the USAEC's Division of Biology, agreed that the tests in the last five years had totalled fifty megatons. They differed widely about what annual amount would be safe in future; some thought an average of ten megatons would be safe; others thought it should be as low as two megatons,[8] if tests are to go on indefinitely. If the lower estimate is

---

[5] See pp. 120 *et seq.*
[6] A. H. Compton, *Atomic Quest*, p. 308. This statement neglects the effects of strontium 90 and the genetic damage; see below.
[7] *The Hazards to Man of Nuclear and Allied Explosions*, Cmd. 9780, p. 57.
[8] *Summary Analysis of Hearings on the Nature of Radioactive Fall-out and its Effects on Man*, p. 16.

right, then the average of the last five years has been dangerously high.

## *The Damage Done to Human Health by Peace-Time Tests*

### SHORTENING THE LIFE-SPAN

All radiation is harmful, in greater or lesser degree, to human health. Small doses, if repeated often, will shorten life.[9] Dr. H. J. Muller, a Nobel Prizewinner, who discovered that X-rays can cause mutations in genes (see below), says that the shortening of the life-span is " by far the most serious of the long-term effects on the exposed person himself." [10]

### CANCER OF THE BONE

Strontium 90 is a radio-active substance produced by the explosion of A-bombs; it is unknown in nature. It has now been spread around the world, but unequally distributed, according to the nature of the soil. Some places in the Welsh hills have fifty times as much as other places. Most people in the world now have some of it in their bones, as the result of eating foodstuffs grown on soil on which bomb dust has fallen. This is a danger, for it may cause cancer of the bone. In 1957 Professor Rotblat wrote:

> " One thing is certain, that each test of an H-bomb will ultimately result in cancer of the bone . . . being incurred by a number of people. . . . Whether this

[9] United States National Academy of Sciences Report on " Biological Effects of Atomic Radiation," June 1956.

The average life-span of radiologists in the United States—that is, of doctors who work with X-rays—is five years less than that of the general population :

|  | *Average age at death* |
| --- | --- |
|  | *Years* |
| United States population over twenty-five years of age .. | 65·6 |
| Physicians having no known contact with radiation    .. | 65·7 |
| Specialists having some exposure to radiation     ..    .. | 63·3 |
| Radiologists  ..    ..    ..    ..    ..    ..    ..    .. | 60·5 |

[10] " Race Poisoning by Radiation," *Saturday Review*, June 9, 1956.

number is measured in tens or in many thousands we shall not know until much more research is done." [11]

A committee of the British Atomic Scientists' Association estimated the number of cases of cancer of the bone at about 1,000 for every megaton exploded in atomic tests.[12] This would mean that over 50,000 people will die of this disease as the result of tests already made. Another British scientist, C. H. Waddington, says: " We know that strontium has a greater tendency to settle in their (children's) bones, and we think they are probably more sensitive to the damage it causes." [13]

## LEUKAEMIA

Dr. E. B. Lewis, of the California Institute of Technology, published a study in 1957 which showed that there is a " direct linear relationship between the amount of radiation received by a person and the occurrence of leukaemia, a fatal disease of the white blood cells," *i.e.*, that any dose, *however small*, may cause leukaemia. Dr. Lewis estimated that if the general population were to ingest the amount of strontium 90 which was considered safe before his work was published—which has probably happened as the result of tests—somewhere " between 150 and 3,000 more people would die of leukaemia each year in the United States alone." [14] One of his colleagues, Professor Harrison Brown, estimated the additional deaths at 10,000 a year.[15, 16]

---

[11] *The New Scientist*, January 3, 1957, p. 39.

[12] Memorandum published on April 16, 1957, and signed by Profs. Rotblat, Haddow, Penrose, Sheppard and others.

[13] " The Biological Effects of Bomb Tests," *New Statesman and Nation*, June 8, 1957.

[14] *The New Scientist*, May 16, 1957.

[15] *San Francisco Chronicle*, July 14, 1957.

[16] The deaths due to leukaemia among radiologists in the United States from 1928 to 1948 were 4·7 per cent. as against 0·5 per cent. in non-radiologist physicians. A detailed study of the survivors of the Hiroshima bombing showed that the deaths among them due to leukaemia in the period 1948–50 were *three–five times more than the normal number in Japan*. See Nobuo Kusano, *Atomic Bomb Injuries*, 1953; cited *Indian Government Report*, p. 84.

## GENETIC EFFECTS OF FALL-OUT

Radiation damages the reproductive organs of human beings, and for these " genetic " effects, says the Medical Research Council, *there is no " threshold dose "*; *i.e.*, any dose, however small, does harm. Radiation may make people sterile; it causes abortions or still-births; it may produce children that are defective in many ways; the general weakening it causes is transmitted to later generations. Four eminent geneticists told Congress in 1957 that the genetic victims of the tests, if tests went on, might number tens of thousands, or even millions. Dr. J. F. Crow estimated that in future generations there will be " 80,000 cases of gross genetic abnormalities, 30,000 childhood deaths and still-births, 700,000 embryonic deaths, plus a larger but unknown number of minor defects." [17] Dr. Linus Pauling, a Nobel Prizewinner, gave a warning in 1957 that—

" if tests are carried on at the present rate, the number of children born in each generation with such serious defects as feeble-mindedness and deformities, will increase by 1 per cent., or 200,000." [18]

Dr. H. J. Muller said in an address accepting the Kimber Genetics Award in 1955:

" No exposure is so tiny that it does not carry its corresponding mutational risk. . . . Each detrimental mutation . . . tends to continue from generation to generation . . . until at last it happens to tip the scales against one of its possessors, and that line of descent then dies out in consequence of the inherited disability. . . . The number of harmful mutations which will be inherited by our own descendants as a result of all test explosions turns out to be not far from the number among the Japanese as a result of the Hiroshima fission explosion." [19]

[17] N.Y.T., June 5, 1957.
[18] N.Y.T., May 1, 1957.
[19] United States *Bulletin of Atomic Scientists*, June 1955, pp. 210–212.

In a paper written for the Geneva Conference of 1955 Dr. Muller said:

"The important quantity in the determination of the total amount of genetic damage is not the amount of harm done to the individuals who have inherited the mutations in question, but only the total number of these mutations. For a mutation doing less harm to an individual will . . . be passed down to a correspondingly larger number of descendant individuals . . . The genetic damage, that to later generations, caused by a given dose is . . . far greater than the damage to the exposed individual himself." [20]

The USAEC is to reduce the present permissible levels of radiation exposure for atomic workers and for populations around atomic installations by one-third. The main reason for this decision is the fear that any additional radiation may cut the life-span and damage the hereditary cells of the people it affects.[21, 22]

## Damage to the Citizens of the Non-Nuclear Powers

The President of the Tenth Assembly of the World Health Organisation, M. Parisot, said in 1957 that the greatest danger from radiation in the nuclear age might come " in the under-developed regions of the world not fully prepared to cope with it. These countries," he said,

"still have much to do in handling the vast health problems of the day. . . . (They) do not yet realise

[20] United States *Bulletin of Atomic Scientists*, November 1955, pp. 329–337.
[21] N.Y.T., September 15, 1957.
[22] *The Times* published three articles, on June 7, 8 and 11, 1957, by their Special Correspondent after he had visited Nevada. Following is an extract from the last article: " On the face of it, coincidence has been playing extraordinary tricks in one Nevada valley. . . . The fall-out was admittedly heavy from one of the bigger explosions two years ago, and within the succeeding months a husky little boy had died of a rare disease—leukaemia—a woman had lost all her hair, cancerous sores and ' big eye ' multiplied at an abnormal rate among the cattle, dogs went blind, and nearly every one of the ranchers complained of varying degrees of eye trouble . . .''

the danger of contamination of soil, water, air and food. The danger of radiation does not stop at their frontiers." [23]

Fall-out from tests is carried all round the world by the upper air currents, and only falls slowly to the ground. But no country can escape it. All the major tests have been held in Siberia or the Pacific, very far from London. But Professor Rotblat has been able to determine the presence in his own body of Caesium 137, a dangerous radio-active substance which, like Strontium 90, is unknown in nature, but results from nuclear explosions.

It is not without reason that the twenty-nine nations of the Afro-Asian group, most of whose territories are nearer than London to the testing sites, and most of whom are " under-developed," and therefore comparatively unprotected, protested at their Conference in Bandung against the policy of the nuclear Powers, and demanded the stopping of the tests, and total nuclear disarmament without delay. They have a no less vital interest in the matter than the peoples of Britain, Russia and the United States, and their Governments speak for three-fifths of the population of the world.

## Nuclear Tests and the Arms Race

Mr. Bulganin said in a letter to the British Prime Minister in 1957 that " every new explosion of an A- or H-bomb . . . leads to the speeding up of the atomic weapons race." [24] Mr. Zorin spelt the argument out in the Sub-Committee:

" Every test explosion of an A- or H-bomb in one country spurs on other countries to adopt similar measures, in order not to be left behind. And in the last analysis this leads to a general intensification of the nuclear armaments race, and makes the world situation increasingly tense and dangerous." [25]

[23] N.Y.H.T., May 8, 1957.
[24] Message of July 20, 1957.
[25] Sub-Committee, August 27, 1957, p. 9.

This is clearly true. The purpose of tests is to make the nuclear weapons cheaper, more efficient, more " versatile," more powerful per kg. of fissile material. In proportion to their destructive power, they are already terrifyingly cheap, light and easy to transport. But further " improvements " can, no doubt, be made. Mr. Sandys said in 1957 that further tests would enable Britain to use less fissile material per bomb, *i.e.*, to increase its total stock of weapons with the fissile material already produced.[26] Dr. Teller and Dr. Lawrence told President Eisenhower that tests must go on, because in five more years of testing they would be able to produce 100 per cent. " clean " bombs.[27]

Dr. Willard F. Libby, one of the scientists of the USAEC, in evidence before a Congressional Sub-Committee, said that the " development of new weapons would be crippled by a cessation of tests," and that " testing must be continued to have warheads for missiles now being developed that are ' so vital to securing the survival of the free world.' "[28] The warheads must be adapted to the missiles; and the missiles must be adapted to the warheads —adapted to carry a given weight to a given destination. The same is true of the other means by which nuclear weapons will be delivered to their targets. " The halting of nuclear tests," said Mr. Hanson Baldwin,

> " must affect other weapons design—particularly in the improvement in the design of the carriers, planes, missiles and ships—which take A-bombs to their targets. The size and design and efficiency of the IRBM and ICBM are directly affected by the capability of nuclear scientists to reduce the present size and weight of nuclear warheads available without reducing their explosive power. The smaller the warhead, the smaller the missiles, the less the amount of fuel required, and the simpler the engineering problems involved."[29]

---

[26] *Hansard*, July 23, 1957, col. 348.     [27] N.Y.T., June 26, 1957.
[28] N.Y.T., June 8, 1957.     [29] N.Y.T. *Weekly Review*, June 30, 1957.

All this testing and redesigning of nuclear warheads and of the means of delivery is immensely costly. It increases the " versatility " of the nuclear weapons, *i.e.*, the variety of different ways in which they can be used in war. As each government learns from its Intelligence sources of the advances which others have made, so it is driven on to further tests itself, and thus the struggle for the " lead," and the anxiety and suspicion it creates, grow more intense. In other words, this testing, re-designing and counter-testing *is* the arms race in one of its most dangerous forms.

## Could the Cessation of Nuclear Tests be Controlled?

Dr. Edward Teller, who is the leading authority in the USAEC,[30] has written:

> " If a nation wants to carry out tests in secrecy, observation will become difficult and uncertain. . . . Of course, it will cost some money and effort to hide nuclear explosions. But the Soviet Union has never been stingy where a military advantage is at stake." [31]

Dr. Teller's words are vague: " difficult and uncertain " imply a risk, not a certainty, that an international control organ could be deceived. It is a risk that his own Government is prepared to take; President Eisenhower himself overruled his objections, and the 1957 Western " package " plan contained proposals for a cessation of tests, subject to

> " the installation and maintenance of the necessary controls, including inspection posts with scientific instruments, located within . . . the Soviet Union, the United Kingdom and the United States, the area of the Pacific Ocean and at such other places as may be necessary." [32]

The Russians had previously proposed the establishment of

[30] See pp. 164–165.
[31] " The Case for Continued Testing," article in N.Y.H.T., January 11, 1958.
[32] Cmnd. 333, p. 98.

such control posts and had suggested that the first period of suspension should be at least two to three years.[33]

In spite of Dr. Teller's view, the majority of experts seem to consider that the Control would be effective. A United States delegate to the Sub-Committee was reported to have said, after the Russian proposal was made: " A fool-proof inspection is feasible, provided access is given to Soviet territory." [34] Mr. Zorin said that " nuclear explosions can be detected at long range. It is also a known fact that not a single A- or H-explosion has so far been set off undetected." [35] The Australian scientist, Professor Oliphant, confirmed that this was true: " We know of every explosion the Russians have made." [35a]

Control could operate in three ways:

1. Nuclear explosions throw radio-active dust high into the stratosphere and it is carried round the earth. As it slowly descends, it can be detected in the increased radio-activity of rainwater. Or the dust can be collected at high altitudes by aircraft carrying special " scoops." Analysis of the dust would show the kind of explosion that had taken place—U235, plutonium, U238, lithium deuteride, or several combined—and its radio-activity would give some indication of the power of the bomb. This is long-distance control.

2. Control Posts manned by scientists with seismographs could detect the physical shock of a nuclear explosion as it travels through the earth's crust—just as earthquakes are detected and recorded.

3. The shock wave from the explosion—the blast—also travels through the atmosphere, and can be detected by a sensitive barometer; though this is likely to be less efficient than the seismic method.

These three methods complement each other. Control Posts at intervals of 500 miles would record *any* explosions

---

[33] Cmnd. 333, p. 76.
[34] N.Y.T., June 11, 1957.
[35] Sub-Committee, June 14, 1957, p. 11.
[35a] M.G., July 29, 1957.

above or on the ground. Explosions under water might require the Control Post to be nearer, perhaps one hundred miles; but, because of the " base-surge " [36] and the radio-active mist they cause, they are very dangerous to those who carry them out. It is in reliance on these three methods, applied by an International Control Organisation, that the Governments of the " nuclear Powers " have agreed that tests could be detected, if any government in violation of its pledges tried to carry them out.

## *The Case for Continuing Tests*

Dr. Teller wants to continue tests, not only because Russia might disloyally conduct secret tests, and so gain a military advantage, but also because

> " further tests will put us into a position to fight our opponent's war machine while sparing the innocent bystanders. One development of the greatest import-ance is the progressive reduction of radio-active fall-out. Clean weapons of this kind will reduce unnecessary casualties in a future war."

Further tests will also help, he says, to produce nuclear anti-aircraft weapons, clean explosives for peaceful use, and so on.[37]

Before Dr. Teller wrote his article, M. Moch had given an answer about " clean " H-bombs. If someone discovered, he said, how to detonate H-weapons without a core of fissile material, *e.g.*, to generate the temperature of scores of millions of degrees that is required by some chemical process, or by a tiny quantity of plutonium, then the whole problem of inspecting and controlling nuclear weapons will become even more difficult than it is today. The making of *fissile* material requires extensive plants, which cannot be concealed; the making of *fusionable* lithium deuteride (a mixture of lithium 6 and deuterium) for H-bombs is

[36] See pp. 124–125.
[37] *Loc. cit.*

done by electrolysis, and the necessary installation can be relatively small. The raw materials are so abundant that no control of them would be possible at all. In fact, " clean " bombs are now the next great danger in the arms race, and the strongest of all reasons for stopping tests.[38]

Dr. Teller's colleague, Dr. Libby, another leading scientist in the USAEC, has given other reasons for continuing tests:

> " It is not contended," he says, " that there is no risk (to human health). . . . Are we willing to take this very small and rigidly controlled risk, or would we prefer to run the risk of annihilation which might result, if we surrendered the weapons which are so essential to our freedom and actual survival?" [39]

This is frankly politics, not science. Dr. Libby and Dr. Teller believe that disarmament is a mirage; Dr. Teller argues this at length in his article. They foresee the arms race going on indefinitely, for decades, with Western experts saving freedom by keeping ahead in armament technique. This is a conception of international relations which armament experts have always held—Dr. Libby and Dr. Teller are only giving it a modern look. But it is repugnant to many of their fellow-scientists. The views of Hahn and Strassmann, who split the uranium atom in 1939, have been quoted above [40]; they and their German colleagues stand for total nuclear disarmament, beginning now. When Dr. Teller sought to persuade President Eisenhower that tests should go on, fifty of his scientific colleagues in the USAEC plant at Los Alamos, where the first A-bomb was made, sent the President a statement to urge on him that the choice today is not between " clean " and " dirty " bombs, but between " a world in which . . . nuclear bombing will occur, and a world in which we shall be free of their scourge." [41]

---

[38] Sub-Committee, July 5, 1957, pp. 14–15.
[39] N.Y.T., June 8, 1957.
[40] See p. 5.                    [41] *San Francisco Examiner*, July 24, 1957.

Dr. Linus Pauling's petition to the UN has also been quoted [42]; he and his 9,000 colleagues from forty countries said:

"Each added amount of radiation causes damage to the health of human beings all over the world and causes damage to the pool of human germ plasm such as to lead to an increase in the number of seriously defective children that will be born in future generations . . ." [43]

The cessation of tests has not yet been agreed to, for the reasons explained in previous chapters. But it is urgently necessary that it should be agreed to without delay. It is the first essential step in preventing other nations from joining in the nuclear arms race. It may, as Dr. Teller thinks, involve a risk; but "the great question facing the West and the world," says Mr. Hanson Baldwin, "is whether the calculated risk of a halt in weapons testing is greater than the calculated risk of uninterrupted development of a nuclear armoury." [44] Dr. Teller and Dr. Libby think that the present arms race can go on indefinitely for many years to come. Dr. Pauling and his 9,000 scientists take a different view. Their words may be repeated: "An international agreement to stop all testing of nuclear weapons now," they say in their petition,

"could serve as a first step towards a more general disarmament, and the effective abolition of nuclear weapons, averting the possibility of a nuclear war that would be a catastrophe to all humanity."

[42] See p. 5.
[43] *The Times*, January 14, 1958.
[44] N.Y.T. *Weekly Review*, June 30, 1957.

# 23

## " *The Cut-Off* "

WHEN the Western Governments changed their policy in 1955, and the UN Disarmament Sub-Committee reached deadlock over the question of secret nuclear stocks, M. Moch proposed that the deadlock should be broken by an agreement to stop the new production of nuclear materials for warlike use.[1] This proposed agreement has always been called for short " the cut-off." He urged this again in 1956, saying that unless the existing nuclear Powers would cease their new production, other nations would be compelled to start:

> " I ask Mr. Gromyko not to compel the countries which have not yet manufactured atomic weapons . . . to do so; I ask him to help me to make this impossible by freezing nuclear stocks at their present level, and by controlling future production with a view to devoting it to peaceful purposes only." [2]

Mr. Nutting repeated the appeal, and also argued that unless the " cut-off " was agreed to, other countries would inevitably join the nuclear race. " Are they," he asked,

> " going to sit by and say: ' All right, we resign superiority to the three or four or five nuclear Powers represented in the Sub-Committee; they will exercise a domination over us all, while we, the smaller Powers, the Powers not represented in the Sub-Committee, will have to disarm '? . . . Does Mr. Gromyko seriously think that all the seventy-five or so countries outside of this Sub-Committee are going to tolerate a situation of that kind? I do not believe it for one moment." [3]

[1] September 6, 1955, Cmd. 9651, p. 751.
[2] Sub-Committee, March 28, 1956, p. 42.
[3] *Loc. cit.*, pp. 47–48.

This argument is unanswerable; but it means that there must be full equality in nuclear disarmament between all nations, great or small, those who at present make nuclear weapons and those who do not. The cut-off might hold the situation for a little while; but, in the end, if there is to be disarmament at all, all States must accept the same duties and obligations and make the same sacrifices of national sovereignty. This is of great importance in respect of stocks [4]; it is of no less importance in the Inspection and Control required to guarantee that the cut-off is faithfully observed. Without it any system will, in the end, break down.

## *Equality of States and Nuclear Control*

Unfortunately, however, an anomalous system of *un*equal rights and obligations has begun, or is beginning, to grow up.

The Western Governments abandoned the UN Plan for international ownership and management of nuclear production in 1955, and said that they would be satisfied with the " safeguards " of Inspection and Control. This was categorically repeated in 1956,[5] and again by Mr. Selwyn Lloyd in 1957.[6] In their 1957 " package " plan, they proposed a formal treaty text for the cut-off whereby all future production of fissionable materials would " be used at home or abroad, under international supervision, exclusively for non-weapons purposes." [7] This undertaking was to be accepted by the United States, Britain, France and Russia, and was to enter into force as soon as " the installation of an effective Inspection system to verify the commitment has been completed." The four Powers were to pledge themselves to " co-operate in the prompt installation " of such an Inspection system, and were to appoint " a group of technical

4 See Chap. 4.
5 Sub-Committee, March 22, 1956, p. 8.
6 *The Times*, September 14, 1957.
7 Cmnd. 333, p. 97.

experts " to " design " its guarantees. There was no indication about what kind of system it was to be; but in all earlier discussions, the Western Governments had insisted that the Control must be rigid, and the Inspectors' rights and powers very wide indeed, so it must be presumed that in 1957 this still held good. The system, under the " package " plan, was to be accepted by the existing nuclear States, and nothing whatever was said about its application to other nations.

But, while all this was going on, the four existing nuclear States, with the co-operation of seventy-eight other nations in the Assembly of the UN, had established the International Atomic Energy Agency. The purpose of this Agency is thus defined in its Statute: " To accelerate and enlarge the contribution of atomic energy to peace, health and prosperity throughout the world," [8] by spreading " throughout the world " the " 2,000 known applications of atomic energy, radio-isotopes and radiation," [9] assisting national and international nuclear research, and helping " a special programme of reactor building." The Statute instructs the Agency to

> " allocate its resources in such a manner as to secure efficient utilisation, and the greatest possible general benefit *in all areas of the world, bearing in mind the special needs of the under-developed areas of the world.*" [10]

To enable it to start its work the United States gave the IAEA a research reactor, an isotope laboratory, a complete technical library on the peaceful uses of atomic energy, five tons of U235 and 200 tons of natural uranium. The value of these nuclear materials was £35m.[11]

Thus IAEA will soon be helping to build new reactors in many countries; and every new reactor, in Germany,

---

[8] Statute of the IAEA, Cmnd. 92, 1957, Art. II, p. 2.
[9] Report of the Preparatory Commission of IAEA, p. 4.
[10] *Loc. cit.*, p. 3.
[11] *The Times*, October 25, and November 1, 1957.

Italy, Japan, the Argentine, Egypt or elsewhere, will be producing fissile material which a government planning aggression might seek to divert to weapons of war. For this reason the Statute lays it down that the Agency must " conduct its activities . . . in conformity with policies of the UN furthering the establishment of safeguarded world-wide disarmament," and confers upon it extensive powers to ensure that no project which it supports shall " further any military purpose." [12]

The purpose of this clause is clear; to ensure that all future developments of atomic energy shall be devoted to peaceful uses, and not to preparation for nuclear war. This purpose can only be fulfilled if the obligation to accept IAEA control is world-wide. But the Statute leaves three great gaps in the obligation:

it does *not* apply to nations which already have their own nuclear industries;

it does *not* apply to nations which may develop their own industries without the help of IAEA (there may soon be a number of them);

and it does *not* apply to industries established by nations under bilateral agreements with one of the existing nuclear Powers (the United States alone have over thirty bilateral agreements with other countries).

Article XII says that IAEA is to have the " rights and responsibilities " of Inspection and Control " with respect to any Agency project " (*i.e.*, where IAEA is a direct participant in the scheme) " *or other arrangement where the Agency is requested by the Parties concerned to apply safeguards.*" But if its right to apply safeguards depends on a request, and the request is not made, the world may soon be full of new reactors and other nuclear plants which, like those of the present nuclear Powers, escape control. This obviously cannot work for long; nor can it be applied for long to seventy-eight nations, if four others retain full

[12] Arts. IX, XI, XII *et passim*.

freedom to make nuclear arms; that is to say, if IAEA's
system of control is not generally accepted, it will soon
become a farce and disappear.

How can universality, and equality of treatment for all
nations, best be secured? It might be done if the nuclear
Powers agreed on a new system of Inspection and Control,
inserted it in a general treaty of disarmament, and persuaded
all other nations to accept it and carry it out. It might be
done more simply, if the existing nuclear Powers accepted
the IAEA system laid down in the Statute; set an example
by applying it to themselves; and persuaded all other nations
to do the same. There is little doubt that they could thus
close all the three gaps in the Statute; if they undertook to
make no bilateral agreements to supply nuclear fuel,
machines or equipment, except on condition that the
receiving countries accepted IAEA control, it is most
unlikely that any receiving country would refuse.

But is the IAEA system sufficiently comprehensive and
far-reaching to ensure that there would be no diversion of
fissionable or fusionable materials to warlike use? Has the
Agency been given the necessary powers to enable it to
overcome the special difficulties of nuclear disarmament set
out in Chapter 8? Are there supplementary measures
which the governments could take to strengthen the system
laid down in the Statute?

## The IAEA System of Control

IAEA's powers to ensure that no project which it supports
shall " further any military purpose " may be summarised
as follows :

1. *The Principle of Accountability.* The Report of the
Preparatory Commission of IAEA says that its safeguard system is based on " ensuring accountability for all
source and special fissionable materials involved in Agency
projects." [13]

[13] *Loc. cit.*, para. 81, p. 21.

" Source material " is defined in the Statute as natural uranium, " uranium depleted in the isotope 235; thorium; any of the foregoing in the form of metal, alloy, chemical compound or concentrate."

" Special fissionable material " means " plutonium 239, U233, uranium enriched in the isotopes 235 or 233; any material containing one or more of the foregoing."

2. *Design of Reactors, etc.* IAEA is empowered to

> " *examine the design of specialised equipment and facilities, including nuclear reactors, and to approve it only from the viewpoint of assuring that it will not further any military purpose* . . . and that it will permit effective application of the safeguards provided in this Article."

In other words, no interference with design or other economic development of atomic energy, *except* to ensure that disarmament obligations are observed.

3. *Operating Records.* IAEA can require governments to maintain and produce " operating records, to assist in ensuring accountability for source and special fissionable materials used or produced " in any project or arrangement which needs control.

4. *Progress Reports.* IAEA may " call for and receive progress reports." Governments in their own interest must maintain operating records, and must receive progress reports, since these documents are the foundation of their " accounting." The documents must be made available immediately to the representatives of IAEA, whose major task will be to ascertain, by Inspection, sampling, analysis, etc., that they are correct.

5. *Chemical Processing.* IAEA must

> " approve the means to be used for the chemical processing of irradiated materials, solely to ensure that this chemical processing will not lend itself to diversion of materials for military purposes."

The design and methods of chemical separation plants like that at Calder Hall must have the sanction of IAEA, and IAEA must make certain by Inspection that the approved methods are adhered to.

6. *Dangerous By-Products.* IAEA may " require that special fissionable materials recovered or produced as a by-product " (*e.g.*, the plutonium at Calder Hall) " be used for peaceful purposes, under continuing Agency safeguards." IAEA must, therefore, keep track of all plutonium or other " dangerous " by-products, to ensure that they are only used for peaceful purposes, under the Inspectors' control.

7. *" Excess Fissile Materials."* IAEA may

> *" require deposit with the Agency of any excess of any special fissionable materials, recovered or produced as a by-product, over what is needed for the above-stated uses, in order to prevent stock-piling of these materials."*

This is an extremely important provision, which imposes duties of great significance on IAEA. IAEA must determine what quantity of fissile material a State requires for peaceful activities which have been approved; it must allow that State to retain that quantity, and nothing more; any excess produced by the State's reactors must be handed over to the Agency, until the Agency is satisfied that the State requires it for peaceful use.

8. *The IAEA Inspectorate.* The basic principle of " accountability for all source and special fissionable material " is to be applied by a system of Inspection, to be conducted by international teams of Inspectors on a permanent basis in every plant or " facility " where it is required.

The Inspectors are to be chosen by the Agency in consultation with the governments of the countries to which they are sent, but they will be wholly responsible to IAEA; will receive no instructions from, and owe no loyalty to, any national government; and will be paid out of UN funds. They will be assisted by national " assessors," who may accompany them on their missions, *provided that the Inspectors are not thereby delayed or hampered in their work*. The Inspectors must have " *access at all times to all places and data and to any person who, by reason of his occupation, deals with materials, equipment or facilities* which are required by this Statute to be safeguarded." This is a far-reaching provision. It means that the Inspectors can remain permanently in any State; can take up residence at any uranium factory, power station, research centre, or other undertaking, exercise continuous supervision of any nuclear process and demand complete information about it; and conduct their own sampling and analysis—for what else can be the meaning of their right to have " all data . . . necessary to account for source and special fissionable materials . . . and fissionable products "? Moreover, they can call on *anybody*, however exalted his position, to explain anything that they think unsatisfactory or obscure.

These powers are very wide; on paper nothing has been denied to the IAEA Board of Governors or their Inspectors that they can reasonably require. Although their " safeguard procedures " are to be so " adapted to the specific character of each individual project and the degree of potential risk of material diversion " [14] as to ensure that there will be no unnecessary interference with national undertakings, nevertheless IAEA will be able, as the Preparatory Commission said, to " apply a combination of material accounting and physical security measures " [15] that should give solid guarantees.

9. *Inspection and " Health and Safety."* The Preparatory Commission of IAEA further suggested that " it would be convenient in practice to associate Inspection under the safeguards functions with Inspection under the health and safety functions of the Agency." [16] This would have many advantages; the health and safety functions of

[14] *Loc. cit.*, p. 22.
[15] p. 21.
[16] p. 22.

the Agency are of great and growing importance (as an accident at the British plant at Windscale showed)[17]; the help of the Agency in such matters will be of much assistance to the signatory governments. This combination of functions might thus promote good relations between governments and Inspectors; it would be welcomed by the Inspectors, who would be enabled to render " positive," constructive service to the world at large. It may be hoped, therefore, that this will be accepted as the standard practice.

10. *Inspection and Other IAEA Operations.* The IAEA is itself to conduct various operations : research; perhaps the construction of power reactors; certainly the construction of stores for stocks of fissile material which, under paragraph 7 above, it is holding for member States. These research and other activities will enable it to recruit the expert staff it needs, and to keep the staff fully qualified to do their job.

The Inspectors will ensure that IAEA health and safety standards are observed in its own activities, and they will make certain that

> " the Agency is taking *adequate measures to prevent the source and special fissionable materials in its custody, or used or produced in its own operations, from being used in furtherance of any military purpose.*"

This is, again, a most important clause. It is difficult to see how the stocks of fissionable materials can be protected without some kind of UN International Force.

11. *The Numbers and Cost of the Inspectorate.* It is not possible to forecast the numbers and cost of the Inspectorate that might be required by IAEA in, say, ten years' time, if it were charged with the task of " safe-

---

[17] The view taken by the Preparatory Commission of IAEA that there is wide scope in health and safety matters for co-operation between national governments and the Agency Inspectors is reinforced by the findings of the Fleck Committee on the Windscale Accident. (The Organisation for Control of Health and Safety in the UKAEA, Cmnd. 342, January 1958.)

guarding " the nuclear provisions of a general disarmament treaty. But M. Moch, with the advice of the French AEC, has made an estimate of the numbers that would be needed to control the atomic energy activities and plants of the three existing nuclear Powers.[18] He says that: The number required for *refineries* and *fuel-manufacturing plants* would vary according to the nature of the operations, and the degree of mechanisation; he suggests an average per plant of twenty, including Inspectors and guards. Each *gaseous diffusion plant* for the separation of U235 and U238 will require twenty to thirty Inspectors, of whom one-third will be scientists and technicians, and two-thirds will be guards. Each *high capacity reactor* would need six, or at most eight, Inspectors, two or three of whom would be qualified to undertake the continuous supervision of operating records, and the sampling, analysis and other work of " accounting " and control. The remainder would be guards, who might also assist with health and safety work.

It may be arranged, as Mr. Maddox suggests, that one *chemical plant for separating irradiated fuel* will serve a dozen high-capacity reactors; M. Moch considers that for each large plant, twenty to thirty Inspectors would be needed, of whom again two-thirds would be guards.

M. Moch adds that safeguards against diversion *during transport* from one processing plant to another, or to the final destination of the fissile material, should present no difficulty; the quantities dispatched from one point must correspond precisely with the quantities received at another. Similarly, there should be no difficulty about the simpler task of *controlling uranium and thorium mines*, and the primary *processing mills*.[19] The number of Inspectors required for these purposes would not be great.

Approval by IAEA of the *design of specialised equipment, facilities and nuclear reactors*, to ensure that they embody maximum safeguards against diversion, will, under

---

[18] In a speech in the Sub-Committee, July 5, 1957, p. 11.
[19] See p. 195.

the Statute, be performed not by Inspectors but by a specialised Division of IAEA's headquarters staff. It does not, therefore, enter into M. Moch's calculations; but if it is to be performed efficiently, and with due regard to the technical progress of nuclear engineering, it should be done by men who are in touch with all developments in research.

On this basis, M. Moch estimated that, for all the plants which existed in the world in 1957, about 3,000 Inspectors would be required, of whom 300 would be scientists, 700 technicians, and 2,000 clerks, guards, etc. The cost of their salaries at international rates would be $15m. a year. Their permanent installations, laboratories, and so on, might cost another $15m. These figures, he says, are a *maximum* estimate; in practice, the numbers and the cost might be much less. There must also be added the staff and the budget of the headquarters of IAEA. Both numbers and cost ought greatly to increase, as nuclear activities spread around the world. But the figures given by M. Moch serve to show that the cost of controlling the new production of fissile material to prevent its diversion to warlike use would be a negligible part of the cost of preparation for nuclear war.

## Technical Factors which will Increase the Efficacy of Inspection

There are special difficulties in the control of nuclear disarmament, as was explained above. But there are also six features of the atomic energy industry which will help to make Inspection easier and more efficacious than it might otherwise be.

1. *Size of Nuclear Plants.* U235 can only be separated from natural uranium in diffusion plants, the buildings of which cover several square miles. It is most unlikely, therefore, that a clandestine diffusion plant could be concealed,

especially if Inspectors had the right to conduct aerial reconnaissance. And although plutonium and U233 can be made in very small quantities in reactors that are smaller than a diffusion plant, to give any significant quantities of weapon material, a large-scale installation is required, including a big chemical separation plant. Windscale alone, without Calder Hall, covers 300 acres of land, and the cooling towers are 300 feet high. Such plants cannot be concealed.

2. *Chemical Analysis in Uranium Plants.* The first of the most " dangerous " activities, namely, the manufacture of natural uranium into " rods " " could not be operated properly, if at all," without an extensive and highly developed service of chemical analysis

> " to control the purity of the finished product; all the materials put into the plant . . . are analysed to determine their purity, and so too are the products at various intermediate stages, and the output metal."

This service of analysis, says Mr. Jay,

> " leads to something more than a control of purity, to the control of the plant as a whole "; it " provides the data by which it is possible to keep an account of all the uranium in the plant; the amount of uranium put in is determined by analysing the ore; and the intermediate and waste products, as well as the output, are then analysed to find out how much uranium is in them. Any discrepancy between the input and total of output must be examined to discover what has happened to the material." [20]

The analyst's work must be exceedingly precise;

> " in uranium accounting, he has to measure accurately one element in the presence of others when its concentration may vary from nearly 100 per cent. in the

[20] Jay, *Britain's Atomic Factories*, p. 19.

finished metal to one part in a million of liquid effluent discharged to the river." [21]

All this must be done by the chemists of the national government which owns the plant. But it is also just what IAEA Inspectors would have to do: their task is to keep track of all the uranium or thorium that enters and leaves the plant; to do so, they must have access to all the phases of the operations, and must have their own laboratories and other facilities for independent weighing, assay and analysis. If this were needed only for international control, the national staff might regard it as a wasteful and irritating imposition, and governments might think it an "infringement of sovereignty." But since, in any case, they have to do it themselves, no great objection is likely to be made. Moreover, the Inspection would simply follow the normal patterns ordinarily used in the control of similar operations in other industries. It would not be something unfamiliar, and therefore, resented.

3. *Diversion of Natural Uranium.* There is a further safeguard in uranium plants. To be dangerous, the diversion of natural uranium must be measured in tons [22]; such quantities would be difficult to conceal.

4. *Analysis in Plutonium Extraction Plants.* The same kind of exact analysis as that described above is needed in the chemical separation plants which extract the plutonium or U233 from the irradiated "rods" of a nuclear power station like Calder Hall. "Samples from all parts of the plant are analysed," says Mr. Jay,

> "not only to determine whether the plutonium is as free from impurities as it should be, but also to find out how much there is of both plutonium and uranium at various points. . . . *It is especially important to account accurately for the plutonium throughout the plant,* not

---

[21] *Loc. cit.*, p. 20.
[22] First UNAEC Report, December 1946, p. 50.

only because it is a very valuable material, *but also because it would be dangerous if allowed to accumulate in one place, and reach explosive dimensions."* [23]

This, again, is precisely what the international Inspectors have to do; they must account accurately for the plutonium throughout the plant. The national staff *must* be able, in their own interest, to do this *with no error at all*; if the international staff can do the same sampling and analysis, they should be able to ensure with equal certainty that there is no diversion of fissile material before it leaves the plant.

5. *Necessity for Nuclear Plants to be Hermetically Sealed.* From the moment the " rods " are exposed to the neutrons in a reactor, and the chain-reaction starts, until the radio-active fission products are finally removed in the chemical extraction plant, they emit a dangerous radiation which makes it necessary for the whole plant to be hermetically sealed [24]; any secret exit would have to be so elaborately shielded that the Inspectors could not fail to find it. Of course, the Inspectors would have to be fully familiar with the whole plant and with every process; this would be a necessary preliminary to their work.

6. *The Use of Instruments.* In 1946 to 1948 the UNAEC were afraid that, in spite of the safeguards described above, diversion of plutonium from a chemical separation plant might be effected, and that in the accounting it might be camouflaged as " normal operating losses." [25] This was one reason why they thought that management of these plants by an international agency was essential.[26] Today, however, there is a further check upon diversion. Control in the separation plants could be effected by instruments; indeed, Mr. Maddox says: " Unattended instruments could probably be used instead of inspectors." [27] Moreover, if, as he

[23] Jay, *op. cit.*, p. 42. Plutonium is also very poisonous; one dust particle is fatal, if ingested.
[24] See pp. 104–106.
[25] *Loc. cit.*, p. 54.
[26] *Loc. cit.*, p. 55.
[27] M.G., July 6, 1957.

suggests, one separation plant could treat the irradiated " rods " from a dozen reactors, this would centralise and simplify control and would mean economy of personnel.

These instruments could also be supplemented by a check on the performance of reactors. Mr. Maddox says:

> " A knowledge of the design of a reactor, and a continuous record of its output of heat, which might also be provided by an instrument and not a person, would be sufficient for an accurate estimate of its potential explosive production. Actual production could then be obtained from a knowledge of how rapidly fuel was discharged from the reactor." [28]

It is probable that IAEA would adopt both these methods of control, and let them check and counter-check each other.

Instruments can also control the separation of U235 from natural uranium in a gaseous diffusion plant. Gaseous diffusion [29] is a continuous process, the same operation being repeated many thousands of times, and the plant must be vacuum-tight from the beginning until the end.[30] Thus secret exits for purified U235 would be extremely difficult to contrive, and the Inspectors should be able to ensure that they do not exist. In spite of this, the UNAEC thought management by the International Agency was needed, because of the " difficulty, under the presently available methods of measurement and with present processes, of any strict accounting of U235 between the input and output materials." [31]

But the " available methods of measurement " have been much improved; Mr. Maddox says that diffusion plants would not require 300 inspectors, as the Lilienthal Report suggested, nor would there be the danger of error which the

[28] *Ibid.*
[29] See p. 100.
[30] Jay, *op. cit.*, pp. 52 *et passim*.
[31] *Loc. cit.*, p. 52.

UNAEC foresaw; the collection of records " need not entail the physical presence of inter-government inspectors; instruments suitably protected from interference could be arranged to collect the required information." [32] If the instruments would give an accurate result, the difficulty of accounting between input and output would no longer exist.

These various technical factors will no doubt help to increase the efficacy of the IAEA system of control over the cut-off by means of Inspection; and it may be hoped that further scientific advance, and improved instruments, will in future help it still more.

## The Attitude of the Western Governments

This outline sketch of the IAEA system shows how the authors of the Statute intended it to work. If sensibly administered, it would be a substantial safeguard against the diversion of fissile material from new production to warlike use; it would not be unduly vexatious to any government that wished loyally to carry out its obligations; it would in no way hamper the peaceful use of atomic energy, or the general economic development of any State; and it would be negligibly cheap.

This system was drawn up, on the initiative of the United States, with the co-operation of Britain, France and Russia, in order that it might be accepted, as the means to their total nuclear disarmament, by the non-nuclear Powers. It is believed to be sufficiently efficacious to prevent the non-nuclear Powers from ever entering the field of atomic armament.

Yet the Western Governments, proposing the cut-off for themselves and Russia in 1957, and saying that a system of control must be " designed," never even considered the application of the IAEA Statute for this purpose; they never thought of the required Control in terms of IAEA at all;

[32] M.G., July 6, 1957.

they suggested a " group of technical experts " to " design " something entirely different and new.

This would be understandable, if it were thought that the IAEA system was adequate to prevent dangerous developments in countries that have no nuclear industries today, but *inadequate* for countries that already have great nuclear industries and great stocks of nuclear weapons. It would be understandable if the " group of technical experts " were likely to devise something much stronger or more radical, something, for example, " akin to managerial control," [33] and if the Western Governments were ready to accept it. But for three years the Western Governments have been saying that a system of Inspection will be sufficient; they have given no hint that they will themselves accept anything more. If it is to be a system of Inspection, then the " rights and responsibilities " of IAEA are, on paper, all that are required. It only remains for the Western Governments to close the three gaps in the Statute (see p. 267); and, as said above, that could best be done by an undertaking in the disarmament treaty that every signatory State, including the existing nuclear Powers, would accept IAEA control for its present or future nuclear activities and plants, and would supply no nuclear material or technical assistance to any other nation, except for peaceful purposes, and under IAEA control.

The IAEA system is not perfect; it does not give 100 per cent. security against the diversion of nuclear materials to warlike use. With a system founded on Inspection there *is* a risk of diversion, as the UNAEC maintained. How grave the risk is will be considered in the next chapter. But there are two other points which must be considered first. Would Russia accept it for herself? And if the Western Governments have doubts about its adequacy, how could they give it added strength, in its application both to themselves and to the non-nuclear Powers?

[33] See pp. 207–208.

## The Attitude of Russia

In the Sub-Committee in 1954, Mr. Selwyn Lloyd gave the following description of Russia's proposals for the control of nuclear disarmament:

> " I think the Soviet Union view was that . . . the system of control should be based upon inspection, accounting for raw materials, the drafting and promulgation of regulations for the technological control of atomic energy production plants and, fourthly, recommendations to governments. . . . It is suggested that the control commission should have access to any facilities for mining, production and stock-piling of atomic raw materials and atomic materials, as well as to facilities for the exploitation of atomic energy. They should have the right of acquaintance with the production and the operations of atomic energy facilities, to the extent necessary for the control of the use of atomic materials and atomic energy. They should have the right to carry out weighing, measurements, various analyses of atomic raw materials, atomic materials and unfinished products. They should have the right to request from the government various data, to request explanations and then make recommendations and suggestions to the government." [34]

Mr. Selwyn Lloyd said: " Some of that seems very good." But he saw two main defects in their proposal: their plan for dealing with violations was inadequate; and they were proposing " *periodic* " instead of *continuous* inspection. The question of violations will be dealt with in the next two chapters; on " periodic " inspection, the Russians changed their attitude in 1955, and accepted " control, including inspection on a continuing basis," and made the other concessions described above.[35] Perhaps they would

[34] May 25, 1954, Cmd. 9205, pp. 122–123.
[35] See p. 20.

not accept the full IAEA system now; but on their past declarations, the chances look good.

## How Could the IAEA System of Control be Strengthened?

The Western Governments could themselves do much to strengthen the IAEA system of control. Here are six examples:

First, they could co-operate to build up the authority and prestige of IAEA itself; encourage it to construct its own uranium factories for making " rods," its own reactors, and its own chemical separation plants; and could offer to have these factories and plants installed on their own soil. They could help it to build up its research centres, and welcome its experts in their own. They could ensure that it has an ample budget; every useful increase in its activity and every development of its experience will increase its influence, and thus strengthen the effectiveness of its Control.

Secondly, its Control would be strengthened, and the danger of diversion much reduced, if IAEA were given the management of chemical separation plants for the treatment of irradiated " rods," and if the signatories of the disarmament treaty all agreed to send their " rods " for treatment to these IAEA plants. The six nations in Euratom are establishing a joint undertaking, called Eurochemic, for the chemical processing of irradiated " rods "; the CEA in Britain is going to send the " rods " from all its power stations to UKAEA separation plants to be processed; if Britain and Eurochemic proposed that IAEA should staff and manage these plants, or at least provide some members of the managerial Boards, they might inaugurate a practice that would be a major guarantee against diversion. This practice would not hamper the development of atomic energy in any country, nor lead to friction with national governments; and it would pay its way.

Thirdly, IAEA has a duty, under its Statute, to encourage the building of reactors; but this must be done, say the Preparatory Commission, " taking into account the need for balanced development of the various regions." [36] This is an echo of the " strategic distribution " of atomic facilities throughout the world, which UNAEC regarded as important for the long-term preservation of peace. [37] The International Bank and the governments of the major creditor nations could much assist this " balanced development," if they planned their loans for nuclear projects jointly with IAEA.

Fourthly, the IAEA system will be strengthened if the disarmament treaty gives UN Inspectors the right of access without notice to all engineering works of every kind. This will make it difficult for an intending aggressor to manufacture the triggering devices, bomb cases, special shell cases, or other products required for nuclear weapons.

Fifthly, IAEA experience will no doubt determine what are the optimum practices and methods of Inspection for making its control effective. Research will produce perfected instruments. The Western Governments could urge the general adoption by all nations of these practices and instruments.

Finally, and most important of all, the Western Governments, quite irrespective of anything that Russia might do, could invite IAEA to appoint consultative members of the managing Boards of their own atomic plants and research installations. These consultative members would perform ordinary managerial functions, would be present at all Board meetings, and would be aware of everything that went on; but they would have no vote on the policy decisions to be made. This would be by far the best system of Inspection. As has been shown above, the functions of an efficient Inspectorate are really parallel to those of an

[36] *Loc. cit.*, p. 13.
[37] See pp. 189 and 193.

efficient management; both have an interest in good accounting procedures, taking proper inventories, checking and improving analytical and assaying methods, detecting the causes of unaccountable losses, etc. The IAEA members, with their wide international experience, might be able to make valuable contributions to good management and to research. Nothing could so effectively eliminate the national rivalries in the development of atomic energy of which the UNAEC were so much afraid, or help to make it " a common enterprise in all its phases." [38] If the Western Governments proposed this plan, and themselves voluntarily carried it out, many other non-nuclear Members of IAEA would almost certainly follow their example—it might, indeed, be made a condition of their technical help; in the end Russia and the other Communist governments might find it difficult not to follow suit. By the mere proposal, the Western Governments could give IAEA a greater authority and prestige than it could gain in any other way. If they are serious in desiring a cut-off, there can be no valid objection to the plan; they can *ex hypothesi*, have nothing they desire to hide about their future production of nuclear materials.

In any case, the Western Governments cannot leave things where they are today. Either the " safeguards " of IAEA Inspection will become the instrument of control for nuclear disarmament for the world at large; or it may soon become a farce. It cannot be made obligatory for nations which need the help of IAEA, and left optional for other nations who can create their own atomic industries, or who get help under bilateral agreements from the nuclear Powers. It cannot be used to keep the non-nuclear Powers disarmed, while the nuclear Powers continue to pile up or to retain great stocks of A- and H-weapons, large and " small." The purpose of IAEA, and the purpose of the cut-off which the Western Governments propose, is to de-militarise atomic

[38] See p. 198.

energy; either that purpose must be fully and speedily achieved, or IAEA, and the hopes built upon it, will all fail.[39]

---

[39] The future of IAEA has been complicated, if not compromised, by the fact that some of the leading Western Governments have taken part in the establishment of the "European Nuclear Energy Agency," which has a Statute largely modelled on that of IAEA. The European Agency is to set up a Control Bureau and its own Inspectorate for ensuring that the projects undertaken with the Agency's help shall, if the governments concerned so request, be subject to control to ensure that they do not "further any military purpose." It appears from Art. 11 of the "Convention on the Establishment of a Security Control," that inspection is only to be "periodic" and that "in each case the government concerned must be notified in advance that the inspection is to be carried out." These are the principles which the UNAEC and the Western Governments resisted for eight years when they were proposed by Russia. See p. 197, above. The Agency came into legal existence on February 1, 1958. The text of the Convention on the Establishment of a Security Control in the field of Nuclear Energy, and a European Nuclear Energy Agency, can be found in Cmnd. 357 (Misc. No. 12, 1958).

## 24

# The Dangers of "Diversion" and Secret Stocks

WHEN the Western Governments abandoned the original UN plan for international ownership and management, and accepted Inspection instead for the control of new production of fissile material, they recognised that this Inspection might not be 100 per cent. effective, and that they must accept the risk of the diversion of a small part of the material to warlike use. This was a new danger, added to the other danger of which so much has been said: the danger that, if an agreement were made to abolish all existing stocks of nuclear weapons, some disloyal government might violate its undertakings, and illicitly retain a secret stock. The purpose of this chapter is to assess and, so far as may be, to quantify these dangers and to consider the risks which they involve.

## The Danger of "Diversion" of New Production

In 1956 the British delegate to the UN Disarmament Sub-Committee—still Mr. Nutting—said that his Government would definitely accept a system of Inspection; but he added: " *I do not claim to know of a system of control which would be 100 per cent. effective in this field* " (new production), " nor can we be sure that other States would be willing to accept the methods of control which we believe would be necessary." [1]

Mr. Stassen was more explicit in 1957:

" It is possible, according to the very best scientific advice we have obtained, to establish an inspection

[1] Sub-Committee, March 22, 1956, p. 8.

286

system under which each nation could be sure . . . that future production of fissionable materials would go entirely, or *almost* entirely, to peaceful, constructive uses." [2]

He amplified " almost " a little later:

" I do not mean to suggest . . . that it is possible to have absolute 100 per cent. efficiency " (of control); " but we believe it is possible to come very close to 100 per cent.—so close that the margin of error would not, in itself, be a basis for rejecting the agreement, or for breaking it." [3]

M. Moch joined with his Western colleagues in saying that a system of inspection of new production could be made to work. But he was bolder than they were; he not only repeated Mr. Nutting's and Mr. Stassen's warnings that Inspection would not by itself be 100 per cent. effective; he went further, and said that, under the detailed system he proposed,[4] the margin of possible diversion by a disloyal government might be 3 per cent.[5]

This is certainly a larger margin than the UNAEC would have been willing to accept. The figures of the actual output of nuclear materials are, of course, not published; but there is other United States information on which a rough estimate may be made. In September 1957 the USAEC reported that in the first six months of the year the production of uranium ore in the United States was 1,706,000 dry tons. In the same period, United States mills " produced 4,141 tons of uranium concentrates," while there were in stock 1,946,000 tons of ore, containing 4,251 tons of uranium concentrates.[6] The phrase " uranium concentrates " is ambiguous; it probably means uranium oxide. If so, the pure uranium, after it had been refined, would be

---

[2] Sub-Committee, March 20, 1957, p. 7.
[3] Sub-Committee, July 3, 1957, p. 12.
[4] See pp. 273–274.
[5] Sub-Committee, July 5, 1957, pp. 9–10.
[6] Official figures given by the USAEC reported in N.Y.H.T. *Economic Review*, September 1957.

about 90 per cent. of the total weight of uranium oxide, *i.e.*, approximately 3,700 tons. This is an enormous figure. One part in 140 (0·7 per cent.) of the 3,700 tons of natural uranium is U235. If all the natural uranium were processed in diffusion plants, and the U235 separated off, it would amount to twenty-six tons.[7]  3 per cent. of twenty-six tons— the margin of possible " diversion " in M. Moch's Inspection scheme—would be about 780 kilograms; enough, at 8 kg. per bomb,[8] for ninety-eight Hiroshima bombs. This would, indeed, be a " very troublesome margin of uncertainty," the more so since Russia's new production of fissile material may be approaching that of the United States, while production in Britain, France and other countries is growing.

But the destructive power of a given amount of fissile material can be much increased, if it is used in H-bombs[9]; and the fusionable material required for H-bombs is both easier to make and cheaper than fissile material, and the installations for its manufacture are more difficult to detect. There is, therefore, with the present rapidly increasing output of fissile material, a heavy risk in nuclear disarmament, if it is guaranteed only by an Inspection system, and if the illicit diversion turned out to be as much as 3 per cent.

## The Danger of Illicit Stocks

Dr. Oppenheimer and others explained from 1946 onwards that, if nuclear disarmament was delayed, there would be another difficulty when it was at length agreed to: the difficulty about secret stocks. It is hard enough to prevent diversion from current production by the method of accounting; it is impossible to discover what total past production may have been, if the producer wants to hide it.

In theory, if the design of a given reactor is known, and the date on which it was started up, and its charge of

[7] See pp. 100–101.
[8] See p. 127.
[9] See pp. 130 *et seq.*

natural uranium or thorium and its consumption of electric power, then its total output of plutonium or U233 throughout its lifetime could be calculated. The calculation could be checked by reference to the plant's records, and by the measurement of the radio-activity of some of its fixed components. But unfortunately, there are various difficulties about relying on this method of estimating what a government's past production of fissile material may have been, and thereby determining its stocks of nuclear bombs.

Experiments at Harwell, Aldermaston and Risley are thus reported by Mr. Maddox:

> " It appears that the variations of the rate of plutonium production from a given reactor which can arise from variations in the length of time for which fuel is left in it are enough to make this simple approach impracticable. The consequent uncertainties in the past output of plutonium " (or U233) " from any reactor would be greater than 10 per cent." [10]

A disloyal government could thus declare that its stocks of plutonium or U233 were 10 per cent. less than in fact they were, and could be sure, on technical grounds, that its word would not be challenged.

But it might much increase this margin of error by deliberate faking of the reactor's records, or by falsely declaring that, at given times since it began its operations, it had been shut down for a shorter or a longer period. The disarmament control authorities might find it very difficult to show that the records were wrong, or that the statements about shut-downs were untrue. The total error in the control authorities' calculations might thus become 20 to 30 per cent.; as M. Moch expressed it to the Assembly, a government planning an aggression might have produced 1,300 nuclear bombs, might declare 1,000, and might keep back 300 in a secret stock.[11] This, again, would be a very " troublesome margin of uncertainty " indeed.

[10] Mr. John Maddox, M.G., July 6, 1957.
[11] 1st Committee, December 6, 1955, p. 241.

The possible error with regard to the production of U235 in a diffusion plant would be little less. If the requisite instruments [12] had been installed from the beginning in all the diffusion plants owned by the nuclear Powers, the total output would be accurately and definitely known. Unfortunately, those instruments were *not* installed at the beginning, and the error in calculation, and due to faked records, might thus be more than 20 per cent.

It must be further remembered that this margin of error might be enormous in absolute amount. Mr. Thomas Murray says that the explosion of 3,500 megatons of fissionable material would wipe out the American and Russian nations and do grave damage to the rest; Dr. Lapp said that the total United States stock of fission and fusion weapons was the equivalent of 10,000 megatons.[13] 20 to 30 per cent. of such stocks as these would constitute an armament that would be instantly overwhelming, if it were used against nations that had, in good faith, abolished all their nuclear arms.

It was of this danger that Dr. Oppenheimer, M. Moch and others had often spoken from 1946 onwards. It was emphasised in sombre terms in the Russian plan of May 10, 1955. The paper said:

" The greatest apprehensions exist among peace-loving peoples in connection with the existence of atomic and hydrogen weapons, *in regard to which the institution of international control is particularly difficult.*

" *This danger is inherent in the very nature of atomic production.* It is well known that the production of atomic energy for peaceful purposes can be used for the accumulation of stocks of explosive atomic materials, and, moreover, in ever greater quantities. This means that States having establishments for the

12 See pp. 277–279.
13 See p. 173.

production of atomic energy can accumulate, in violation of the relevant agreements, large quantities of
explosive materials for the production of atomic
weapons. . . .

" Thus there are possibilities beyond the reach of
international control for evading this control and for
organising the clandestine manufacture of atomic and
hydrogen weapons, even if there is a formal agreement
on international control. In such a situation, the
security of the States signatories to the international
convention cannot be guaranteed, since the possibility
would be open to a potential aggressor to accumulate
stocks of atomic and hydrogen weapons for a surprise
attack on peace-loving States." [14]

This stated the major difficulty of total nuclear disarmament in extreme, not to say extravagant, terms. If it was
all to be taken at face value, it might well be asked why
Russia, in the same paper, proposed total nuclear disarmament, accepted the terms (the " 75 per cent. arrangement "
and the rest) put forward by the West, and went much
further than ever before in agreeing to international control
by continuous and unrestricted Inspection. The reason
why the passage appeared in the paper of May 10 has been
explained above [15]; it was a justification for the major
breaches in the Iron Curtain to which, by these Inspection
proposals, and by her spontaneous proposals for Ground
Control Posts, Russia had agreed. The Kremlin may well
have felt that, to explain this major change of policy, both
to the Russian people and to the outside world, some new
and very cogent reason was required. They adduced the
danger of a secret nuclear stock, and painted it in the
grimmest colours they could find. They did so, not with
the purpose of suggesting that nuclear stocks should be
retained, but of proposing measures which would inspire

[14] Cmd. 9650, pp. 613–614.
[15] See p. 23.

confidence, in their own people and in the Western Governments, that the danger of nuclear aggression would not arise. Both in 1955, and ever since, they have vigorously protested that what they said in their paper of May 10 was *not*, and *could* not be, a ground for abandoning total nuclear disarmament, including the abolition of stocks.[16]

Yet the Western Governments, who up till May 10 had urged total nuclear disarmament, and whose delegates had often spoken of this difficulty of secret stocks, chose to regard this passage in the Russian paper as a conclusive reason for throwing over everything that they had previously proposed.[17]  And they stated their new position in language quite as extravagant as that which the Russians had used. Mr. Nutting said in April 1956: " Science simply will not permit us to go forward with an arrangement for eliminating nuclear weapons.  It just is not possible; we cannot detect them." [18]  By 1957 the argument had been developed and was stated thus by Mr. Stassen:

> " Can all nuclear weapons be removed from the face of the earth? . . .  This idea has much attraction.  But . . . nuclear weapons are materials, plus knowledge, plus fabrication.  The materials are and will be available on every continent.  The knowledge exists in the minds of men; it cannot be erased.  It is spreading and will continue to spread.  The fabrication, given the knowledge and the materials, is relatively simple." [19]

This defeatist exordium made nonsense of the proposal for the cut-off of new production, which Mr. Stassen had been urging, and went on urging, with great force.  It really meant that, even if all existing stocks had been effectively abolished, they could easily be built up again; which also certainly went much too far.  But the purpose of the exordium was to lead into Mr. Stassen's main argument

[16] The Kremlin dealt with this point in vigorous terms in their Memorandum to the UN Assembly of September 20, 1957.
[17] See Chap. 2.
[18] Sub-Committee, April 23, 1956, p. 41.
[19] Sub-Committee, March 20, 1957, pp. 5–6.

that existing stocks could *not* be effectively abolished. " We also find," he said,

> " that when such weapons are fabricated, or when the material is available, either the weapons or the material can be very easily shielded from detection and discovery. One hundred of the most powerful multi-megaton H-bombs can be placed in storage and shielded by relatively simple methods, and then the most sensitive detection apparatus thus far invented by science would give no indication of the presence of this storehouse, even if it were brought within 100 yards of its location."

And the *bulk* of the stock will be relatively small; it will be less than a millionth part of a reserve supply of conventional ammunition of equal power.

Thus, argued Mr. Stassen, a disloyal government could either keep a part of its existing stocks, instead of converting them all, or could " divert, without the knowledge of the Inspectors, a quantity of fissionable material from which twenty, forty or even fifty multi-megaton bombs could be fabricated. All of this could be carried out without discovery by Inspectors, and without the knowledge of other nations, until it was completely accomplished."

He asked:

> " Is it not clear . . . that no nation could agree that all nuclear weapons should be removed from the face of the earth, if it meant that *in the ten years ahead, and in the decades thereafter,* some nation might suddenly have and exercise a tremendous overpowering military force against all other nations solely by reason of having within its hands a clandestinely developed and secretively maintained storehouse of multi-megaton bombs?"

Thus he reached his substantive conclusion:

> " On the basis of present scientific knowledge, and unless and until there is some new scientific break-

through which makes controls more effective than anyone can now prescribe, the United States has reluctantly
concluded that it would not be sound, that it would not
be consistent with the security of the United States or
of other nations, to agree to the complete elimination
of all nuclear weapons, and that such an agreement
would be a bad agreement—a tragic mistake." [20]

The words in italics should be noted: " In the ten years
ahead, and in the decades thereafter." In their context,
they meant that the United States Government proposed
to keep some part of their existing nuclear stocks for very
many years to come.

## *Nuclear Armaments and Nuclear Disarmament: The Balance of Risk*

Under a system of nuclear disarmament controlled only by
Inspection there is thus a double risk: diversion of fissile
material from new production, which may be as much as
3 per cent. of current output; and disloyal retention of a
secret stock, which may be from 20 to 30 per cent. of past
production. These are grave dangers, and no attempt
should be made to underestimate them.

But against them must be set the dangers of failing to
disarm, *i.e.*, of failing to get the cut-off and to abolish
stocks. The risks of failing over the cut-off and over stocks
must be taken in turn.

### THE RISK OF FAILURE OVER THE CUT-OFF

Why did the Western Governments accept the risk of diversion from new production, a risk which they all recognised
as serious, and which M. Moch quantified at 3 per cent.?
For two reasons. First, they felt that *something* must be
done without delay. They had spent twelve years in
arguing for a better plan, and all the while the stocks of

[20] *Ibid.*

nuclear weapons had grown and grown. Better—infinitely better—a 97 per cent. result than no result at all. " I know of nothing that has occurred in our time," said President Eisenhower in July 1957,

> " where greater optimism must be maintained . . . than in this whole business of beginning disarmament, of relieving tension in the world. The alternative is so terrible that you can merely say this: *All the risks you take in trying to advance are as nothing compared to doing nothing, to sitting on your hands.*" [21]

Second, they hoped that a first disarmament treaty could be made which would secure the cut-off, but which would allow them to retain for many years a large part of their existing stocks.[22] They would thus, so they believed, have a powerful nuclear safeguard against the 3 per cent. diversion risk.

But in proposing to retain their stocks they accepted different, but very serious, risks.

## THE RISK INVOLVED IN FAILING TO ABOLISH STOCKS

The first risk is that, if they *do* retain their stocks, no disarmament treaty will be made. It was on this question of nuclear stocks that Russia broke off negotiations, and left the Sub-Committee and the Disarmament Commission, in 1957. It will remain the crux of all disarmament discussions until it has been solved. It seems certain that Russia will not accept the cut-off without the abolition of stocks, so long as the United States, in quality and quantity of nuclear weapons, is as far ahead as President Eisenhower asserts they are.[23] It would mean accepting a permanent inferiority in the decisive instruments of modern war—and that is something the Kremlin will never do. Nor will Russia accept the United States Government's " equitable

[21] Press Conference, July 17, 1957.
[22] See pp. 26–28.
[23] See p. 27.

transfers " of fissile material from weapon stocks to peaceful uses, so long as they propose that Russia should transfer 47 kg. for every 53 transferred by the United States; for, if the United States has at present the great advantage which the President claims, every transfer on these terms would merely mean a further weakening of Russia's relative strength.[24] It seems likely, therefore, if the Western position on nuclear stocks is adhered to, that no disarmament treaty will be made, because Russia will not sign.

And even if Russia signed, it would still not be certain that the seventy-eight non-nuclear nations would agree. Indeed, it is most unlikely that they will accept indefinitely the position of complete military inferiority which the retention of stocks by the three nuclear Powers would mean. Mr. Selwyn Lloyd said in the Sub-Committee in March 1957 that it was vitally important to prevent other countries from entering the nuclear arms race[25]; but in July he said that for the United Kingdom " the advent of nuclear weapons has provided greater security." [26] The United States Government say that they must keep a " substantial part " of their enormous stocks " for decades ahead "; Mr. Dulles says almost every day that nuclear weapons are a legitimate and a necessary means of self-defence. How long will it be before France, Germany, China, Japan, perhaps India under a new government, begin to say the same? Italy is sure to follow France, and Yugoslavia, Turkey and others would follow Italy. In short, if Mr. Nutting's argument about the seventy-eight non-nuclear powers[27] is valid for the cut-off, as it is, then it is valid for stocks as well.

---

[24] During the 1957 session of the Sub-Committee, Mr. Stassen made several other proposals, including one for an initial transfer of 12 per cent. of existing stocks; as this would have meant revealing the total existing stock, it was dropped. So was the 53:47 proposal, and in the end nothing appeared in the Western " package " plan, except the vague suggestion that there should be a future negotiation about it. (See p. 26.)

[25] March 18, 1957, p. 3.

[26] July 2, 1957, p. 2.

[27] See p. 264.

But if no disarmament treaty is made, the arms race will go on, stocks of nuclear weapons will increase, these other nations will acquire them, and the danger that they will actually be used in war as the result of fear, of malevolent design or simple accident, will constantly grow greater. It is unfortunately true, as Marshal Zhukov said, that " the mere existence of atomic weapons implies the possibility of their use." [28] This means, as said above, that the abolition of stocks remains the crucial issue in all disarmament debates.

But how can the risks which it involves be dealt with? How can the nations avert the danger that clandestine stocks will be retained from past production, and further stocks built up by the diversion of 3 per cent. of new production? So far, the Western Governments have only discussed the problem in the context of Inspection, and of the sanctions which might be imposed if a violation of a nuclear disarmament agreement should occur. As has been shown, Inspection may be a most important safeguard, especially if the Western Governments accept it for themselves whole-heartedly and without reserve, and apply it in the spirit and by the methods described above. Sanctions may also have a real restraining power, if they are well conceived, and if the leading governments make it plain that they will be resolutely and loyally applied. But there are also other measures, of wider scope, and more profound importance, which ought to form a part of a disarmament treaty, and which would be additional and powerful safeguards against the potential dangers of total nuclear disarmament. The next chapter will set out these measures, and will discuss the degree of safety which they might bring.

[28] Quoted by M. Malik, Sub-Committee 1955, Cmd. 9651, p. 826.

# 25

## *Additional Safeguards*

THE last chapter showed that Inspection by itself would not provide absolute security either against " diversion " by a disloyal government of fissile material from new production to warlike use, nor against the danger that a government which possesses nuclear weapons might try, in violation of the disarmament treaty, to retain an illicit stock.

When this admission has been made, it must be added that an agreement for total nuclear disarmament, and the establishment of a world-wide system of Inspection by international teams of UN officers, could not fail to make a profound impact on the public thinking of all nations, on both sides of the Iron Curtain. It would produce a psychological change which, in turn, might increase the efficacy of the Inspection, and its restraining power. It would convince the peoples that their governments were resolved to end the arms race, and to free them from the nuclear menace; and the hopes and enthusiasms which this would undoubtedly arouse would be a factor of great practical importance. For any government which thereafter broke its pledges by threatening the use of an illicit stock of nuclear weapons, would have to reckon with the deep hostility of every other nation in the world.

But, while this is true, the danger of possible evasion of the disarmament treaty would nevertheless remain, and since the consequences of nuclear aggression would be so catastrophic, Inspection must be supplemented by every other reasonable safeguard that can be devised. These other safeguards will be of various kinds. Some of them will certainly be part of any disarmament treaty that comes into force; for example, the general Inspection of all engineering works and similar plants, and of all military

298

depots and installations,[1] and the establishment of Ground
Control Posts and air photography, to prevent surprise
attack.[2] Other safeguards, like the international co-operation of scientists, and the establishment of sanctions, would
be natural developments of the IAEA system of Inspection
and Control; yet others would consist in measures of
conventional disarmament that are hardly less important
than nuclear disarmament itself, and in a " pooling of
sovereignty " that is historically overdue. In the pages that
follow, these various safeguards will be considered in turn.

## *Sanctions*

When Mr. Baruch first put forward the United States plan
in the UNAEC he spoke much about the " condign
punishment " of any State that might violate the agreement to abolish nuclear arms.[3] But Western views have
changed. The scheme proposed in the IAEA Statute [4] is
much more modest than Mr. Baruch's; it does not necessarily follow that it will be less effective.

The Statute provides that the Inspectors shall verify the
" accounting " described in Chapter 23, and shall be responsible for " determining whether there is compliance with
the undertaking " to do nothing that will " further any
military purpose." They are to " report any non-compliance to the Director General, who shall thereupon transmit
the report to the Board of Governors." The Board is to call
on the offender " to remedy forthwith any non-compliance
which it finds to have occurred "; it must report the non-
compliance to all the Members of IAEA, and to the Security
Council and the Assembly. If the offending State does not
" take fully corrective action within a reasonable time," the
Board may itself:

---

[1] The importance of this was explained on p. 283.
[2] See Chap. 43.
[3] See pp. 190–191.
[4] See p. 266.

(i) curtail or suspend the assistance being given by IAEA or by another member State;

(ii) call for the return of materials and equipment made available to the offending member;

(iii) suspend the offending member " from the exercise of the privileges and rights of membership."

This action can be taken by the Board itself; there is no question of a veto in the Security Council. In some circumstances the suspension of assistance might be a heavy material sanction. The Statute does not lay down what action the Security Council or the Assembly might take to restrain a recalcitrant member which persisted in its offence. The action would depend on many things: the gravity of the offence, the imminence of nuclear aggression, the level of general disarmament which had been carried out, and the collective security system which the disarmament treaty had set up.[5] What the IAEA Statute does is to ensure that immediate measures would be taken against any government that broke its pledges, and that world opinion would be focused on the crime. This is all that *could* be done in the Statute; but if the IAEA system comes to life at all, these " sanctions " may be an important supplementary safeguard against the danger of diversion.[6]

It has been suggested that the effectiveness of IAEA action would be increased if the principle of the Nuremberg trials were applied to acts which violated a nuclear disarmament agreement; that is to say, that the individuals who committed the treaty-breaking acts should be personally liable to prosecution and punishment, and could not shelter behind the orders which they had received from their government. This suggestion deserves consideration, but the argument is not all on one side.

[5] See Chap. 44.

[6] In the Convention on Security Control drawn up by the European Nuclear Energy Agency, there is a regrettable provision (Art. 9) that Inspectors and other Control Personnel shall never, even after they have left the Agency, divulge any information which has come to their knowledge in the performance of their duties. This, presumably, is to protect " trade secrets "; it is the negation of the sharing of knowledge and information which the UNAEC said was essential to the de-militarisation of atomic energy.

# *A Standing IAEA Commission to Study Inspection and Control*

In 1957 Professor Otto Hahn [7] proposed that there should be " talks between serious scientists from the Western nations and from Russia as well." But *not* for the purpose of making declarations; " rather," he said, " they should consider what might be done, and they should think what advice to give their Governments." He had led his German colleagues in demanding total nuclear disarmament, and he wanted the scientists to consider how it could be made to work.

Mr. Nutting had made a similar proposal in the UN Sub-Committee in 1955. He suggested that " a group of scientists " should be invited by the UN to study the problem of the control of nuclear disarmament in general, and the problem of detecting secret stocks in particular.[8] It was a good suggestion, but unfortunately it was never made again; and when the Foreign Minister of the Lebanon revived it in the Assembly it was swept aside.[9] But if the UN now invited IAEA to set up a Commission to perform this task, it might be a valuable supplementary guarantee for the observance of a nuclear disarmament agreement. To produce the maximum effect the Commission should be permanent; a majority of its members should be drawn from nations which have no nuclear arms; its members should receive expenses and remuneration from UN funds; they should be responsible, *not* to the governments of their respective countries, but to the IAEA, and to the UN Assembly as a whole. They should choose their own staff, and be given an adequate budget; while their primary task should be research into the methods of detection, they should be free to travel, and should have the privileges, and the rights of access to all nuclear " facilities " which the IAEA Inspectorate will have. The existence of such a

[7] See p. 5.
[8] Cmd. 9652, p. 992.
[9] Committee 1, December 8, 1955, p. 269.

standing Commission with power to make inquiries on the spot, and to present independent reports to IAEA and the Assembly, might be a valuable adjunct to the Inspectorate, and might help to bring home to an intending violator of the disarmament treaty the risk of being found out.

## *Internationalisation of Research and Free Intercourse between Scientists*

The more both fundamental and applied nuclear research are internationalised under IAEA, and the closer the co-operation between national research establishments and IAEA's research staff, the better the chance that a violation would be detected at an early stage. The words of the UNAEC may be recalled:

" Co-operative development " (of atomic energy) " and complete dissemination of information alone promise to remove fears and suspicion that nations are conducting secret activities." [10]

Clauses should, therefore, be inserted in the disarmament treaty, providing (i) that there shall be free intercourse between scientists of different countries, by the grant of visas, right of access to university and national laboratories, right to hold unofficial international scientific conferences, etc.; (ii) that individual citizens, including scientists, should have a personal obligation to reveal to IAEA or UN Inspectors any violation of the treaty of which they knew.

This last proposal may sound academic, but its potential importance is shown by the action of the fifty USAEC scientists recounted in Chapter 22 above.[11] This incident could not have happened in the Russia of today, but it would be wrong to disregard the hope that even there new standards may ultimately prevail. The making of a disarmament treaty, and the introduction of an Inspection system, will be a major breach in the Iron Curtain; future

[10] Third Report, May 17, 1948, p. 4.
[11] See p. 262.

Geneva Conferences on the peaceful uses of atomic energy will promote co-operation; scientists in every country are conscious that their work is hampered by restrictions on the exchange of information on their personal travel, and on their right to correspond and to discuss. If the disarmament treaty laid a personal duty on them to report a violation of its undertakings, it would create a strong sense of obligation in their minds. No government could well refuse to sign such clauses, and they might lead to practical results.

## Reward for Information

In 1955 the United States Congress passed a law offering " a reward of up to $500,000 to anyone who uncovers an effort to smuggle atomic bombs or nuclear material into the United States." The reward was recommended by the Joint Congressional Atomic Energy Commission, and the law was backed by the Department of Justice, the USAEC, and the Central Intelligence Agency. It was believed that the offer of large rewards would help to detect saboteurs who tried to " smuggle nuclear devices or special nuclear materials " into the United States in order to " destroy vital targets " before an enemy attack.[12]

If this was considered by these high authorities to be of practical value for the defence of the United States, the same system might be of value to the UN in securing the observance of nuclear disarmament. The disarmament treaty might authorise the offer of large rewards to anyone who gave evidence to IAEA or UN Inspectors which led to the detection of a " diversion " of fissile material or of a secret weapon stock. This idea may be repugnant to some people, as inconsistent with the dignity of the UN. But it might be a useful safeguard, particularly in under-developed countries, where the informant's escape would be easy, and the attraction of a large sum of money very great; and it

12 N.Y.T., July 7, 1955.

might also be useful in totalitarian States.  The rulers of
most totalitarian States know that many of their subjects
want to escape abroad; to such people the reward would
mean not only freedom, but wealth for the rest of their
lives; and they could give their information with the
clearest conscience, and with the certainty of safe asylum.
This would mean a serious risk to any government that
tried to violate its treaty obligations.  However carefully its
measures were carried out, they would be known to some
dozens of its subjects, and perhaps to many more.  Even if
the personnel were meticulously screened, the government
would be assailed by doubts about their loyalty, and would
live in constant fear that its crime might be divulged to
the UN.

## An International Stock of Nuclear Weapons

In their " package " plan of 1957 the Western Governments
proposed, as a safeguard against nuclear aggression, that
each of the present nuclear Powers should retain a substantial part of its existing stocks of nuclear weapons.  The
United States delegate defended this proposal by saying that
" so long as there does exist *on various sides* in the world a
remaining nuclear weapons capability, there would not be
the incentive " for clandestine diversions, nor the terrible
consequence that a treaty-breaking government might be
able to blackmail other nations, or to gain world domination, by the possession of a secret stock.

The phrase " on various sides " implies the assumption
that the world will remain " for decades ahead " [13] divided
into the present power blocs of the Communist and
democratic nations; and the rest of what the United States
delegate said assumed that the other seventy-nine nations
would remain content to leave a monopoly of A- and H-
weapons in the hands of the three existing nuclear Powers.

[13] See pp. 293–294.

Neither of these assumptions is realistic. The argument makes a powerful case, not for the Western Governments' proposal but for the maintenance of a stock in international hands. As shown in the last chapter, an intending aggressor *might* be able to retain a secret stock of 20 per cent. to 30 per cent.—say a quarter—of the nuclear weapons he possessed when the disarmament treaty came into force. Thus three-quarters of his stock would be abolished, and perhaps a good deal more; for the larger the proportion he retained, the greater the risk that he would excite suspicion, and be found out. The abolition of so great a part of the existing stocks would be in itself a considerable result. To cancel out the danger from the quarter that might possibly be retained, the UN could keep an international stock amounting, say, to 40 per cent. of the nuclear armament of the strongest nuclear power. This would give a decisive nuclear advantage to the members of the UN who united to resist aggression; this advantage could hardly fail to be a powerful dis-incentive to attempts to evade the treaty's obligations. M. Moch put forward this suggestion in the Sub-Committee in 1955:

> "These difficulties" (of detecting secret stocks), he said, "have obliged us to envisage alternative means of elimination, which, strange though they may seem at first sight, may offer at least a partial solution. . . . Some ideas that have been suggested are: to internationalise stocks of fissile materials, to concentrate them on some distant island, or to deposit them for safekeeping with some supra-national authority." [14]

In 1957, after he had proposed the total abolition of stocks by five annual instalments of 20 per cent.,[15] M. Moch said:

> "I will just mention one idea which we reserve the right to take up again . . . that of a United Nations

[14] Sub-Committee, September 28, 1955, Cmd. 9652, p. 898.
[15] Sub-Committee, April 15, 1957, p. 18.

> Army, which . . . would garrison sensitive areas or
> vital strategic points, and which might assume custody,
> during a first stage . . . of stock-piles of fissionable
> materials before denaturing." [16]

And he added: " I believe profoundly in them " (these
ideas) " *for they are indispensable.*"

But the proposal for an international stock has not
remained wholly in the realm of vague suggestions. The
Statute of IAEA lays upon the Agency the specific duty of
maintaining an international stock. It says " Members
may make available to the Agency such quantities of special
fissionable materials as they deem advisable." (This may
mean large amounts.[17])

> " The Agency shall be responsible for storing and
> protecting materials in its possession. The Agency
> shall ensure that these materials shall be safeguarded
> against: (1) the hazards of the weather; (2) unauthor-
> ised removal or diversion; (3) damage or destruction,
> including sabotage; and (4) forcible seizure." [18]

Of course, this " special fissionable material " will not be
weapons, but in a form adapted for peaceful use. But such
materials, as has been shown, can be very easily transformed
into weapons; and it is against the dangers of their diversion
to military use that the Agency must " protect " them,
and " must ensure the geographical distribution of these
materials in such a way as not to allow concentration of
large amounts of such materials in any one country or
region of the world." [19]

But if IAEA is to " store and protect " large quantities
of these " dangerous " fissile materials against " diversion,"
" sabotage " or " forcible seizure," it must have its own

---

[16] Sub-Committee, May 28, 1957, pp. 7–8. Admiral Lord Fraser of North Cape
made a similar proposal in the House of Lords, *Hansard*, December 7, 1955,
cols. 1198–1202.
[17] See p. 266.
[18] Cmnd. 92, 1957, p. 8.
[19] *Loc. cit.*, p. 9.

very powerfully constructed buildings for their storage, and a UN Force for their protection. It clearly cannot rely on forces made available to it by a national Government. And if this is to be done for " dangerous " materials for peaceful use, why can it not be done for an international stock of nuclear weapons, too? This would add to the gravity of the responsibilities laid on IAEA, but it would not change their character.

There would, of course, be problems of political control; they would probably be solved, as they were for the UN Emergency Force in 1956, by the appointment of a standing Commission of the Assembly. This system has worked well. If the international stock were strategically distributed " in such a way as not to allow concentration of large amounts . . . in any one country or region of the world," the aggressor could not hope to seize it, or even to knock it out. If the Western Governments' purpose in proposing the retention of their stock is simply, in the United States delegate's phrase, to " cancel out " the nuclear power of a potential aggressor, then an international stock in the hands of the UN is far more realistic than the plan of leaving a large part of their existing stocks under the exclusive national control of Britain, Russia and the U.S.A.

People are apt to dismiss proposals such as this as " Utopian." But one British Minister of Defence said in 1955 :

"Genuine disarmament . . . must include all weapons . . . conventional and unconventional. . . . Control must provide effective international, or, if we like, supranational authority invested with real power. Honourable Members may say that this is elevating the United Nations, or whatever may be the authority, into something like world government. Be it so, it is none the worse for that. In the long run, this is the only way out for mankind." [20]

[20] Mr. H. Macmillan, *Hansard*, March 2, 1955, col. 2185.

Another British Minister of Defence said in 1957:

" If once the great Powers could agree to disarm
and to set up a system of international control, we
should have gone a long way towards the establishment
of a world authority with a world police force. ' You
may think that is starry eyed optimism. Maybe it is.
But as Minister of Defence, with my feet fairly well
on the ground, I believe that in the long run nothing
short of that will really work. We must aim at total
peace.' " [21]

If nothing short of this will really work, then there
should be no difficulty about accepting the proposal for a
UN nuclear stock, as a guarantee for total nuclear disarmament. If Britain would propose it, that might be a
long step forward to total peace.

## " *Means of Delivery* ", *Military and Naval*

There is another safeguard against the dangers of " diversion " and the secret stock: the abolition of the means by
which nuclear weapons are delivered to their targets—
guided missiles, bombing aircraft, aircraft-carriers and
submarines.

" A stockpile of bombs big enough to destroy every inch
of an enemy's industrial heartland would be of little value,"
wrote Mr. Gordon Dean, " unless the means existed of
getting those bombs through the defences and on to the
target." [22]

The significance of this obvious, but vitally important,
fact has often been recognised by Western Government
spokesmen, both in the Sub-Committee and elsewhere.
" We all know," said the United States delegate, Mr.
Wadsworth, in the Sub-Committee in 1955, " that the

[21] Mr. Duncan Sandys at Brighton, *The Times*, October 11, 1957.
[22] *Report on the Atom*, p. 110. " The nuclear weapon and its means of
delivery are indivisible; they can constitute a deterrent only when they are
together ": *The Times*, leading article, March 19, 1958.

effectiveness of nuclear weapons depends in large measure upon the effectiveness of the means for delivering them." [23] Mr. Nutting endorsed this view. Mr. Stassen, arguing in favour of " open skies," quoted with approval words which the Russian delegate had used: " The atom bomb cannot be effective in itself. . . . *It is useless without the means of conveying it to its destination.*" [24]

In other words, it has been widely recognised by men in authority that the problem of nuclear aggression, which threatens the future existence of mankind, could be solved if the " means of delivery " required for nuclear weapons were abolished. And all the " means of delivery," bombing aircraft, missiles, aircraft-carriers and submarines, are, in themselves, weapons that help attack against defence; they are weapons that favour surprise and encourage intending aggressors to think that a sudden and unprovoked attack may rapidly succeed. It will be argued in Part Six that, for these reasons, quite apart from the nuclear menace, their abolition—to be effected, no doubt, by stages, and over a period of years—is the most essential of the measures of conventional disarmament which a general treaty must contain. It is also a most essential measure of nuclear disarmament as well.

The point need not be further dealt with here, except to say that, if they were abolished, there would be no problem of control; neither their manufacture nor their construction, nor their tests, nor the training of troops or crews to use them, could be concealed from UN Inspection teams. If they were abolished, the temptation to a disloyal government to divert fissile material to weapons, or to retain a secret stock, would be virtually removed. If the governments genuinely desire to eliminate the danger of nuclear aggression, this is the most important single measure they can take.

---

[23] Sub-Committee, May 3, 1955, Cmd. 9650, pp. 528–529. See also Mr. S. Lloyd, *Hansard*, July 30, 1954, col. 900.
[24] September 8, 1955, Cmd. 9651, p. 787.

## Other Means of Delivery

If the above military and naval means of delivery were abolished it is unlikely that even the most reckless dictator would ever seek to use nuclear weapons. But there are, in theory, three other methods of delivery that might be adopted.

*Civil Aviation.* The abolition of bombing aircraft would entail a very strict control of civil aviation and, perhaps, the creation of an international air police. Surprising as it may seem, neither of these measures should present great difficulty, if once the decision to abolish bombers had been made.[25]

*Smuggling.* The competent United States authorities thought the risk of smuggling sufficiently serious to make it worth while to pass the law described above.[26] But smuggling would be a very hazardous proceeding. A nuclear weapon would be brought in in parts; each part would be liable to detection by customs officers or by counter-espionage; the parts would have to be assembled—no simple job; the weapon would be exploded by a time-fuse, sufficiently delayed to allow all the nationals of the aggressor State to leave the vicinity attacked. All this elaborate preparation might or might not go well. The number of the targets that could be attacked would inevitably be small; there could be no follow-up without the large-scale use of conventional military forces, which the international Inspectors would discover. In short, if missiles, bombers, aircraft-carriers and submarines had been abolished, no aggressor could hope to subjugate his victim by smuggled bombs alone.

*Merchant Ships.* The same is true of nuclear weapons left with a time-fuse in the holds of merchant ships. With

[25] See pp. 438–440 on Civil Aviation and an International Air Police. This view of the practicability of an International Air Police was confirmed by the experience of the R.A.F. with squadrons of Allied pilots and "mixed squadrons" during the 1939 War.

[26] See p. 303.

this plan the difficulties of transport would be nil, and the risk of detection would be smaller—though by no means negligible, if the plan of UN rewards to informers were adopted; the inducement to the crew, and their chances of safely and successfully informing, would be great. But by this method only ports could be attacked. A great disaster might be inflicted on a maritime nation like the British; but subjugation of the victim could not be achieved.

## The Final Safeguard : A "Robust" Disarmament

The final safeguard against clandestine treaty-breaking diversion of fissile material, and against the retention of secret stocks of nuclear weapons, lies in a drastic reduction of all national armaments of every kind. This was the conclusion reached by Dr. Oppenheimer in 1953, when he thought the nuclear arms race was out of control, when he was gravely anxious about the disasters that would happen in any nuclear war, and after he had given long delibera-tion to the dangers of a secret stock. Writing of the future time when " serious discussion of the regulation of armaments " could be resumed, he said:

" There will by then have been a vast accumulation of materials for atomic weapons, and a troublesome margin of uncertainty with regard to its accounting— *very troublesome indeed if we still live with vestiges of the suspicion, hostility and secretiveness of today. This will call for a very broad and robust regulation of armaments, in which existing forces and weapons are of a wholly different order than those required for the destruction of one great nation by another, in which steps of evasion will either be too vast to conceal or far too small to have, in view of then existing measures of defence, a decisive strategic effect.*" [27]

[27] *Foreign Affairs*, July 1953, pp. 534–535.

If this kind of armament reduction and control is carried through no aggressor, even if he succeeded in making or retaining some nuclear weapons, could hope to win his war.

Even if all the measures above proposed were soon agreed to, they would take a period of years to carry through. During that period a danger of nuclear aggression, even if slight, will still remain. The governments no longer have a choice that will give *absolute* security to their nations, immediately, and in the early years. They must make a balance between the risk of keeping stocks of nuclear weapons, and the risk of agreeing to their abolition, with the safeguards here proposed. These safeguards assume that the nations will accept limitations of national sovereignty, and practices of international co-operation, greater than have yet been tried. But for forty years the governments—all the governments—have been committed, by the League of Nations Covenant, the Kellogg Pact, and the UN Charter, to ending the international anarchy in which they live, and to the acceptance of the rule of law. Total nuclear disarmament, with the safeguards needed to eliminate its risks, might herald in the ultimate fulfilment of these pledges, by which, for so many years, the governments have been bound.

# PART FIVE

# OTHER WEAPONS OF MASS DESTRUCTION

# 26

# *What are the Weapons of Mass Destruction?*

IN 1948 the UN Commission on Conventional Armaments adopted the following definition:

> "Weapons of mass-destruction should be defined to include *atomic explosive weapons, radio-active material weapons, lethal chemical and biological weapons, and any weapons developed in the future which have characteristics comparable in destructive effect to those of the atomic bomb or other weapons mentioned above.*" [1]

This definition was endorsed by the Security Council in August 1948. It was still unchallenged when the Assembly adopted the Resolution which set up the Disarmament Commission in January 1952. This Resolution instructed the Commission to prepare treaty clauses providing "for the elimination of all major weapons adaptable to mass destruction." [2] The wording should be noted; "weapons adaptable to" can only mean "*weapons which can be used to cause* mass destruction." The point is very important.

The Assembly of 1953 elaborated this instruction; its Resolution said that the Commission should prepare a co-ordinated plan for "the elimination and prohibition of atomic, hydrogen, bacterial, chemical and all other such weapons of war and mass destruction, and for the attainment of these ends through effective measures." [3] Again, the wording should be noted; apart from the specific inclusion of bacterial and chemical weapons, the Resolution

[1] Security Council, Official Records, 2nd Year, Document S/C3, August 13, 1948.
[2] Adopted January 11, 1952.
[3] Adopted November 28, 1953, Cmd. 9204, p. 12.

speaks of "*all other such weapons of war* and mass destruction." This is very wide; it must, on any rational interpretation, include the methods of radiological warfare, which have often been mentioned in UN discussions; it must also, it will be argued in Chapters 28, 30 and 31, include incendiary weapons and guided and ballistic missiles.

The 1954 Assembly reaffirmed that the Commission should prepare a " draft international disarmament convention," which should include " the total prohibition of the use and manufacture of . . . weapons of mass destruction *of every type.*"

A year later the United States Secretary of the Army, Mr. Brucker, approved a Report drawn up by a Committee of four well-known civilians. *The Times* gave the following account of the Report:

> " Their underlying conception seems to be that gas and germ weapons are inherently less ' horrifying ' than nuclear weapons, and should have their proper place in military planning. They urged that *new ' uninhibited' research be undertaken in developing a complete family of chemical, biological and radiological weapons for actual use, if necessary, and pointed to their advantages in subduing an enemy without destroying property which the victor might wish to save.*"

The words of the Report are these:
" Recognition must be given to these weapons as having unique potential in warfare without associated destruction of facilities and the attendant problems of rehabilitation."

" The Committee conceded," says *The Times,*
" that ' current concepts of warfare ' did not envisage the use of chemical and biological weapons by the United States, but such developments, it insisted, must be capable of adaptation to America's military needs. Research should be imaginatively directed to the

development of weapons of maximum potential, irrespective of particular concepts of warfare; they were essential for their deterrent effect or for their actual use, as new concepts and policies might dictate."

This reads like the " Kriegsraison " theory of the Kaiser's General Staff.[4] But it was endorsed by Mr. Brucker, who " approved detailed proposals for three major commands under the Chief Chemical Officer for Research and Development; Engineering; and Material." [5]

The NATO Civil Defence Bulletin for December 1957 quoted from an article in the United States monthly Service magazine, *Army*, which was circulated, and therefore, presumably, endorsed, by the Federal Civil Defence Administration. The author of the *Army* article commented on a speech by Zhukov as follows:

" He . . . declared that any new war would see the mass use of air power, various types of missiles, and means of mass destruction like nuclear, chemical and biological weapons. The threat is very real, and *the fact that we disagree with Zhukov in classifying chemical and biological weapons in the ' mass destruction ' class does not detract from the warning.*" [6]

In the 1957 United States Handbook on the Effects of Nuclear Weapons there was the following passage:

" For some time consideration has been given to the possibility of using radio-active material deliberately as an offensive weapon in what is called radiological warfare. The basic idea is that radio-active contamination of areas, factories, or equipment would make their use either impossible, or very hazardous, without accompanying material destruction."

---

[4] See Julius Stone, *Legal Controls of International Conflict*, pp. 351 *et seq.*
[5] *The Times*, November 8, 1955.
[6] *Loc. cit.*, p. 31.

The Handbook explained the difficulties of preparing radio-active isotopes for this purpose, and then continued:

" The situation has undergone a change with the development of bombs having high fission energy yield. The explosion of such bombs at low altitudes could cause radio-active contamination over large areas that are beyond the range of physical damage. Consequently they are, in effect, weapons of radiological warfare. Instead of preparing and stockpiling a contaminating agent in advance, with its attendant difficulties, the radio-active substances are produced by fission at the time of the explosion. Radiological warfare has thus become an automatic extension of the offensive use of nuclear weapons of high yield." [7]

This really means that, after research, no weapon of radiological warfare had been discovered except the three-decker fission-fusion-fission bomb, which covers thousands of square miles with fall-out.[8] This confirms what Professor Frisch had said four years before; that " taking radio-active material from a pile and scattering it over an enemy town " was " probably not a useful weapon." [9] The effects of three-decker bombs have been already considered in Part Two; radiological warfare need not, therefore, be dealt with further in this Part.

But the other weapons of mass destruction raise questions of the utmost gravity. Those most intimately concerned with these weapons regard them as hardly less potent—that is to say, hardly less dangerous to mankind—than A- and H-bombs. Of course, it has been common knowledge that all the leading governments have been preparing them, for defence and for retaliation, for many years. Russia, no doubt, has done as much as any other Power to develop them to a high degree of efficiency. But the fact that a Western Government has gone so far towards abandoning

[7] United States *Handbook*, 1957, pp. 427–428.
[8] See pp. 135 *et seq.*
[9] *Atomic Energy : A Survey* (Rotblat), pp. 17–18.

the " current concepts of warfare," and to preparing them
" for actual use " on grounds of " military need," and that
there was no mention of them in the Western Governments'
" package " plan of 1957, gives them a new significance.
When the Kaiser's generals and Hitler's Nazis first used
chemical and incendiary weapons, the whole world united
in horrified protest at their violation of accepted international law.  Missile warfare stems from Hitler's V 1s and
V 2s.  If the author in *Army* is reflecting the view of his
Government and nation; if chemical, incendiary, and biological weapons, and missiles, are not to be regarded as
weapons of mass destruction, but are to be accepted as
normal and legitimate means of war; if this is to be the
basis of a disarmament treaty, then the treaty might as well
never be made.  If the treaty is to bring safety and confidence to the nations, it must abolish these weapons without
delay, and must make " a co-ordinated plan . . . for the
attainment of these ends through effective measures."  The
purpose of the following chapters is to show what these
measures ought to be.

# 27

# *Chemical Disarmament:*
## *Poison Gas*

" The wounded began to pour in on us; French and British and Indian troops, and Zouaves. The first poison gas sufferers. This horror was too monstrous to believe at first. . . . Far as we had travelled from our civilised world of a few months back, the savagery of it, of the sight of men choking to death with yellow froth, lying on the floor and out in the fields, made me rage with an anger which no cruelty of men, not even the degradation of our kind by the hideous concentration camps in later Germany, ever quite rekindled; for then we still thought all men were human. . . .

" ' Gas wall, a hundred feet high and two miles long; the Huns are through, but it's stopping them too.' So two wounded English officers reported." [1]

THIS is an account, by an eye-witness who was already accustomed to the sights and sounds of battle, of the first German gas attack at Ypres. It shows how the use of this new weapon horrified the world. It was, indeed, a terrible development in the cruelty of war. From primitive times, the use of poison had been forbidden by the laws of war; and the laws had been obeyed. This gas attack was the first major breach in the accepted rules of the Hague Conventions; it was followed by the unrestricted use of submarines to sink merchant ships at sea; by aerial bombardment of open towns; by the use of fire, first in the field, and after the destruction of Guernica in the Spanish Civil War, against civilians. It heralded the development of the weapons of mass destruction we know today.

[1] G. Winthrop Young, *The Grace of Forgetting*, p. 233.

## *Poison Gas in the 1914 War*

This first attack was made by a cloud of chlorine released, when the wind was in the right direction, from stationary containers. It cost the British and Canadians 59,000 casualties, and might have given the Germans the Channel ports if they had assembled the reserve divisions needed to exploit their break-through.

The Western Allies did not reply by verbal protests. They improvised a primitive form of gas-mask, and proceeded to prepare poison gases of their own. Within five months they had made a successful gas attack at Loos; they produced not only chlorine, but new gases of various kinds: tear gases; mustard gas, which blistered and burnt the body; Blue Cross or arsenic gases, which were expected to penetrate the German gas-masks, and many others. They invented the Livens projector, a great advance on the German containers; they put gases into shells, fired from guns and mortars. The Germans produced their own type of mustard gas; they introduced phosgene gases, and made various other developments of their own.

Even these primitive gases, used on the field of battle in the 1914 War, were inherently a better weapon than high explosive. A gas shell covered a greater area than the blast and fragmentation of a high explosive burst; everyone within that area was subjected to its effect—shell-fire hit some and missed many; its effect lasted longer—even the most fleeting gas clouds lasted many minutes, while a high explosive shell's effect was over in an instant; it had a searching effect—a shallow trench gave shelter against high explosive; not even buildings or a copse of trees were a protection against gas. All the 1914 War gases had these four advantages; but in all four points mustard gas was undoubtedly the best. A recent (1955) *British Service Manual* says that it was the " most effective," because it had hardly any smell, and was " difficult to detect "; it " could attack all parts of the body not protected by a gas-mask " and rendered contaminated ground dangerous for some time.[2]

These were qualities which, in all subsequent research into poison gas, the chemists sought to perfect. But when they were first introduced, not only mustard, but almost all the compounds used did well. Indeed, gas had a good claim to the title of the most successful weapon of the 1914 War. Although it was only used against soldiers who had gas masks and protective clothing, and who had been trained in their use, and although the gas shell was relatively inefficient, gas produced, pound for pound, several times more casualties than high explosive.[3] Moreover, the United States Army had prepared a new gas, Lewisite, for the campaign of 1919, which would have been used, if the German resistance had not collapsed in the previous year; it was claimed that Lewisite was invisible, that it would reach down to cellars and dugouts; that it was fatal if inhaled; a small quantity on the skin would produce almost certain death; it was persistent; it had *fifty-five times* the " spread " of any previous poison gas; and it would compel the victim to tear off his gas-mask, and so to die.[4] If these claims were true, Lewisite had all the merits of mustard gas, but in much greater degree.

## Preparations for Chemical Warfare Between the Wars

After the 1914 War, the general staffs all came to think of gas as a normal weapon, and they made their plans on that assumption. They decided that aircraft would be by far the best method of delivery, and that the general industrial populations of the belligerents would certainly be attacked.

[2] *Medical Manual of Chemical Warfare*, 4th ed., 1955, p. 1. This Manual was issued by H.M.S.O. for the Admiralty, War Office and Air Ministry.
[3] United States General Fries said that 75,000 out of 275,000 United States casualties were due to gas, " and yet the Germans used it in a feeble, comparatively halting manner." Quoted by V. Lefebure, *The Riddle of the Rhine*, p. 182.
[4] Heinz Liepmann, *Death from the Skies*, p. 117.

Some of them made the most alarming predictions. General Frey, of the United States Army, said: " An aero-chemical bomb weighing half a ton and filled with Lewisite, could render ten districts of New York uninhabitable." [5]

*General Bradner, Chief of Research of the Chemical Warfare Service of the United States Army*, spoke at a congressional hearing about a certain gas-generating compound: " *If Germany had had 4,000 tons of this material and three or four hundred planes equipped . . . for its distribution, the entire First American Army would have been annihilated in ten to twelve hours.*" [6]

General Fries and Major West of the United States Army wrote:

> " Mustard gas, which is a third again as heavy as water . . . may be sprinkled through a small opening, such as a bunghole, in a tank that simply lets liquid flow out. The speed of the aeroplane will atomise it. In this way gas can be sprinkled over whole areas. . . . Lewisite will be used. . . . The burns from a quantity equal to three drops will usually cause death. The material can be made up by hundreds and even thousands of tons per month." [7]

The views of General Sir Frederick Sykes,[8] who had been Chief of Air Staff in 1918, of Major Victor Lefebure,[9] who had played a large part in the development of various gases for the British Army in the field, and of other authorities, were thus summarised by General P. R. C. Groves in an official League of Nations document in 1923:

> " The gas bomb is probably by far the most effective weapon for use from aircraft. This form of attack upon great cities, such as London or Paris, might entail the loss of millions of lives in a few hours. . . . All gas

[5] Cited by Liepmann, *op. cit.*, p. 118.
[6] Cited by Irwin, *The Next War*, pp. 46–47.
[7] *Chemical Warfare*, p. 380.
[8] *Aviation in Peace and War*, p. 100.
[9] " Chemical Warfare—Possibilities of its Control—Problems of Peace and War," *Grotius Society Transactions*, Vol. VII, p. 166.

experts are agreed that it would be impossible . . . to protect the civil population from this form of attack." [10]

These men were not pacifists or pamphleteers. They were soldiers who had conducted gas warfare operations in the First World War, and most of whom were still responsible army or air force leaders when they wrote. They may have overstated their case. Lewisite may have been less deadly than they thought. After they wrote, Radar was invented, and the other means of defence against aircraft were improved. But so long as the bomber could get through, the dangers of which they spoke were real.

And their views were accepted by all the governments between the Wars. Although a treaty banning the use of chemical and biological weapons had been drawn up by a League of Nations Conference in 1925, the Staffs all continued their preparations; research into new and more effective compounds went on; troops were given offensive and defensive training; when the 1939 War began, the civilian populations had all been furnished with gas-masks, and taught how to make their houses as gas-proof as might be. Meanwhile Mussolini had shown in Abyssinia what mustard gas could do, if it was distributed against civilians from the air.

## Gas in the 1939 War

Gas was taken to the battlefields of all the big land actions throughout the 1939 War. It was ready for use by bombers on all the airfields. Why was it never used?

For the Western Governments, there is a clear answer; they had signed the Geneva Protocol of 1925, and they intended to honour their signature and to observe what they regarded as the binding laws of war, until the enemy, by using it first, obliged them to retaliate in kind. This is

[10] L.N. Document C.T.A. 210, 1923. General Groves was Director of Air Operations in 1918, and later representative of the British Air Ministry to the League.

what they did in other forms of warfare, for example, the air bombardment of civilians, and the indiscriminate sinking of merchant ships at sea. No doubt they also bore in mind that, if the horror of gas bombardment was unloosed on their civilian populations, the casualties would be very heavy, and the suffering severe.

But why was it never used by Hitler, Mussolini and the Japanese? The Western Governments confidently believed that it would be. In January 1941 Sir Winston Churchill wrote: " Many and increasing indications point to the early use of gas against us." [11] In August 1941 he wrote: " We must expect gas warfare on a tremendous scale. It may break out at any moment." [12] Why did this not happen? No one believes that it was the legal obligations of the Geneva Treaty of 1925 that held the Axis Powers back; they had broken too many other treaties by their aggressions. Various other explanations have been suggested.

Some authorities [13] believe that it was due to Hitler's own experience; he had been gassed seriously twice in the 1914 War, and when it ended, he was recovering from mustard gas in a military hospital. His general staff must also have reminded him of what an error it had been for Germany to start gas warfare in 1915; no doubt they showed him the memorandum written by Haber, the German Nobel Prize Winner who first proposed it in 1914:

" If there is even the remotest possibility that the war will last beyond the summer of 1915, reject all schemes for gas warfare. If you disregard my warning, we shall be beaten by the use of our own weapons. Our enemies have a hundred times as much raw materials as we, and, should the war last beyond the summer of 1915, they will have time to overtake us in our stride, and to drench us with quantities of gas enormously greater than we shall ever be able to produce." [14]

[11] Churchill, *The Second World War*, Vol. IV, p. 642.
[12] *Loc. cit.*, p. 726.
[13] *e.g.*, General Prentiss, see *Civil Defence in Modern War*, p. 67.
[14] Quoted by Liepmann, *op. cit.*, pp. 73–74.

Events had proved that Haber was right; before 1918 Germany had lost heavily by the use of gas.

Major-General Porter, Chief of the Chemical Warfare Service of the United States Army, writing in March 1942, suggested other strategical considerations. " A persistent gas," he said,

> " is primarily a defensive weapon. In the fall of 1941, its use would have been of much more value to the retreating Russians than to the advancing Germans. Hitler understands well that mustard gas on British beaches would add materially to the precariousness of an invasion." [15]

This reasoning alone would explain why Hitler did not use gas early in the war. By the time he was preparing to use it against the Russians in the spring of 1942, Sir Winston Churchill issued broadcast warnings that, if he did so, Britain would retaliate by carrying gas warfare " on the largest possible scale far and wide against military objectives in Germany." [16] And by then we were building up our air superiority, which meant that the advantage in gas attack would inevitably lie with us, and that Germany would suffer very heavily indeed.[17]

But there remains a mystery. Before 1944, the German chemists had discovered a new class of " nerve gases " which they called Tabun. These, says Dr. Bush, " far exceeded in deadliness " the gases of the 1914 War, including Lewisite.[18] Before 1945 the Western Allies had developed the Tabun gases, too, and all the leading governments possess them now. The British Service *Manual* already quoted says that Tabun was " an acute systemic poison active in extremely low dosage "; other similar compounds now exist " which are even more toxic "; they are " colourless liquids," which " in vapour form are invisible and some are

---

[15] Quoted by Prentiss, *op. cit.*, p. 67.
[16] Broadcast of May 10, 1942. See also Churchill, Vol. IV, p. 294.
[17] Vannevar Bush, *Modern Arms and Free Men*, p. 156.
[18] *Op. cit.*, p. 154.

virtually odourless." Some are as persistent as mustard, they "rapidly penetrate mucous membranes, and more slowly skin." Both liquid and vapour pass through fabrics, so that " clothing cannot be relied on for protection "; " relatively small doses may prove fatal "; a " few drops of liquid on the bare skin may kill within half an hour," [19] and " anti-gas ointment is ineffective against nerve gas." [20] General Prentiss gives a ghastly description of its physical effects upon the human body.[21]  How did it happen that in the months of mounting disaster before his final fall, Hitler did not order the use of this new and terrifying weapon?

He *had* sent it to his forces in the field. In April 1945 the advancing Allied troops discovered 16,000 gas bombs, some of them weighing 550 lb., at a place called Ossa; thousands more were found a little later; they contained Tabun. And Hitler intended that it should be used; he was disobeyed by his Minister of Production, Speer. This is the evidence given by Speer at the trial of the major War Criminals at Nuremburg:

> " I was not able to make out from my own direct observations whether gas warfare was to be started, but I knew from various associates of Ley's and Goebbels' that they were discussing the question of using our two new combat gases: Tabun and Sarin. They believed that these gases would be of particular efficacy, and they did in fact produce the most frightful results.[22] . . . These two gases both had a quite extraordinary effect, and . . . there was no respirator, and no protection against them that we knew of. So the soldiers would have been unable to protect themselves in any way. For the manufacture of this gas, we had about three factories, all of which were undamaged and which until

---

[19] *Manual*, p. 12.
[20] *Ibid.*, p. 16.
[21] *Op. cit.*, p. 57.
[22] There is an account of a secret report made to Speer about the effect of Tabun on a herd of goats; the goats were violently ill, then became rampant maniacs and killed each other in a fury of uncontrollable destruction: L. Farago, *UN World* (N.Y.), February 1948.

November 1944 were working at full speed. When rumours reached us that gas might be used, I stopped its production in November 1944. . . . Beginning with a letter . . . which I wrote to Hitler in October 1944, I tried through legal methods to obtain his permission to have these gas factories stop their production. . . . Hitler informed me that the gas production would have to be continued whatever happened, but I gave instructions for the preliminary products not to be supplied any more.

"In military circles there was certainly no one in favour of gas warfare. All sensible Army people turned gas warfare down as being utterly insane, *since, in view of your superiority in the air, it would not be long before it would bring the most terrible catastrophe upon German cities.* . . .

"MR. JUSTICE JACKSON: And your reasons, I take it, were the same as the military's, that is to say, it was certain Germany would get the worst of it if Germany started that kind of warfare? . . .

"SPEER: Not only that. It was because *at that stage of the war* it was perfectly clear that under no circumstances should any international crimes be committed which could be held against the German people after they had lost the war. That was what decided the issue." [23]

Thus it was by a series of lucky chances that the " most terrible catastrophes " in the cities did not occur. All the belligerents were ready to use gas, and some of them would have used it, if they had been certain that it would pay.

## Developments Since 1945

Today, all the leading military Powers still assume that gas might be used, if another war broke out; all have gone on with research and large-scale preparation for its actual use.

[23] *Records of the International Military Tribunal*, Vol. XVI, pp. 527–528.

The United States Army Chemical Corps states that " nerve gases have been developed to the point where they are *ten times* as toxic as the best chemical agents previously known." [24]   Mr. Hanson Baldwin said ten years ago that they had " already made obsolete the Second World War gas-mask and protective clothing . . . it seems certain that not a square inch of skin can be safely exposed." [25]   Troops on exercises are made to inject themselves with an antidote, atropine, after a simulated gas attack.[26]  The Chief Chemical Officer of the United States Army said in 1955 that the danger of chemical weapons was as great a threat as that of A-bombs, and that by their use " mental derangement might be deliberately inspired." [27]   The threat is increased by the development of missiles; General Prentiss believes, and other authorities agree, that " air-breathing " missiles will be the best means of delivery for chemical attacks on cities in any future war.[28]

Political developments have been no less alarming.  The United States Government decided in 1955 to treat gas as a conventional weapon, when Mr. Brucker accepted the Report described above.[29]  The British Government *Manual* contains these sentences :

> " The advent of the atom bomb and the fact that gas was not used in World War II do not exclude the possibility of gas being used again in war.  *The experiences of World War I indicate that gas is a useful strategic and tactical weapon.  It can affect personnel in both forward and rear areas.*
>
> " During World War I gas was only used in land weapons, and not from aircraft; consequently gas casualties were due mainly to vapour, and were largely

[24] Quoted by Prentiss, *op. cit.*, p. 57.
[25] *The Price of Power*, p. 71.
[26] The United States F.C.D.A. says that " the effectiveness of atropine . . . would be limited against massive saturation by nerve gas to be expected in an all-out onslaught ": *NATO Civil Defence Bulletin*, December 1957.
[27] *The Times*, June 22, 1955.
[28] See *op. cit.*, p. 29.
[29] See pp. 316–317.

confined to troops in the field. In a future war, gas may be dispersed by other methods on to selected targets far removed from the fighting line, *such as cities, dockyards and factories. It therefore seems probable that the nature and severity of casualties may differ from those recorded in World War I.*" [30]

This was written in 1955. It is a very genteel way of saying that nerve gas will be delivered by aircraft and missiles; that it will *probably* be used against the civil population; and that it will be a weapon of mass destruction. If what the United States Chemical Corps and Mr. Hanson Baldwin say is true, there can be little hope of any real defence for civilians, and not much for troops.

## Total Chemical Disarmament

### British Proposal in 1933

Since this is so, there is no need to argue that the total abolition of chemical weapons must form part of any disarmament treaty worthy of the name. That has always been accepted by every government, both between the Wars, and since the Second ended; it has only been in doubt since 1955.

But the technical problems of chemical disarmament have never been fully explored. The subject has never been discussed in the UN; and the proposals considered by the League Disarmament Conference were the least complete part of all its work. Having decided, however, that poison gases were " specifically offensive," " especially efficacious against national defence," and " most threatening to civilians," the sixty governments represented in the Conference did unanimously arrive at certain definite conclusions which the British Government embodied in their Draft Convention of March 1933. All preparations for chemical warfare were to be prohibited in time of peace as

[30] *Loc. cit.*, p. 2.

in time of war; so were the manufacture, import, export or possession of appliances or substances suited for chemical warfare, and the instruction or training of armed forces in the use of chemical weapons and means of warfare.[31] The Permanent Disarmament Commission to be established under the British Draft Convention was empowered to investigate any complaint that preparations for chemical warfare were being made.[32] Proposals for some form of sanctions against the violation of these clauses would, no doubt, have been added, if the Convention had been signed.

## Other Proposals made between the Wars

These provisions were not regarded as wholly adequate, even by the authors of the Draft Convention. There was a general view that drastic disarmament would greatly reduce the risk that any aggressor would challenge world opinion by resort to a barbarous and illegal weapon; but many delegations shared the view of Denmark, which urged that the abolition of national air forces and the creation of an international air police force was a necessary supplementary guarantee against the disloyal preparation or use of chemical weapons. The Danes also proposed that the prohibition of preparations for chemical warfare should be supervised by " an international cartel of manufacturers of chemical products under the supervision of the (Disarmament) Control Commission." [33]

This had been suggested earlier by M. Jouhaux, the representative of the International Federation of Trade Unions, in the League Preparatory Commission; he proposed an international cartel which, " being managed by international employers and experts, would see to it that none of its branches went astray." The only spokesman of the chemical industry in the Commission, a Frenchman, immediately " declared himself ready to accept it straight-

---

[31] Conference Documents, Vol. I, p. 135.
[32] Conference Documents, Vol. II, pp. 489–490. The Report of the Special Commission of the Conference is at p. 370. See also *United States Green Book*, 1955, pp. 170–189.
[33] Conference Documents, Vol. I, p. 141.

way "; he favoured " a loosely knit federation of national industries which would submit when necessary to the inspection of a ' syndic,' " *i.e.*, a League commission of control.[34]

This idea had been worked out in greater detail by Major Lefebure, who has already been quoted; Major Lefebure was an able chemist, with a practical knowledge of the chemical industry, and a pioneer in making gases operational in the field. Of all who wrote about the subject, he foresaw most clearly the danger which a continued arms race in chemical weapons would involve. Already in 1923, having explained the difficulties of producing an atomic bomb, he forecast " the use of chemicals which may attack human functions hitherto immune," [35] *e.g.*, the nerve gases which now exist; and proposed for the chemical industry a system remarkably like that suggested by Dr. Oppenheimer for atomic energy. His scheme involved:

(i) The abolition of chemical warfare research, which, with the co-operation of Scientific Associations, he believed could be made effective;

(ii) The abolition of testing grounds and plants, and the prohibition of all tests; this, he said, would effectively prevent the production of *new* chemical weapons;

(iii) The prohibition of " actual bulk manufacture." This Major Lefebure thought quite simple, so far as government plants for poison gas were concerned; they could simply be closed down. But the control of ordinary chemical plants was more difficult, for the reason that they could be very rapidly converted to the production of poison gas. " It took forty years and more," he said, " to develop these (German dye) factories; yet forty days saw many of these plants producing huge tonnages of poison gas, and as many hours were sufficient for others." [36]  Moreover, this could be

[34] S. de Madariaga, *Disarmament*, 1929, p. 163. S. de Madariaga gives a fascinating account of the discussion.
[35] *Op. cit.*, pp. 232–236.
[36] *Loc. cit.*, pp. 250–251.

done without the knowledge of the general body of workers in the industry, since in many cases only the last stage in the preparation of a lethal compound is toxic; only the directors would need to know.

Since for this reason the chemical industry is the " most perfect type " of an industry readily convertible to war, Major Lefebure thought it necessary to secure a " strategic " distribution of chemical plants throughout the world; to control these plants by a kind of international directorate imposed upon the private firms; and to establish a system of close inspection by experts acting for the League.[37] He believed that " the cumulative effect " of these measures would be watertight, but in any case, he thought that " the risks of unhampered and unlimited development of the new agencies of war are far greater than those which will accompany a really comprehensive and effectively operated attempt to control them." [38]

## Total Chemical Disarmament Today

These words were written in 1923; they were written by a man who had thought through the problem of chemical disarmament much more thoroughly than anyone else before or since. They are still the vital propositions about poison gas. There is still no reason to believe that its abolition could not be effectively controlled. With the kind of inspection now projected,[39] it would be impossible for a disloyal government to maintain a clandestine government plant for making poison gas. Control over private or nationalised government chemical plants, in Russia or elsewhere, could be secured either by Major Lefebure's international directorate, or by the Danish international cartel of manufacturers. But now, as then, the most essential guarantees against a treaty-breaking manufacture of poison gas would lie in the three simplest of the measures which

[37] *Loc. cit.*, pp. 161–162 and 244–257.
[38] *Loc. cit.*, p. 286.
[39] See Chap. 43.

were proposed, all of them measures contained in, or forecast by,[40] the British Draft Convention of 1933, and all of
them measures in which no serious problem of control
would arise:

> (i) the abolition of the means of delivery, *i.e.*,
> missiles and military and naval aircraft;
>
> (ii) the abolition of the manufacture or possession of
> the necessary "appliances"—bombs, sprays, airborne
> and other containers, etc.;
>
> (iii) the prohibition of the training of troops in the
> use of poison gas.

The last of these three would in itself have a powerful
restraining effect even on the most reckless would-be
aggressor; it would be a grave risk to use gas, if the troops
who used it had not been given adequate protective clothing
and equipment, and if they had not been adequately trained.
And this training could not be concealed from UN Inspectors. This is even more true of modern methods of chemical
warfare than it was between the Wars. The risks of
abolition ought therefore to be accepted now, even more
readily than they were accepted by the governments in 1933.

[40] See pp. 330–331 and 417

# 28

## *Chemical Disarmament: Fire*

DURING the Second World War, fire became a very potent weapon.  But it has received singularly little attention, either in the histories of the War, or in the disarmament discussions of the post-war years.  As will be seen, it must, on any rational interpretation of the words, be classed as a weapon of mass-destruction, yet it has never been mentioned among the weapons that must be abolished.  It has come to be accepted as a normal, conventional means of war, both for attacking troops in the field, and against the civilian population of industrial or " strategic " towns.

### *Incendiary Weapons and the Laws of War*

This is the more surprising, since the use of fire was strictly prohibited by international law, as it was established before 1914, and reaffirmed between the Wars.  The First and Second Hague Conferences both included the following provisions in their Convention on the Laws and Customs of War on Land:

> " Besides the prohibitions provided by special Conventions, it is especially forbidden . . . to employ arms, projectiles or material of a nature to cause superfluous injury." [1]

This was interpreted by international lawyers to mean that " cannons . . . must not be loaded with . . . red-hot balls and the like," and *a fortiori*, fire was without doubt " especially forbidden." [2]  This was still the unanimous view of the

---

[1] A. Pearce Higgins, *The Hague Peace Conferences*, p. 235.
[2] *e.g.*, Oppenheim's *International Law*, 5th ed., Vol. II, p. 282.

sixty governments assembled in the Geneva Disarmament Conference in 1932; in their Resolution of July 23 they declared that " incendiary warfare shall be prohibited under the conditions unanimously recommended by the Special Committee." [3]   This meant total prohibition of every form of incendiary weapon for any purpose, or in any circumstances whatever.   The Special Committee had agreed on this, because, if used against urban centres, incendiary weapons are " particularly threatening to civilians," while, if used in flame projectors against troops in the field, " the cruelty inherent in the use of these appliances causes suffering that cannot be regarded as necessary from the military point of view."   The majority of the Special Committee also held that all incendiary weapons were specifically weapons of offence.   In pursuance of this finding, the British Government's Draft Convention of March 1933 laid it down " as an established rule of international law " that no incendiary weapons should be used, either as projectiles, in " flame projectors," or in any other way.[4]

There was no doubt, therefore, that, up to 1939, incendiary weapons were forbidden by the accepted laws of war, and that they were universally condemned by the moral conscience of mankind.

## Fire in the 1914 War

Perhaps it was not surprising that the Germans, after they had violated the Hague Conventions by using gas at Ypres in April 1915, should have committed a further breach by using flame-throwers in July.   Field-Marshal Sir John French reported:

> " A new device has been adopted by the enemy for driving burning liquid into our trenches with a strong jet. . . .   Most of the infantry occupying these trenches were driven back, but their retirement was due far more

---

[3] Conference Documents, Vol. I, p. 269.
[4] Conference Documents, Vol. II, p. 488.

to the surprise and temporary confusion caused by the burning liquid than to the actual damage inflicted."

Major Lefebure comments on this dispatch and on the later development of the flame-thrower in the 1914 War:

> "There exists a mistaken notion that the flame-projector was a negligible quantity. This . . . is certainly not true of the very efficient portable flame-projector which was the form officially adopted by the German, and later by the French, Armies."

The German troops jocularly called the chief of their Flammenwerfer service (who was also the inventor of the weapon) the "Prince of Hades," and his units the "fire-spouters." *Flame-throwers were mostly used to break the resistance in front-line machine-gun nests in fixed entrenchments,* i.e., *in attack.*[5]

## Fire in the 1939 War

Fire was much more important in the Second World War. Before it began, Hitler, in the course of his aggression in Spain, had tried out his incendiary bombs; in a few hours his aircraft burnt Guernica to the ground. With this plain warning of his intentions, the British Government planned to use fire too; in 1940 they drew up the scheme called the "Flame Defence of Britain," for the purpose of repelling the Nazi forces, if they crossed the Channel. A Petroleum Warfare Department was set up to organise the use of petroleum with flame barrages on beaches, flame traps, flame fougasses, fire cars, and simple forms of flame-throwers. Two hundred flame traps were prepared in Southern England and Scotland and 40,000 flame fougasses were installed along the roads of Britain.[6]

---

5 Lefebure, *op. cit.*, pp. 44 and 72–74.
6 Chambers's *Encyclopaedia*, 1950 ed., Vol. III, pp. 333–337, "Chemical Warfare."

## The " Tactical " Use of Fire

Naturally, having used fire against Guernica, Hitler did not hesitate to use flame-throwers in all his campaigns. The Italians and the Japanese were equipped with them. The Russians used small flame-throwers in street fighting, particularly in Stalingrad and Berlin. The United States used portable flame-throwers against the Japanese and developed a long-range weapon for use by tanks. The British Army was furnished with a flame-thrower known as the " Wasp " and used on the infantry carrier. Its success in 1944 " led to its general adoption as an infantry weapon." It was subsequently developed for use with the Churchill tank, and the so-called " Crocodile " apparatus had a range of more than 150 yards. Three " Crocodile " regiments were formed and took part in over one hundred separate actions.[7]

## The " Strategic " Use of Fire

But the tactical use of fire in battles on land was of small importance compared to the strategical developments that followed from Guernica. The German general staff did with fire what everyone had expected that they would do with poison gas. They made large-scale attacks from the air with incendiary bombs on Coventry, London and other targets. In due course, the Western Allies replied in kind, and, as with gas in the 1914 War, the Germans paid a heavy price for their criminal disregard of international law.

## The Development of Incendiary Weapons

Of course, scientific research was brought to bear on the improvement of the incendiary materials used both in land battles and from the air. The purpose was to find something that would burn for a long time; develop a very hot flame; render inflammable all the combustible materials in a considerable area; and present no great problems of manufacture, cost or transport.

[7] *Ibid*. See also *Flame-Thrower*, by Andrew Wilson, 1956.

Hitler's early bombs fulfilled these requirements. They weighed only 2 lb., and consisted of thermite as the primary igniting substance, and metallic magnesium as the principal incendiary material. This combination was called *thermate*. The bombs were completely consumed by combustion, burnt with a dazzling white heat, and could not be extinguished by water. The British and United States Air Forces found that 4 lb. thermate bombs were better, because they would penetrate a heavy roof and one or more wooden floors as well. The thermate was ignited on impact; it burnt fiercely at a temperature of 3,000°C. for approximately one minute, throwing pieces of molten magnesium as far as fifty feet. The magnesium casing of the bomb burnt less fiercely for fifteen minutes. The bombs were dropped in " clusters " of up to 150, so that they followed the trajectory of standard high explosive bombs, and the clusters were scattered at the height which gave them the maximum useful " spread " over the town or city attacked. There were also heavy bombs up to 500 lb. in weight for attacking special targets or buildings that were more difficult to set on fire. These bombs were filled with thermate as igniter, and solid oil mixed with magnesium shavings. They were not used in great numbers, but were extremely efficient.

During the 1939 War, the Western Allies developed two other incendiary agents of the solid-oil type; the more important was gasoline saponified in napalm. This was a stiff jelly, loaded into light metal bombs, and ignited by the bursting charge. The napalm scattered in small lumps which adhered firmly to any material (including clothes and human flesh) with which it came in contact. It burned fiercely for long enough to set fire to any ordinary inflammable material. It was especially effective against the light wooden structures which made up so much of the cities of Japan.

Like gas, incendiary agents were also adapted for spraying by low-flying aircraft. This gave a uniform coverage of a large target area with a relatively small amount of material, and was well-suited for setting forests and grain fields on fire. The incendiary oil mixture would also float and burn on water; it could therefore be used to set fire to docks and ships in harbour.

## Results of Strategic Incendiary Bombing

The British raids on Hamburg in July and August 1943 first showed what fire could do. Hamburg had a population of 1½ million. In raids spread over nine days, the R.A.F. destroyed 75 per cent. of the city. In the first raid, they dropped 2,300 tons of bombs, of which a large proportion were incendiaries; the tonnage in the second raid was even greater. The fires continued burning between the raids; Hamburg had had the best fire brigade in Germany, but it was helpless; at one time the houses on 133 miles of street were ablaze; thirty miles of quay, docks and arsenals were devastated. 80 per cent. of the damage was done by fire. Altogether 70,000 to 100,000 people perished, most of them burnt to death, many of the rest poisoned by the carbon monoxide which filled their shelters, and against which their gas masks were no good. " Terror . . . terror . . . terror . . . pure, naked, bloody terror," was the cry of the commentator, Dr. Carl Hofmann, after the fourth raid. " No subsequent city raid shook Germany as did that on Hamburg," says the United States Strategic Bombing Survey. " Hitler himself thought that further attacks of similar weight might force Germany out of the war." [8]

In March 1945, United States bombers made an even more terrible attack on Tokyo. From the low height of 7,000 feet, they dropped 1,667 tons of incendiaries, with some high explosives too. They burnt fifteen square miles of the city to the ground; 83,000 persons, most of them

---

[8] J. M. Spaight, *Air Power can Disarm*, pp. 74–76; Prentiss, *op. cit.*, pp. 79–80. Prentiss gives an aerial photograph of Hamburg showing the area of fire damage.

civilians, perished in the flames; the heart of Tokyo lay in smoking ruin. This, says Mr. Spaight, "was the most destructive attack ever made from the air, the attacks on Hiroshima and Nagasaki with atomic bombs not excluded." [9]

The United States Strategic Bombing Survey estimated that, in the Allied air attacks on forty-nine German towns and cities, between 75 per cent. and 80 per cent. of the damage and casualties were due to fire. In the last six months of the war against Japan, sixty-five cities were attacked by fire, and on the average 50 per cent. of the cities was destroyed. After the war, United States surveying parties were able to determine that, ton for ton, the incendiaries used against Germany were 4·8 times as effective as high explosive. [10]

## Fire Weapons in Korea and Indo-China

The practice of the 1939 War had so completely demolished the old laws of war that the United Nations Forces in Korea used incendiary weapons from the start. The weapons were extremely effective; a commentator wrote about the mountain fighting in 1952:

> " Infantry dug into hill positions—especially where timber is used instead of concrete—can be burnt out by napalm more quickly and thoroughly than they can be blasted out by explosive. Either way the result is hideous." [11]

Napalm also proved to be a most efficient weapon against tanks. " Experience in the field " (in Korea), says Colston Shepherd,

> " seems to show napalm as a superior weapon to the rocket against tanks. Napalm has been taken to be an

[9] Spaight, *op. cit.*, pp. 151–152. In later attacks fifty-one square miles of Tokyo were destroyed. See also Prentiss, *op. cit.*, pp. 81–82.
[10] *Fire and the Air War*, p. 80. (National Fire Protection Association. Boston, 1946.)
[11] M.G., March 10, 1952.

improvement on the fragmentation bomb for use against troops. . . . A napalm bomb is reported to spread over an area of 100 feet by 150–200 feet. In relation to a tank, this allows such a margin of error that the rocket cannot compete. . . . With napalm a near-miss usually means that the tank is put out, because the intense heat destroys insulation and other rubber fittings, and frequently explodes the ammunition carried inside the tank." [12]

After the Communist forces captured Seoul, the capital of Korea, in 1950, the UN forces burnt it to the ground.[13] The French forces also used incendiary weapons, and in particular napalm bombs from aircraft, throughout the war in Indo-China.

## The Abolition of Incendiary Weapons

There were some protests in 1952 against the cruelty of the napalm bomb. They were inspired by a description of the effects of napalm given by a B.B.C. correspondent in Korea:

"In front of us a curious figure was standing, a little crouched, legs straddled, arms held out from his sides. He had no eyes, and the whole of his body, nearly all of which was visible through tatters of burnt rags, was covered with a hard black crust speckled with yellow pus. A Korean woman by his side began to speak, and the interpreter said: ' He has to stand, sir, cannot sit or lie.' He had to stand because he was no longer covered with a skin, but with a crust like crackling which broke easily." [14]

[12] *Brassey's Annual*, 1952, pp. 343–344.
[13] " So murderous were the enemy's small arms volleys that Col. Puller was obliged to call for another air raid on the city. Planes dropped a fresh rain of napalm fire bombs on districts already consumed by yesterday's dropping of bombs ": N.Y.H.T., September 22, 1950.
    " American flame-throwing tanks stabbed flimsy Korean houses, igniting whole blocks ": N.C., September 27, 1950.
[14] R. Cutforth, *Korean Reporter*, p. 174.

No one can read these words without a feeling of mingled nausea and shame. But Mr. Cutforth goes on to say that napalm is *less* cruel than

> " phosphorus and flame-throwers, which have been with us for years: I would rather die by napalm than by phosphorus. . . . Napalm reaches a temperature of more than 1,000°C. in a few seconds and the vast majority of its victims are killed outright." [15]

So far, this is unanswerable. By the same argument, the atomic bomb at Hiroshima was, in its immediate effect, less terrible than the fire-raids on Hamburg and Tokyo. This is the view of Dr. Bush, who says that, nevertheless, the people of the United States as a whole, " took the use of fire-raids in their stride; *either they did not understand*, or, understanding, they did not object."

Certainly they did not understand. It needed the gift of imagination to take in the fact that the fire-raids on Hamburg and Tokyo were more ghastly in their cruelty to great multitudes of men, women and children, than anything that has happened in modern war. But if the arms race goes on, the potency of the incendiary weapons will certainly increase, and if war should come, they will be used again. [16]

Fire was much used by torturers in bygone days; in a modern fire-raid, it is still a means of torture, but the torture has become a weapon of mass-destruction too. If there is to be any disarmament worthy of the name, the fire weapons must be abolished. Their manufacture, and the training of troops to use them, must be wholly prohibited. These prohibitions can be made effective by the same machinery of inspection and control that is required to enforce the abolition of poison gas. Since incendiary bombs must be delivered by aircraft, the abolition of military aviation will again be the most important of supplementary guarantees.

[15] Letter to M.G., March 17, 1952.
[16] See General Prentiss, *op. cit.*, p. 82.

# 29

## " *Biologicals* "

ON January 3, 1946, the United States War Department
published a Report by Mr. George W. Merck, Special
Consultant for Biological Warfare to the Secretary of War,
which described the work done by his Service during the
1939 War; it said that, in making plans for lasting peace,
" the potentialities of biological warfare cannot safely be
ignored," and it set out what still remain the three most
important facts about this new means of waging war : first,
the major military Powers are all making large-scale
preparations, offensive and defensive, for the use of biological weapons; secondly, these weapons have not yet been
tested in large-scale operations against an enemy; thirdly, it
is still uncertain how effective they would be. But the
potential dangers they involve are so great that they cannot
be ignored in a disarmament treaty; the treaty *must* include
an agreement for biological disarmament by *all* the signatory
Powers.

No government has yet deployed the case for this view in
any document readily available to the public. The United
States Government has published a large number of special
studies on various technical aspects of biological warfare;
using this material, Dr. Theodore Rosebury,[1] who held an
important post in Mr. Merck's Research Service during the
war, General Prentiss [2] of the United States Army, and
others, have published studies on the subject; the British
Home Office have issued a Civil Defence Manual entitled
*Biological Warfare* [3]; the American Association of Scientific
Workers presented a Memorandum on it to the UN General

[1] *Peace or Pestilence*, 1949.
[2] *Civil Defense in Modern War*, 1951.
[3] Pamphlet No. 7, H.M.S.O., 1955.

Assembly in 1947. A brief summary must be made of the salient facts which these documents reveal.

## Historical Development

Biological agents may be used against men, animals or plants. Mr. Merck said in his Report that:

> " there is incontrovertible evidence . . . that in 1915 German agents inoculated horses and cattle leaving United States ports for shipment to the Allies with disease-producing bacteria,"

and other similar attempts were made elsewhere.[4] In 1932, a Commission of the Geneva Disarmament Conference published a Report which said: " Beyond question, in certain countries, preparations are being made for bacterial warfare," and Dr. Madsen, the famous Danish biologist, who was Chairman of the League Health Committee, declared that biological science was sufficiently advanced to render the dissemination of frightful epidemics a possible means of making war. Dr. Rosebury believes that the Japanese may have tried to spread plague among the Chinese in the late 1930s.[5] In any case, Mr. Merck made it plain in his Report that the Japanese were working intensively on biological weapons from 1936 until 1945; Hitler is known to have started large-scale work in 1936.[6] In 1938, Russia, against whom Hitler uttered constant threats, issued a public warning. Marshal Voroshiloff said:

> " If our enemies use such (biological) methods against us, I tell you we are prepared, and fully prepared, to use them also, and to use them against aggressors on their own soil." [7]

It was generally believed that this was no idle boast, and

---

[4] These were recorded by a German, Dr. Hellmut Klotz, at one time high in the counsels of the Reichswehr, in an article published in *Les Annales*, September 14, 1934.
[5] *Op. cit.*, p. 109.
[6] Heinz Liepmann, *Death from the Skies*, pp. 262 *et seq.*, gives many details.
[7] N.Y.T., February 23, 1938.

that by then the Russians' biological work was well advanced.

After the fall of France in 1940, Britain developed her biological research at the Ministry of Supply Station at Porton. In 1942 the United States set up a research station at Camp Detrick, near Frederick, Maryland; before 1945 Camp Detrick had a personnel of close on 4,000.[8] In 1948 the Soviet Army newspaper, *Red Star*, published a description of a biological warfare station which the Japanese set up near Harbin in Manchuria during the 1939 War; *Red Star* alleged that its " capacity was nearly a ton of bubonic plague bacteria a month," and that during the 1939 War the Japanese " used prisoners of war for tests, usually killing them in the process." [9]   Russia is said to have had her main experimental station near the Caspian.

All this work has continued and, no doubt, developed since 1945. The United States Army organised a separate Biological Warfare Command after Mr. Brucker's decision referred to above [10]; no doubt Camp Detrick has been given new and greater resources since then. In 1954 the British Ministry of Supply issued an official statement, saying that it was working on " methods of defence against all possible forms of attack, including even such forms as biological warfare, which are expressly forbidden by the rules of war," and that trials were being carried out.[11] The Russians are known to have many eminent biologists; it would be surprising if they were not as far advanced in the techniques of biological, as they are in those of missile, war.

In short, the arms race in biological weapons has developed with no less intensity than in other fields; and Mr. Brucker's decision shows that the fact that these weapons are " expressly forbidden by the rules of war " is fast losing its restraining power.

[8] Prentiss, *op. cit.*, p. 85.
[9] *Red Star*, July 28, 1948.
[10] See p. 316.
[11] *The Times*, March 12, 1954.

## The Biological *" Agents "*

Dr. Rosebury describes the broad classes of " germs," or " agents " of infection (the British *Manual* calls them " micro-organisms "), which are likely to be used in biological war; bacteria, protozoa, spirochetes, fungi, actinomycetes, pleuropneumonia forms, rickettsiae, and viruses.[12] More than forty of these agents have been considered for possible use in war; some are air-borne; others water- and food-borne; vector-borne (*i.e.*, carried by insects, *e.g.*, fleas), or contact-borne (*i.e.*, contagious). Anthrax may be both air-borne and contact-borne; it is dangerous both to animals and men; brucellosis (undulant fever) may be air-borne, water- and food-borne, and contact-borne. Psittacosis (parrot fever), plague, dysentery, cholera and syphilis are those which promise the best results.

To be useful, says the British *Manual*, an agent must be virulent; tough enough to " withstand destructive forces "; and capable of being produced in bulk. In particular—and this is important—there are only " relatively few biological agents that are suitable for dissemination from aircraft in area cloud attacks." [13] Of all the agents, botulism (food poisoning) and psittacosis are most likely to have these characteristics. Botulism is the most potent of all; such a deadly poison that a single gram contains seven million lethal doses for man. But it is a poison, not a self-propagating disease; and it would be less easy to distribute than psittacosis. For this reason, the American Association of Scientific Workers spoke of psittacosis as the greatest danger; they said that a routine unpurified preparation of this virus contains enough respiratory doses per *millilitre* to kill twenty million men; *i.e.*, a quart of psittacosis virus preparation would contain enough virus to infect more than seven billion human beings, or about three times the total population of the earth. The American scientists went on to say that " even if the efficiency were as low as 0·01 per

12 *Op. cit.*, p. 21.
13 *Manual on Biological Warfare*, p. 8.

cent. the potency of this material would still be extra-
ordinarily high." [14]

## *Delivery of Biological Agents*

The crucial problem of biological warfare is not the production of the agent, but delivery. This might be done by
enemy spies, who could spread infection by bringing in
diseased animals, polluting food, contaminating reservoirs,
and so on. But this would not give a big result; it is only
by the large-scale dissemination of air-borne agents that
biological warfare can become a major weapon of war. The
agents must, in short, be delivered by aircraft, either in
bombs or by sprays, or else by missiles.

Specially designed bombs would, of course, be needed;
bacteria will be destroyed if the bursting charge which
opens the bomb is too powerful; the bomb's fall must be
retarded by a parachute; the bomb will probably be small;
the bacterial culture it contains may be either in liquid or
in powder form. The tanks needed for spraying biological
agents in liquid form from aircraft would, however, be very
like those used for spraying poison gas; agents in powdered
form would need a spray like that used for distributing
DDT against malaria-carrying mosquitoes.

The British *Manual* dismisses the danger of spraying, on
the ground that the aircraft would have to fly so low that
they would be very vulnerable to ground attack. Other
authorities believe that low altitude attacks would have the
advantage that the aircraft fly below the radar screen, and
at modern speeds they might be difficult to bring down.

Some types of biological agents may also be delivered by
missiles. Speaking of the V 1s used by Hitler in 1944, Dr.
Vannevar Bush says: "There was no guarantee that the
warhead would not contain toxic materials instead (of high
explosive). It was a real threat." [15] This supports what is
said by Major-General Chisholm in his statement below.

[14] Memorandum dated September 26, 1947.
[15] *Modern Arms and Free Men*, p. 85.

## Methods of Defence

The British *Manual* frankly explains the difficulties of
defence against biological agents. It says they are
" invisible to the naked eye "; " they can multiply
rapidly "; " during their incubation period there is no
visible indication of their presence." They differ from
chemical agents " and are more difficult to deal with
because they cannot be detected by the senses and, . . .
their presence . . . is not revealed by the use of chemical
detectors "; the process of establishing their presence and
identifying them is " slow and difficult and may take
several days "; " it is very difficult to define infected
areas "; the decontamination or disinfection process for
persistent agents is " slow, laborious and uncertain." [16]

The *Manual* describes many precautionary measures that
might be taken for the defence of civilians; but other
authorities are not optimistic about the defence either of
civilians or of troops. Dr. Selman Waksman, the discoverer
of streptomycin and a Nobel Prize-winner, said in 1954 that
" sulfa drugs and antibiotics . . . should be of great value
in defeating this type of warfare "; but he added:

" The dangerous potentialities are there, however. We
will never feel safe from new diseases and new epidemics
unless the nations of the world find ways and means of
living together in peace." [17]

Dr. Rosebury discusses possible methods of defence; he
points out the inevitable delays in taking action, the
inadequacy of the vaccines available, and the difficulties
involved in the general vaccination of the population. His
conclusion is that there seems to be no adequate defence.[18]

## Is Biological Warfare a Major Danger?

Nevertheless, the British *Manual* appears to discount the
suggestion that biological warfare could cause any great

[16] pp. 13–14.
[17] N.Y.H.T., November 12, 1954.      [18] *Op. cit.*, p. 136.

disaster, like the Black Death which started in China in 1343, reached Europe in 1348, and is estimated to have killed in all 62 million people. The *Manual* says that " startling claims " for biological agents " as a mass destruction weapon " have been made.

> " These claims assume that the agent can be disseminated in a vast number of small dosages with little or no loss from the many hazards to which it would ordinarily be subject, among a population completely unprotected in every sense. The truth about biological warfare lies somewhere between completely untenable claims of this type and those which assume that the difficulties and hazards of dissemination and the natural resistance of the individuals comprising the population would between them reduce the effectiveness of a biological warfare attack to negligible proportions. Just where between these extremes truth lies can be determined only if and when this weapon is ever used in war." [19]

This seems to dismiss the view that " biologicals " may be a weapon of mass destruction. But other authorities take a different view. Dr. Vannevar Bush says :

" The terrors of the possibilities of biological science, turned loose for destructive purposes and guided by skilled minds, are very real." [20]

The American Association of Scientific Workers say biological warfare " is the pre-eminent terror weapon. . . . [It] epitomises the total war that is now or will very soon be ready for use." [21]

Dr. Rosebury says that there is little doubt that biologicals would be effective, and that, if they were used on a large scale, the results would be " *incalculable* " and *might be " irremediable.*" [22]

[19] p. 14.
[20] *Op. cit.*, p. 164.
[21] Memorandum to the UN, September 26, 1947.
[22] *Op. cit.*, p. 136.

Some governments seem to share this view; M. Moch said in the Sub-Committee in 1954 that:

> " some forms of bacteriological warfare now already devised are infinitely more dangerous . . . *are cheaper to manufacture . . . easier to produce . . . they kill far more people than the atomic bomb and moreover inflict ghastly suffering.*" [23]

Very significantly the Russian delegate, Mr. Malik, replied: " M. Moch states that bacteriological weapons *at their present stage of development* are more destructive and more terrible than the hydrogen bomb. . . . *I grant this to be the case.*" [24]

## Major-General Chisholm's Statement

But perhaps Major-General Brock Chisholm is the best qualified and most persuasive witness. Major-General Chisholm was Director-General of the Royal Canadian Army Medical Corps during the latter part of the 1939 War; in that capacity, he was well informed about biological warfare research in Canada, and about the " agents " that were prepared for possible use. At the end of the war he was unanimously selected as the first Director-General of the World Health Organisation. As Director-General of WHO, and since his retirement, he has given many warnings of the dangers of biological warfare. In 1947 he said:

> " Known methods of bacteriological warfare provide the ' final ' offensive weapons and may soon enable even a small country to kill all living persons on any continent very quickly. Any number of millions of human beings can be killed in a few hours by methods now available." [25]

This view was challenged by Mr. Forrestal, then the United States Secretary for Defence.[26] Major-General

[23] Cmd. 9205, 1954, p. 207.
[24] *Loc. cit.*, p. 211.
[25] N.Y.T., October 16, 1947.
[26] N.Y.T., March 13, 1949.

Chisholm was not convinced. In 1949 he told a Press Conference at the UN headquarters in New York that:

> " most of the world's inhabitants will be wiped out in any future war in which virulent bacteria now developed are used as a weapon. . . . One bacteriological weapon, developed late in the Second World War, could wipe out all human life in a given area within six hours and yet leave the area habitable afterwards." [27]

Recent developments have confirmed Major-General Chisholm in this view. At a private conference in Clarens, Switzerland, in September 1957, he delivered a speech, a summary of which was made at the time. This summary is now reproduced with his consent. It recounts some of his personal experiences in the Second World War.

> " 1. British Intelligence learnt without long delay that the German Nazi authorities had begun to work seriously on biological weapons in 1936. We naturally followed suit, and by 1940 all the major Powers were hard at work.
>
> " 2. In 1943–44, when we saw the V 1 launching sites in Northern France and Belgium, we thought that they might be for the use of biological weapons. There was one biological in particular of which we were afraid. It is so deadly that a dose in a microscopic quantity is fatal in six hours. If you could secure perfect distribution to all the world's people (which, of course, is impossible) you could kill everyone in the world with a quantity amounting to about eight ounces.
>
> " 3. This weapon has the further advantage that while it kills everybody in six hours, it is itself oxidised in twelve hours, leaving the ground perfectly safe to occupy, so that there is no danger that the troops of the Power which used it will be contaminated.

[27] *Montreal Gazette*, October 14, 1949.

" 4. A toxoid was developed in Canada which gives protection against this particular weapon, but it requires two doses administered with an interval of some weeks. It is not known how long immunity will last; it has been known to last at least two years, but it may be longer.

" 5. We knew that if the Germans used this biological in their flying bombs they could kill millions of people, and perhaps everybody south of the Tweed, within six hours, and there would be nothing, repeat nothing, that we could do about it.

" 6. In order to warn them that we were ourselves prepared with biological weapons, Chisholm brought over from Canada 235,000 doses of prophylactic toxoid, which was duly administered to 117,500 British, American and Canadian troops. The information that this had been done was carefully fed into the German Intelligence sources, so that they knew that we were ready for biological warfare.

" 7. When at last the V 1 attack was launched in June 1944, and the first flying bomb went off with a big bang, showing that it only contained normal high explosive, the general staffs all heaved an immense sigh of relief. The dangers of biological warfare had not yet been let loose against us.

" 8. We had, of course, stocks of this biological for use in retaliation, if Hitler in fact had used it. *There are very large stocks of this weapon available today.*

" 9. The potential dangers of biological warfare are much greater now than they were in 1944. Research is at present going forward with a view to making the bacteria of the more general diseases, *e.g.*, cholera, typhus, etc., much more virulent, so that the vaccination, etc., now carried out might not serve as a protection to anybody who was infected. This line of investigation is very dangerous to the future of mankind.

" 10. There is at present probably no exchange of information between any nations on this subject, although the major military nations all know that the others are carrying on research. The military authorities of all countries have almost always pursued a policy of total secrecy. In 1939 an American published a somewhat superficial book describing the general character of the biological and chemical weapons which then existed. The United States General Staff authorities traced down every copy and confiscated it; not one remained available to the public.

" 11. This policy has had the dangerous result that public opinion and Parliaments are almost totally without information on the nature and power of biologicals.

" 12. But the most sinister fact about biologicals was the fact that they can be prepared and administered by a very small number of people whom it would be extremely difficult to detect. One really competent biologist, working in a small laboratory, could prepare enough to be decisive in a war against any country."

## *Is Biological Disarmament Possible?*

In 1946 Mr. Merck gave a second warning:

" Above all," he said, " there should be careful and serious consideration of the subject in whatever deliberations take place concerning the implementation of a lasting peace . . . for the potentialities of this type of warfare cannot be ignored. This is the most important peacetime implication of biological warfare." [28]

Is effective, controlled disarmament possible in this field at all? The United States Government said it was in 1952; they submitted a Working Paper to the UN Disarmament Commission in which, starting from the Six Principles, they said:

[28] " Peacetime Implications of Biological Warfare," published in *Chemical and Engineering News*, May 25, 1946.

" Safeguards must be devised to ensure the elimination of bacterial weapons and facilities and appliances for their production and use, along with the elimination of all armed forces and armaments not expressly permitted to States to maintain public order and to meet their Charter responsibilities. The principal safeguards to ensure the elimination of bacterial weapons are to be found in an effective and continuous system of disclosure and verification of all armed forces and armaments. . . . It is proposed that, at appropriate stages . . . agreed measures should become effective providing for the progressive curtailment of production, the progressive dismantling of plants, and the progressive destruction of stockpiles of bacterial weapons and related appliances. Under this programme, with co-operation in good faith by the principal States concerned, all bacterial weapons and all facilities and appliances connected therewith should be completely eliminated from national armaments and their use prohibited." [29]

What detailed measures would be needed to make this policy effective?

## 1. *Prohibition of Preparation, Possession and Use*

There would have to be a clause in the disarmament treaty enjoining on all signatory Powers the complete and unconditional renunciation of the right to prepare or possess biological weapons of any kind, or to use them in any circumstances whatever. The Geneva Conference agreed in 1932 that this must include the renunciation of the right to use them even in retaliation against an aggressor who used them first; they said that, if use in retaliation was allowed, competitive preparation could never be stopped. [30]

[29] 2nd Report of the Disarmament Commission, p. 154.
[30] Conference Documents, Vol. II, p. 372.

## 2. Inspection and Control

There are four main stages in the preparation of biological agents for use in war: (i) research and development; (ii) large-scale or field testing; (iii) manufacture of the containers, sprays, bombs or other devices required for the employment of the agents in battle or against enemy cities or territory; (iv) training of military personnel in use of the agents, and in self-protection against them.

(i) In respect of *research and development*, the same kind of measures as those suggested for nuclear disarmament are required. The same effort should be made to secure the co-operation of biologists as was proposed for physicists.[31] In 1947 Dr. Rosebury urged the bacteriologists of all nations to co-operate in studying the possibilities of effective control. The bacteriologists immediately responded; in July of that year the International Cytological Congress responded to Dr. Rosebury's suggestion; they " resolved to set up a Committee to offer technical advice and assistance to the UN . . . on this subject." [32] This offer was never taken up, but it should be taken up now, and the UN should furnish all the funds and facilities they may require.

All government, university and other biological laboratories should be open to qualified UN Inspectors; the control would evidently be less effective than that for nuclear or chemical weapons; but it would not be worthless.

(ii) and (iv) *Military Depots and Stations.* Inspection and control of military depots and stations would inevitably hamper, and very possibly discover, large-scale field experiments; it might also hamper or discover the secret training of Service personnel in the use of biologicals; it would render impossible the provision of masks, vaccination, or other measures which an intending aggressor might wish to take to protect his troops.

[31] See pp. 302–303.
[32] Quoted by Rosebury, *op. cit.*, p. 179.

(iii) The close *UN inspection of engineering works and military depots* might discover the manufacture, storing or transport of the containers, sprays, bombs, etc., which would be required.  An intending aggressor might take a considerable risk if he began the large-scale manufacture and distribution of such apparatus and appliances.  And if biologicals were to be used as a major weapon, large-scale supplies of these things would be required; very small doses of the agents are lethal, but the wastage in distribution would be so great that large tonnages, and many and repeated deliveries, would be needed to produce a major result.

The United States Government expressed this view with vigour in 1952.  Their delegate in the UN Commission said:

> " It may be true that there is theoretically no fool-proof safeguard which would prevent the concoction of some deadly germs in an apothecary's shop in the dark hours of the night.  But when the United States proposes the establishment of safeguards to ensure the elimination of germ warfare along with the elimination of mass armed forces and all weapons adaptable to mass destruction, it demands what is possible and practical, and not the impossible.  The United States is seeking action to ensure effective and universal disarmament, not excuses for inaction.  Bacterial weapons, to be effective in warfare, require more than the dropping at random of a few infected spiders, flies or fleas.  They require industrial establishments, facilities for maintaining the agents, transport, containers and disseminating appliances.  Such arrangements and facilities will not readily escape detection under an effective and continuous system of disclosure and verification of all armed forces and armaments." [33]

[33] 19th meeting, August 15, 1952.

## 3. *Abolition of Means of Delivery*

Dr. Vannevar Bush wrote in 1951: "Now we have more powerful toxins. The question of their use, of their relative effectiveness, still depends upon methods of delivery . . . There remain three main methods, by projectiles, by aircraft, and subversive methods."[34] Like the British *Manual*, he discounted the results likely to be achieved by saboteurs; this left aircraft and projectiles, which now mean missiles. Of these, Dr. Bush and the authors of the British *Manual* think aircraft are at present the most important. This furnishes another argument, identical with that used about nuclear weapons,[35] for the abolition of military aircraft, and of missiles. This would be the greatest single safeguard against the danger that an aggressor might try to use biologicals to win a war.

## 4. *A General Disarmament Treaty*

But a safeguard of no less importance lies in the fact that biological disarmament will never be agreed to except as part of a general disarmament treaty by which, in gradual stages, drastic reductions in the present levels of armament will be made. This is an important safeguard for the reason stated by Mr. Merck in his Report: "Biological warfare is still in the realm of theory rather than fact, in the sense that it has not actually been used in military operations." An intending aggressor might hope to evade the controls suggested above, especially if military aircraft and missiles were *not* abolished. But he would be rash indeed if, his other armaments having been drastically reduced, he relied for victory on a weapon whose efficacy was still in doubt.

## 5. *The International Organisation of Biological Research*

One other safeguard, of a "positive" kind, might also help. The biological research done at Camp Detrick, at

34 *Op. cit.*, pp. 124–125.
35 See pp. 308–309.

Porton, and in Canada during the 1939 War produced results which are, or may be, of the highest value for the health both of men and animals. It developed improved techniques which, says Dr. Rosebury, may be "as fruitful for human welfare" as Pasteur's pioneering work.[36] Camp Detrick, Porton, and the other great research stations for biological war, have resources, apparatus, and skilled personnel never given to bacteriology before. If they could be used in common as international centres, with the leading specialists of France, Germany, Russia, Japan, Denmark and the rest; if research in all countries could be pooled and guided on a common plan designed to exterminate the natural plagues of man—tuberculosis, malaria, influenza, and many more—what a revolution in thinking might that not produce, and what prospects of relief from suffering might it not offer to mankind?

## *Conclusion*

If all that is proposed above were carried out, there might still be risks in a general international agreement to abolish the present preparations for biological war. But would they be as great as the risk of allowing the present competitive preparation to go on?

[36] *Op. cit.*, p. 197.

# 30

## *Missiles and the Missile Race*

" In the long haul," said General Schriever, the Commandant of the United States Western Missile Development Division, at Los Angeles in 1957, " our safety as a nation may depend upon our achieving space superiority. *Several decades from now* the important battles may not be sea battles or air battles, but space battles "—and the United States must not lag in the struggle for " space supremacy." [1] The officer who does the official briefing for journalists and VIPs at General Schriever's headquarters begins his talk like this: " Flight time from Los Angeles to Moscow is just a matter of minutes. . . . Flight time from Moscow to Los Angeles is exactly the same. . . . The race for the ICBM is a race we cannot afford to lose." [2]

In 1955 more than 100 German-born rocket experts at the United States Army Redstone Arsenal in Huntsville, Alabama, acquired United States nationality. Among them was Dr. Wernher von Braun, chief of the guided missile development division of the Arsenal.[3] They had all helped Hitler to develop the V 1 and V 2, which he launched on London in 1944. Missile warfare is one of the bequests which Hitler left mankind. It is a commonplace among those who write about armament policy to say that the general development of missile warfare was " inevitable " once the V 1 and V 2 had appeared. It *was* inevitable, unless the nations who conquered Hitler were ready to end the arms race after 1945. Events have proved that they were not, and so the development of missile weapons has continued with increasing intensity for a dozen years. General Schriever's conviction that it will continue for

[1] *The Times*, June 13, 1957.
[2] Bruce Rothwell, N.C., March 12, 1957.
[3] N.Y.H.T., March 28, 1955.

" several decades from now," and his vision of what space warfare will then be like, makes it essential to consider if some other policy cannot be found.

## Air Breathing and Ballistic Missiles

There are two main categories of missiles:

First, those which, like the V 1, approximate to pilotless aircraft, operate within the earth's atmosphere, use the oxygen of the atmosphere in the engines which propel them, and are therefore called " air-breathing." They travel at relatively low speeds, but they can be steered by various kinds of guidance mechanisms over the whole of their course, and right on to the targets they are intended to destroy.

Second, those which approximate to the artillery shell, are driven by rocket propulsion, and require no oxygen. They may go up to great heights, far outside the earth's atmosphere; they travel at immense speeds, up to twenty times the speed of sound (Mach 20): but they are not guided, except in the early stages of their journey; they are rather aimed, like a shell or a bullet from a gun.

## The Four Military Uses of Missiles

The missiles now being developed serve four different military purposes. They are for use:

1. From surface (land or sea) to surface. These missiles replace land or naval artillery; in the longer ranges they replace the bomber.

2. From air to surface. These are only for use from aircraft, and they replace the conventional bomb and torpedo. As the missiles may have a range of many miles, and can be guided to their targets, they enable an aircraft to accomplish its mission without entering the zone where it will be subjected to the heaviest attack by AA guns, short-range AA missiles, or enemy fighters.

3. From air to air. These again are only for use by aircraft; they replace the cannon and unguided rockets previously used by fighters to attack bombers, or by bombers to defend themselves against fighters.

4. From surface to air. These are at present only for use against enemy aircraft, although anti-missile missiles are also planned. They replace the AA guns; the British Defence White Paper of 1957 forecasts that they will also soon take over the task of air defence from the piloted fighter.

Missiles are also generally classified by range:

1. *Short range missiles.* These originally had ranges of eighteen to twenty miles, like the first surface-to-surface Corporal, mentioned below, and the first British AA missiles. But " short-range " is now used to include everything up to 200 miles; this is the longest range the United States Army are allowed to have; anything longer is confided to the United States Navy and Air Force.

2. IRBM. These include missiles with a range from 200 to 1,500 miles. But not all missiles with this range are ballistic; the United States " air-breathing " Matador has a range of 500–1,000 miles.

3. ICBM. These include missiles with a range from 1,500 to 5,500 miles. Again, the United States Snark, which is inter-continental, is an air-breathing machine.

## How Missiles Work

*Air-breathing missiles*

There is nothing unfamiliar about the propulsion of an air-breathing missile; it is propelled by a jet or a ram-jet engine, and uses its wings for lift.

It may be guided in either of two ways: by commands given by ground or airborne observers, who radio orders to the weapon, and " tell " it what course to take; or by mechanisms contained within the missile itself. A missile, for example, may contain a radar transmitter which makes a beam on to the target—*e.g.*, an enemy bomber; the missile will then " ride " the beam until it strikes and destroys the bomber, or is exploded close to the bomber by a proximity fuse. An alternative mechanism makes the missile " home " on the heat-energy given off by the target; the missile follows the path of the heat to its source, the target.

## Ballistic missiles

The problem of ballistic missiles is more complex.

" Rocket engines . . . set in the tail burn various combinations of highly volatile chemicals. They spew hot gases out of the tail and the reaction lifts the rocket. The fuels can be liquid or solid propellants; most of those used for the giant rockets so far are liquids— alcohol and liquid oxygen for the V 2; acid-aniline combinations for the United States Army's Corporal." [4]

The ICBM has a propulsion system which is built in " stages ";

" several rocket motors are hooked up either in tandem or in parallel. After one of the motors utilises its available supply of fuel it drops off, and the missile, lightened, is pushed upward and along its trajectory faster and faster by another motor. By far the greater part of the weight of an ICBM is fuel. . . . In the first three or four minutes of flight all of the fuel will be burned, and at point of burn-out the rocket-engines will drop off, and the warhead and upper rocket body will continue climbing at terrific speeds." [5]

A ballistic missile is " aimed " rather than guided. The problem is the same as that of putting an artillery shell on to its target, but greatly magnified by the enormous ranges of the missiles. The exact co-ordinates of the target must be known, and the missile when launched must be travelling at exactly the right speed towards the right point in space.

[4] Hanson Baldwin, N.Y.T. *Weekly Review*, April 29, 1956.
[5] *Ibid*.

The course of the ICBM is calculated in advance; as it climbs, electronic devices report what it is doing, and if necessary its course can be adjusted by the ground control station—either by swivelling the motors, or by altering the angle of the vanes which are set in the path of the jet blast. But this control lasts only until the rocket-engines drop off. After that, the missile is in " free " flight, and no one can guide it any more.

But new guidance systems are now projected, which will keep the ballistic missile on its proper course after control from the ground has ceased.   They are called " inertial "; they are installed inside the missile, and require no aid from radar beams, " star-tracking " or anything else; they cannot, therefore, be detected or jammed by enemy action. They consist of " ultra-precise gyroscopes," " accelerometers," and other automatic electronic mechanisms.[6] The electronic brain " remembers " where the rocket started and what is its destination, and causes the other instruments to make the necessary adjustments to keep it on its course.

Every missile is a miracle of engineering.  It is founded on three sciences: supersonic aerodynamics; miniature electronics; and these immensely intricate new systems of propulsion.  A small air-to-air missile, the British " Fireflash," has 15,000 component parts; " a single failure of any of the components leads to a complete catastrophic failure of the missile." [7]  An ICBM has 300,000 parts [8]— pumps, gyroscopes, computers, and thousands of radio valves.   A thrust equivalent to 10,000 horsepower is obtained from a simple tube twelve inches in diameter.[9] To make a missile which will carry three rocket motors on

[6] Mr. Ansel Talbert, N.Y.H.T., October 19, 1957.
[7] *The Times*, August 15, 1957.  In 1957 Mr. J. E. Serby, Director-General of Guided Missiles, Ministry of Supply, discussing this problem, said: " If component reliability does not . . . improve at the same rate as the complexity of equipment is increasing, a serious situation might well arise," both for missiles and military aircraft: *The Times*, November 22, 1957.
[8] R. Witkin, N.Y.T., April 7, 1957.
[9] Bristol Aeroplane Co. advertisement in *Economist*, October 23, 1954.

its back, and stay on its course when each of them successively drops off and the next takes over, is a technical achievement almost equal to the release of nuclear energy. When that has been achieved, an H-warhead must be designed which will withstand the immense heat generated by the friction of the rocket's re-entry into the earth's atmosphere. After that, a large enough number of the missiles must be made to be decisive, the launching sites must be constructed, and the troops must be trained to maintain and operate them.

## Missiles and H-Warheads

All missiles have one grave defect from the military point of view: they are much more costly than the artillery shell, and yet, like the shell, they can be used only once.

The ballistic missile has another defect; it can achieve great ranges, but at these ranges it is extremely difficult to make it strike the earth again sufficiently near its target to serve a useful military purpose. An IRBM, for example, with a range of 1,500 miles, would have an average error of at least two miles; even with an A-warhead this might be too much to make the missile of practical military use.

Both these defects were overcome when it was discovered, in 1953, how to make an H-warhead small enough and light enough to be carried by an IRBM or an ICBM. Major-General Brentall, Assistant Chief of Staff of the USAF, told a Congressional Committee that " the advent of light-weight high-yield warheads made ballistic missiles attractive, because it simplified many problems and insured that thermonuclear weapons would be light and handy enough to be carried by a long-range missile of reasonable size." [10]

Views about the General's adjective may differ; only a missile enthusiast would have said " attractive." But the point he made was fully valid; H-warheads cause sufficient

[10] N.Y.H.T., April 30, 1956.

devastation to justify the cost of a missile that can be used only once; they destroy so great an area that an error of five to ten miles in their accuracy is quite " acceptable."

## The Missile Race: United States, Russia, Britain

The leading military Powers are now engaged in a desperate race for "missile supremacy." This is more costly, and more dangerous, than their earlier race in nuclear-weapon-carrying bombers.

### U.S.A.

The United States have 110,000 workers employed on producing missiles. They have thirty-nine different missiles sufficiently developed to have been given names. Ten of them are already " operational," five with the Navy, three with the Army, and two with the Air Force.[11]

The thirty-nine in use, in production, or "under development" vary in size from the Mighty Mouse—so small that a fighter plane " shot 194 . . . in one pass " [12]; the Falcon, which weighs 100 pounds; up to the Atlas, which is intended to have a range of 5,500 miles, and which, when ready to fire, will weigh 100 tons.

The most successful air-breathing types are the Matador and the Snark.

The Matador flies at supersonic speed, at 35,000 feet, and has a range between 700–1,000 miles.[13] There is a squadron of Matadors on Formosa,[14] and others in Europe and Korea.

The Snark has a range of 5,000 miles—it is inter-continental. It flies at 700 m.p.h. at 50,000 feet, but it reaches greater, supersonic, speeds as it descends on its target. A first production order for Snarks was placed in 1957; it is believed that the contract was for about seventy.

[11] R. Witkin, N.Y.T., February 5, 1958.
[12] N.Y.T., March 5, 1957.
[13] N.Y.T., February 5, 1958.
[14] *The Times*, May 7, 1957.

The most successful short-range missiles are the Army's A.A. Nike, now protecting eighteen industrial centres in the United States; the Army's surface-to-surface Corporal, with a range of ninety miles, and an atomic warhead about as powerful as the Hiroshima bomb, now furnished to United States troops in Europe, and to the British Army; and the Navy's surface-to-surface anti-aircraft missile, the Terrier.

The most successful United States intermediate range ballistic missile is the Jupiter. It is alleged to have travelled 3,600 miles in 1956 [15]; it certainly did travel 1,500 miles in 1957.[16] It can be launched from a ship. It goes 300 miles up into space, and travels at 10,000 m.p.h.

The ICBM Atlas has had no successful long-range trial. Designed to have a range of 5,500 miles it will go up 600 miles into space, will travel at 15,000 m.p.h.—Moscow to New York in twenty minutes; it will, like the Jupiter, carry an H-warhead powerful enough to destroy any city in the world. The United States have other ICBM projects which are rivals to the Atlas, but the trials of none of them are yet complete.

*Russia*

Some military commentators have said consistently since 1945 that the Russians were ahead in missiles. The Russian forces used many types of rockets in the 1939 War; they captured as many German experts as the Western Powers; they have done large-scale research and development ever since. In 1955 the Killian Committee reported to the United States National Security Council that Russia would enjoy " an important predominance in inter-continental guided missiles from 1960–65." [17] This prediction seemed to be confirmed by the successful trials of two Russian ICBMs in 1957,[18] and by the launching of the first earth satellites.

[15] N.Y.T., September 7, 1957.          [16] N.Y.T., August 14, 1957.
[17] N.Y.H.T., September 21, 1955.        [18] *The Times*, September 18, 1957.

A Russian expert, Major-General Pokrovsky, wrote an article in 1957 which no doubt described their successful ICBM. He says that " the major part of the flight of a modern inter-continental ballistic rocket takes place at an altitude of 1,000 kilometres." The rocket would then plunge to its target at an " unimaginable speed " which " may be 25,000 kilometres an hour." The essential characteristic of the modern rocket, he says, is its great accuracy. " It can be assumed that possible errors amount to no more than ten to twenty kilometres (six to twelve miles)." Since these rockets can carry hydrogen warheads, " their accuracy guarantees the destruction of any given target." The launching sites, he adds, are small, easy to erect, and easy to camouflage.[19]

The Russian success with the IRBM may be more practically important than their ICBM. " The Russians are known," said Mr. Hanson Baldwin in 1957, " to have test-fired about fifty rockets at a range of about 800 miles. This would indicate that Moscow may soon be ready to standardise and start production of an IRBM . . . The Russians seem to have a development lead in the IRBM category. Even though the range of the weapon they are testing is only 800 miles, this is sufficient to put virtually all of the Allied bases and positions in Europe, including Britain, within range of positions now occupied by Soviet troops." [20] In 1957 Mr. Sandys said there was " every reason to believe " that they had developed a " rocket with a nuclear warhead " and that its range " would probably be sufficient to reach Britain." [21] It is believed that the Russians have stockpiled great numbers of missiles of shorter range, and it is reported that they have prepared a complete system of

---

[19] Maj-Gen. G. I. Pokrovsky, *Sovyetskaya Avyatsya*. Quoted by M. G., August 29, 1957. He has since described the guidance system: " Radio waves form a sort of tunnel." Mr. Maddox says it could be jammed. M.G., January 23, 1958.

[20] N.Y.T. *Weekly Review*, March 3, 1957.

[21] *Hansard*, February 13, 1957. Captain Liddell-Hart confirms that Russian IRBMs were then reaching targets 1,000 miles away. Brighton Conference Paper No. 26, p. 3.

launching sites, pointing at Sweden, Norway and other countries of Western Europe.

It is evident that the Russian effort to develop missiles has been conducted on a gigantic scale, and that their scientists and engineers have been given all the resources and facilities they could desire. (Sir J. Cockcroft says that the Sputniks must have cost £300m.) Perhaps Mr. Khruschev had more grounds than usual for his claim: " I shall not be revealing any military secrets if I tell you that we now have all the rockets we need; long-range rockets, rockets of intermediate range, and close-range rockets. Of course, these are not the limits of what can be achieved, for engineering is not marking time; but these means fully ensure our defence." [22]

## Britain

It would be a mistake to think that Britain is wholly out of the missile race. So far the work has been mainly confined to short-range surface-to-air, or surface-to-surface, missiles for anti-aircraft and naval tasks. But by 1953 there had been 1,500 test firings at the Woomera range in Australia [23]; there have since been 1,000 at Aberporth in Cardigan Bay, and others at Larkhill. [24] In 1956 more than 350 firms were " already deeply concerned in guided weapon development." [25] Britain was spending in 1956, " at a conservative estimate," £50m. a year on missiles. [26] It is unlikely that British scientists and engineers will have failed to produce extremely serviceable weapons.

Mr. Sandys said in Australia in 1957 that " our emphasis is now being placed on the inter-continental missile, which can carry an atomic warhead." [27]

[22] Mr. Khruschev to Mr. James Reston, reported in *Soviet News*, October 14, 1957.
[23] M.G., August 25, 1953.
[24] *The Times*, February 21, 1956.
[25] M.G., May 9, 1957.
[26] Hugh McLeave, N.C., October 24, 1956.
[27] N.Y.H.T., August 21, 1957.

The missile race has reached a point of great intensity. Governments are throwing unlimited resources into the effort to gain "supremacy," as they did in the naval race before 1914. As then, the race is causing grave anxiety. The feeling it has aroused is shown by the words of a respected United States commentator. If there were more sense of urgency about the United States Government's missile programme, this commentator said, together with absolute priority, "Atlas might be in production two years ahead of the most hopeful present schedule—perhaps even this side of 1960. It may sound melodramatic to say so, but these two years could make the difference between national life and death." [28]

## Progress and Accuracy of Missiles

The Russians publicise their successes, and conceal their failures. The United States publicise their failures too. General Pokrovsky writes as though the Russian ICBM is so well tested, is so reliable and accurate, that it will soon be in quantity production. It may be so, but it seems unlikely that there will be many of them for a number of years.

It would be equally unwise to attach too much importance to the failures in the United States. The Snark had many unsuccessful tests; one got loose, and lies still undiscovered in the jungles of Brazil; at one time people spoke of the "Snark-infested waters of the Caribbean." [29] But in 1957 the Snark flew from California to Washington, D.C., and landed in a circle ten yards across.[30] Large-scale production orders have been placed. There is no reason to doubt that similar success would come with Jupiter and Atlas too; stories of six missile tests going awry in recent months [31] have little meaning. The experts often learn more from failure than from success.

[28] S. Alsop, N.Y.H.T., March 14, 1955.
[29] R. Witkin, N.Y.T., January 22, 1957.
[30] N.Y.H.T., September 20, 1957.          [31] *The Times*, June 13, 1957.

No missile will ever score 100 per cent. hits on its target. Indeed, the head of Hitler's missile research, Dr. Dornberger, has said that " if 100 missiles were fired, perhaps twenty-five would land on the wrong *country*." [32] The dangers involved in their use are illustrated by the story that one Atlas, after launching, turned back and headed for the United States. They will always be dangerous weapons —30 per cent. of Hitler's V 2s failed at launching, due either to engine or guidance trouble.[33] But 40 per cent. of the V 1s and V 2s hit London—a far better record than that of British bombing in its early stages, *e.g.*, in 1941. In ten months V 1s and V 2s killed 24,000 people; in fifty months Hitler's bombers killed 37,000 people. It is said that Nike, at its first public showing, only got one certain kill in eight firings, though the United States Army claimed more. But one in eight is incomparably better than any other form of AA fire.[34]

The true conclusion from experience up to date is that " though the missile era has been born, it is still in its infancy." [35] Ten years ago Mr. Hanson Baldwin wrote: " Today missiles are still relatively inaccurate, chiefly valuable for use in barrage fire or against target areas. Tomorrow they will be ocean-spanning, and all but human." [36] It is already clear that his prophecy will come true.

## Missiles and Submarines

The efficacy of missiles, and especially of the IRBM, with ranges of 200 to 1,500 miles, may be enormously increased by the fact that they can be fired from submarines. The United States Government finds this plan " attractive," not only because submarines reach distant targets with smaller

---

[32] *The Times*, August 22, 1957.
[33] Dr. von Braun, to United States Senate Sub-Committee on the Air Force. 1957 Report, pp. 783–791.
[34] N.Y.T., May 24, 1956.
[35] Washington Correspondent of *The Times*, June 13, 1957.
[36] *The Price of Power*, p. 91.

missiles, but because they need no bases, and are not subject
to the veto of a foreign government. A United States
project is in hand for a submarine to fire an H-missile
(Polaris) without even coming to the surface of the sea.[37]
But this is of minor importance. If an aggressor planned
a large-scale attack, he would send his submarines under
water to the points from which they could attack the targets
they were ordered to destroy; it would be impossible to
track them, and in a matter of minutes they could fire their
missiles from the surface, and submerge again before the
unsuspecting victim could prepare his counter-attack. This
might make the IRBM a far more effective weapon than the
ICBM; every target in Britain and nearly every target in
the U.S.A. could easily be reached.

Russia, Senator Jackson told the United States Senate in
1957, already has submarines which can launch missiles
with a range of 200 miles; she will soon increase the range
to 1,000 or 1,500 miles.[38] She now has " more than 400
submarines. Nazi Germany at the start of World War II
had less than sixty and was able to tie up the North
Atlantic. At the rate Russia is building, she will have 1,000
submarines by 1960." [39]

## Missiles and Air Forces

Missiles are immensely expensive; a Snark costs $1m., and
can be used only once; before Nike's first public test it had
cost $1,000m.; it costs the United States Government
$20,000 to train a missile technician. But there is an offset
on the other side; missiles will undoubtedly reduce the
numbers and the cost of the military aircraft which
governments now maintain.

Indeed, they have already begun to do so. In 1956 the
United States Secretary for Defence, Mr. Wilson, " called

---

[37] M.G., January 18, 1958.
[38] Chairman, Military Applications Sub-Committee of the Joint Congressional
Committee on Atomic Energy, reported in M.G., May 28, 1957.
[39] Sen. Jackson, N.Y.H.T., January 30, 1957.

for a cut in the 137 Wing goal of the United States Air Force because of the increasing power of Army AA rockets and missiles (Corporal, Honest John and Redstone) for battlefield support "[40]; the United States Air Force accordingly scrapped four Wings of its tactical Air Command.[41] General Twining, the Chairman of the United States Chiefs of Staff, said that Matadors would replace other Air Force Groups.[42] Altogether the target for the United States Air Force had been reduced by March 1957 by fourteen Wings—a Wing may have from thirty to seventy-five aircraft.[43] In 1957–58 the U.S.A.F. ordered 350 fewer aircraft than in 1956–57, but *more* missiles, especially Matadors and Bomarcs.[44]

The 1957 British White Paper on Defence announced that research and development on supersonic bombers and fighters was to be stopped, because their task could be better done by missiles.[45]

> " The fact that the Soviets have cut back sharply on production of their long-range Bison bombers has been absolutely confirmed by the (United States) Intelligence. And logic suggests that they would not do so unless they were already producing operational ICBMs to replace the bombers." [46]

This may explain why Mr. Khruschev said so confidently that bombers could be " thrown on the fire," and that " we are now entering a period when fighters and bombers will have to be consigned to museums, because they have already been superseded by rockets." [47] General Twining strongly disagrees; he says that missiles will not be accurate enough to " replace bombers entirely " [48]; and no doubt bombers will still be used for years. But the day can be foreseen,

40 N.Y.T., November 27, 1956.
41 Hanson Baldwin, N.Y.T. *Weekly Review*, January 20, 1957.
42 M.G., August 15, 1957.
43 Hanson Baldwin, N.Y.T., March 15, 1957.
44 *The Times*, April 23, 1957.
45 Cmnd. 124, para. 61, p. 9.
46 S. Alsop, N.Y.H.T., October 15, 1957.
47 M.G., October 9, 1957.
48 M.G., August 15, 1957.

and it may be near at hand, when most of the bombing and nearly all the interception will be done by rockets. And Mr. Khruschev was certainly right in saying that " when the guns begin to boom, the rockets will begin to fly." [49]

## The Anti-Missile Missile

From the point of view of national defence, the chief significance of the switch from aircraft to missiles is not that missiles are even more costly; it is that they are even harder to intercept. Mr. Hanson Baldwin always calls them " the least stoppable " of weapons.[50]

Service experts maintain, however, that they can be stopped. General Gavin, the Chief of United States Army Research, said in 1957 that the Army's goal was " a 100 per cent. effective air defence system." [51] His colleague General Daley said: " We are confident that we can achieve a successful counter-weapon against ballistic missiles . . . in time to meet the described threat of 1960 or 1961 " [52]; and United States scientists have worked out in theory a system of defence, and initial contracts have been signed. Mr. Hanson Baldwin has described it thus:

> " Huge radar antennae—as big as football fields— capable of picking up the enemy rocket as soon as it rises above the curvature of the earth; high speed calculating machines and a system of 10,000 mile-an-hour intercepting missiles, with electronic and homing guidance and nuclear warheads, may actually, in years to come, be able to seek out, and destroy an ICBM in flight, like a bullet intercepting another bullet." [53]

The nuclear warhead of the intercepting missile, exploded by a proximity fuse, would, by the heat it generated, burn the conventional high explosive of the triggering device of the enemy bomb before it could go off.

[49] *Ibid*.
[50] *e.g.*, N.Y.T., September 11, 1956.
[51] N.Y.T., June 15, 1957.
[52] N.Y.H.T., June 20, 1956.
[53] N.Y.T., June 3, 1956.

Thus the whole enemy missile, including the fission and fusion explosives, would be harmlessly vapourised in outer space.[54]

Mr. Baldwin does not think that this system of defence promises to give a 100 per cent. result. He calls it " minimal "; he says:

> " Even radar will not be able to pick up the ballistic missile until it is falling toward its target at the rate of 12,000 to 15,000 miles an hour. In time it is quite possible that some sort of an anti-missile system may be devised. But in the meantime, and even if and when such a defence is developed, the best defence will be more emphatically than ever, offence . . . the capability of retaliating with crippling blows." [55]

This is to say that missiles are, of all weapons, those which most certainly and most devastatingly help surprise attack. Dr. A. H. Compton's view upon the point may be recalled; it was even more emphatic.[56] It may safely be said, therefore, that there is not now, and there will not soon be, any effective defence against missiles. This would be true, even if General Schriever were not also at work on another missile to counter the anti-missile missile.[57] The layman, indeed, will not readily believe that missiles will ever be made which, themselves vertically ascending at fifteen times the speed of sound, can be relied on to intercept other missiles falling at twenty times the speed of sound. Nor will he feel confident that the lives of millions of human beings can safely be entrusted to the simultaneous functioning of several thousand electronic valves, some of them being subjected to severe strain inside a rocket driven at stupendous speed by a motor of stupendous power. He will ask whether there is not a better way by which the dangers of missile aggression can be met.

[54] Mr. M. D. Martin, Head of the Weapons Engineering Division of the University of California Radiation Laboratory, N.Y.T., June 14, 1957.
[55] N.Y.T. *Weekly Review*, August 4, 1957.
[56] " It would appear foolhardy to rely for safety " on stopping missiles, *op. cit.*, p. 312.                                             [57] See p. 382.

# 31

## Missile Disarmament: Total or Partial Abolition

"This" (the ICBM) "is really a matter of deterrence," said General Schriever in 1957; "we have to build it as a deterrent and therefore it is a weapon of peace."[1] This is a reasonable and satisfactory proposition to a missile expert. It makes nonsense of the governments' talk about disarmament.

There is a better way of dealing with the missile danger than simply trusting to deterrence, and hoping that some day a more or less successful anti-missile missile may be made. It is proposed that missiles should be altogether abolished by the disarmament treaty.[2]

### Missiles and Qualitative Disarmament

This would be an obvious and a necessary part of any treaty in which the principle of qualitative disarmament is applied.[3] If missiles are abolished, it will much reduce an aggressor's hope of a sudden and overwhelming surprise attack; it will correspondingly increase the victim's hope of successful national defence. This is true of *all* missiles, whether they carry conventional or nuclear warheads, whether they are large or small. The danger to national defence of nuclear warheads, and especially of H-warheads, is much greater than that of the conventional high explosive used in V 1s and V 2s. But no one can doubt that V 1s and V 2s were aggressive weapons, which helped attack against defence. Modern missiles with conventional warheads would be more dangerous still; they should, therefore, on

[1] N.C., March 12, 1957.
[2] See pp. 382–383.
[3] See Chap. 33.

376

the principle of qualitative disarmament, be abolished altogether and at once.

But the fact that virtually any missile can now carry a nuclear warhead greatly strengthens the case for abolition. It is still the declared policy of all the governments to abolish all nuclear weapons in the end. If this is ultimately done, then, as President Eisenhower said in 1956, most missiles will become quite useless.[4] If the governments are serious in what they say about abolishing nuclear weapons, the immediate abolition of missiles will save appalling waste.

The governments constantly repeat that, even if existing stocks of nuclear weapons are not abolished, it is nevertheless their ardent hope that none of these weapons, and above all no H-bombs, shall ever be used. As was argued in Chapter 25, the abolition of missiles would be the most effective way of ensuring this generally desired result.

If these propositions are accepted, it is clear that the proposal in the Western Governments' " package " plan of 1957 is quite inadequate. They suggested that " a technical committee " should " study the design of an inspection system which would make it possible to assure that the sending of objects through outer space will be exclusively for peaceful and scientific purposes." [5]

This would leave the way open to an intensive race in air-breathing missiles; their range, speed and power would be constantly increased, and their guidance systems, like that of the British Bloodhound, rendered impervious to jamming or other interference by the defending State. It would also leave the way open to a race in short-range ballistic missiles, which, like air-breathing missiles, would serve as a delivery system for an aggressor's secret stock of nuclear bombs.

The Russian proposal of March 1957 was not very clearly worded, but it can only mean the total abolition of all

---

[4] " It is a . . . paradox to urge that we work just as hard as we know how on the guided missile, and that we stop all research on the H-bomb, because one without the other is rather useless ": President Eisenhower, quoted in the N.Y.H.T., April 27, 1956.

[5] Cmnd. 333, p. 98.

missiles that can be used for war. Mr. Zorin said that "short and medium range rockets . . . are no less dangerous to the security of States" than the ICBM; Russia

> "considers necessary a complete prohibition of A- and H-weapons, including the use of all types of rocket missiles . . . which are suitable for employment as A- and H-weapons." [6]

The text of the Russian plan reads thus:

> "International control shall be instituted over guided rockets in order to ensure that all types of such rockets which are suitable for use as A- and H-weapons shall be used exclusively for peaceful purposes." [7]

It is, perhaps, possible to read this formula as being intended to permit the manufacture, possession and use of missiles with conventional warheads, and it is believed that Russia had begun to make large stocks of missiles with conventional warheads before the nuclear warhead had been devised. But a missile which will take a conventional warhead will also take a nuclear warhead; Mr. Zorin's words quoted above are really quite clear; so are Mr. Khruschev's speeches. There seems no doubt that Russia was proposing the total abolition of all missiles in March 1957.

If the general principle of abolition is accepted, must there be no exceptions to the rule? Are not small air-to-air and surface-to-air missiles effective against bomber attack?

This raises the question, also mentioned in Chapter 25, whether bombers are not weapons which cause mass destruction and help surprise attack; it will be considered further in Chapter 34. If bombers are abolished, as they should be, then the small anti-bomber missiles cease to have a *raison d'être*. But if bombers are *not* abolished, and if, for that reason, agreement is not reached on the general abolition of all missiles, it would be relatively simple to fix a maximum size for those which the disarmament treaty would allow.

---

[6] Sub-Committee, March 18, 1957, pp. 25–26.     [7] Cmnd. 333, p. 27.

If they were restricted, *e.g.*, to one ton laden weight (*i.e.*, with fuel) they would remain effective for short-range AA work; and this would be a restriction which it would be possible to control.

## *The Control of the Abolition of Missiles*

But control would be much simpler, and more certainly effective, if the manufacture, use and possession of *all* missiles were forbidden. In that case, inspection could beyond all doubt ensure that the treaty was faithfully observed.

There are three main reasons why control by Inspection could be made 100 per cent. effective:

1. Missiles, even small missiles, are a big engineering job. The British AA supersonic homing missile, the Bloodhound, weighs a ton. Its manufacture could never be concealed from Inspectors who had the right to visit all engineering shops. The Corporal is forty-five feet long and weighs five tons; the Snark is seventy feet long and weighs twenty tons; no such missile could ever be concealed.

2. Surface-to-air and surface-to-surface missiles (these two categories cover twenty-nine out of the thirty-nine missiles being developed by the United States) cannot work without elaborate radar systems: the early warning system; the tactical control radar, which locates the hostile target in the air; the radar in the missile itself; the fire-control system. These would make the manufacture of the missile, and the siting of its launcher, much harder to conceal.

> "The successful development of . . . a (missile) system calls for very large resources in manpower, floor space and special facilities. . . . Such a (production) team must also be supported by elaborate research facilities as well as having within its control extensive production resources." [8]

All this could hardly be concealed.

[8] E. L. Beverley, "How a Guided Weapons System Works," *The New Scientist*, May 16, 1957, pp. 9–11.

3. Missiles must be subjected to elaborate and constant tests; troops must be trained to maintain them and to use them in the field. The testing and the training could not be kept secret from UN Inspectors with the right to move freely both by air and on the ground.

In short, if the nations desire to free themselves from the deadly menace of missile war, they have only to decide to do so; unlike nuclear weapons, missiles present no problem of control.

## Missiles and Budgetary Limitation

" A missile system calls for very large resources "; even small, short-range missiles are very costly; *e.g.*, the British Bloodhound costs £30,000; the United States Terrier, without its launcher, £60,000. This means that budgetary limitation will furnish another factor of control. Whether there were total abolition, or abolition of all missiles of over, *e.g.*, one ton, it would be impossible for a government to divert undetected the large sums of money needed to produce and to maintain such weapons and to give their troops the long and costly training needed for their use.

## The Need for Early Action

But if any kind of missile disarmament is ever to be done, then the sooner the necessary decisions are taken the better it will be. The longer the present developments continue, the harder they will be to stop; greater and greater vested interests will grow up; more and more armed forces will be reorganised around the missiles; more and more nations will add them to their armament—even Japan has purchased Swiss Oerlikon missiles [9]; as these things happen, the resistance to their abolition will be correspondingly increased. The competition for missile export orders to the

[9] M.G., November 22, 1957.

nations which do not make them has already begun, and it is becoming an unhealthy influence in world affairs.

Moreover, if the production of missiles is continued, and they are distributed in large numbers to their launching sites, the control of any subsequent disarmament would be much harder than it would be today, and the risks of secret stocks would be much greater. The V 1s and V 2s were beaten because, before the first was used, the Allies had discovered and heavily bombarded 450 of the 500 launching sites which Hitler had prepared. If the launching sites have been constructed before the disarmament treaty enters into force, and if they are scattered in forests, mountains, or other places where they can be camouflaged, the UN Inspectors might find them difficult to detect.

In any case, there is no sense in allowing an immense world-wide missile system to develop, and then deciding later to do without it after all. The governments at the Washington Conference of 1922 decided that they could not make a disarmament treaty about their military aircraft, because " the state of development of air services differs widely . . . and *in no case can these services be considered as complete* "; ten years later their nations bitterly regretted that the development of air forces had been permitted to go on.[10] It would be madness to repeat this folly with missiles today.

There may be peaceful uses for guided missiles—express mails from New York to London, Tokyo or Moscow; space travel " several decades from now." These potential benefits can hardly be considered to outweigh the perils which the preparation for nuclear missile war involves. But if missiles are genuinely required for peaceful uses, there will be no difficulty in organising an effective international control.

General Schriever is not alone in believing that the struggle for space supremacy must inevitably go on, and that the Western nations' hope of peace depends on keeping a " lead." General Gavin, whom *The Times* calls " the

[10] See pp. 413–414.

retiring Chief of the Army Research Division, and probably one of the most knowledgeable of the prophets," predicts that " space cavalry " forces will be patrolling the earth within ten years. There will be " task forces " of about 500 men each, travelling—or should it be " riding "?—in space vehicles, " each group armed with about fifty men carrying nuclear missiles," and equipped with " communications eyes " (TV and infra-red devices). This type of force, he said, " will control a major portion of a continent." [11]

Senator Johnson told the Senate that:

> " Scientists had said that control of space means control of the world far more totally than any control that has ever or could ever be achieved by weapons or by troops of occupation. From space, the masters of infinity would have the power to control the earth's weather, to cause drought and flood, to change the tides and raise the levels of the sea, to divert the Gulf stream and change temperate climates to frigid."

" The race in which the United States must now enter," Senator Johnson emphasised,

> " is not merely the race to perfect long-range ballistic missiles. More important than any ultimate weapon is the ultimate position—the position of total control over earth that lay somewhere out in space." [12]

These are developments that may become the realities of tomorrow if the race in missiles goes on. Immense resources are being given to perfecting the missiles, and to producing them in large numbers. There is no prospect that the anti-missile-missile can be made operational in an early future; when it is, it may be cancelled out by General Schriever's anti—anti-missile-missile—missile. In other words, there is no present hope of any real defence. The missile with the nuclear warhead is pre-eminently a weapon of offence, a

[11] *The Times*, January 15, 1958.
[12] M.G., January 8, 1958.

weapon which would help aggressors to make a sudden and devastating attack.

The total abolition of missiles would be in itself a most important measure of disarmament; it would enormously reduce the risk that the present stocks of A- and H-bombs would ever be used; there would be no problem of control, since neither the manufacture, nor the testing, of missiles, nor the training of troops in their maintenance or use, could be concealed from UN Inspectors.

If total abolition is not agreed to, because governments desire to retain short-range missiles for AA defence, it would be quite practicable to fix a maximum permitted weight, *e.g.*, one ton, which no missile might exceed. Again, there would be no problem of control. But action is urgently required. The missile race, month by month, and year by year, is adding to the tension in international affairs. The time to end " the missile era " is now, while it is " still in its infancy." Urging speedy action, *The Times* in a leading article said in 1957:

"The sad lesson of many attempts at control—especially over nuclear weapons—is that agreement would have been far easier to reach *in the initial stages.*" [13]

If developments such as those described in this chapter and the last are to continue for even *one* more decade, it would be better for the governments to give up talking about disarmament altogether. For their talk will only camouflage a danger that may be mortal and that may be near.

[13] November 10, 1957.

# PART SIX

# PRACTICAL PROPOSALS FOR CONVENTIONAL DISARMAMENT

# 32

# *The Work of the League and the UN*

In 1932 Mr. Stanley (Lord) Baldwin said that " all disarmament hangs on the air." Since Hiroshima was destroyed, everyone has tacitly assumed that all disarmament hangs on the atom; and many people have believed that, if nuclear disarmament were achieved, there would be no trouble about the rest. Unfortunately, this is not true; and it would be of no avail to secure nuclear disarmament, and to leave the race in conventional armaments still going on.

" We are in favour of general disarmament," said Mr. Macmillan in 1957,

> " We are not in favour of the abolition of the unconventional, that is the nuclear, weapon without such corresponding reductions in conventional forces as will make Europe secure from Soviet aggression. . . . I have been through two major wars fought by conventional weapons. Some people now talk as if those were quite harmless and quite respectable operations. The contrast between the new and the old is great, but let nobody think that if we could ban all nuclear weapons it would be all right to have a massive third world war with conventional weapons. That is the reason I believe we must strive for full disarmament covering unconventional and conventional weapons alike." [1]

Mr. Selwyn Lloyd said in 1957:

> " We " (the Government) " believe that a world war fought with so-called conventional weapons, similar to those of the last war, but improved upon, will be just as terrible for the world as a war fought with nuclear

[1] *Hansard*, April 17, 1957, cols. 2048–2049.

weapons. It may take longer for society to destroy itself, but it will happen just the same." [2]

This view has always been accepted in the United Nations. The General Assembly's Resolutions have year by year declared that there must be " regulation, limitation and balanced reduction of *all* armed forces and *all* armaments." [3] This is only common sense.

### THE FACTORS OF CONVENTIONAL MILITARY STRENGTH

In 1954, the United Kingdom delegation put in a paper about " what weapons and armed forces and other matters should be covered by a disarmament convention," *i.e.*, about the factors of military strength to be dealt with. They started from the proposition " that the Disarmament Convention should cover all types of weapons, all types of armed forces and military facilities of all kinds." [4] In respect of conventional armaments this meant that the treaty must deal with manpower; weapons, for use on land, on the sea and in the air; other warlike equipment and installations; military, naval and air transport; arms factories, proving-grounds and research stations; land, naval and air bases; dockyard, tank and aircraft repair depots, airfields, etc.; and, not least, the budgetary appropriations for military purposes which will be allowed.

When this has been agreed, it must further be decided what conventional weapons, if any, shall be abolished, and which of the remainder shall be reduced and limited; how this shall technically be done; and what shall be the permitted strength of each nation in each of these factors. In this way, the so-called " ratio " between the Powers, the proportionate strength of each nation relatively to the rest, must be determined. There must be agreement about the times, and the stages, at which the abolitions shall become

---

[2] *The Times*, September 14, 1957.
[3] *e.g.*, Resolution establishing the UN Disarmament Commission, adopted on January 11, 1952.
[4] Sub-Committee, May 21, 1954, Cmd. 9204, p. 15.

effective, and the reductions made. There must be agreement about the methods of Inspection and Control by which the parties to the treaty will be assured that the other nations are carrying out its terms.

Under each of these broad headings, a number of complicated questions will arise. Manpower must be defined by a common formula; a system of reduction and limitation must be devised that will apply both to conscript armies and to armies of long-term volunteers; it must maintain the agreed balance of strength by limiting the numbers, and the effective military value, of trained reserves. Some conventional weapons—that is, weapons used by all belligerents in the two World Wars—ought to be abolished; others ought to be limited both in quality (*i.e.*, in destructive power) and in numbers; others ought to have no limit but that of an overall budgetary appropriation. Transport, depots, bases, research, total permitted military expenditure, may all be of great importance in increasing the defensive or offensive power of a given number of men and a given amount of arms; they must, therefore, be dealt with in the treaty. All these questions will be discussed, and solutions will be suggested, in this Part of the book and in the next.

It is unfortunate that none of these technical problems of conventional disarmament have been discussed at all in the UN Disarmament Commissions and Sub-Committee. There is thus no guidance of any sort to be obtained from a study of their records. This is unfortunate, because it means that Ministers and general staffs—those who must make the necessary decisions—are not yet familiar with the merits of the questions they must decide. But it is of less importance than might appear, because the conventional forces and armaments of today, though improved in quality and performance, are in character substantially the same as the forces and armaments maintained by the nations between the Wars; and the problems of reducing and limiting these forces and armaments were very throughly threshed out in the disarmament debates which were conducted in the

League of Nations for a dozen years. Before the World Disarmament Conference met in February 1932 almost every question concerning manpower, the reduction and limitation of armaments and weapons, and the limitation of military expenditure, had been meticulously debated, and in many matters a practical solution had been found. These solutions were embodied and improved in the proposals laid by many governments before the Conference; some of them were adopted in the comprehensive plan put forward by President Hoover in June 1932; and in the Draft Disarmament Convention put forward in the Conference by the British Government in March 1933. None of these proposals succeeded. But for the present purpose they are not only relevant but of the greatest value. Much of the "conventional" sections of a disarmament treaty—naval, land and air—could be lifted without much change from the Washington and London Naval Treaties, from the British Draft Convention, or President Hoover's plan. These documents, and the League discussions, will be referred to, when they throw much-needed light on the problems to be faced today.

### Reduction and Limitation of Military Expenditure

A few words may be said about the place of budgetary limitation in a system of conventional disarmament.

It is, in itself, an important measure of armament reduction, and not least because it is the one that the ordinary taxpayer will readily appreciate and understand. It has a special value in various ways. In respect of some vital factors of military strength, e.g., research and development, it is the most essential method of securing the desired result.[5] In respect of other factors, e.g., manpower and the purchase of new weapons, it is an indispensable supplementary instrument of control, to ensure that the obligations of the disarmament treaty are carried out.[6] For some

---

[5] See pp. 495–496.
[6] See p. 500 and pp. 506–507.

classes of weapons and equipment it may be a more satisfactory method of reduction than a numerical or quantitative system.[7]   It is an extremely complex matter, but one on which the League of Nations' work was particularly thorough and complete.   Some readers may find the chapter on the subject to be exceptionally dull; but if they labour through it they will recognise how great a part budgetary limitation ought to play in any sound system of armament reduction, limitation and control.   But, for reasons that will appear in Chapter 40, budgetary limitation is not, by itself, enough to secure disarmament.

## THE RATIO

In theory, the problem of the " ratio " between the parties to a disarmament treaty, the proportionate strength of each nation relatively to the rest, is one of great complexity.

In practice it can be, and has been, used as an excuse for endless talk by those who wish to delay or obstruct disarmament.[8]   Obstructionists can suggest a large number of different principles or criteria by which the proportionate strength of the nations should be settled: size of population; length of frontiers; natural aids to defence, *e.g.*, the sea, mountain ranges, etc.; degree of industrialisation; *potential* military strength; the *status quo*.   They can argue that there ought to be separate ratios for air forces, navies and armies, and that these three should then be combined. The possible complications are immense.   In practice, in most of the disarmament treaties which have been made,[9] and in most of the proposals put forward,[10] the matter has been settled by rule of thumb: arbitrary levels of manpower or armament have been laid down, based broadly on the

[7] See p. 500.
[8] See pp. 448 *et seq.*
[9] *e.g.*, the Washington and London Naval Treaties of 1922 and 1930 established the following ratio of strength between the five principal naval Powers: United States 5; Britain 5; Japan 3; France 1·75; Italy 1·75.   See pp. 446–448.
[10] President Coolidge's Naval proposals of 1927; President Hoover's Naval, Land and Air proposals of June 1932; the British Government's Draft Disarmament Convention of 1933.

principle of the *status quo, i.e.*, on the proportionate existing strength of the parties when the treaty or proposal was
drawn up. Even so, the application of this principle has
been a difficult affair. In Washington, in 1922, many
anxious weeks were spent in working out the agreed ratio
of 5:5:3 between Britain, the United States and Japan,
in terms of ships to be scrapped and ships to be retained.

The UN Commission and Sub-Committee have not
dealt with the problem of the ratio, except in the 1952
manpower proposal of 1 to 1·5 million men for the United
States, Russia and China; 700,000 to 800,000 for Britain and
France [11]; and " less than 1 per cent. of the population "
for the rest. This, again, was an arbitrary rule-of-thumb
proposal, but it served an invaluable purpose when it was
made; Russia's ultimate acceptance of this ratio may yet
prove to be of much importance, and may avoid great
difficulties when a disarmament treaty is drawn up. Difficulties may arise with other nations about the principle of
" less than 1 per cent. of their population." But the nature
of these difficulties cannot be foreseen, and a further
discussion of the ratio would serve no useful purpose here.[12]

## THE PRINCIPLE OF QUALITATIVE DISARMAMENT

There was one principle of conventional disarmament
which was ultimately accepted by almost all the sixty
governments who took part in the League Disarmament
Conference of 1932, and which became the foundation of
the British Government's Draft Convention. This was
the principle of qualitative disarmament. It applies to
naval, and land and air armaments alike, and is of dominating importance in any consideration of conventional
disarmament.

---

[11] Subsequently amended to 650,000.
[12] There is a long theoretical discussion of the ratio in Chap. XIII of *Disarmament*, by P. J. Noel-Baker, 1926; and a discussion of the practical difficulties
that arose in the Coolidge Conference in *The Coolidge Conference* by the
same author, 1927.

# 33

## *Qualitative Disarmament*

QUALITATIVE disarmament is the phrase adopted between the Wars to describe the abolition by international agreement of weapons which help attack against defence. When this plan was first suggested, many people said it was absurd to try to establish a distinction between weapons that were primarily offensive and others that were primarily defensive; the only real difference, they said, lay in whether you were behind a weapon or in front.

This sophistry has been repeated in UN debates, and some delegates have urged that the Disarmament Commission and the Sub-Committee should not waste their time on a barren, intellectual exercise in which the League of Nations failed. The falsity of this view is shown by two recent statements by men in authority. The British Minister of Defence said in 1957: " The power of defence is, for the time being, at a very low ebb, in relation to the power of attack." [1] A year earlier Dr. Cockburn, the chief scientist in the Ministry of Supply, had written:

> " Although a balance will always be achieved eventually between offence and defence, there can be long periods when one or the other is clearly superior. Thus the 1914–18 War was essentially defensive, because of the development of automatic fire-power. By the 1939–45 War the petrol engine had restored armoured mobility on the ground and made air power practicable. This swung the balance in favour of the offensive." [2]

These statements establish beyond dispute that, in the opinion of those who determine the policy of weapon

[1] *Hansard*, February 13, 1957, col. 1311.
[2] *Journal of the R.U.S.I.*, February 1956, p. 25.

production in Britain, there *are* weapons that are primarily defensive, and others that help attack. This view is in no way undermined by Dr. Cockburn's introductory proviso, or by the rest of what Mr. Sandys said in 1957:

> " So far no weapon has ever been invented to which there was no answer, and I am confident that the ballistic rocket will prove no exception. But it would be absurd to pretend that we shall be quick to evolve an effective defence against this form of attack." [3]

The fact that a successful counter may ultimately be found to an offensive weapon does not mean that that weapon is not offensive; if it had never been invented, the power of defence would have remained by that much greater; if, having been invented, it could be abolished, the power of defence would be correspondingly restored.

It is, indeed, unanswerably established that the theory of qualitative disarmament is right; that the general abolition of weapons that assist attack would strengthen the power of national defence, and increase the general security of the world. It has been shown in Parts Two to Five that nuclear weapons and all other weapons of mass destruction are offensive weapons, against which there is no adequate defence, and which, therefore, ought to be abolished, since defence is the only legitimate purpose for which national armaments should be used. What conventional weapons, if any, can be said primarily to help attack? Is it practical to propose their abolition? A brief outline of the debates between the Wars will throw light on this important question.

## Qualitative Disarmament Between the Wars

In 1919 the victorious Powers imposed on Germany and her allies the system of Part V of the Treaty of Versailles; it

[3] *Hansard, loc. cit*

had a double purpose: " to render possible the initiation of a general limitation of the armaments of all nations," and to render it impossible for Germany " to resume her policy of military aggression." To carry out this second purpose German manpower was drastically reduced, and Germany was forbidden to have the following weapons:

*Army*: mobile guns of over 105 mm. (4·1 in.) calibre; tanks, armoured cars, and " all similar constructions "; all forms of poison gas.

*Navy*: surface vessels of over 10,000 tons displacement; aircraft carriers; submarines.

*Air Force*:

" The armed forces of Germany must not include any military or naval air forces." [4]

This was the origin of the doctrine of qualitative disarmament, and these were the weapons which the general staffs of the victorious Allies considered as primarily offensive, and likely to help attack against defence.

It was Lord Cecil who made qualitative disarmament the dominant issue in the League Conference when it met in 1932. He urged that the chief task which the Conference should perform was " the prohibition for all nations of those kinds of armaments which are now forbidden to the vanquished Powers." This, he said, would

" tend to decrease the offensive power of armaments, while leaving defensive power untouched. That eventually must be the chief object of any disarmament proposals. If I am right in this representation of our proposals, it is evident that they will produce a very important increase of security. Carried to its logical conclusion, the removal of the power of aggression would eventually bring about a complete security, and anything which diminishes the power of aggression proportionately to the power of defence necessarily increases the safety of the world."

[4] Treaty of Versailles, Arts. 164–198.

Accordingly, battleships and other warships of over 10,000 tons should be abolished; they had " no real reason for their existence, except to fight one another. They are not the vessels most suitable for the protection of commerce, or indeed, for any other defensive operation." [5] If big battleships were abolished, the argument of the smaller Powers that they needed submarines for coastal defence " would be to a great extent destroyed." In any case, " the real strength of the submarine was in the destruction of merchant ships, which is a purely offensive operation."

On land, Lord Cecil proposed the abolition of tanks and heavy mobile guns.

> " The great purpose of both these weapons is the destruction or penetration of defensive entrenchments. In the late war it was found that, with modern rifles and machine-guns, the power to hold an entrenchment was very great, especially with the aid of wire entanglements. . . . In other words, these weapons are essential to attack. . . . It is true to assert that without them no offensive against properly organised defences is practicable."

In the air, Lord Cecil proposed the abolition of all military aircraft. They were, he said, " of use in attacking entrenched positions." But " their main offensive purpose was to bomb buildings and other objects of military importance," including great cities; in any future war their power of destruction, and their menace to civilian populations, would be " enormously increased."

> " If, therefore, the Conference would agree to the abolition of military aircraft, it would not only render offensive military operations more difficult, it would abolish what is surely a most barbarous form of warfare." [6]

---

[5] *Verbatim Records of Plenary Meetings*, Annex, p. 197.
[6] *Loc. cit.*, pp. 197–198.

After prolonged debates, which centred principally on Lord Cecil's proposals, the Conference referred the following resolution to its land, naval and air commissions, which consisted of generals, admirals and air marshals:

"In seeking to apply the principle of qualitative disarmament . . . the Conference is of opinion that the range of land, sea and air armaments should be examined by the competent Special Commissions with a view to selecting *those weapons whose character is the most specifically offensive or those most efficacious against national defence or most threatening to civilians*." [7]

After six weeks of intensive discussion the Commissions made Reports to which reference will be made in the chapters on land, naval and air disarmament. Before they had finished, the British Foreign Secretary, Sir John Simon, had made an important speech in the House of Commons:

"There are certain weapons mentioned in Part V of the Treaty of Versailles which are prohibited to Germany, and there are certain other weapons which Germany is permitted to have. Will anybody who thinks that qualitative disarmament is all nonsense be good enough to tell me why the Allied and Associated Powers selected those particular weapons and prohibited Germany from having them? The answer is written on the face of the Treaty of Versailles, and it is that those weapons were then regarded as weapons which would have enabled Germany, had she been so minded, to undertake operations of offence." [8]

Still more important, President Hoover's proposals to the Conference in June 1932 were wholly founded on Lord Cecil's principle. "The Briand-Kellogg Pact," the President said,

"to which we are all signatories, can only mean that

[7] *Minutes of the General Commission*, Vol. I, p. 116.
[8] *Hansard*, May 13, 1932, col. 2334.

the nations of the world have agreed that they will use their arms solely for defence. . . .

"This reduction should be carried out, not only by broad general cuts in armaments, but by increasing the comparative power of defence through decreases in the power of attack."

He accordingly proposed: "in order to reduce the offensive character of all land forces as distinguished from their defensive character . . . the abolition of all tanks, all chemical warfare, and all large mobile guns"; the abolition of "all bombing planes" and "the total prohibition of bombardment from the air"; and the reduction by one-third of battleships and submarines, and by one-quarter of aircraft carriers, cruisers and destroyers; no nation was to retain a submarine tonnage greater than 35,000 tons.

"This plan," added the President, "would greatly reduce offensive strength compared to defensive strength in all nations." [9]

The President's whole programme was thus founded on the principle of qualitative disarmament; his naval proposals were avowedly intended to abolish capital ships, aircraft carriers, and submarines in successive stages, of which this was to be the first.

The British Government's Draft Disarmament Convention of March 1933 was equally founded on the principle of qualitative disarmament. The Minutes of the General Commission of the Conference record:

"Mr. Eden said that earlier declarations by his delegation had made it quite clear that the United Kingdom had always been impressed with the desirability, in the interests of real disarmament, of depriving the armed forces of all countries of those heavier and more powerful weapons which the last war had brought to such perfection for the specific purpose of overcoming resistance by organised defences and

[9] *Minutes of the General Commission*, Vol. I, pp. 122–123.

thereby ensuring a success for direct attack. These more powerful weapons had been generally classified as those essential for the success of offensive warfare.

"The Conference had therefore approved the principle of the prohibition of certain kinds of weapons, and it remained to be determined what kinds of weapons should come under this ban, and what methods should be adopted for their disposal." [10]

In their Draft Convention the British Government left naval armaments to be dealt with in a conference two years later; they proposed the abolition of land guns over 4·1 in. calibre; of all tanks over sixteen tons (the British Government later suggested that *all* tanks might be abolished); of all poison gases, and incendiary and biological weapons; of aircraft over three tons unladen weight (*i.e.*, bombers), with proposals for a plan to abolish *all* national military and naval aircraft within five years; and the prohibition of all air bombardment.

President Franklin Roosevelt, who had come to power in the United States, endorsed the British Draft Convention in the following message, sent in May 1933: "The programme for immediate reduction of aggressive weapons, now under discussion at Geneva" (*i.e.*, the British Draft Convention) "is but a first step towards our ultimate goal." He did not believe that "the proposed immediate steps go far enough"; he wanted the naval reductions proposed by President Hoover, and the immediate abolition of national air forces. He therefore said that his Government would "exert its influence towards the attainment of further successive steps of disarmament."

The "ultimate goal" he defined as follows:

"Modern weapons of offence are vastly stronger than modern weapons of defence. Frontier forts, trenches, wire entanglements, coast defences—in a word, fixed fortifications—are no longer impregnable

[10] Vol. II, pp. 344–345.

to the attack of war planes, heavy mobile artillery, land battleships called tanks, poison gas.

" If all nations will agree wholly to eliminate from possession and use weapons which make possible a successful attack, defences automatically will become impregnable, and the frontiers and independence of every nation will become secure.

" The ultimate objective of the Disarmament Conference must be the complete elimination of all offensive weapons. The immediate objective is a substantial reduction of some of these weapons, and the elimination of many others." [11]

President Hoover's proposals and, indeed, the full application of Lord Cecil's principle, had been endorsed throughout the Conference by Russia, Germany (until Hitler came into power), Italy and virtually every " middle " and small Power. Lord Cecil had been opposed by many military experts, but after eighteen months of intensive international discussion in the Conference, in national parliaments, and outside, the principle of qualitative disarmament by the abolition of aggressive weapons had been specifically endorsed by the leading governments of the world.

# Qualitative Disarmament and the 1939 War

Within ten years the experience of war entirely confirmed what those who favoured qualitative disarmament had said.

In 1935–36 the Abyssinians successfully resisted Mussolini's powerful armies, until he crushed them by air bombardment and mustard gas. Hitler conquered Europe by a series of sudden, smashing, " blitzkrieg " attacks, which were conducted by aircraft, tanks and heavy mobile guns. Without these weapons his campaigns in Poland, Denmark,

[11] *Minutes of the General Commission*, Vol. II, pp. 461–462.

Norway, Holland, Belgium, Jugoslavia, Greece and France would have been impossible.[12]

He almost brought Britain to her knees in a blockade conducted by submarines. He almost isolated Russia by his attacks on the Allied convoys to Archangel and Murmansk conducted by battleships, aircraft and submarines.

The Japanese had argued in a Memorandum at Geneva that aircraft carriers were vessels that helped attack; they proved at Pearl Harbour that this was true; without battleships, aircraft carriers and submarines, that sudden aggressive onslaught could never have been made.

The weapons which the qualitative disarmers had sought to abolish at Geneva were the weapons with which the militarist dictators of the Axis came near to conquering the world. The petrol engine had beaten automatic fire. If the dictators had not had these weapons, their aggressions could never have been planned.

## Qualitative Disarmament in the UN

Those who urged qualitative disarmament between the Wars argued that the abolition of offensive weapons would prevent the swift victory of an aggressor, and would thus give the peaceful nations more time to uphold the law.[13] They predicted that if the arms race in the *quality* of weapons went on, then the power of an aggressor to mount a sudden devastating blow would progressively increase. This has happened in a measure which none of them could then foresee. Already in 1947 Lord Tedder said that:

> " One of the features of modern scientific and technical development is that more and more the scales are being weighted in favour of the blitzkrieg; as modern weapons develop, the potentiality of the initial blow tends to grow and grow." [14]

---

[12] " The tank is now a familiar, conventional weapon; it was the tank that overran vast areas of Europe and was responsible for the deaths of millions and the enslavement of millions more ": Sir J. Slessor, *Strategy for the West*, p. 16.

[13] *e.g.*, Sir J. Simon, *Minutes of the General Commission*, Vol. I, p. 100.

[14] *Air Power in War*, Lees Knowles Lectures, 1947, p. 17.

This is more true in 1958 than it was eleven years ago. As a result, the principle of qualitative disarmament has begun to emerge in a rudimentary form in the UN debates. The clearest statement was made in 1957 by the British delegate:

> " We should, in my opinion, give very special attention to other weapons of a particularly drastic character. When I spoke in the United Nations First Committee on January 15 this year, I mentioned in this connection the long-range submarines, and I said '. . . They can be used as launching platforms for guided missiles. *Such submarines are offensive and not defensive weapons.*' Later I mentioned military aircraft, warships, armoured vehicles, guns of all types, flame-throwers, rockets and other weapons, and I suggested that the Sub-Committee of the Disarmament Commission should embark on a study of the problems posed by these weapons." [15]

This clearly stated the principle of qualitative disarmament, and suggested that its application to all these categories of " particularly drastic " conventional weapons should be studied. It is regrettable that this study was not undertaken long ago, for no conventional disarmament measures will make sense, unless they are designed to reduce the power of surprise attack, and to increase the power of national defence against aggression. This means the application of the principle of qualitative disarmament in the greatest measure for which agreement can be secured.

## How Qualitative Disarmament Might be Applied

The acceptance of the principle of qualitative disarmament must mean, as will be argued in Chapter 39, the abolition

[15] Commander Noble, Sub-Committee, April 4, 1957, p. 6. Cmdr. Noble had also said in the First Committee that '' under the Anglo-French Plan . . . all weapons of mass-destruction, including chemical and biological weapons, would eventually be banned.''

of military research; certainly no qualitative limitations would be of value if military research went on. It must mean, also, a prohibition of the introduction of " radically new " weapons, and, if possible, of " modifications of existing types," since these " modifications " are immensely costly, and almost always increase the weapon's offensive power.[16] The further it goes in securing the abolition of weapons that help attack against national defence, the easier it will be to control, and the more it will assist to establish lasting peace.

But abolition can be effected by a series of successive reductions, as President Hoover proposed for battleships, aircraft carriers and submarines, or as M. Moch proposed for nuclear stocks.[17] This system could easily be applied to air forces, to tanks, heavy mobile guns, flame-throwers and other conventional weapons that help attack.

The full acceptance of the principle of qualitative disarmament is in the interest of every nation. The introduction of a weapon which helps attack may seem to give a military advantage to the nation that first brings it out, but in the end all other nations get it, and the national security of them all, including the nation which introduced it, is undermined. The whole history of weapon development, from Britain's Dreadnought to the United States' and Russia's H-bombs, proves this true.

---

[16] See pp. 493–495. The rivalry in quality of weapons is now so intense that £1,000s of millions are spent by the nations every year on replacing existing weapons with others that are somewhat better. It is clearly a desirable application of qualitative disarmament that this, if possible, should cease.

[17] See p. 221.

# 34

## *Air Disarmament*

### *Military Aircraft: Weapons of Attack*

#### DEVELOPMENT OF AIR WARFARE 1903–1932

ORVILLE WRIGHT flew the first heavier-than-air machine on December 17, 1903. Within fifteen years—by November 11, 1918—aircraft had become a major weapon of war; general staffs had come to see that "air superiority" was essential to victory; many scores of thousands of pilots of many nationalities had perished in the air.

#### OPINION FROM 1919 TO 1932

In the twelve years that followed the 1914 War many far-seeing Service experts foresaw, and warned their nations against, the dangers inherent in air armaments. Sir Frederick Sykes, who had commanded the Independent (Bombing) Air Force, and who had been Chief of Air Staff, and Brigadier-General P. R. C. Groves, who had been Director of Flying Operations in 1918, predicted that in a future war aircraft would be used, not to bomb military objectives only, as military objectives were then defined, but to bomb railways, harbours, shipping, mobilisation zones—and also the enemy's "centres of population." [1] They forecast that the use of incendiary bombs would mean large-scale fires which no fire brigade could control. They believed that in air warfare attack would continue to establish its supremacy against defence. Lord Trenchard, while he was Chief of Air Staff (he held that post for eleven years), felt so deeply about the dangers that this involved that he said:

[1] Sir F. Sykes, *Aviation in Peace and War*, pp. 100–103. Groves, *Behind the Smoke Screen, passim.*

" I do not want you to think that I look upon Air as a blessing altogether. It may be more of a blessing for this Empire than for any other country in the world, but I feel that all the good it will do in civil life cannot balance the harm that may be done in war by it; and, if I had the casting vote, I would say: abolish the Air. *I feel that it is an infinitely more harmful weapon of war than any other.*" [2]

## Findings of the Disarmament Conference, 1932

The view that aircraft were weapons of attack was strikingly endorsed in the Disarmament Conference of 1932. When the Air Commission, which consisted for the most part of high-ranking staff officers, was invited to consider what air armaments were " most specifically offensive," " most efficacious against national defence," or " most threatening to civilians," they gave the following replies:

" All air armaments can be used to some extent for offensive purposes, without prejudice to the question of their defensive uses. *If used in time of peace for a sudden and unprovoked attack, air armaments assume a particularly offensive character. In effect, before the State victim of the aggression can take the defensive measures demanded by the situation, or before the League of Nations or States not involved in the conflict could undertake preventive or mediatory action, the aggressor State might in certain cases be able rapidly to obtain military or psychological results such as would render difficult either the cessation of hostilities or the re-establishment of peace.*" [3]

This was a full-blooded endorsement of the view that aircraft are " most specifically " weapons of attack.

---

[2] Speech to the Cambridge University Aeronautical Society, *Daily News*, October 25, 1925.
[3] Conference Decuments, Vol. I, pp. 245 *et seq.*

The Air Commission further said: "*The Commission was unanimously of opinion that air bombardment is a grave threat to civilians.*" [4]

## THE STRUGGLE IN THE BRITISH CABINET, 1932

While these technical discussions in Geneva were taking place, a struggle had begun in the British Cabinet about the air proposals which the United Kingdom delegates should support. Mr. Stanley (Lord) Baldwin, then Deputy Prime Minister, and Sir John (Lord) Simon, the Foreign Secretary, wanted not only to accept the plan which President Hoover had put forward in June for the abolition of bombers and air-bombardment, but also to propose the total abolition of national air forces. They were defeated by the Secretary of State for Air, Lord Londonderry; and in July the British Government rejected President Hoover's proposal, and put forward instead counter-suggestions for restricting the size and number of aircraft, and for regulating bombing by rules of international law. [5] The British Government's attitude on this, and on the President's Naval proposals, killed the Hoover plan. But Mr. Baldwin did not accept his defeat as final; he had come to think that total air disarmament was essential to make the Geneva Conference succeed, and that unless it succeeded civilisation might be doomed. In November he made a speech in the House of Commons, one sentence of which is still quoted: "The bomber will always get through." This prophecy was fulfilled in the 1939 War; but it was the rest of the speech that deserved to be remembered. He spoke of the "appalling speed which the air has brought into modern warfare," and he went on:

"I think it is well for the man in the street . . . to realise that there is no power on earth that can prevent him from being bombed. Whatever people may tell him, the bomber will always get through. . . . The

[4] *Loc. cit.*, p. 251.
[5] *Loc. cit.*, p. 265.

only defence is in offence, which means that you have to kill more women and children more quickly than the enemy if you want to save yourselves . . .

"Fear is a very dangerous thing. It is quite true that it may act as a deterrent in people's minds against war, but it is much more likely to make them want to increase armaments to protect themselves against the terrors that they know may be launched against them. We have to remember that aerial warfare is still in its infancy, and its potentialities are incalculable and inconceivable."

He then spoke of the " futile attempts " so far made to deal with the problem, such as " reduction of the size of aeroplanes, prohibition of the bombardment of the civil population, the prohibition of bombing." As this was precisely what his government had put forward in their counter-proposal of July 7, his sense of frustration must have been strong to make him say in November that such proposals " reduced him to despair."

"What would be the only object of reducing the size of aeroplanes? . . . Immediately every scientific man in the country will turn to making a high explosive bomb about the size of a walnut, and as powerful as a bomb of big dimensions.

"The prohibition of the bombardment of the civil population . . . is impracticable so long as any bombing exists at all. . . . If a man has a potential weapon, and is going to be killed, he will use that weapon, whatever it is, and whatever undertaking he has given about it. . . . We remember . . . the cry that was raised when civilian towns were first bombed (in the 1914 War). It was not long before we replied . . .

"On the solution of this question hangs . . . in my view, our civilisation . . .

"*I am firmly convinced myself, and have been for some time, that, if it were possible, the air forces ought*

*all to be abolished. . . . All disarmament turns on the
air.*" [6]

This was a resounding endorsement of the proposition
that all military aircraft are weapons of attack, and as such
ought to be abolished.  It was a whole-hearted rejection of
the theory of " limited war," with bombing restricted by
rules of international law, and it was a prophetic forecast
of the dangers of the air and nuclear armaments of today.

### Experience in the 1939 War

Mr. Baldwin finally failed, and another World War began,
as he predicted, within a short period of years.  The words
used by the Air Commission of the Disarmament Conference about the role of aircraft in " sudden and unprovoked attacks " might almost have been written to describe
what happened in Poland on September 1, 1939.  " The
Polish Air Force was virtually destroyed on the first day,"
says Lord Tedder.[7]  This was entirely due to the immense
advantage given by aircraft to an aggressor who makes a
sudden and unprovoked attack.  The Polish Air Force had
a large number of good fighter planes, and the Polish pilots
later proved in the R.A.F. that they were very good; with
any warning, they would have put up a tough resistance.
Yet they were almost instantly overwhelmed.  Lord
Trenchard's dictum was proved to the hilt: " Air is pre-
eminently the weapon of surprise."

The bombing of Polish Army Headquarters, railway
junctions and mobilisation centres was equally effective.  It
disrupted the whole defensive system, and inflicted blows
from which the Polish Army never recovered.  The Army
numbered 1,750,000 very courageous, highly disciplined and
well trained men.  Yet within a week it was a rabble;
within a month it had ceased to exist; the conquest of
Poland was complete.  In this result, German aircraft, both
bombers and fighters, had played a major part.

---

[6] *Hansard*, November 10, 1932, cols. 631–637.
[7] *Air Power in War*, p. 35.

The same was true of Hitler's " sudden and unprovoked attacks " against Denmark, Norway and Holland in 1940, and against Jugoslavia, Greece and Crete in 1941. In all these six campaigns offensive operations were undertaken which would have been completely impossible without the German Air Force, and in all of them the " national defence " was quickly overwhelmed.

Fortunately for Britain the Luftwaffe's offensive of 1940 had not the overwhelming advantage of surprise. Even so, it may well be that without radar, an unforeseen but immense help to the defence, " the Few " would not have been able to prevail.

Throughout the war the " specifically offensive " power of air forces continued to be a major factor whenever armies or navies went to the attack. Von Rundstedt summed up the causes of the Allied success in the invasion of Normandy —the most hazardous of all offensive operations—in these words :

> " The main difficulties which arose for us at the time of the invasion were the systematic preparations by your Air Force; the smashing of the main lines of communications, particularly the railway junctions. . . . The second thing was the attack on the roads. . . . That also meant that the bringing up of the armoured divisions was also out of the question, quite impossible. And the third thing was this carpet-bombing. . . . These were the main things that caused the general collapse." [8]

Lord Tedder explained the " carpet bombing " : " Before any major Allied advance, the German troops facing the advance were smothered in a sudden deluge of high explosive from the air—as much as 7,000 tons of bombs in half an hour." [9]

At sea, aircraft, unsupported by surface vessels, were able to undertake offensive operations against enemy

[8] Cited by Tedder, *op. cit.*, p. 113.
[9] *Ibid.*

warships, convoys and merchantmen; and they won great
victories.[10]   On land, as at sea, bomber aircraft conducted
offensive operations, and won important victories of their
own.   They compelled Hitler to organise a force of 900,000
for AA defence, and AA guns took over 25 per cent. of
Germany's total weapon production.   The German transport system received only 138,000 tons of bombs during the
six years of war; yet the railways were utterly disorganised
by 1945, and rail deliveries of coal were down to 4 per cent.
of normal by March of that year.   Oil targets received only
98,000 out of a total of 955,000 tons dropped on Germany;
yet when Speer was asked after the War: " Do you believe
that strategic bombing alone could have brought about the
surrender of Germany?" he replied " The answer is Yes.
The attacks on the synthetic oil industry would have
sufficed, without the impact of purely military events, to
render Germany defenceless." [11]   No one could speak
with greater authority than Speer about the " specifically
offensive " power of bomber aircraft using " conventional "
bombs.

Aircraft also proved to be " most threatening to
civilians."   When Hitler began his all-out onslaught on
London in 1940 all restraints were set aside, as Mr. Baldwin
and General Groves had forecast that they would be.   By
1943 the R.A.F. had developed " target-area " or " saturation " bombing; and by 1945 virtually all the towns and
cities of Germany had learnt what this could mean.   A
correspondent who made a tour of 2,500 miles in Germany
in 1945 wrote as follows:

> " There is something terrifying in the devastation
> of a whole country, its cities smashed beyond repair,
> its industries ruined, its communications utterly dis-
> rupted.   Almost without exception, every large city I
> passed through was 80 to 90 per cent. wrecked, with
> mile after mile of burnt-out shells of houses, with

10 See pp. 452–453.
11 Cited by the Rt. Hon. J. Strachey, *Hansard*, March 12, 1946, col. 966.

debris piled in some places 40 feet high on the pavements, with huge filled-in bomb craters straddling the main thoroughfares." [12]

The heaviest weight of bombs ever dropped on London was 590 tons, on May 10, 1941; it took the Luftwaffe all night to do it. On Hamburg, in 1943, the R.A.F. dropped 2,300 tons in half an hour, and continued raids on that scale for a week. Later the United States Air Force did the same to Dresden. This cost 100,000 human lives in Hamburg, and 200,000 in Dresden [13]; the overwhelming majority were civilians. The total number of civilians killed by air attack in Germany was officially declared to be 1,100,000.

The same thing happened in the East; in Burma the Japanese bombed civilians in order to spread panic and alarm, and they rained down incendiaries from a low level, and burnt the towns. The reckoning had come before the atom bombs were dropped on Hiroshima and Nagasaki. With conventional high explosive and incendiary bombs, the United States airmen had wiped out many of the cities of Japan.

## Developments since 1945

By 1945 air power had become the dominating factor in every campaign, both by land and sea. Until missiles take their place, military aircraft will continue to dominate strategy and national preparedness for war. Their offensive power against national defence has rapidly increased, and is still increasing. The bomber has already made conventional AA guns obsolete, and is rapidly diminishing the usefulness of fighters. Air Chief Marshal Sir Ralph Cochrane, Deputy C.A.S., said in 1954: " Assuming that we devote equal scientific and technical resources and brain power to each, there is yet no sign that a successful countermeasure can be produced far enough in advance of the bomber to neutralise it." [14] Lord De L'Isle and Dudley,

---

[12] Douglas Williams, *Daily Telegraph*, May 30, 1945.
[13] Rt. Hon. A. Henderson, *Hansard*, March 10, 1955, col. 649.
[14] *The Listener*, September 16, 1954.

Secretary of State for Air, said in 1955: " For the next ten years at least the relative advantage of offence over defence in air strategy was likely to be maintained." [15]

If one of the purposes of a disarmament treaty is to strengthen national defence against attack, there must be a drastic measure of air disarmament. Indeed, if missiles and nuclear and other weapons of mass-destruction are abolished, then it will still be true, as Mr. Baldwin said in 1932, that " all disarmament turns on the air." The partial or total abolition of national air forces is thus the central problem with which the conventional section of a disarmament treaty must deal.

## *Proposals for Air Disarmament, 1919—1932*

### THE " AIR INTERESTS "

From 1919 onwards there were always far-seeing Service experts who understood the dangers of air warfare, and who drew the logical conclusion. Lord Trenchard's view has been quoted; he was ready, not only for total air dis-armament, but for the abolition of aviation itself, because he thought it " an infinitely more harmful weapon of war than any other."

But, in spite of the lead given by such men, proposals for air disarmament were always resolutely, not to say violently, opposed by what were called the " air interests "—many staff officers, the aircraft manufacturers, " patriotic " Air Leagues, the technical air journals, the air correspondents and commentators.[16] The Air League of the British Empire opposed all proposals for the abolition of national air forces because, as it said in a pamphlet: " It denies the premise, so often assumed, that air power is essentially inhumane, and must be specially discriminated against " [17]; but when its secretary and spokesman discussed proposals for an International Air Police Force, he rejected

---

[15] M.G., October 12, 1955.
[16] See P. J. Noel-Baker, *Private Manufacture of Armaments*, pp. 320 *et seq. et passim*.                              [17] Pamphlet issued in 1934.

them in the name of " morality itself." " Imagine," he said, " the feelings of any nation *suffering from the most feared and hated means of warfare* in the name of peace and the League of Nations. It was not for such bloody tasks that the League of Nations was formed. . . ." [18]

It was against such opposition, organised and conducted with great resources, that those who proposed air disarmament had to contend, not only in Britain, but even more in France, Italy, Germany, Japan, and elsewhere.

### VERSAILLES AND WASHINGTON

There was no difficulty over the first issue that arose after the 1914 War. The purpose of Part V of the Treaty of Versailles was that " of rendering it impossible for Germany to resume her policy of military aggression." [19]  No one doubted that an air force would help her to do that, so she was forbidden to have any military aircraft at all or to do any air training of military personnel.

Things were different when the Washington Conference met in 1921. This is always called a " Naval Conference," but it was intended by the United States Government, who summoned it, to deal with land and air armaments as well. Air armaments, however, were left to a Committee of Service experts; and this Committee produced a Report which deserves to be remembered as a classic statement of the view that disarmament is both impracticable and pernicious. Their main conclusion was that " the problem of finding a suitable ratio between the air forces of various Powers is . . . at the present time almost insuperable." [20] The reason given for this view was that:

> " The *status quo* cannot serve as a starting point, since the state of development of air services differs widely in the case of the various Powers, *and in no case can these services be considered as complete.*"

[18] *Air Review*, November 1934, p. 12.
[19] Note to German Delegation to the Peace Conference, June 16, 1919.
[20] Cmd. 1627, 1922, p. 31.

" *In no case.*" If the starting point of a discussion about disarmament is that all the parties are firmly resolved to expand their armaments, it is not very likely that they will reach a definite result. But in addition to this conclusive proposition, the Committee produced six other reasons, political and technical, why air disarmament was impracticable; they examined and rejected five methods of reducing and limiting air forces, urging among other things that " detailed inspection by a foreign commission would be intolerable." Their Report, in fact, was a verbose and disingenuous way of saying: " We do not intend, now or ever, to disarm," and it repeated *ad nauseam* that it was impracticable and *undesirable* to control civil aviation in any way, since the increase of aviation would " largely act to bring about . . . the removal of some of the causes of war " [21]—an optimistic view not borne out by subsequent events. Their almost passionate belief that air disarmament was not only " impracticable," but also pernicious, because it was, as they thought, inevitably the enemy of aeronautical progress and expansion, was generally shared by the " air interests," and it became an important factor in the following years.

LEAGUE PREPARATORY DISARMAMENT COMMISSION 1926–30

Things took a different turn when the League Preparatory Commission began the serious discussion of air disarmament in 1926. No one then suggested that air disarmament was impracticable; on the contrary, everyone, including all the five governments whose experts had drawn up the Washington Report, agreed that it was essential; and delegates from various countries proposed all the five methods of reduction and limitation which these experts had rejected. Before the P.D.C. had finished its work, it had proposed a technical plan by which the numbers of aircraft and air personnel in national forces could be reduced and limited, and by which the quality of aircraft could be limited directly by horsepower, and indirectly by budgetary

[21] *Loc. cit.*, p. 29.

expenditure. The proposal that the number of long-term regulars should be limited was, for air forces, of particular importance.

## PROPOSALS IN THE DISARMAMENT CONFERENCE OF 1932

But when the 1932 Conference met, many governments were prepared to go much further than the P.D.C. A large number of delegations took up Lord Cecil's proposal for the total abolition of national air forces; others proposed the abolition of bombers; others proposed new and more stringent methods of reducing the numbers and offensive power of whatever military aircraft might be permitted. In the Air Commission, eighteen delegations suggested that the *unladen weight* of an aeroplane was by itself an adequate criterion of its capacity for carrying bombs, and therefore the most satisfactory method of limitation. The Commission's Report in June 1932 came near to endorsing this point of view: "It was . . . agreed that unladen weight was an essential criterion for aeroplanes." [22] The idea of relying on unladen weight alone had the great merit of simplicity, and it was soon to be taken up again.

This Report of the Air Commission was dated June 8. On June 22 President Hoover's plan was laid before the Conference. The President said:

"Air Forces. All bombing-planes to be abolished. *This will do away with the military possession of types of planes capable of attacks upon the civil populations,* and should be coupled with the total prohibition of all bombardment from the air." [23]

The President said nothing about restrictions on the fighter aircraft that would still be allowed. But the discussion in the Air Commission had made it certain that if any treaty was made at all, these aircraft must also be restricted in size, and, of course, limited in number.

[22] *Conference Documents,* Vol. I, p. 250.
[23] *Minutes of the General Commission,* Vol. I, p. 123.

The Hoover plan marked the climax of the first stage in the British Cabinet conflict which has been described. Five months later, Mr. Stanley Baldwin made the speech in which he urged that all national air forces ought to be abolished; but he made this proposal with the following proviso: if they were abolished, he said, " there would still be civil aviation, and in civil aviation there are the potential bombers. It is all very well using the phrase ' international control,' but nobody quite knows what it means, and the subject has never been investigated. *In my view, it is necessary for the nations of the world concerned . . . to devote the whole of their minds to this question of civil aviation, to see if it is possible so to control civil aviation that such disarmament will be feasible. . . .*"

It was on this basis that the compromise plan contained in the British Government's Draft Convention of 1933 was drawn up. The Air section of this Draft Convention was based on the principle of qualitative disarmament; it embodied the plan for an inquiry into civil aviation which Mr. Baldwin had expounded to the House of Commons; and it provided for a drastic interim measure of air reduction and limitation. Thus:

1. An unladen weight of three tons was taken as the size of aircraft which could not be used for bombing or other purposes of offence.

2. Aircraft of over this weight were to be destroyed within five years.

3. Exceptions were made for troop carriers and flying boats, which might weigh more than three tons; but particulars of such aircraft had to be furnished to the Permanent Disarmament Commission.

4. The total number of aircraft " in commission in the Land, Sea, and Air Armed Forces of each of the H.C.P." was to be drastically reduced; the major Powers—Britain, United States, France, Italy, Russia, Japan, were allowed 500, including troop carriers and flying boats; Poland was allowed 200, Sweden 75, and so on.

5. Each Party was also allowed to keep a number of aircraft " in immediate reserve," not exceeding in each case 25 per cent. of the number which it had in commission.

6. There was to be "complete abolition of bombing from the air " (a reservation about the N.W. Frontier was withdrawn).[24]

7. Air force personnel, including long-term personnel, were to be limited as proposed by the Preparatory Commission.

8. But by far the most important provision of the British Draft, and the only one which gave it any hope of general acceptance, was Mr. Baldwin's plan:

" The Permanent Disarmament Commission . . . *shall immediately devote itself to the working out of the best possible schemes providing for*:

" (a) *The complete abolition of military and naval aircraft*, which must be dependent on the effective supervision of civil aviation to prevent its misuse for military purposes. . . .

" The schemes prepared by the P.D.C. shall be reported to the second Disarmament Conference " (in five years time).[25]

These proposals, drastic as they appear today, were received with disappointment in March 1933. But if they had been accepted, they would have meant something like a 60 per cent. cut in the numbers of aircraft then possessed by Britain, France and the other major Powers, and a far greater cut in their offensive power; they would have stopped the development of the heavy bomber; and would have given time for public opinion to force the adoption of the measures needed for the total abolition of military aircraft, and for the internationalisation or international control of civil aviation.[26]

[24] Sir A. Eden, *Hansard*, July 5, 1933, cols. 370–371.
[25] The full text of the British Draft Convention and its Annexes is given in *Conference Documents*, Vol. II, pp. 476 *et seq.*
[26] See pp. 435 *et seq.*

As has been said above, if the Draft Convention had been put forward six months sooner, it might well have brought success. If, when it *was* put forward, it had been bolder, it might still have brought success. An able observer of the Conference wrote that the debate on the Draft Convention "revealed an almost unanimous opinion in favour of the complete abolition of military and naval air forces." [27] In any case, there had been an immense evolution of opinion since the experts' Washington Report of 1921; all the major governments had changed their view; and concrete plans for drastic air disarmament, designed to lead to the total abolition of national air forces, had been prepared.

## Proposals for Air Disarmament, 1958

This development of thinking about air armaments has been described, and an outline of the proposals for air disarmament made between the Wars has been given, because they furnish the only guidance for present action that now exists. None of the issues discussed above have been raised in the debates of the UN since 1946. There have been *no* proposals for a " ceiling " in the numbers of permitted aircraft, nor for the abolition of certain types of aircraft, *e.g.*, bombers; no mention of the advantages or the dangers of total abolition of national air forces; no discussion of the technical problems of their reduction and limitation; no examination of the residual problem of civil aviation.

But all these problems were thoroughly discussed between the Wars. And since everything that was then urged by those who wanted air disarmament has been proved correct by subsequent events, it is useful to remember what they said, and to reconsider the plans which they devised. It is still true, as they said, that all conventional disarmament " hangs on the air "; that what can be done about land and naval armaments will depend on what is

[27] M.G., May 29, 1933.

done about air forces; that aircraft are still weapons which are " specifically offensive," " most efficacious against national defence " and " most threatening to civilians "; and that no disarmament treaty will, therefore, be worth while that does not either abolish or drastically reduce and limit the air forces which national governments maintain.

How can this be done? Three alternative methods must be considered: (i) total abolition of all military and naval aircraft; (ii) the abolition of bombers, and perhaps other types, together with the reduction and limitation of the remaining permitted aircraft; (iii) reduction and limitation of air forces, without the abolition of any existing types.

### ABOLITION OF ALL MILITARY AND NAVAL AIRCRAFT

This is obviously the most satisfactory solution, and the easiest to control, if governments can be persuaded to agree. At the time when the British Draft Convention was being prepared, Major-General Temperley wrote of the fear of " that instant and overwhelming attack which haunts governments and general staffs today." [28] In 1934 Sir Anthony Eden said that: " If the menace from the air was to be entirely removed, military and naval aircraft must be completely abolished." [29]

This is still true; no one has ever answered Mr. Baldwin's case. So long as national air forces exist, there will be a risk that secret stocks of aircraft may be built up. The rules, for example, about the replacement of crashed or worn out aircraft will be difficult to draft, and their application will not be easy to control; and the larger the permitted air forces, the greater the risk of evasion.

There will likewise be a risk that *qualitative* competition will go on. The progress of aeronautical engineering is so rapid that, whatever restrictions on the character of aircraft are imposed, it will be difficult to ensure that they remain effective, and that they maintain approximately the agreed

[28] *The Whispering Gallery of Europe*, p. 273.
[29] *Observer*, July 29, 1934.

balance of strength between the signatory Powers. Each government will fear that its rivals are producing, within the permitted limits, better or more powerful aircraft than its own.

But the strongest reason for abolition is that aircraft are now, and will for years remain, the best "means of delivery" for the weapons of mass-destruction, whether nuclear, chemical, incendiary or biological. What are now classed as small fighter aircraft could be used to carry out a biological, a chemical, an incendiary, an atomic or perhaps even a hydrogen attack. With the first four of these weapons, a few hundred fighter aircraft might achieve a devastating result.

As aircraft are by far the most powerful weapons of conventional attack, their abolition would be of great significance in measures of conventional naval and land disarmament. How true this is, will appear in Chapters 36, 37 and 38.

Finally, with abolition there would be no difficulty about control. If there were any UN Inspection worthy of the name, the manufacture of military aircraft, and training in their use, could not possibly be concealed. There would remain, of course, the problem of civil aviation; that could be dealt with by the methods discussed in the next chapter.

In short, while every reasonable person would welcome any measure of practical air disarmament to which the governments may agree, it is plain that the safest and most satisfactory plan would be, as Sir Anthony Eden said a quarter of a century ago, that "military and naval aircraft should be completely abolished."

## The Abolition of Bombers

If total abolition is rejected, the second best is obviously "partial abolition"; if possible, on the basis of the Hoover plan and the British Draft Convention, *i.e.*, the abolition of bombing planes.

To make the abolition of bombers effective, a number of questions must be decided, and a number of supplementary guarantees agreed to:

1. If bombers are abolished, what method of determining and restricting the size and power of permitted aircraft will be accepted as effective and fair?

Probably the best method would still be that of the Eden Draft of 1933: to fix a maximum unladen weight for permitted aircraft, and to agree that all above it shall, by stages, be destroyed. The definition of " unladen weight " given in the Draft would still be adequate.[30] Probably three tons would be regarded as extremely small; hardly any modern fighters weigh as little as that. Every aircraft must today carry much more radar and electronic equipment than existed in 1933; it is needed not only for combat, but for safe flying by night, and, in bad weather, by day. This equipment is very heavy. On the other hand, aero-engines give much more power per lb. than they did then, the design of airframes has improved, and the lifting power per square metre of wing area has been increased. On balance, the " useful load " and the range of a three-ton aircraft might not be much greater than it was then. In any case, *an unladen weight should be fixed that would eliminate any aircraft that could carry nuclear bombs*; other things being equal, the less the permitted weight, the more effective the disarmament will be, and the less the risk of inequality of " performance " in the aircraft of the various signatory Powers.

2. In order to minimise the danger that permitted fighters, or civil aircraft, should be used for bombing, the following provisions should be inserted in the disarmament treaty:

(i) The manufacture, possession and use of all kinds of aerial bombs and projectiles, of bomb-racks, bomb-release mechanisms, bomb-aiming devices, torpedo-carriers and torpedo-release mechanisms should be forbidden.

[30] Art. 41, Annex I.

This would greatly reduce the danger of illicit preparation for an aggressive air attack. The mechanisms required for bombing are extremely complex and extremely costly; it would be very difficult to conceal their manufacture.

(ii) The testing of bombs and bombing devices should be forbidden. This would be easy to control; bombing tests could not be concealed, and the making of bombs is so intricate a business that much testing is required.

(iii) The training of air personnel for bombing should be forbidden. This again would be easy to control; bombing practice, like bombing tests, could not be concealed. This would be an important safeguard against illicit preparation for an aggressive air attack; the training of bomber pilots is long and costly. It would, in particular, be a safeguard against the use of nuclear bombs, which involve special dangers to the bombing crew.

Thus, if these provisions were inserted in the disarmament treaty, the signatory nations could have a reasonable degree of confidence that the abolition of bombers would be effective, and that the temptation to a disloyal government to attempt aggression by air bombardment would be much reduced.

## REDUCTION AND LIMITATION OF PERMITTED AIRCRAFT

If bombing aircraft were abolished, and a maximum unladen weight accepted for the permitted aircraft, the disarmament treaty would have to establish an agreed balance of air strength between the signatory Powers, by the reduction and limitation of the residual air forces that they were respectively allowed to have. To this end, the methods of limitation of the British Draft Convention should be adopted. Thus:

### First-Line Aircraft

The unladen weight (*e.g.*, three tons) of the permitted aircraft should be laid down, and the maximum armament which they might carry; and the numbers of these aircraft which each signatory might keep in commission should be fixed.

## Reserve Aircraft and Air Material

The treaty should also fix the numbers to be kept in " immediate reserve " (to replace crashes, for use while aircraft in commission were undergoing extensive maintenance and repair, etc.). Perhaps, as in the British Draft, this might be fixed at 25 per cent. of the first-line machines. It should further fix the numbers of other reserve aircraft and aero-engines to be kept, assembled or in unassembled component parts, and the depots at which they might be stored.

## Replacement of Aircraft

It should lay down rules for the replacement of permitted aircraft, when they reach the term of their useful service life. This is a difficult matter, but one of great importance, as it will help to check the race in the *quality* of permitted aircraft that may all too easily take place.

## Budgetary Limitation

Strict budgetary limitation of the money allowed to air forces would also help to prevent the development of a race in the quality of permitted aircraft. There should be :

(i) A limitation of the total amount allowed to be spent on the air force. This would help to prevent, or to detect, the illicit expansion of air personnel.

(ii) A sub-limitation of the amount permitted to be spent on aircraft, air armament, equipment and other air material. This would greatly help to prevent the constant development of new and more powerful types of aircraft, and the over-rapid replacement of existing aircraft with these new and better types.

## Limitation of Personnel

(i) The *total numbers* of the permitted personnel of each national air force should be limited.

(ii) A fixed ratio should be established between the number of permitted aircraft and the number of permitted men.

(iii) There should be a sub-limitation of the number of permitted long-term " *regulars* "; again, a standard ratio of regulars to conscripts—perhaps one officer for every twenty men, and one N.C.O. for every fifteen—might be agreed.

This point is of great importance in respect of air forces, in view of the long-term training and experience which are required; it might, therefore, be agreed that air forces should have a larger proportion of long-term men than armies or navies.

(iv) There should be a sub-sub-limitation of the number of permitted *pilots*. This was proposed by the Italian officer in the Washington Committee of Experts in 1922. It was a most intelligent proposal, and it would be an even more effective safeguard now against evasion of the disarmament treaty than it would have been then. A rigid limitation of the number of military pilots would effectively limit the fighting strength of an air force, and attempts at evasion by passing numbers of reserves through the training courses would certainly be found out by the inspectors.

All the technical restrictions proposed above are relatively straightforward. Political decisions would, of course, be needed: about the ratio of strength between the signatory Powers, about the unladen weight of permitted aircraft, the numbers of permitted aircraft which each signatory might have, the number of personnel per aircraft, etc. On any of these points, agreement might be difficult to secure; *e.g.*, Russia probably employs considerably more men per aircraft than the Western Powers. But such political decisions must be made about every kind of armed force and armament, if there is to be a disarmament treaty at all. The difficulties in respect of air forces would be much reduced if the governments adopted the method of the British Draft, *i.e.*, took an arbitrary figure for the number of permitted aircraft, far below the strength of the existing forces, and built the rest of the reduction and limitation system around that.

It is not to be expected that, with air forces at their present strength, the governments, at the first stage, would accept anything like the British figure of 1933: 500 fighters for the major Powers, and proportionately fewer for the rest. But even if the figure were much larger, a proposal for a big reduction, for some arbitrary ratio of strength reflecting roughly the present military *status quo*, would be more likely than other plans to secure acceptance. If the major Air Powers agree to a large reduction, there is unlikely to be much trouble over the numbers permitted to the rest.

It must be repeated that the smaller the numbers that are allowed, the easier it will be to detect evasions, if they occur.

### REDUCTION AND LIMITATION OF AIR FORCES

If bombers are not to be abolished, if all the existing types of aircraft are to be retained, and if air disarmament is to consist simply in the reduction and limitation of the numbers of these existing aircraft which each signatory nation may possess, then the making of an air disarmament treaty becomes difficult in the extreme. Since this appears, from the vague phrases used in the Sub-Committee, to be precisely what the Western Governments now intend, it may be useful to try to visualise what such a treaty would be like.

The treaty would have to be founded on the kind of system adopted for the Washington and London Naval Treaties. That is to say, the aircraft of the national air forces would have to be divided into classes, according to their unladen weight, which determines their capacity for carrying bombs—that is, their main offensive power; the number allowed to each signatory in each class would have to be fixed; the armament permitted in each class would have to be laid down. As aircraft at present vary from one ton up to 250 tons, while even larger types are projected, the treaty would need schedules which, over-simplified, might look like this:

| Class | Maximum Unladen Weight | Maximum Calibre and Nature of Armament |
|---|---|---|
| Heavy Bombers | 250 tons | (i) 5″ rocket launchers, air-to-ground.<br>(ii) Air-to-air guided missiles.<br>(iii) $x$ machine guns. (This kind of armament might be needed by bombers for self-defence against fighters.) |
| Transport Aircraft | 250 tons | ditto |
| Tanker Aircraft for refuelling in the air | 100 tons | ditto |
| Medium Bombers | 50 tons | ditto |
| Photographic Reconnaissance Aircraft | 30 tons | (i) Air-to-air guided missiles.<br>(ii) $x$ machine guns. |
| Fighter-Bombers | 12 tons | (i) 5″ rocket launchers, air-to-ground.<br>(ii) Air-to-air and air-to-ground guided missiles.<br>(iii) $x$ machine guns. |
| Fighters | 6 tons | (i) Air-to-air guided missiles.<br>(ii) $x$ machine guns. |

This is a very crude suggestion of the kind of classification that would be required; once negotiations about the limits to be imposed on the different classes were begun, innumerable points of great difficulty would arise. How complex the negotiation would become can be readily understood, if an attempt is made to imagine the United States delegates and the Russians arguing about how to fit B 47s, B 52s, B 58s, and T.U. and Bison bombers into the Table.

The difficulties would be greater still when, in each class, a figure had to be inserted for the number of aircraft permitted to each signatory Power.

Indeed, it seems all too likely that the experts, if they were once let loose in this jungle of technical complications and potential disputes, would fail to find a way out. Even if the cut were as large as 50 per cent. of the present numbers, the difficulties would remain very formidable indeed. If the cut were only 10 or 15 per cent., as has been suggested, and if the qualitative race in the " performance " of aircraft were allowed to go on, it is doubtful whether it would be worth while to try to make a treaty at all. A 10 per cent. cut would leave the United States with over 37,000 aircraft in its forces; it is hard to see how, with such enormous figures, the faithful execution of the cut could ever be controlled. If the race in the speed and range of aircraft is to continue, it might be better, as with missiles, to give up talking about disarmament at all.

## Conclusions

By 1918 aircraft had become a major weapon of war. Between the Wars, there was a growing consensus of opinion that they were " specifically offensive," " especially efficacious against national defence," and " most threatening to civilians." This led to proposals for the total abolition of national air forces, to which by March 1933 many leading governments had given their support. During the 1939 War, all the predictions of those who had favoured total air disarmament were fulfilled. The case for the total abolition of all national air forces, with international control of civil aviation, is now stronger than ever before. It is the only method that would effectively and certainly end the threat of a sudden and unprovoked air attack. Total abolition has also other great advantages; it enormously reduces the danger from the mass-destruction weapons; it is the simplest and the safest method, and the easiest to control. It could be carried out by stages, if the ultimate obligation to abolish were agreed.

But if this is not agreed to, the abolition of bombers, bombs, bombing devices, bombing training and the right to bomb would mean a great reduction in the danger of air aggression; it would not be difficult to control; it would mean that a disloyal government would have little hope of using air power to win a victory by " sudden and unprovoked attack." To secure this result, and to ensure that the disarmament treaty was not evaded, all the methods of limitation described above—limitation of numbers and types of aircraft, of air personnel, air training and air force budgets—should be adopted and combined; they will serve to check and counter-check each other.

Either of these proposals for total or " partial " air disarmament would be a practicable and realistic policy today —far more realistic than seeking to defend a nation against air attack by the retention of the present air forces with all the types of aircraft they now possess. But, as has just been said, it is doubtful whether any minor cut in the numbers of existing aircraft, without the abolition of bombers or other significant limitation of aircraft types, would serve a useful purpose. A treaty of this kind would be very difficult to draft, and even harder to control.

Every nation has a vital interest in ending its present haunting fear of " instant and overwhelming attack." But no nation has so great an interest as Britain. If the fear of air aggression were abolished, Britain would regain the island security she used to have. If we think of armaments in terms of what will ensure effective national defence, the abolition of national air forces should be a major purpose of our policy.

# 35

## *The Problem of Civil Aviation*

### *Military and Civil Aviation*

MERCHANT ships have always been valuable auxiliaries to national navies. Civil aviation constitutes a similar reserve for national air forces. The greater the number of civil aircraft a nation has, the larger is its aircraft industry, the greater the number of its maintenance technicians, the larger its total of trained flying personnel. It has always been accepted, and it is still accepted, that a flourishing civil aviation is an important factor in air power. In 1955 Mr. Quarles, the United States Secretary for Air, said that a " huge commercial order " for jet-propelled air-liners would " help greatly in maintaining the qualitative superiority of our air force." Mr. Robertson, the Deputy-Secretary of Defence, said that the jet fleet would be " a welcome addition to our reserve." [1]

For this reason, many governments have given, and still give, large subsidies from public funds to build up their national air lines, and to foster commercial and private flying in every way they can.

### *The Problem Between the Wars*

It was believed between the Wars that civil aircraft could be readily transformed into bombers, and that their crews could almost instantly become efficient air force personnel; and this view was put forward, from 1922 onwards, as constituting a major difficulty in air disarmament. Mr. Baldwin set out this difficulty in the speech which has been

---

[1] N.Y.T., October 14, 1955.

quoted; national air forces could not be reduced and limited, unless adequate measures could be devised to ensure that a disloyal government would not evade its treaty obligations by increasing its civil aircraft, and making them readily adaptable for war.  Still less could national air forces be abolished, unless means were found to ensure that an aggressor could not successfully use his civil aircraft in a sudden and unprovoked attack.

## Proposals of the League Preparatory Disarmament Commission

To meet this danger, the League Preparatory Commission included in their Draft Convention provisions which forbade the parties to enjoin on their aircraft manufacturers " the embodiment of military features in the construction of civil aviation material . . ."; to make preparations in peace-time to convert civil into military aircraft by installing armaments; to require civil aviation enterprises to employ personnel trained for military purposes; or to subsidise, directly or indirectly, air lines " principally established for military purposes instead of being established for economic, administrative or social purposes." The parties, moreover, were to " encourage . . . the conclusion of economic agreements between civil aviation undertakings in the different countries, and to confer together to this end."

The observance of these undertakings was to be ensured by a system of international inspection.

## Proposals at the Disarmament Conference, 1932

When the Disarmament Conference met in 1932, many delegations proposed much bolder schemes, and some spoke in general terms of " internationalising " all the civil air lines of the world.  In June 1932 the Belgians carried the matter beyond the stage of general terms; they put forward a detailed plan for the international ownership, management and control of civil air lines; its financial basis was a scheme for speedy, and extremely cheap, air postal services.

Other detailed proposals were put forward by the French, the Swedes, the Dutch and the Spaniards.[2] Among them, these nations had a great fund of practical experience in the running of air services; the Dutch and the Swedes had what at that time were regarded as the finest air lines in the world; their plans were a solid basis on which a practical system could have been prepared.

In November 1932 the French Government proposed that civil aviation should be controlled by the methods suggested by the P.D.C.; that there should also be created a " European Air Transport Union," which should manage and supervise all public air transport in Europe, and apply safeguards against the use of civil aircraft for military purposes; and that an international air force, to serve the League, should be set up. The personnel of the force were to be found by " direct recruiting from volunteers of different nationalities, in accordance with a quota system to be laid down." [3] The Swedes also proposed an international air police force, putting forward a carefully considered scheme based (like NATO) on a system of national contingents.

These detailed and authoritative plans were in existence when the Baldwin-Eden plan for an inquiry into the best means of supervising civil aviation was put forward; and they had received the endorsement of many of the Air Powers. If the British Draft Convention had been accepted, and national air forces had been drastically cut, as it proposed, an adequate system for guarding against the dangers of civil aviation could certainly have been drawn up. If this had been done during the five-year period for which the Draft Convention provided, the way would have been open to the total abolition of national air forces in 1938. The support of public opinion for this solution would have been extremely strong.

[2] The text of these proposals can be found in *Britain's Air Policy*, Jonathan Griffin, 1935, pp. 189 *et seq.*
[3] *Conference Documents*, Vol. II, pp. 435–439.

## Military Value of Civil Aircraft in the 1939 War

The predictions made about the military value of civil aircraft were not fulfilled in the 1939 War. Nowhere were they used for any more directly military purpose than the transport of troops, petrol and other supplies. Indeed, already in 1943 General Mance could write:

> " We have . . . long passed the stage when fighter aircraft can be improvised from any class of civilian plane, and have already reached in the present war a stage of development where a transport aircraft is no more readily adaptable for bombing than is the merchant ship at sea for conversion to a naval vessel. . . . We can without doubt put gun turrets on transport aircraft and adapt them to the carriage of moderate bomb loads. We shall not be able to fit them for the carriage of the heaviest bombs. . . . Thus, in spite of the fact that many parts are the same, *the divergence between military and civil types is continually increasing.*" [4]

Writing after the war, Mr. J. M. Spaight said:

> " (The argument) that air liners could be easily converted into night-bombers is no longer of much substance . . . civil aircraft can be used in war, but only for transportation and similar services. . . . They are extremely vulnerable. That was proved over and over again in the Second World War. . . . Civil machines are at the mercy of fighters." [5]

## Civil and Military Aviation Today

It is still true that civil aviation constitutes a potential reserve for national air forces, insofar as it increases the number of trained air personnel, enlarges the capacity of a national aircraft industry, and so on. Indeed, the numbers, speed

[4] *International Air Transport*, 1943, p. 103.
[5] *Air Power and War Rights*, 3rd ed., 1949, pp. 395–396.

and load-carrying capacity of civil aircraft are all growing so fast that their relative importance as a factor in air power is much greater than it was before the war; and there is no foreseeable limit either to the increase in their numbers or to the improvement in their performance.[6]   Other things being equal, this adds to the gravity of the problem of civil aviation under a system of air disarmament, *i.e.*, to the danger that an intending aggressor might try to use his civil aircraft for a sudden attack, if national air forces had all been abolished or very drastically reduced.

But other things are not equal.   The divergence between military and civil types of aircraft has continued.   Major-General R. H. Bower wrote in 1954:

" Civil aircraft are tending to develop farther and farther away from the military requirements, and are rapidly becoming one-purpose aircraft.   Being jets or turbo-props, they are pressurised, and therefore have small side doors and are difficult to load or unload. Due to these and other factors they could not drop parachutists, still less equipment.   They have relatively weak floors, a high landing speed, need long and good runways, and would therefore be unable to operate in many areas where they might be required." [7]

Further, civil machines are as vulnerable as ever to fighter attack, if not more so.   Their speeds are being increased, but much less quickly than the speed of interceptor planes.   However great their progress, they will probably remain hundreds of miles-an-hour slower.

## Civil Aviation and Air Disarmament

How do these facts affect the hope of air disarmament?

It can still be argued, as some people used to argue, that air disarmament, even without special measures to deal with

[6] See, *e.g.*, Sir Arnold Hall, Director of Royal Aircraft Establishment, Brancker Lecture, *The Times*, February 15, 1957; Sir Roy Fedden, *Britain's Air Survival*, 1957.
[7] *Brassey's Annual*, 1954, p. 184.

civil aviation, would be much safer than the continuance of competitive preparation for air war. But few governments are likely to accept this proposition. They will certainly argue, as they argued between the Wars, that, if there is total or drastic air disarmament, civil machines may be used to make a sudden attack. They will maintain that, however great the general divergence between civil and military aviation, some types of civil aircraft could be adapted to drop the smaller nuclear weapons, and perhaps even an H-bomb; floors, they will say, can easily be strengthened by clamping steel plates (" pods ") on the outside; research and tests are constantly reducing the size and weight of nuclear bombs. They will, therefore, argue that the increase in the numbers, speed and load-capacity of civil aircraft makes " safeguards " of the kind discussed in Chapter 32 *more*, and not *less*, necessary than they were then.

To many people concerned with aviation this argument, so potent between the Wars, will now seem quite unreal. The modern air-liner, and indeed most modern civil aircraft, they say, would be extremely difficult to adapt for bombing; the aeronautical risks involved in fitting bomb-racks, or other bombing devices, would be great; the preparations for the adaptation, the hoists, etc., required for loading bombs, would be so large and elaborate that they would be difficult to conceal. In short, the nightmare fear that civil aircraft will be abused is no longer the powerful argument that it was.

Nevertheless, this argument will certainly be used, and it might become again a major obstacle to the acceptance of air disarmament. Safeguards against the use of civil aviation for aggression are, therefore, required as a complement to air disarmament. Of what kind can these safeguards be? Two separate hypotheses must be considered: the *partial* and the *total* air disarmament, discussed in the last chapter.

PARTIAL AIR DISARMAMENT: THE ABOLITION OF BOMBERS

What is the danger, on this hypothesis? What measures should be taken to meet it?

If bombers were abolished, some civil aircraft could, no doubt, carry General Mance's "moderate bomb loads," and therefore the light-weight nuclear bombs which now exist. They have "relatively weak floors"; they might need strengthening even to carry a single H-bomb. They would certainly need *some* conversion—the fitting of bomb-racks, bomb-sights, etc.; the pilots and aircrew would need *some* training—the launching of a nuclear bomb is a risky business for the men who do it; it must be done from great heights, and at a great distance from the target area. These measures of training and conversion would inevitably take time, and cause the aggressor both trouble and delay.

*Regulations for the De-Militarisation of Civil Aviation*

The first step required, therefore, to prevent the misuse of civil aircraft is to make these measures of training and conversion as difficult as possible to carry out and to conceal:

(i) There must be in the general disarmament treaty, stringent rules of the kind proposed in the Draft Convention drawn up by the Preparatory Commission of the League, and reproduced in the British Draft Convention of 1933.

(ii) There must be stringent rules prohibiting the manufacture of bombs, bomb-racks, bomb-sights, bomb-hoists, and the other technical equipment which bombing requires, and all military training of air personnel.

(iii) The observance of these restrictions must be subject to regular and continuous inspection by the expert international officers of the UN. This would be no paper guarantee; the chances that attempted evasion would be discovered would be great.

## UN Control of Civil Air Traffic

UN Inspectors could also be used to diminish the risk that attacks by civil aircraft could be successfully camouflaged as ordinary peaceful flights. The Inspectors could be permanently stationed on every airport, and charged with ensuring that no aircraft should take off without permission, to be granted only after an Inspector had examined the aircraft and its cargo immediately before its engines were started up.

These arrangements would be costly, in cash and manpower; but the cost would be negligible, compared to the cost of national air forces. They would mean the minimum of interference with the normal working of civil aviation. They would not be a fool-proof guarantee against aggression; the aggressor, if he were ready to go to war, might not hesitate to dispose of or even kill the UN Inspectors. But they would be one more serious deterrent, for the aggressor's preparations would take him a considerable time, and there would be the constant risk that the Inspectors, whose duty it would be to visit every aircraft every day, might at any moment find him out.

## Defence by Fighter Aircraft

On the hypothesis now being discussed, the signatory Powers would retain their fighter aircraft and their radar warning screens. If the first attacks were successfully camouflaged as ordinary peaceful flights, as they might be, the victim's fighters would not be warned in time. But once the first bomb had been dropped, the chances of survival for the aggressor's civil aircraft would be slight; they would be at the mercy of the defending fighters, and they would be lucky if any of them reached their base.

### Total Air Disarmament

If all national military and naval air forces were abolished, including fighters, other and more drastic guarantees against the use of civil aircraft for aggression would be

demanded, as they were in 1932. These guarantees might
be of three kinds:

## 1. *Internationalisation of Airports*

The airports of the world might be placed under the
management of an international authority appointed by the
UN. This sounds ambitious, but in reality the technical
difficulties would not be great. Ninety-five per cent. of the
personnel of each airport could be recruited locally; only
the higher ranks of the staff need be appointed by, and be
responsible to, the international authority. International
management would have considerable advantages from the
civil aviation point of view. Almost every air service is
international, and most civil aircraft cross several countries
every day; it would be of value in many ways if on each
airport the aircrews could deal with men of their own
nationality. International management would mean that
every airport would be developed to, and maintained at, the
highest standards of equipment and efficiency; shortage of
capital, and national shortcomings, would be eliminated.

But, more important, it would be an even better
guarantee than a permanent team of UN Inspectors that
an aggressor could not secretly prepare his civil aircraft for
a sudden and unprovoked attack.

## 2. *International Directors on Boards of Civil Air Lines*

Internationalisation of civil aviation would have been a
fairly simple matter in 1932, when the French, Belgian and
other governments proposed their plans. Today the
number of national civil air line corporations and private
companies is greater; the volume of traffic has enormously
increased; the vested interests involved are much greater.
Much of the wasteful and dangerous competition which
then existed has been eliminated, or mitigated, by the work
of the International Air Transport Association. It is

probably true that international ownership and/or management, of the kind proposed for atomic energy by UNAEC,[8] would still have economic and political advantages for civil aviation too. There is certainly scope for more co-ordinated planning of services, maintenance and investment in the industry than exists today, and a need for " a publicly accountable authority" to decide matters in which " different aspects of the public interest," or public and private interests, conflict.[9] International management, if it were accepted, would effectively eliminate the danger that civil aircraft could be mobilised and used for aggressive war. As the French Minister for Air said in 1932, when he was urging the internationalisation of civil air lines, and the creation of an international air police, the greater the degree of internationalisation, the less the need for an air police.

But it would certainly be very difficult to secure acceptance for so radical a change as this would mean. Nor, perhaps, is it necessary. International co-operation has been carried very far in IATA. It might be practicable to entrust the system of inspection to IATA, and to make them responsible to the UN for ensuring that civil aviation was not prepared for use in war. There is little doubt that they could effectively perform this duty.

## 3. *An International Air Police*

Until recently, the creation of an international air police seemed Utopian. With the success of the UN Emergency Force in Sinai, and the pledges of many governments to co-operate in the establishment of a standing UN Force, it has become practical politics.

*Technically*, the organisation of an international air police presents no difficulties. Either the French or Swedish plans of 1933 could be taken as a starting point for drawing up a scheme.[10] Since the air police would

[8] See pp. 194 *et seq.*
[9] See Stephen Wheatcroft, *The Economics of European Air Transport*, Part III.
[10] See p. 431.

only have civil aircraft to oppose them, their mastery of the air would be complete. It would probably be decided that they would only need fighters; if it were also felt that the weapon of retaliation by bombing must be retained as an ultimate deterrent against aggression, agreement for a bomber force could probably be obtained.

Probably the simplest and safest basis for an international air police would be direct UN recruitment of individual volunteers, with appropriate quotas for the different nationalities. It might be easier to secure acceptance of the plan, and the force, when created, might inspire greater confidence, if its personnel were chosen only from the " middle " and smaller Powers. The " middle " and smaller Powers could certainly furnish officers and men who, both as aviators and as international citizens, would pass the most exacting tests.[11]

An international air police would not only be a guarantee against the use of civil aircraft for aggression; it could perform useful functions in maintaining peace and order, and in serving the standing UN Force, in many parts of the world.

Thus there would be no insuperable difficulty in devising technical measures to deal with the danger of the aggressive use of civil aircraft, if either total or partial air disarmament were carried through. They would require international co-operation more extensive than has hitherto been agreed to; but this international co-operation might have economic, as well as political, advantages. The major difficulty will still be, as it was between the Wars, to secure the agreement of the governments. But if they once made the decision to abolish all national military and naval aviation, that would bring such a profound change in the whole character of international relations that the other " surrenders of sovereignty " proposed above might seem a natural result.

[11] For a detailed discussion of the problems involved in the creation of an International Air Force, see P. J. Noel-Baker, *Challenge to Death* (Ed. S. Jameson), 1934, Chaps. X and XI.

If these far-reaching decisions are made, aviation will have a brilliant future; it will become a major factor in the growth of international institutions and the unification and pacification of the world. But if these decisions are not made, aviation, together with missiles, may be the instrument for the annihilation of mankind. This is the choice which those concerned with aviation, military and civil, must help to make.

# 36

# *Naval Disarmament:*
# *British Interests and the*
# *Lessons of The Wars*

## *Britain's Dependence on the Sea*

NAVAL disarmament must be a matter of special concern to the British people. It is a sphere in which, above all others, they cannot afford to make mistakes.

For almost four centuries the British Navy was the strongest in the world. It successfully performed a great variety of tasks. It contained and defeated the naval forces of Britain's enemies in war—the Spanish Armada; Napoleon's fleet at Trafalgar; the Kaiser's fleet at Jutland; Mussolini's fleet in the Mediterranean. It ensured the safe passage of British armies to countries overseas; in both World Wars this meant to Europe, Africa, the Middle East and Asia. It maintained contact with the other countries of the Commonwealth, and with the British Bases, such as Gibraltar, Malta, Suez, Aden and Hong Kong. It suppressed piracy and ensured the safety of the world's commerce in time of peace. In time of war it brought to British ports the merchant ships without whose cargoes Britain's war effort would have ceased.

In both World Wars this last task was the most important, and the most difficult to fulfil. During the 1939 War there were never less than 2,500 British merchant vessels on the high seas, scattered over scores of thousands of miles of trade routes, and requiring protection in all weathers, and at all seasons of the year. There were about the same number of Allied ships helping to maintain our military and civilian supplies. If the ocean trade routes

441

had been closed, and if imports into Britain had ceased for as long as six weeks, the population of the island would have been close to starvation; much of its transport system would have been immobilised; its industries, including those producing arms, would have come to a standstill.

Britain's dependence on the sea is not likely to grow less in future. In 1957 about fifty million tons of dry goods, and about thirty million tons of oil were imported from abroad. There is every reason to believe that these quantities will grow, and that, as the standard of living rises both in this country and in the under-developed countries, the volume of British overseas trade, and the numbers and size of British merchant ships, will continue to increase.

## The British Navy and the Arms Race

The arms race of the last fifty years has gravely affected the position of the British Navy, and has made all its tasks harder to fulfil. In 1907 it was not only the strongest navy in the world, it was as strong as any other two Powers together (the two Power standard) or even more, not only in battleships and battle cruisers, but in every other category of ship. Today, it is only third in strength to the United States and Russia, and, if the arms race goes on, it is not certain that the navies of other nations with greater populations—Germany, China, Japan—will not some day exceed it in the numbers and the power of their ships.

Moreover, the constant improvement of naval armaments over half a century, and the increasing predominance of attack against defence, have made it much harder for the navy to fulfil its traditional tasks. In 1906 the construction of the Dreadnought began to imperil the supremacy of the Battle Fleet [1]; by 1917 the German submarines made it very difficult for the British cruisers and other escort

---

[1] See pp. 32–34.

vessels to protect our merchant ships; only the tardy adoption of the convoy system saved us from defeat. It was
also shown that aircraft could be used efficaciously against
surface vessels.

While Hitler was maturing his plans for the 1939 War
he said to Rauschning: "Aircraft and the U-boat have
turned surface fleets into the obsolete playthings of the
wealthy democracies." [2] He was so far right that, thanks
to aircraft and submarines, surface vessels suffered as never
before. In the 1939 War 40,000 British merchant seamen
and 70,000 naval officers and men were killed, together
with a large number of Allied seamen. There were periods
when it seemed beyond the power of the British navy to
defeat the enemy attack on our merchant vessels. Indeed,
it is almost certain that it could not have done so without
the massive naval and merchant shipping help of the United
States.

Since 1945 the changes in the methods of war at sea have
still further increased the power of attack as against defence.
Modern aircraft, guided missiles with nuclear warheads,
nuclear-powered submarines, will certainly reduce the
chances of survival for surface ships. Even if nuclear
weapons were not used, aircraft, missiles and submarines
might constitute a mortal danger to surface ships in any
future war. The ending of the arms race, and, if possible,
drastic naval disarmament, are thus a major British interest,
and by far the best hope for the defence of Britain on the
sea.

## The present Naval Arms Race

Before 1914 the competition in naval building was regarded
as the most dangerous single factor in the arms race which,
in Lord Grey's view, caused the First World War.[3] In
1912 the British Navy comprised 522 ships [4]; its manpower
was 137,000; its annual cost, including a large programme

[2] Herman Rauschning, *Hitler Speaks*, p. 129.　　　　[3] See pp. 79-81.
[4] Of which only five were over 18,000 tons displacement, *i.e.*, larger than the
Sverdlov cruisers; a great number were of 700 tons displacement or less.

of new battleship construction, was £45·6m.[5] By 1957 the Navy had become the third in scale, cost, and numbers, of our Services; yet in 1957–58 its manpower was 121,500, and its expenditure £316m.[6]

In 1957 the United States Navy had over 800 ships in commission and more than 4,000 in reserve; its manpower was 620,000, plus nearly 200,000 Marines, who are an integral part of the United States Naval Forces; its cost was close on £3,500m.—more than ten times the cost of the British Navy; it ordered one new ship—a nuclear powered aircraft carrier—at a price of £120m.[7]

The Russians have acted in accordance with Marshal Zhukov's dictum that " In a future war, the struggle at sea will be of immeasurably greater importance than it was in the last war." [8] Since 1945 Russia has built twenty-two cruisers of the Sverdlov class, faster, larger and more heavily gunned than any British cruiser; many destroyers, and about 500 submarines. Russia's rate of submarine output is seventy-five to eighty-five a year; they are now designed to serve as launching platforms for nuclear missiles of the IRBM class, with ranges up to 1,500 miles. The manpower in her Navy is 750,000; she spends one-fifth of her military budget on it; her total naval expenditure in the decade that followed 1945 was £12,000m.

Thus naval armaments play an important part in the present arms race; other nations, according to their means, are joining in, and their forces and expenditure will certainly increase; nuclear propulsion will be applied to all classes of warships, with a vast increase in their cost.

## Naval Disarmament Treaties Between the Wars

Since the competition in naval building before 1914 had been regarded as so dangerous, it was natural that the men

---

[5] Cmd. 127 and 300, 1912.                    [6] Cmd. 151, p. 3.
[7] N.Y.T., August 17, 1957.
[8] 20th Communist Party Congress, February 1956.

who set up the League should seek to deal with it without delay. In the fourteen years that followed the 1914 War there was constant international discussion of the subject, there were numerous conferences, and six treaties were made; four of them imposed drastic naval disarmament on Germany and her allies; the other two reduced and limited the naval forces of the remaining leading Powers.

These treaties were all effective, in the sense that their provisions were carried out; they were faithfully observed over a period of fifteen years; they produced the political results that had been hoped for; they were only abandoned when it was certain that no general treaty of disarmament would be made. They solved all the technical problems of a treaty for the reduction and limitation of the naval armaments that then existed. Many, if not all, of their provisions may serve as a model when the general disarmament treaty comes to be drawn up. A brief outline of the three most important of these treaties is, therefore, worth while.

## The Treaty of Versailles

The Naval Clauses of the Treaty of Versailles were founded on the full application of the principle of qualitative disarmament: they forbade Germany to have any warships or naval weapons that would help her to make aggressive war. She was allowed no capital ships of over 10,000 tons displacement, no aircraft carriers, no naval aircraft, and no submarines; she was permitted six battleships of 10,000 tons displacement; six cruisers of 6,000 tons; twelve destroyers and twelve torpedo boats. The ships might only be replaced after a fixed period of years—twenty for battleships and cruisers, fifteen for the rest; the manpower of the Navy was limited to 15,000. Fortifications and naval bases are of great importance in increasing the effective fighting strength of a navy; stringent restrictions were placed on those which Germany might retain, and some (*e.g.*, on the islands of Heligoland and Dune) were wholly forbidden and destroyed.

## The Washington Naval Treaty of 1922

It was intended by the authors of the Treaty of Versailles that the same kind of naval disarmament should in due course be accepted by all other nations. But since the preparations for a general disarmament treaty were evidently going to be protracted, and since a dangerous naval race between the United States, Japan and Britain had begun, the leading Powers made a preliminary Naval Treaty at Washington in 1922. This Treaty contained the following provisions:

1. It limited the permitted size and armament of three categories of ships, as follows:

| Class | Maximum Permitted Displacement | Maximum Permitted Armament |
|---|---|---|
| Capital ships | 35,000 tons | 16 inch gun |
| Aircraft carrier | 27,000 tons | 8 ,, ,, |
| Cruisers or other ships | 10,000 tons | 8 ,, ,, |

2. It limited the permitted total tonnage in capital ships and aircraft carriers as follows:

| | Capital Ships | Aircraft Carriers |
|---|---|---|
| Britain | 525,000 (15 ships) | 135,000 |
| U.S.A. | 525,000 (15 ,, ) | 135,000 |
| Japan | 315,000 ( 9 ,, ) | 81,000 |
| France | 175,000 ( 5 ,, ) | 60,000 |
| Italy | 175,000 ( 5 ,, ) | 60,000 |

These figures represented the long-term balance of strength agreed to on the basis of the famous " ratio " of 5:5:3: 1·75:1·75. The actual tonnage of the ships retained in 1922 was slightly different, because a number of the British ships were older and less well armed than those of Japan and the United States.

3. The reductions of capital ship tonnage thus agreed to by the three leading Powers were as follows:

$$
\begin{array}{ll}
\text{U.S.A.} & 829,800 \\
\text{Britain} & 593,100 \\
\text{Japan} & 780,900
\end{array}
$$

Part of this tonnage was of ships still under construction, on which a great deal of money had been spent, but which were now abandoned. Apart from ships under construction, the three nations scrapped about 40 per cent. of their existing strength.

4. The Treaty provided a " naval holiday "; no new capital ships or aircraft carriers were to be laid down for a period of ten years. Together with the scrapping of existing tonnage, this meant the saving, for each of the signatory nations, of many scores of £ millions.

5. The Treaty did not limit the total tonnage of cruisers, destroyers, submarines or other classes of ship, for the reason that France categorically refused to agree.

6. The signatories to the Treaty agreed that, in respect of a specified area in the Pacific, they would maintain " the status quo at the time of the present Treaty with regard to fortifications and naval bases."

In spite of its limitations, the Washington Treaty was regarded at the time as an outstanding success. It ended a naval race in which Japanese expenditure on the Fleet had risen from £19m. to £54½m. in four years, while United States expenditure had risen from £27½m. to £94m. It immediately produced a striking détente in the tension between Japan and the United States. Further, as a result of this Treaty, it became a physical impossibility for the United States successfully to attack Japan, and for Japan to attack the United States. Moreover: " These agreements, so far as England and the United States are concerned, have also removed the possibility of war. They have nipped in the bud an impending struggle for the supremacy of the seas." [9] There is no doubt that the Treaty played a major part in creating the relation between Britain and the United States that exists today.

[9] R. L. Buell, *The Washington Conference*, p. 200.

## The London Naval Treaty of 1930

This completed the work of the Washington Conference by securing the agreed reduction and limitation of the cruisers, destroyers, submarines and other warships maintained by Britain, the United States, and Japan. The Treaty contained the following provisions:

1. Total tonnage was limited thus:

|  | Cruisers | Destroyers | Submarines |
|---|---|---|---|
| British Commonwealth | 339,000 | 150,000 | 52,700 |
| U.S.A. | 323,500 | 150,000 | 52,700 |
| Japan | 205,850 | 105,500 | 52,700 |

This meant big cuts in the programmes which had been proposed by all the signatory governments.

2. The Treaty extended the " Naval Holiday " to 1936 —no new capital ship or aircraft carrier construction until then.

3. It limited the maximum displacement of destroyers to 1,850 tons, and of submarines to 2,000 tons.

The London Treaty saved Britain £70m. and the United States £100m. over the following five years. It would have been accepted by Italy and France if a general disarmament treaty had been made.

## The Coolidge Conference of 1927

The London Treaty followed the disastrous failure of a conference summoned in Geneva by President Coolidge in 1927. It was only remarkable for the doctrine of " absolute requirements," which the British Admiralty advanced, and on which the negotiations failed.

The Admiralty argued that Britain's ocean trade-routes were 80,000 miles in length; that on any given day there were nine and a half million tons of British shipping on the seas; that to protect these merchant vessels there must always be available one cruiser for every 2,500 miles of trade-route; that this meant an absolute minimum " requirement " of seventy cruisers, with correspondingly large numbers of destroyers and other craft. These numbers, they said, were necessary, however much the naval tonnage of other nations might be reduced. This argument was deployed before the conference by Lord Jellicoe, the victor of Jutland. President Coolidge had proposed a large reduction in the existing tonnage of the principal Powers; Lord Jellicoe demanded an *increase* for Britain of no less than 220,000 tons.

The doctrine of " absolute requirements " was palpable nonsense. Lord Jellicoe showed in his own speeches that the advantage *always* lay with commerce-raiders against the ships engaged in commerce defence; it followed that the security of British merchant vessels could be best secured by reducing the number of potential enemy ships. The argument was thus expressed by Commander Sir Stephen King-Hall:

> " Granted that all warships were destroyed, the British Empire would automatically enter into a state of potential mastery of the sea transport of the world, such as it has never had in the past and is not likely to be allowed to have in the future. . . . In such a case as soon as a war broke out a nation such as the British with a strong sea spirit and half the merchant tonnage of the world would make a fleet of armed liners capable of dealing with the combined fleets of Europe, if not of the world!" [10]

The doctrine of " absolute requirements " was not only nonsense; it challenged the basis of any disarmament agreement of any kind. The United States delegate, Mr. Gibson, made this plain in the Coolidge Conference. " The United States delegation," he said, " had never been able to reconcile the conception of absolute naval needs with the negotiation of a treaty to fix limitations on the basis of mutual concessions." And he added that acceptance of this conception would " render impossible any effective limitation by international agreement." [11]

[10] *Imperial Defence*, 1926, p. 183.
[11] United States Senate Document No. 55, pp. 63–70.

This is obviously true, and not only of naval armaments. In various countries, and at various times, the conception of " requirements " has been used to justify a great expansion of military preparation in the air. Mr. Stassen came near to advancing it when he said in 1957 that the United States could not accept a manpower ceiling for her forces of less than 2·5 million men.[12] It is a fallacy which has been widely and dangerously accepted, and which is still often consciously or subconsciously allowed to influence thought. That is why the Coolidge Conference has been mentioned here. Its failure was a disastrous set-back which the subsequent success of the London Conference only partially made good.

### Naval Disarmament in the 1932 Conference

The most important naval proposals laid before the Conference of 1932 have been mentioned in Chapter 33 above. They were intended to secure the abolition by stages of capital ships of over 10,000 tons displacement, of aircraft carriers, and of submarines. President Hoover's proposal for an immediate reduction of one-third was clearly intended to be followed by further similar reductions after a period of years. As the Conference progressed a great majority of delegations, including a great majority of the maritime nations, came to accept the view that those three classes of warships were likely to help attack against defence.

Throughout the Conference the British delegation urged that submarines should be abolished, on the ground that they were chiefly useful for law-breaking attacks on merchant ships. Other nations argued that they required submarines for defence against large capital ships and aircraft carriers. It became plain that, if the leading naval Powers would give up their big ships, they could obtain the abolition of submarines in return. A bargain on these lines, agreed to in the early months of the Conference, to

[12] See pp. 25 and 29.

be carried out by President Hoover's stages, might have ensured that a disarmament treaty would have been made. By then all the technical problems had been thoroughly examined, and solutions, both for large and small navies, had been found.[13] But unfortunately the British Admiralty still stood in the way; another of its spokesmen, Admiral Sir Dudley Pound, declared that capital ships could not be classed as " specifically offensive " or " especially efficacious against national defence "; Britain must retain them because they were " more precious than rubies to those who possessed them." It was this British naval stand more than anything else that defeated the Hoover proposals and thus prevented the Geneva Conference from coming to what might have been a quick agreement and a big success. As a direct and inevitable consequence the Versailles, Washington and London Treaties were all denounced. Seven years after Admiral Pound made his speech the 1939 War began; Britain's capital ships played a negligible part in our national defence; Hitler's submarines almost brought us to our knees. In 1945 another pre-war Naval Chief-of-Staff added the final comment on this tragic episode; speaking in the House of Lords, Admiral of the Fleet Lord Chatfield said: " The use of the capital ship is to destroy the enemy's capital ship. *If the enemy has no capital ship, we need none either.*" [14] This was obvious common sense, constantly urged by many delegations in Geneva, but it had required the experience of a second World War to bring it home.

## Naval Qualitative Disarmament and the 1939 War

The experience of the 1939 War also supported the view of those who had urged in the Geneva Conference that

---

[13] The adaptations of the Washington and London Treaties required for smaller Navies were all worked out by the League Preparatory Commission and embodied in their Convention. See *Conference Documents*, Vol. I, pp. 11 *et seq.*
[14] House of Lords, December 2, 1954, col. 139.

aircraft, aircraft carriers and submarines are "specifically offensive" and "especially efficacious against national defence."

## The Role of Aircraft in Naval Operations

Aircraft, shore-based and carrier-based, proved in almost every theatre to be the most efficacious weapon of attack against surface shipping, both warships and merchant ships alike. Lord Tedder has recorded that in the area of the Baltic and the N.W. European seaboard north of Dover, of 2,471 enemy ships sunk and damaged, 289 fell to surface and under-water vessels; the rest, over 88 per cent., to aircraft, either by direct attack or by mines which aircraft laid. In the coastal and enclosed waters from the North Cape to the Bay of Biscay 920 ships were sunk—22·7 per cent. by surface vessels and submarines, 77·3 per cent. by aircraft attack and mines, mostly laid from the air. Lord Tedder adds that the German loss of trade due to the blockade was twice the loss due directly to sinkings—a most effective blockade, conducted mostly from the air.

In the attack on Rommel's supplies to North Africa, which the R.A.F. and the Navy carried on from Malta, and which ensured his ultimate defeat, aircraft played a major part; in the last quarter, August to November 1942, 205,000 tons of Axis shipping was sunk, 35 per cent. by submarine, 61 per cent. by air attack.

In the battle of the Pacific and the blockade of Japan nearly nine million tons out of a total available ten million tons of Japanese shipping was out of action at the end of the war, either sunk or seriously damaged; nearly 55 per cent. was due to submarines and 40 per cent. to air action of various kinds.

During the operations in Crete, which the Germans captured with airborne troops, Britain lost to air attack: three cruisers and six destroyers sunk; one battleship, one aircraft carrier, three cruisers and one destroyer seriously damaged; one battleship, four cruisers and six destroyers in need of extensive repairs.[15]

## Aircraft Carriers

The Japanese had argued in the Geneva Conference that aircraft carriers were " specifically offensive "; they said in their Memorandum:

> " Being highly mobile aerodromes, and capable of acting independently of the fleet, these vessels are not only most suitable for making surprise attacks, but are capable of working havoc upon inland regions far removed from the sea. . . .
>
> " These vessels enhance the capacity of a fleet for reconnaissance, observation, and especially for attack; they also accentuate the aggressive character of a fleet, and enable it to operate in the neighbourhood of the coast of an adversary which even possesses coast-defence air forces.
>
> " The character of these vessels permits of their being employed more advantageously for aggressive than for defensive purposes. Coast-defence air operations can be carried out more effectively and more economically by a shore-based coast-defence air force than by aircraft carriers.
>
> " Being a new arm, they may serve destructive purposes as yet unforeseen." [16]

This was a remarkable document, the full significance of which the Japanese demonstrated at Pearl Harbour in 1941. Sir Winston Churchill has given the following account of their " sudden and unprovoked attack " on the United States:

> " The idea of a surprise attack on Pearl Harbour originated in the brain of Admiral Yamamoto, the

---

[15] These facts are from Marshal of the Royal Air Force Lord Tedder, *Air Power in War*, Lees Knowles Lectures, 1947.
[16] *Conference Documents*, Vol. I, p. 221.

Japanese Commander-in-Chief. Preparation for this
treacherous blow before any declaration of war went
forward with the utmost secrecy, and by November 22
the striking force of *six carriers*, with a supporting force
of battleships and cruisers, was concentrated in an un-
frequented anchorage in the Kurile Islands, north of
Japan proper. Already the date of the attack had been
fixed for . . . December 7, and on November 26 (1941)
the force sailed under the command of Admiral
Nagumo. Keeping far to the northward of Hawaii,
amidst the fog and gales . . . Nagumo approached his
goal undetected. Before sunrise on the fateful day the
attack was launched from a position about 275 miles
to the north of Pearl Harbour. *360 aircraft* took part,
comprising bombers of all types, escorted by fighters.
At 7.55 a.m. the first bomb fell. Ninety-four ships of
the United States Navy were present in the harbour.
Among them the eight battleships of the Pacific Fleet
were the prime targets. . . . By 8.25 a.m. the first
waves of torpedo and dive-bombers had struck their
blow. By 10 a.m. the battle was over and the enemy
withdrew. Behind them lay a shattered fleet hidden
in a pall of fire and smoke, and the vengeance of the
United States. *The battleship Arizona had blown up,
the Oklahoma had capsized, the West Virginia and
California had sunk at their moorings, and every other
battleship, except the Pennsylvania, which was in dry
dock, had been heavily damaged.* Over 2,000
Americans had lost their lives, and nearly 2,000 others
were wounded. The mastery of the Pacific had passed
into Japanese hands, and the strategic balance of
the world was for the time being fundamentally
changed." [17]

Admiral Yamamoto had probably first thought of the
Pearl Harbour plan when he read of the success of an

[17] Churchill, *The Second World War*, Vol. III, p. 545.

earlier aircraft-carrier operation conducted by the British Fleet a year before. Sir Winston Churchill has thus described this operation:

" Taranto lies at the heel of Italy, 320 miles from Malta. Its magnificent harbour was heavily defended against all modern forms of attack. . . . The British plan was to fly two waves of aircraft from the Illustrious, the first of twelve and the second of nine, of which eleven were to carry torpedoes and the rest either bombs or flares. The Illustrious released her aircraft shortly after dark from a point about 170 miles from Taranto. For an hour the battle raged amid fire and destruction among the Italian ships. . . .

" By this single stroke the balance of naval power in the Mediterranean was decisively altered. The air photographs showed that three battleships, one of them the new Littorio, had been torpedoed, and in addition one cruiser was reported hit and much damage inflicted on the dockyard. Half the Italian battle fleet was disabled for at least six months." [18]

These episodes prove that the Japanese had been right to argue in 1932 that aircraft carriers make possible *offensive* operations against distant targets that could not otherwise be attempted; and that they favour sudden and unprovoked aggression.[19]

But other actions in the 1939 War showed that aircraft carriers were not nearly so effective in *defence*. In August 1941 a convoy of fourteen merchant vessels was despatched from Gibraltar to Malta, with an escort of three aircraft carriers, two battleships, and other auxiliary warships; five merchantmen reached Malta; the rest were sunk, while the carrier *Eagle* was also sunk, and the carrier *Indomitable* damaged. Many other episodes besides the sinking of the

[18] Churchill, *The Second World War*, Vol. II, p. 481.
[19] They also demonstrate the point which was made on p. 443, above: that capital ships, like all other surface vessels, are extremely vulnerable to air attack. During the 1939 War, many other such warships were sunk by aircraft, both on the high seas, and at their moorings in port.

*Eagle* showed that aircraft carriers could not even defend themselves. In the Pacific, the two decisive battles, the battle of the Coral Sea and the battle of Midway, were both fought far out of range of the ships' guns; the Japanese lost six aircraft carriers, the United States two, to air attack. The value of the aircraft carrier in defence is far outweighed by its value for attack.

## Submarines

There is no need to argue the case that submarines proved to be weapons that were " specifically offensive " in the 1939 War. They were primarily used by all the belligerents to attack merchant shipping. Their attack on British and Allied shipping in the Atlantic had a devastating success, until air cover for the convoys was fully organised. Lieutenant-Commander Waters recalls " how crippling were our shipping losses and how heavy the loss of life " before air defence was organised by shore-based, escort carrier, and " macship " aircraft.[20] In the Pacific, as was said above, United States submarines sank or severely damaged something like five million tons of Japanese merchant shipping. Allied submarines sank sixty-eight enemy submarines during the course of the war—a small proportion of the total destroyed. This was their principal contribution to defence.

The facts recalled above make a tragic story. For many decades Britain has been increasingly dependent on her foreign trade; if her merchant vessels and those of friendly nations could not sail the seas, her people would soon be hungry and her industry would largely cease. The development and improvement of naval armaments, which resulted from the arms race, continually increased the difficulty of defending ships at sea; in both World Wars

[20] *Journal of the R.U.S.I.*, February 1956, pp. 109–112. " Macship " was the name given to merchantmen that were adapted to carry fighter aircraft.

safe passage across the Atlantic was so gravely menaced that for long periods Britain was faced by the prospect of defeat. These dangers could have been averted, and British interests served, by a general Disarmament Treaty, in which a naval agreement, establishing a fair and stable balance of armed strength at sea, would have played a major part. British Ministers, moved by their memory of the danger of the naval race before the 1914 War, took the lead in starting naval disarmament by the Treaties of Versailles, Washington and London. Other British Ministers threw this work away, and helped to defeat the making of a general disarmament treaty, by their reluctance to give up the capital ship and the aircraft carrier. The consequences of their action were wholly disastrous; they have helped to create the dangerous situation which every maritime nation confronts today.

# 37

# *Naval Proposals for 1958*

## *Developments in Naval Armaments since 1945*

As was said in Chapter 36, all the major developments in naval armament since 1945—the increased speed and carrying capacity of aircraft and of aircraft carriers, nuclear-powered submarines, nuclear weapons, guided missiles—have helped to increase the power of attack against defence. The principal changes in the leading national navies have been as follows:

### Capital Ships

Admiral Jerould Wright, Supreme Commander of the NATO forces in the Atlantic, said in 1956 that the United States then had only three of its battleships in commission, and that " they are now regarded as obsolete in the face of modern air power." [1]

Both the British and United States Governments have now decided to scrap the battleships they had previously kept either in commission or in reserve.

### Aircraft Carriers

These vessels have had the extraordinary development described above.[2] They are now regarded as having " replaced the battleship as the backbone of the modern navy." [3]

The main attraction of the aircraft carrier was explained by the United States Assistant Secretary for the Navy, Mr.

[1] *The Times*, April 25, 1956.
[2] See pp. 62–63.
[3] Admiral J. Wright, N.C., December 11, 1956. Lord Mountbatten, M.G., July 26, 1955.

J. H. Smith, when the *Forrestal* was commissioned in
1955; it was capable, he said, of "*deep invasion of an
aggressor's land mass.*" [4] This means, of course, that the
aggressor's carriers would equally be capable of deep
invasion of its victim's land mass. In other words, they
are especially efficacious against national defence.

A carrier is an extremely mobile air base, capable of
covering 500 miles a day, very difficult to find on the high
sea, and therefore less vulnerable than a land base to sudden
attack by guided missiles from fixed launching sites on land.
It is not expected that a carrier would long survive submarine or air attack with large nuclear weapons. After
the NATO naval exercise " Strike Back " in 1957, Mr.
Hanson Baldwin wrote:

> " In all-out nuclear war in which thermonuclear
> weapons in the megaton range as well as small atomic
> bombs were employed, the life expectancy of any
> carrier would be short indeed. But . . . the carrier
> would have fulfilled its mission if it had stayed afloat
> long enough to deliver its atomic strikes on selected
> land targets." [5]

But post-war events have proved that in " limited " war
the carrier may be of great help to an aggressor in other
ways. " These mobile airfields," said Field-Marshal Lord
Montgomery in 1957, " are greatly valued by the army.
As an example, take the Suez operations in November last
year. In those operations the bulk of the air support for
the army came from naval aircraft operating from
carriers." [6] In fact, the navy's carriers " had to provide
50 per cent. of the preliminary air strike, the whole of the
subsequent close tactical air support, and a proportion of
the airborne troop landings." [7]

[4] Reported by Mr. Hanson Baldwin, N.Y.T., October 2, 1955.
[5] N.Y.T., October 1, 1957.
[6] M.G., October 22, 1957.
[7] Navy League Pamphlet, 1957.

In short, it is probably true to say that the offensive operations at Suez, like the attack on Pearl Harbour, could never have been attempted without aircraft carriers.

## Submarines

There have been four main developments in submarines since 1945.

1. The leading naval powers have begun to build them, as was noted above, in far greater numbers than ever before.

2. The use of nuclear propulsion has given them far greater range, and a capacity for staying almost indefinitely under water. The first atomic submarine, the United States *Nautilus*, cruised 60,000 miles—two and three-quarter times around the world—without refuelling; for 34,500 miles it was submerged; it used up 8·3 lb. of uranium 235; to cover the same distance by conventional propulsion it would have needed three million gallons, or 10,000 tons, of fuel oil.[8] It can attain high speeds; it made one voyage of 1,200 miles *under water* at an average of " well over 20 knots an hour." [9] Later atomic submarines are to have a new reactor which is far more efficient than that which propels the *Nautilus*.

3. There has been a big advance in the submarine's *silent* speed. " A submarine may stalk silently up to the speed at which a noise begins to be set up by the collapse of bubbles produced by the blades of her propeller. During the war this was about three knots; now it is at least eight." [10] This is a fact of immense importance; combined with the increased endurance under water, it makes the submarine extremely difficult to find. Admiral Rickover, who developed the *Nautilus*, said in 1957 that hunting it would be like " trying to find a black cat on a vast and empty plain on a moonless and starless night." [11]

[8] J. Raymond, N.Y.T., March 9, 1957.
[9] Mr. C. S. Thomas, United States Secretary of Navy, *Sunday Times*, April 7, 1957.
[10] *The Times* Naval Correspondent, April 30, 1956.
[11] M.G., September 16, 1957.

4. Submarines are being adapted to fire short-range and intermediate-range missiles either from the surface or when still submerged. Since these missiles might have ranges up to 1,500 miles, no country, and almost no city in the world would be immune from surprise nuclear attack. The submarine, equipped with IRBMs is, in fact, an alternative to the intercontinental ballistic missile; and it is likely to be more accurate.

A great array of new defensive devices have been produced to counter submarine attack—radar; sonar; helicopters; aircraft reconnaissance screens; automatic quick-firing, self-aiming naval mortars; atomic depth charges that will crush any submarine within a square mile, and which become the more effective, the greater the depth at which they are exploded. All these were in use in the NATO exercise, " Sea Watch," in 1957. Yet when the exercise was over, one of the Joint Commanders, East Atlantic, Admiral Sir John Eccles, said:

> " *In recent years the submarine has without any doubt at all gone a very long way ahead of the devices with which we are at present equipped to sound and destroy it.*" And he added: " We are desperately short of all the hardware needed to fight this battle." [12]

A few days later, the Supreme Commander, Admiral Wright, said: " I support all that Admiral Sir John Eccles said last week." [13]

*Missiles*

Missiles with nuclear warheads have been produced for all classes of naval ships. Their use would render the life of any surface vessel extremely precarious. An under-water explosion of a Hiroshima bomb at Bikini in 1946 caused a " base surge "—an immense tidal wave—which was extremely radio-active and was fifty feet high. The larger fission weapons might constitute a grave danger to any

[12] M.G., September 28, 1957.          [13] M.G., October 3, 1957.

surface vessel within a distance of several miles. Admiral Clark of the United States Navy, when asked by the Senate Committee on Armed Forces to comment on the fact that a Russian IRBM could cover 1,500 miles in twenty-five minutes, during which time a carrier could move fifteen miles, replied: " I would not want to be within fifteen miles of a megaton bomb." [14]  There are other methods than that of the IRBM (*e.g.*, missile ship, submarine, aircraft) by which megaton bombs could be aimed at a carrier, or at a convoy, and with much greater accuracy than an error of fifteen miles. A large A-bomb (*e.g.*, 200 kiloton, ten times Hiroshima) might bring disaster to a whole convoy. If, to avoid this danger, a convoy, or, indeed, a battle fleet, were to scatter, it would greatly increase the danger of submarine attack.

## Radar

Radar has been much improved since 1945, and its range has been increased. This helps defence in many ways, in particular by giving earlier warning of air, and possibly of missile, attack. But at sea it also helps attack. " A great ship alone on the sea," says Dr. Vannevar Bush, " is a clear target to radar, and a clear target for a guided bomb." [15]

## Ports

It is useless to bring convoys safely into port, if they cannot be unloaded when they arrive. But the British Admiralty clearly think that the ports might be heavily damaged in another war. Speaking in 1955, the First Sea Lord, Admiral Lord Mountbatten, said:

> " Convoys might have to be run into smaller ports, or unloaded over the beaches, if the main ports were damaged. The navy would also have to be prepared to use landing ships and landing craft to get the imports ashore." [16]

[14] Quoted in King-Hall Newsletter, June 12, 1957.
[15] *Modern Arms and Free Men*, p. 50.
[16] M.G., July 26, 1955.

It is, at least, doubtful whether the British people *could* be fed, or British industry kept working, through the smaller ports, or over the beaches. In any case, an enemy attacking Britain would choose the ports as early targets. All of them could be made unusable for months or years by a single hydrogen mine, laid off the coast days before the attack was due, with a time fuse; the submarine which laid it need never surface, and could be a thousand miles away before the mine exploded; the tidal wave created would simply blot out the port attacked.

The same is true of naval bases. *The Times* Naval Correspondent, commenting on the work of an Admiralty Committee set up by Lord Mountbatten, said:

> " (The Navy's) first task in war would be to get out into open sea, on the assumption that its shore bases at home, vulnerable targets for nuclear weapons, would quickly become untenable." [17]

The developments sketched above show that the power of attack at sea has greatly increased since 1945; that defence has never been at " so low an ebb "; and that, in consequence, if the arms race goes on, the dangers to British merchant vessels and surface warships will continually increase. Indeed, the words used by the Minister of Defence may be adapted: " There will be no real safety (for British ships) until there is disarmament." [18]

## *Naval Disarmament Today*

It has been argued in earlier chapters, and in different contexts, that all nuclear weapons, missiles, and military and naval aircraft should be abolished. If this were done, the problem of naval disarmament would become once more what it was when the Geneva Conference met in 1932. The solutions then proposed would be appropriate. The naval armaments which were then considered to be " specifically

[17] *The Times*, August 31, 1955.
[18] *Hansard*, April 16, 1957, col. 1761.

offensive " or " especially efficacious against national
defence " would be so still; now, as then, it would be the
part of wisdom for all peace-loving nations to accept their
total abolition, by stages as few and as short as could be
agreed. This time capital ships would cause no trouble;
aircraft have abolished them, and no one wants to bring
them back. Aircraft carriers would serve no purpose, if
naval air forces had been abolished; but they might be used
as a counter to secure the abolition of submarines. The
West is so strong in carriers that such a bargain might
appeal to Russia; proportionate reductions of aircraft,
carriers and submarines might be arranged for, at each
stage, that would be fair to all. And the abolition of the
submarine is of greater importance than ever before to all
peace-loving nations, and above all to Britain. " The
U-Boat," wrote Admiral Doenitz on September 1, 1939,
" will always be the backbone of warfare against England,
and of political pressure on her." [19]  Lord Montgomery, in a
general review of Western defence, said in 1956, that " the
submarine must be eclipsed. . . . It is one of the key
factors of survival in a future war—to get the submarine
mastered." [20]  But there is no present prospect that it *can*
be mastered, except by an international agreement for its
abolition; if the naval race goes on, the offensive power of
the submarine against defence will, in all human probability,
*increase*.

If this East-West bargain could be made, the vessels
remaining in the national navies would be cruisers,
destroyers, mine-sweepers and smaller craft. There would
be no difficulty of any kind in drawing up the treaty clauses
needed for their reduction and limitation; the Versailles,
Washington and London Treaties, and the work of the
League Preparatory Commission's Draft Convention would
furnish a ready model for everything required. The only
problem would lie in fixing the ratio of naval strength to be

[19] Quoted by *The Times* Naval Correspondent, April 30, 1954.
[20] Speech to the Royal United Service Institution, October 10, 1956.

allowed to the signatory Powers; as at Washington and London, this would probably be settled by negotiations based on the principle of the *status quo*.

But what can be done about naval disarmament, if nuclear weapons, missiles, and military and naval aircraft are *not* abolished?

The answer, as in respect of other armaments, is: " Probably nothing at all." The dangers of war at sea would remain so great, the menace to merchant vessels so deadly, that it would hardly be worth while to try to secure a limitation of the number or the tonnage of the naval ships allowed. It would be very difficult to get agreement on such limitations; the limitations, if agreed to, would probably be worthless; new scientific devices would quickly render them of no avail.

## Summary of the Case for Naval Disarmament

1. For nearly two centuries Britain has depended on imports from overseas. She is increasingly dependent on them today.

2. The arms race, in naval as in other armaments, has increased the power of attack against defence. This process has been going on for half a century; aircraft, submarines, nuclear propulsion and missiles with nuclear warheads have greatly accelerated its pace since 1945. It now seems probable that there will be no real defence in any future war either for merchant vessels or for surface warships.

3. Drastic naval disarmament is therefore a vital British interest.

4. It is doubtful whether any attempt at naval disarmament will be worth while, unless nuclear weapons, military and naval aircraft and missiles are all abolished.

5. If these weapons are abolished, then aircraft carriers and submarines should be abolished, too. This, again, is a

major British interest; modern naval aircraft and submarines are a deadly menace to merchant ships.

6. The abolition of these weapons and warships would, of course, be carried through in stages, spread over a period of years.

7. If these measures were agreed to, the drafting of the naval section of the disarmament treaty could be based on the model furnished by the Naval Treaties and Draft Conventions made between the Wars.

8. Everyone who cares for peace should support this programme. The naval arms race is more intense, and more dangerous, than before the 1914 War.

9. Everyone who cares for navies should support it, too. " In an all-out nuclear war," wrote Mr. Hanson Baldwin in 1957, " the United States Sixth Fleet " (which includes eighty-five ships and 10,000 marines)

> ". . . must be considered expendable. The strategic success or failure of the Sixth Fleet in the Eastern Mediterranean would not be judged by whether or not it was sunk—it would almost certainly be sunk—but by whether or not it had accomplished its mission of bombing Soviet objectives with nuclear weapons before it was wiped out." [21]

Mr. Hanson Baldwin was only explaining the thinking of the United States Naval Staff. But this thinking is based on the philosophy of the Japanese suicide pilots, applied to an armed service as a whole. Such a conception of naval war should be intolerable to all civilised men. Naval disarmament of the kind proposed above would bring back relatively small national navies of small surface ships, which could act together to keep the seas open for peaceful commerce and, under a system of collective security,[22] to crush aggression in the bud.

---

[21] *Foreign Affairs*, July 1957, p. 659.
[22] See pp. 552–553.

# 38

## *Land Disarmament*

LAND campaigns have in the past been the bloodiest, the costliest, and the most destructive part of war. Land armies have absorbed the greater part of the total military budget, and of the manpower trained to war. In 1938–39 Hitler's standing forces were as follows:

| | |
|---|---|
| Army | 750,000 |
| Navy | 50,000 |
| Air | 206,000 |
| Total | 1,006,000 [1] |

Today the relative importance of land armies is considerably less; the change is shown in the figures for the United States Forces in 1957–58:

| | |
|---|---|
| Army | 900,000 |
| Navy | 645,000 |
| Marines | 180,000 |
| Air | 875,000 |
| Total | 2,600,000 [2] |

This shows that both the Navy and the Air Force are now regarded as relatively much more important than they used to be. The figures for the Russian Forces indicate the same trend. If the arms race continues, the trend will be progressively increased.

But the land armies are still the most numerous, if not the most costly, of the armed forces of the world, and their armament is becoming increasingly expensive. The United States has developed "Pentomic" divisions, adapted and equipped for nuclear, chemical and biological war, with a

[1] *Encyclopaedia Britannica Book of the Year 1939*, pp. 69 and 458.
[2] Targets for June 1958, United States Secretary of Defence, Mr. C. E. Wilson, N.Y.H.T., September 20, 1957.

great increase of fire-power, maximum mobility, and maximum flexibility of operation in the field. A Pentomic division consists of five " battle-groups," each with five companies, comprising among them 13,700 men; all moved by air; ready to start in four hours; armed with powerful automatic small-arms, machine-guns and bazookas, five batteries of 4-inch howitzers, and four Honest John rocket launchers; the rockets have 30-kil. atomic warheads (1½ times Hiroshima). It has air-borne television and radar to watch the enemy, and infra-red ray equipment to spot troop concentrations at night. This reorganisation and re-equipment is immensely expensive, but the United States Army " plans to have all divisions converted to the new command and combat doctrine within two years." [3]   Other armies will be compelled to follow suit. If there is to be any disarmament at all, it is clearly desirable that the waste involved in these developments should be averted.

## The Factors of Military Strength on Land

There are four main factors of military strength on land, with which a disarmament treaty must deal: manpower, the quality and quantity of weapons and ammunition, transport, and budgetary appropriations.

### Manpower

Of these factors, manpower was much the most important until the 1914 War. In that War, weapons and supplies of ammunition—the " weight of metal "—began to count for more than men. In 1922, a French general went so far as to assert that, in calculating the efficiency of a military force, French experts gave one point to their numerical strength, and six to their weapons and material. The balance has swung much further in favour of weapons and material since then; an army of 50,000 with modern conventional weapons could probably defeat an army of a

[3] N.Y.T., July 21, 1957.

million with the weapons of 1922.  Nevertheless, manpower remains of great importance; in 1952, when they put forward their proposal for a manpower ceiling of " 1 or at most 1·5 million men " for the forces of the major Powers, the British, United States and French Governments argued that " a numerical limitation on armed forces is a major element " in any disarmament programme.  They gave three reasons :

> " (a) All armaments programmes depend upon manpower and therefore must to a greater or less degree be affected by limitations on permitted armed forces.

> " (b) A substantial reduction of armed forces . . . in itself would tend to reduce the likelihood of successful aggression.

> " (c) Agreement on a substantial and balanced reduction of armed forces, minimising the likelihood and fear of successful aggression, should greatly facilitate agreement reducing and restricting the armaments supporting these armed forces." [4]

These arguments are all still valid, and all apply with special force to the manpower in land armies.  But limiting manpower alone would not prevent the competition in the quantity and quality of weapons and equipment, and no stable balance of strength could be secured; indeed, unless both the quality and quantity of land weapons and equipment are dealt with, it is improbable that any agreement on land armies will be reached.

## Transport

The mobility of land forces has become a most important factor in their strength.  In the 1914 War, mechanical transport replaced animals; it made possible the maintenance of much greater numbers in the field, and the supply of enormously greater quantities of weapons and ammunition. With the threat of nuclear attack, the staffs are now striving to reduce the dependence of land troops on road transport;

---

[4] Para. 6 of Working Paper dated May 28, 1952, Cmd. 8589, pp. 13–14.

helicopters and transport aircraft are to take its place. But helicopters and transport aircraft are very costly and could give a great advantage to forces that possessed them against forces that did not. Transport, therefore, must be limited by the disarmament treaty, together with all equipment for bridging, making airstrips, etc., which facilitates aggressive assault.

### Budgetary Appropriations

If the purpose of a disarmament treaty is to create a stable balance of strength, then the budget allowed to each nation for its army must be reduced and limited. There are many elements of military strength on land which would be difficult to control by direct quantitative restrictions, but which could be effectively limited by fixing a total appropriation for an army as a whole.

## UN Consideration of Land Disarmament

The formulation of the treaty clauses to deal with these four factors would present real difficulties, none of which has been considered in the discussions in the UN. The Western Governments' manpower paper of 1952, which suggested " ceilings " for the total permitted strength of the armies, navies and air forces of the various nations, mentioned some of these difficulties—*e.g.*, how to deal with " para-military and security forces "; the danger of evasion by the " building up of large forces of trained reserves," etc.; but it suggested no solutions, nor have any of the other papers which have been presented to the UN Commission or Sub-Committee done so since then.

There is thus no guidance to be found in the UN debates about the methods by which land disarmament can be carried through. Fortunately, as with air and naval disarmament, this is not true of the discussions conducted between the Wars. In the Treaty of Versailles, in the Reports of the League Commissions, in the proposals laid before the Geneva Conference of 1932, in the British Government's Draft Convention, every problem of conventional land disarmament was meticulously dealt with, and concrete solutions, embodied in treaty clauses, were worked out. Since conventional land armaments have remained in essential character very similar to what they were then this work is still relevant, and it may be worth while to review briefly its more important features.

## *Proposals Between the Wars*

### THE TREATY OF VERSAILLES

The Treaty of Versailles imposed provisionally unilateral disarmament on defeated Germany; it was designed to deal with the most efficient army the world had ever seen, and to render it incapable of future aggression [5]; it was declared to be the starting point for a general world-wide system. It defined the purpose for which the German Army was in future to exist: it "shall be devoted exclusively to the maintenance of order within the territory and to the control of frontiers." This conception became of great importance in subsequent discussions, and was the foundation of President Hoover's proposals of 1932.

Germany was allowed an army of 100,000 long-term volunteers; conscription, believed to be the source of German militarism, was abolished; the proportion of officers was fixed at 4,000, *i.e.*, one to twenty-five other ranks. A tactical organisation (seven infantry and three cavalry divisions) was imposed upon this army, with the numbers of each unit laid down, the purpose being to make it difficult for the German Staff to expand its forces beyond the treaty strength; other measures were designed to prevent the building up of trained reserves.

Germany was forbidden to have any of the weapons which were considered to assist attack: tanks and armoured

[5] *Cf*. the Six Principles, see pp. 12–14.

cars; poison gas; guns of over 4·1-inch calibre (105 mm.) (except for a small number of fixed guns in certain specified fortified works). The weapons per division were fixed at twelve 4-inch howitzers; twenty-four 3-inch field guns; 268 machine guns and 12,000 rifles. Very small stocks of ammunition were allowed.

There were two notable omissions in Part V of the Treaty of Versailles. There was no limitation on the proportion of N.C.O.s; by 1932 " there were something like one for every two private soldiers " [6]—a fact which made it much easier for Hitler to expand the army when he seized power. And there was no limitation of the budgetary appropriations; in consequence defence expenditure rose from 459m. Reichsmarks in 1924 to 788m. in 1930.[7] There can be no doubt that this meant an increase in military strength.

The omission about N.C.O.s was made good in the treaties with Germany's allies; N.C.O.s were not to exceed 1/15th of the total effectives. These treaties also allowed the infantry division to vary between a minimum of 8,300 and a maximum of 11,194 officers and men. In consequence, it was not possible to prescribe the number of weapons and quantity of ammunition permitted to each division; instead, a fixed number and quantity were allowed per 1,000 men: three field guns or howitzers, two trench mortars, fifteen machine guns, and 1,150 rifles. Such a fixed relation between a unit of manpower, weapons and ammunition may be useful in the drawing up of treaty clauses for land disarmament.

## THE LEAGUE COMMISSIONS

Only a few points need be noted from the long and constructive debates of the League Commissions between 1920 and 1932.

---

[6] Temperley, *The Whispering Gallery of Europe*, pp. 221–222.
[7] G. Scheele, *The Weimar Republic*, 1946, p. 112.

*Manpower*

It was soon evident that the majority of nations were unwilling to give up conscription, and that, therefore, on this point, at least, the Versailles system could not be generally applied. This led to a search for some method of equating conscripts with long-term volunteers; attention was focused on the fact that the long-term professional is of greater military value than the conscript; it was agreed that the shorter the conscript's service, the more quickly does the effect of his training wear off; that, if the period of service is short enough, the conscript will not be capable of playing a part in offensive operations; and that, even if the period is longer, he will only be useful as a " trained reserve " for a short period of years.[8] This was the origin of the formula for the limitation of " man-days with the colours," which became the foundation of a workable system to reduce and limit both " effectives with the colours " and " trained reserves," by a common method applicable both to conscript armies and to long-service volunteers. This system was embodied in the Land Chapter of the Draft Convention which the League Preparatory Commission drew up. It provided for the limitation of the total number of men in the army of each signatory State, and also of the numbers in " formations organised on a military basis," *i.e.,* " police forces of all kinds, gendarmerie, customs officials, forest guards," and para-military formations such as the Stahlhelm in Germany. It also provided for separate limitations on the numbers of officers, N.C.O.s, and other long-term regulars. The numbers in each of these separate categories of effectives were to be, for each High Contracting Party, " the average daily effectives laid down for such Party in the corresponding column in the tables." The Draft Convention then provided that " the average daily effectives are reckoned by dividing the total number of days' duty performed in each year by the number of days in such year "

---

[8] For a detailed discussion of this point, see P. J. Noel-Baker, *Disarmament*, 1926, pp. 140 *et seq*.

(Article 3). Thus each government would be obliged to keep a careful check of the total man-days of service performed by all ranks in all its armed forces and other military formations, and to ensure that the average per day did not exceed the figure allowed by the Convention. The P.D.C.'s Draft Convention also laid down the " maximum total periods of service " for a conscript, and provided that this period of service should include all the days spent in re-training, after his original term of service was over.

This system solved a number of problems which had arisen in debate, and which will still arise if the reduction and limitation of armies is seriously discussed. For example:

(i) Not only the standing army was to be limited, but all other para-military formations too; and para-military formations were adequately defined.

(ii) Colonial forces were to be limited.

(iii) Special limitations were to be placed (a) on the number of officers and (b) on other long-term professional soldiers who could serve as the cadre for expanded forces, if mobilisation occurred.

(iv) Reserves doing re-training service were to be counted in the " average daily effectives " which were allowed.

(v) A limit was placed for each signatory Power, not only on the number of these " average daily effectives," but on the maximum period for which conscripts might be trained.

(iv) and (v) together, if low figures were inserted in the disarmament treaty, would mean a very effective limitation of trained reserves.

If conscription was to be allowed by the disarmament convention (as was inevitable), and if no common tactical organisation of armies could be agreed, it is difficult to see what better system for reducing manpower could be devised than this. In long months of study and debate the Conference of 1932 cleared up some outstanding obscurities and doubts, and made some small improvements, but did not find it necessary to make any substantial change.[9]

## War Material

The P.D.C. were less successful on war material, *i.e.*, weapons, ammunition and equipment. There were prolonged debates about the rival merits of " direct " limitation by numerical lists and schedules (as in the Versailles Treaty), and of " indirect " limitation by budgetary appropriation. In the end, only budgetary limitation appeared in the Commission's Draft Convention; the debates of the Disarmament Conference soon showed that this was not enough.

## Forces for Internal Order and Frontiers

One other point of lasting interest arose in the League discussions. A Commission made an inquiry, based on the Versailles stipulation that the German Army should be " devoted exclusively to the maintenance of order within the territory, and to the control of the frontiers." They asked the governments to establish " as far as possible a distinction between the forces intended for the maintenance of order " (in their respective territories) " and the forces whose purpose was to provide for defence against an attack from outside." [10] Commenting on the replies made by the governments, the Third Committee of the Third Assembly said in its Report:

> " The statements . . . show that the forces maintained by the various governments for the maintenance of internal order are relatively very small; that, in consequence, the military effort made by the various

[9] See p. 477, below.
[10] A.31.C.631.C.T.A.175.1922. The replies of the governments are in the same document.

countries is almost exclusively intended as defence against aggression from without." [11]

President Hoover based his land disarmament plan on this finding in 1932.

## DISARMAMENT CONFERENCE, 1932

*Manpower*

The President said:

" I propose . . . that there should be a reduction of one-third in the strength of all land armies over and above the so-called police component.

" The land armaments of many nations are considered to have two functions. One is the maintenance of internal order in connection with the regular police force of the country. The strength required for this purpose has been called the ' police component.' The other function is defence against foreign attack. The additional strength required for this purpose has been called the ' defence component.' While it is not suggested that these different components should be separated, it is necessary to consider this contention as to functions in proposing a practical plan of reduction in land forces. Under the Treaty of Versailles and the other peace treaties the armies of Germany, Austria, Hungary, and Bulgaria were reduced to a size deemed appropriate for the maintenance of internal order, Germany being assigned 100,000 troops for a population of approximately sixty-five million people. I propose that we should accept for all nations a basic police component of soldiers proportionate to the average which was thus allowed Germany and these other States. This formula, with necessary corrections for Powers having colonial possessions, should be sufficient to provide for the maintenance of internal order by the nations of the world. Having analysed these two

[11] A.124.1922, p. 8.

components in this fashion, I propose, as stated above, that there should be a reduction of one-third in the strength of all land armies over and above the police component." [12]

Mr. Hoover's plan was not accepted, but the principle of the two " components " which he thus set out was later accepted by the Conference, and by the British Government, when they came, nine months later, to draw up their Draft Convention.

Shortly before this British Draft Convention was prepared the Conference made eighteen " decisions," which interpreted or completed the manpower proposals drawn up by the P.D.C. The most important of these decisions were as follows:

" (1) That the European continental armies should be standardised by being converted into armies with short-term service and limited effectives . . .

" (3) That pre-military training should be reckoned in the period of training;

" (4) That military training received in any form elsewhere than in the army should be reckoned in the period of training;

" (5) That professional or long-service military personnel should be limited on common bases;

" (6) That the effectives of police forces of a military character should be limited on common bases; . . .

" (10) That the division of effectives stationed in the home country into two components, one irreducible and the other reducible, should in principle be accepted. (President Hoover's Plan.)"

It was in the light of these decisions that Sir Anthony Eden, General Temperley and their colleagues drafted the Manpower Chapter of the British Government's Draft Convention.

[12] *Conference Documents*, Vol. I, p. 260.

*War Material: Tanks*

The Land Commission of the Conference said in its Report on what Land Weapons were " specifically offensive " :

" A large number of delegations is of opinion that all tanks should be included in the list of weapons to which the resolution of April 22 applies.[13] They consider that the possession of such vehicles considerably facilitates offensive operations based on surprise, operations which are in the highest degree dangerous to national defence. . . . Several of them point out that even modern fortifications are exposed to the attack of tanks."

The Commission's " Committee of Experts " further stated that even light tanks " can usually cross trenches and make breaches in the usual wire entanglements of the battlefield." [14]

This memorandum confirmed what Ludendorff and the German General Staff had said about the rôle of tanks in the 1914 War.[15] The more the experience of that War was debated in the Conference, the more opinion hardened in favour of the view that tanks were " specifically offensive."

Before the Conference ended hardly anybody denied that tanks were " aggressive " weapons, which helped attack against national defence.

*Guns*

The Report of the Land Commission said that:

" As a rule, artillery of a calibre up to about 100 mm. can only be effectively used against the least strongly protected personnel and objectives of the battlefield.

" Artillery of a higher calibre—particularly of about 150 mm., which is the calibre most commonly

[13] See p. 397.
[14] *Conference Documents*, Vol. I, pp. 230–231.
[15] Groves, *Behind the Smoke Screen*, pp. 79–83.

employed—and up to a calibre of 220 mm. inclusive, is capable of effective action against most entrenchments, field works and other objectives of the battlefield, which can be organised and constructed in a short time with limited personnel and material." [16]

This seemed decisive against the 150 mm. (6-inch) gun, and this view was accepted in a British White Paper dated November 17, 1932:

"Under the Treaty of Versailles the maximum calibre of large mobile guns permitted to Germany is 105 mm. *This figure is obviously intended to limit these guns to a type which is suited for defence. . . .* The obvious way of according Germany equality of treatment in regard to this weapon, while at the same time making a great advance in disarmament, is to press for a general reduction to this figure." [17]

## THE BRITISH DRAFT CONVENTION OF MARCH 1933

The British Government's Draft contained the following provisions:

### Manpower

The draft provisions drawn up by the P.D.C., together with the eighteen Conference " decisions " referred to above, were reproduced as Articles 7–18.[18] These proved to be generally acceptable; although the general staffs' views had been widely divergent when the Conference began, close and constant discussion, which often seemed futile at the time, had in the end produced solutions that were technically sound, and politically acceptable. The British Government added a table of the actual strengths which they proposed:

[16] *Loc. cit.*, p. 228.
[17] Cmd. 4189.
[18] *Conference Documents*, Vol. II, pp. 477–479.

" Table of Average Daily Effectives which are not to be Exceeded in the Land Armed Forces

| Party | Land Armed Forces | |
|---|---|---|
| | Stationed in home country | Total including overseas |
| Germany | 200,000 | 200,000 |
| Belgium | 60,000 | 75,000 |
| Bulgaria | 60,000 | 60,000 |
| Spain | 120,000 | 170,000 |
| France | 200,000 | 400,000 |
| Greece | 60,000 | 60,000 |
| Hungary | 60,000 | 60,000 |
| Italy | 200,000 | 250,000 |
| Netherlands | 25,000 | 75,000 |
| Poland | 200,000 | 200,000 |
| Portugal | 50,000 | 60,000 |
| Rumania | 150,000 | 150,000 |
| Czechoslovakia | 100,000 | 100,000 |
| U.S.S.R. | 500,000 | 500,000 |

They further provided that " the maximum total period of service for the effectives in the Land armed forces stationed in continental Europe . . . shall not exceed eight months."

Thus the British Government proposed that European continental armies should be transformed into short-service militias, incapable, by their lack of training, of conducting the offensive operations of aggressive war. (This was the application of the principle of qualitative disarmament to manpower.) They fixed figures for the standing armies of Europe so low that today they look Utopian.

## War Material

On war material they accepted the principle of both qualitative and quantitative disarmament.

On *tanks*, they did not at first go as far as President Hoover, who had proposed the total abolition of *all* tanks; they proposed instead the abolition of tanks over sixteen tons. They added a limitation on the *number* of permitted tanks, and offered to re-consider the question of abolition.

On *mobile guns*, the British Government, as said above, proposed that the maximum calibre for replacement should be 105 mm. (4·1 inch).

They proposed no limitation of small arms, machine guns and other equipment. This was not illogical, since small arms and machine guns are pre-eminently defensive weapons. But if the Draft Convention had succeeded, the Conference would have insisted on dealing with them by means of a budgetary limitation.

The British Draft Convention did not succeed, for reasons which have been discussed above.[19]    As has been said, many people thought it would almost certainly have done so, if it had been put forward six or nine months earlier; Major-General Temperley believed it might even have succeeded in March 1933 if it had been vigorously pressed; he had expected that his table of figures would evoke universal imprecations; he records that, in fact, " the figures were . . . very well received.    Several of the delegates came to see me, and asked for increases of their own, but there was almost an entire absence of general criticism." [20] He believed that by bold leadership at the highest level it could have been forced through.    " It is a deep conviction of mine," he wrote in 1938,

> " that it would have succeeded, and as time brings an added perspective, the more certain am I that I am right.    I was in close touch with the general feeling at the time and I am sure that there was very great anxiety about the fate of the Conference and the gathering storms.    The immense advance by the French towards the German point of view was a most favourable sign, although it proved to be too late. . . . We should have been sure of American and Italian backing and the French and Germans could hardly have said ' No '. . . .    The chance was lost because it was never realised by those at home what a winner we had in our stable." [21]

## The Principles of Land Disarmament Today

The proposals made for land disarmament between the Wars have been described at length for two reasons.

[19] See pp. 7–8, 406–408, 450–451.
[20] *Op. cit.*, pp. 235–236.                    [21] *Op. cit.*, pp. 243–244.

First, they produced, in the British Draft Convention, the technical solutions for the problems of conventional land disarmament that are required today. Much of the Land Chapter could be taken as a basis of discussion by the UN, or could, indeed, be written straight into a disarmament treaty. This might be of great importance; as Mr. Selwyn Lloyd said to the Sub-Committee in 1957:

> " The appointed task of this Committee is to draft a disarmament convention, and *to solve the technical problems involved. An agreement on the technical problems would undoubtedly contribute to the solution of the other issues.*" [22]

Second, the British Draft Convention was produced at a moment of doubt and confusion, after long and seemingly fruitless debates, in which the question of land armies, tanks and guns had been bitterly controversial subjects. Yet the action of a leading government, putting forward a draft with sound technical solutions and actual figures of permitted strengths, created out of chaos an opportunity for success. The same thing might happen again today, if a similar initiative were taken, and more vigorously pressed.

If this were done, the principles of the Land section of a disarmament treaty are clearly indicated by the work done between the Wars. They are:

## Manpower

The adoption of the system contained in Articles 7–18 of the British Draft Convention. One new point of difficulty would arise. Russia proposed in 1957 that civilians who work full-time for the Services should be included in the totals of permitted manpower; the United States in that year employed 1,173,752 civilians with its forces [23]; Britain employed 494,100. [24] The point is one of great substantive importance, for the civilians do, no doubt,

[22] March 18, 1957, p. 11.
[23] N.Y.H.T., May 22, 1957.
[24] *Hansard*, February 7, 1958, col. 222

perform many services which used to be done by men in uniform, and which add to the military strength of the Services.

## Tanks

The application of qualitative disarmament, if agreement could be obtained, by abolition; if not, by restriction to a low maximum tonnage, coupled with a limitation of the numbers allowed.

## Guns and Mortars

The application of qualitative and quantitative disarmament, by the abolition of guns over 105 mm. calibre, and a limitation of the numbers allowed.

## Small Arms, Machine Guns and other weapons and ammunition

Limitation by a budgetary appropriation, since " direct " numerical limitation would be difficult to agree, and is, in any case, much less important than the limitation of the " heavy " arms.[25]

## Transport

Road and tracked vehicles and troop carriers, transport aircraft, helicopters, bridging and other equipment, to be limited by a budgetary appropriation.[26]

### STAGES

The reduction of the period of service, and of total effectives with the colours, would, of course, have to be carried out in stages over a period of years, with, *e.g.*, 20 per cent. of the agreed reduction being made each year. So would the abolitions or reductions of weapons, ammunition and other war material, and the reduction of budgetary appropriations.

[25] See p. 500.
[26] See pp. 500–501.

The drafting of treaty clauses for land disarmament on these principles would present no technical difficulty for which a ready solution is not available.

The filling in of the figures in the manpower schedule could be based on the proposals for " ceilings " approved by the majority of the UN Disarmament Commission in 1952 and since accepted by Russia.

The quantities of permitted " heavy " weapons, and the budgetary appropriations for other war material, should be fixed in strict proportion to the manpower ceilings, but at the lowest level per 1,000 men [27] for which agreement could be secured.

These cold phrases convey no sense of the issues involved, of the ferocity of land-fighting in modern wars, or of the magnitude of the reform in the life of most nations, and in world affairs, which would be effected, if drastic land disarmament were carried through. On land, as on the sea and in the air, " partial " measures, small reductions of manpower, small limitations of the sums spent on weapons, are not enough; they would produce no significant or worth-while change. Modern armies have been equipped to overcome the power of national defence, and utterly to devastate the country attacked. The only sure way to prevent this kind of war is to transform the armies, and to abolish the weapons with which it can be fought.

[27] See p. 472

# PART SEVEN

# OTHER PARTS OF A DISARMAMENT TREATY WHICH AFFECT ALL ARMAMENTS AND ARMED FORCES

# 39

## *Military Research*

As Mr. Stassen said to the UN Disarmament Sub-Committee in 1957, the purpose of a disarmament treaty is to create a stable balance of armed strength among the nations at a lower level of armament than they had before it was signed.[1]

The purpose of any nation's military research and development is to upset the existing balance of strength in favour of that nation, by securing for it better, cheaper, more powerful weapons than those possessed by other States.

Each nation is driven by the arms race into an endeavour to secure a technical " lead " over its possible enemies; its posssible enemies are driven to do the same. Military research and development are thus inherently incompatible with a stable system of disarmament. Mr. Selwyn Lloyd recognised that this was so when he asked in the Sub-Committee " whether we cannot now see that *this common loathing of war should halt the pursuit of ever more deadly devices, and the perfection of ever more efficient means of delivering them.*"[2] This means that we should seek by international agreement to halt all military research and development, for its sole purpose is " the pursuit of ever more deadly devices, and the perfection of ever more efficient means of delivering them."

## *The Growth of Military Research*

For more than seventy years the engineering, metallurgical, and chemical advances due to science have been progressively applied to increasing the striking power of armaments

[1] March 20, 1957, p. 10.
[2] March 18, 1957, p. 5.

by land, sea and in the air. But it is only since 1939, as
Professor Rabi said,[3] that governments have come to think
of scientific research as a major factor in armament policy.
The following figures of expenditure speak for themselves.

EXPENDITURE ON MILITARY RESEARCH AND DEVELOPMENT
ALL DEFENCE DEPARTMENTS

|  | Britain | U.S.A. | Sweden |
|---|---|---|---|
|  | £ millions | $ millions | kr. millions |
| 1938–39 | 5·7 | – | – |
| 1939–40 | 7·9 | 26·4 | – |
| 1945–46 | – | – | 2 |
| 1947–48 | 40·0 | 529·2 | 7 |
| 1951–52 | 80·0 | 821·0 | 14·4 |
| 1953–54 | 100·0 | 1,569·2 | 17·4 |
| 1954–55 | 160·0 | 1,550·8 | 19·4 |
| 1955–56 | 160·0 | 1,450·6 | 18·7 |
| 1956–57 | 204·0 | 1,407·9 [4] | 21·8 [5] |

On these figures, British expenditure, since the last year
before Hitler's war, has increased by thirty-five times;
United States expenditure by fifty-six times; while since
1945, after the world conflict was over, the expenditure of
neutral Sweden has increased by eleven times. Even allowing for the fall in the purchasing power of money, these
figures mean that there has been in these three countries,
as in Russia, France, Italy and elsewhere, a great increase
in the real resources given to military research and development. Nor do these figures tell the whole story. In 1957
it was revealed that the full cost of research, weapon
development and testing in the United States in that year
amounted to the fantastic figure of $5,300m.[6] This was
an increase of $1,600m. (£570m.) over the fiscal year 1956.

The number of highly qualified scientists and engineers
engaged in military research and development has correspondingly increased since 1939. To begin with, this was
a War policy; by 1945 scientists were " engaged not only

[3] See p. 3.
[4] These figures were kindly provided by the United States Embassy in London.
They are taken from *Federal Funds for Science*, National Science Foundation,
p. 41.
[5] These figures were kindly provided by the Swedish Embassy in London.
[6] N.Y.H.T., May 10, 1957. President Eisenhower, Radio Address, November
7, 1957.

in developing and producing new techniques and in training the Services in their use, but also in the analysis of operations, the development of new tactics, and even the planning of campaigns." [7] But it has continued in peace, and the scientists' share in all military work has further increased; in 1956 there were in Britain alone over 10,000 graduate scientists and technologists doing research and development.[8] The British Government Research Establishments are the core of the peace-time service; but " there is continuous interchange of experience with industry, with the Universities, and with government laboratories in other countries." [9] During the War the United States had 30,000 scientists at work on weapon development, under the leadership of Dr. Vannevar Bush.[10] There are many more today, their resources are much greater, and their equipment and facilities much more extensive.

## Facilities and Equipment

Funds are granted by governments for military research and development on a scale that would never be accepted for civil purposes.[11] " The (Government Research) Establishments," says Dr. Cockburn, " have built up resources which are too elaborate for any one firm in industry, or for the most highly endowed universities, to maintain." [12] The scientists are given their head; Mr. Gordon Dean describes how a Congressional Committee in 1950 asked him what the Savannah River plant was going to cost. He replied: " In the neighbourhood of $600m., but I would hate to be frozen to that." Four months later the estimate had risen to $900m.; four months later still to $1,200m.; in the end it cost $1,500m.[13] Congress never complained.

[7] Dr. Cockburn, Chief Scientist to the Ministry of Supply, *Journal of the R.U.S.I.*, February 1956, p. 23.
[8] *Hansard*, April 18, 1956, col. 983.
[9] Dr. Cockburn, *loc. cit.*, p. 24.
[10] Vannevar Bush, *Modern Arms and Free Men*, p. 7.
[11] Zeta may be an exception.
[12] *Loc. cit.*, p. 24.
[13] *Report on the Atom*, pp. 93–94.

Mr. Dean points out that these unheard of risks and errors in estimating the sums required would never have been sanctioned by Congress, or by any other parliament, except to meet an urgent military demand.

## Peaceful Value of Military Research

It is true that military research may give, as an accidental but welcome by-product, a return in valuable civil results. " The submarine, aircraft and large ship reactor programme," says Mr. Dean,

> " are spawning a myriad novel alloys and ceramics, designs and techniques that would not have seen the light of day for many years had there been no strong incentive to build power reactors where cost was not of primary importance." [14]

The same thing has happened in aviation and other peaceful industries. But this does not mean that military research is, therefore, a desirable activity, still less that it is essential to human progress. Aircraft would certainly have been invented, atomic energy would certainly have been discovered, even if the second Hague Conference had made a disarmament treaty in 1907, and the two World Wars had been avoided. Perhaps, in a disarmed world, the governments would have noticed sooner how much civil research could do for human betterment, and would have given far greater resources to it. Military demand has diverted a large proportion of the best scientific brains and much costly instrumentation and plant away from their proper function of promoting the well-being and happiness of man.

## Research and Armament Costs

" The greatly accelerated advance of technical knowledge," said Mr. Selwyn Lloyd to the Sub-Committee in 1957,

[14] *Op. cit.*, p. 149.

" . . . is imposing an increasing, indeed almost intolerable, strain on the economies and resources of all countries seeking to maintain their armed forces equipped with modern weapons." If Britain tried to keep its forces at the numbers at which they stood in 1957, and to give them modern arms, " the defence budget, instead of being at the level of £1,600m. . . . would rise quite quickly to £2,000m. a year." [15]

The complication of modern weapons is such that the cost of training troops to use them is much increased. It costs the R.A.F. £150,000 for the training of the five members of a V-bomber, " up to the time of joining V-bomber squadrons " [16]; it costs the United States Army $10,000 to train a radar technician, and " in certain cases more " [17]; and the effective service life of these men may be very short.

The pace of military research is such that new weapons are often obsolescent, sometimes actually obsolete, and abandoned, before they are in operational use.

" The changes in the types of weapons are so rapid and continuous," said Sir Winston Churchill in 1954, " that if war should come at any time in the next decade, all the countries engaged will go into action with a proportion—a large proportion—of obsolete or obsolescent equipment."

These words give a vivid picture of the waste of human brain-power and technical resources which military research involves, and a no less vivid picture of the instability and strain of the arms race which it creates.

## *Purpose of Military Research : a Technical " Lead "*

The United States Republican Party " Platform," on which President Eisenhower was re-elected in 1956, promised that:

[15] March 18, 1957, p. 7.
[16] *Hansard*, March 26, 1958, col. 403.
[17] *The Times*, January 27, 1955.

"In order that American youth in our armed services shall be provided with the most modern weapons, we . . . will continue to support an effective and well-directed program of research and development, staffed by men of the highest caliber and ability in this field. *There is no substitute for the best* where the lives of our men and the defense of our nation are concerned." [18]

A British Minister said in 1954:

"To be prepared over a long period means that much money and effort must be devoted to research and development. *It is imperative that we should retain a strong technical lead at all costs.*" [19]

Yet Dr. Cockburn says that "it is the rule rather than the exception for developments to occur at almost the same time in different countries, even though they may be isolated by strict security measures." Thus in 1939 both sides had developed radar to the same point, "each thinking it was first in the field"; in 1945 both were introducing jet aircraft; in atomic energy "progress is proceeding at very much the same pace in different countries." Yet he concludes that we must maintain the impetus of our own research; "*once the lead has been lost, it takes a very long time indeed to regain.*" It is not clear from this what Dr. Cockburn means by "the lead"; but whatever it is, it supports the proposition that "we must expect the demand for research . . . to *increase* in the future" [20]; and the *New Scientist* says that "its cost is rocketing, as projects become more complex."

If every nation strives to get "the lead," and if it does so by *increasing* its research above the fantastic levels which now obtain, this will certainly contribute to greater instability and tension. At given moments some nation,

[18] N.Y.T., August 22, 1956.
[19] *Hansard*, March 4, 1954, col. 1374.
[20] *Loc. cit.*, pp. 29–30.

perhaps a nation whose government contemplates aggression, will get a genuine " lead " that may be a grave danger to the world. Other new weapons will be produced; when Mr. Khruschev said "you might as well throw them (bombers) on the fire," he also said that the Russian ICBM was " only one of the many things we are doing," and " we have more up our sleeves." This was certainly no idle boast, and he was right to offer—if it was a serious offer— to " bring all new scientific developments under control," and so avoid " the dangers of even more horrible weapons that science was bringing on the horizon." [21]

## Disarmament and Military Research

One thing is certain: if these " new scientific developments " are *not* " brought under control," no disarmament treaty, even if signed and ratified, would long endure. It is absurd, as Professor Rabi said,[22] to think that the development of armament technique in the next decade would be less than the development in the last. And this development would infallibly destroy the balance of armed strength which the Treaty laid down.

How true this is can be shown by reference to the Working Paper on *The Relation of Armaments to Manpower*, presented to the Sub-Committee by the British delegate in 1957. The final paragraph of the Paper reads as follows:

> "*Introduction of New Types of Weapons.* The procedure for introducing a new type of armament would depend on whether the new armament was a modification of an existing type, or radically new.
>
> "(a) For a modification (*e.g.*, a new type of fighter plane) no new manpower ratio would be necessary, and the change could be made after notification to the Control Organisation.

[21] M.G., October 9, 1957.
[22] See pp. 3 and 561.

" (b) For radically new armaments, however, a new manpower ratio would need to be agreed in order to decide whether the total number of armaments held by any one State were consonant with its manpower level." [24]

Imagine that a disarmament treaty had been made in June 1945, and that this suggested clause had been in force since then. How would it have worked?

Under (a), the arms race in the quality of existing weapons would have continued, with a multitude of " notifications " of " new types " every year. The expenditure, the mutual distrust, and the tension would have gone on mounting, too. Weapons are now incomparably more significant in assessing military strength than manpower; to take the British delegate's example, one 1957 fighter plane could probably defeat one hundred of the fighters of 1945. A disarmament treaty with such a clause could not bring a stable balance of strength.

And, under (b), what would have happened to the disarmament treaty when the first A-bomb was " notified," or the first H-bomb, or the poison gases and " biologicals " which the United States and other governments have made? How would a " radically new " form of armament be defined? Does the term apply to the proximity fuse, the effect of which was " equivalent to having ten times as much artillery at work "? [25]  At what range does it apply to rockets and guided missiles, of which there are already so many existing types? Does it cover a submarine driven by nuclear power? (The British people would certainly have thought so if it had been the Russians who built the first.) How could " a new manpower ratio " offset such new weapons as these? And can it be hoped that, in such circumstances, a new manpower ratio would really be agreed?

[24] Cmnd. 333, p. 40.
[25] Vannevar Bush, *op. cit.*, p. 33.

These questions suggest the answer: a disarmament treaty which allowed military research to go on would be inherently unstable; it might lead to serious friction, and in the end would infallibly break down. The truth is that the nations do not need either new and better types of existing weapons, or weapons that are radically new. The machinery of destruction has been perfected for long enough. It may be nonsense to talk about disarmament, or to believe that any system of armament reduction can be made to work. But if disarmament is attempted, even by small and gradual stages, then military research must stop.

## The Elimination of Military Research and Development

How can it be stopped? How can "all new scientific developments" in armament be "brought under international control"? Many methods might be suggested, some more ambitious and others less. The most radical solution is the most likely to succeed. If a real reduction, and a stable limitation, of armaments is desired, then the disarmament treaty should:

1. Prohibit all forms of military research and development, together with the testing of new weapons and training in their use.

2. Open all national research establishments of every kind to international inspection by scientific experts of the highest grade.

3. Lay on governments collectively, and on scientists individually, an obligation to assist the UN Inspectors to ensure that the treaty is observed.

4. Forbid any allocation of money in national defence budgets to military research and development.

If these provisions were once accepted, they would be in great measure self-policing; military research is conducted in big establishments, which cannot be concealed; weapon research is useless without field testing of the weapons and field training of the troops, which likewise cannot be concealed; it is very costly, and with a proper system of budgetary limitation and budgetary control [26] any significant expenditure on weapon development would certainly be found out.

Would the scientists help? The answer must be that given in earlier chapters.[27] But men like Dr. Linus Pauling and his 9,000 colleagues, and the fifty USAEC scientists at Los Alamos might create a movement of opinion which even the governments of Communist countries might find it difficult to resist. In any case, it cannot be doubted that the scientists of these countries would desire, like their colleagues elsewhere, to be freed from the necessity, now laid upon them, of seeking for " ever more deadly devices " for destruction. If they withheld their co-operation there would be some risk that the obligations of the disarmament treaty might be disregarded by a disloyal nation, and some small-scale research be carried out. But the chances of detection would be great; the risk taken by the loyal nations would be far less than the risk of allowing military research and development to continue unrestrained.

## Conclusion

Military research has helped to bring the arms race to the point of frenzy; indeed, it *is* the arms race in its most dangerous form. The pace of the change in armaments which it brings has immeasurably increased since Hitler fell and Japan surrendered; and it is increasing still. In 1949 an eminent authority, who had held a high position in weapon research in a democratic country, expressed the view that the future of armament development was far less frightening than many people said, and that, for example, the atomic bomb could not be sub-divided, there would be no atomic shells, torpedoes or rockets, and that nuclear

[26] See pp. 505–506.
[27] See pp. 262 and 302.

weapons (a " few bombs on cities ") could not determine the outcome of a war. Within four years all this optimism was blown to pieces by military research. The present rapidity of change in weapons would end all hope of the stable balance of military strength which it would be the purpose of a disarmament treaty to obtain. Thus, if military research were permitted to go on, it would add greatly to the difficulty of drawing up a disarmament treaty; and even if a treaty were agreed, signed, ratified and brought into force, its system might soon be undermined. But, if military research were ended, and the scientists with their present funds and equipment were diverted to peaceful projects, there is no limit to the benefits which they might bring to the peoples of the world.

# 40

## *Budgetary Limitation*

IT has often been proposed since 1920 that disarmament could be effected by the budgetary limitation of the military expenditure of each of the signatory Powers; let each nation cut a given percentage of its annual budget, all would be relieved, and their relative military strength would remain the same.[1] The simplicity of such proposals is attractive; unfortunately, when they are examined, they prove to be unsound. They would not establish a stable balance of military strength between the signatory Powers; there would be many loopholes for evasion; they would not, therefore, create confidence among the governments.

Budgetary limitation may, however, be a valuable supplementary guarantee that quantitative and qualitative reductions and limitations of armaments and forces would be observed. It would be a powerful instrument in the hands of UN Inspectors; it would enable them to keep the armament policy of every government under constant supervision; it would give early warning of a disloyal government's attempts to violate the undertakings of a disarmament treaty, either by secretly increasing the numbers of its effectives, or by illicit purchases of arms.

To produce these results, however, a number of difficult problems must be solved, and the solutions embodied in a complex system, which all the governments must accept. None of these problems has been considered in the UN debates, although delegates have sometimes said in general terms that military expenditure should be reduced and

[1] For a discussion of early proposals, see P. J. Noel-Baker, *Disarmament*, 1926, Chap. VI. For a plan based on this principle, and put forward by the French Prime Minister, M. Edgar Faure, at the " Summit " Conference in 1955, see Cmd. 9543, pp. 14–16.

limited.[2] Fortunately, this is not a serious matter, for the whole question was fully examined, and a satisfactory system drawn up in treaty form, by the League Preparatory Commission and the Disarmament Conference of 1932.

## The Preparatory Commission and the Committee of Budgetary Experts' Scheme

Early League discussions showed that specialised knowledge and experience would be required if any useful plan was to be prepared. The Commission, therefore, set up a Committee of Budgetary Experts; its Chairman was M. Jacomet, *Comptroleur* of the finances of the French army, and its other members were also genuine experts with special experience in this field. The Committee spent many months on its work; it prepared answers to questions put to it by the Commission, and in its Report it drew up proposals for the specific provisions which a disarmament treaty should include.

It started from the proposition that " taking countries or regional groups as a whole, a comparison of expenditure on armaments cannot furnish any precise information as to relative size of the actual armaments." [3] A sum of money is not a measure of military power; an equal reduction made in their expenditure by different States will not mean an equal reduction in their armed strength. This is one reason why budgetary limitation by itself is not a satisfactory basis for a disarmament system. But

" if the facts are correctly interpreted, and above all, if variations in the purchasing power of the currencies are taken into account, the comparison of the expenditure returns of the same State from year to year will

---

[2] The Western " package " plan of 1957 proposed that information about military budgets and expenditure should be exchanged, and said: " The categories of information to be supplied will be agreed in advance and annexed to the Convention," *i.e.*, not even this elementary point had been considered.

[3] Report of the Technical Committee: L.N. Document, Disarmament, 1933, IX.3, p. 231.

enable the evolution of its expenditure on armaments to be followed, and will provide very useful information as to the variations of its armaments themselves," [4]

*i.e.*, the obligation to make an annual return of expenditure, and to have it examined by international experts, will be a useful factor in a system of armament inspection and control.

Other advantages of budgetary limitation were recognised: it may be *impossible* to set out in the schedules of a disarmament treaty all the permitted quantities of all types of arms or material, *e.g.*, rifles; it may be very difficult to limit the " quality " of arms by direct limitation—it would mean specifying in detail the *character* of every item; but if certain major weapons were limited by " quantitative enumeration," then the *quantity* of the rest, and the *quality* of all, could be limited by fixing sums which might be spent each year by each signatory State on the purchase, manufacture and maintenance of war material.

The " quality " of *effectives* might also be limited in the same way. Other things being equal, the instruction of the individual officer or soldier will vary according to the amount expended on his training—" schools," academies, special courses, exercises and the rest. A global limitation on military expenditure would automatically limit what the governments could spend on improving the quality of their troops.

The Committee of Experts therefore proposed a limitation of the total defence expenditure of each State, and a separate limitation of the sums allowed for the purchase of arms and war material for the army, navy and air force. It added that to make this system workable the following measures were required:

1. An agreed definition of what items should be included in " defence expenditure." This should, so far as possible, cover everything that increases or affects

[4] *Ibid.*

military strength, from fortress guns and oil supplies to chaplains' salaries; it must include items that in many countries appear in civil budgets; it must be accepted by all the signatory Powers.

2. As no definition can by itself afford the necessary degree of legal precision, there must also be a list of items of military expenditure for which every signatory Power must account, together with instructions for its application. It must, of course, cover both the armed forces and " formations organised on a military basis."

3. There must be an appropriate heading in the military budget of every Power for every item of expenditure, and the figure entered under each head must be " verifiable "; it must not be possible for items of expenditure to be moved from one head to another unperceived.

4. There must be a model statement, or " uniform framework in which governments must enter all national defence expenditure within the meaning of the Convention " (*i.e.*, as defined in accordance with paragraph 1 above), "irrespective of the nature and origin of the resources out of which that expenditure is met." [5]

This model statement is a most important part of the system proposed; without it budgetary limitation could not work.

> " The structure of these (defence) accounts differs . . . widely from State to State, and furthermore, the line of demarcation between national defence expenditure within the meaning of the Convention and expenditure which, although having military value, is not to be regarded as national defence expenditure, does not appear in these accounts." [6]

If, therefore, governments tried to draw up a complete account of their defence expenditure on the basis of the

[5] *Loc. cit.*, p. 214.
[6] The French *gendarmerie* "which is a police force organised on military lines, is divided half and half between the Ministry of National Defence and the Ministry of the Interior." M. Moch, Sub-Committee, April 3, 1957, p. 29.

definition and their accounts alone, it would be necessary
for the international inspectors " to proceed to a variety of
researches, interpretations and calculations which would
necessitate familiarity with the administrative practice and
institutions of each country." [7] This would be an extremely
difficult, if not an impossible, task for any international
supervising body; it would be no less difficult for the
governments to prove that they had loyally complied with
their obligations. This difficulty is overcome by an agreed
international model statement.

5. But the filling in of the model statement is an
extremely complex operation. The key to it is supplied
by " reconciliation tables," which show in detail how each
figure of the accounts has been transferred to the model
statement. Such an instrument will enable all States to
certify their national defence expenditure in an identical
form.

6. The mechanism of budgetary limitation having been
decided, it would then be necessary to insert into the disarmament convention the figures of the sums of annual
expenditure (total defence expenditure, expenditure on the
three separate Services, expenditure on war material for
land, sea and air forces) allowed to each signatory Power.
These figures would be settled by negotiation among the
Powers. As a starting point, a sum might be taken calculated on the average expenditure per annum per effective
in the three forces over the four preceding years.

7. Adjustments in permitted expenditure must be
allowed to meet changes in the purchasing power of
national currencies. Such changes might considerably
reduce the cost of a nation's forces, and thus enable a
government to *increase* their number; or they might increase
the cost of the forces, and thus compel a government to
*reduce* their number. In either case, an adjustment of its
permitted budgetary appropriation would be required. Such
adjustments should not be made by allowing automatic

---

[7] *Loc. cit.*, p. 214.

increases, on the basis of changes in cost-of-living indices. These indices vary from country to country; they are all imperfect, and some extremely so; they bear no close relation to the cost of armaments. Adjustments must, therefore, be authorised by what the Committee called " a living organisation "; *i.e.*, by a body of specially trained international officials, acting as part of the international inspectorate, and charged with the duty of supervising the budgetary limitation system, and ensuring that it was observed. A government desiring an " adjustment," *i.e.*, an increase in its permitted expenditure, would lay the necessary evidence about the change in the purchasing power of its currency before these officials; they would submit it to the Permanent Disarmament Commission, and the Commission, or some higher political authority, would then decide.

This, again, is a vitally important part of a budgetary limitation system; without a workable arrangement for adjustments, no such system would ever be agreed.

8. The sums allowed to each signatory Power would have to be the *actual payments* for their armaments which they made in any given year. The task of supervision would, therefore, have to be conducted by the international officials on the basis of each State's closed accounts (*i.e.*, not estimates or budgets).

But to render their task easier to fulfil, every signatory Power should furnish not only its closed accounts, but also its draft estimates, its budget proposals, and two other statements each year, at given intervals, showing any changes in actual expenditure from that for which provision was made in the budget. The international officials would thus be able to check changes in armament policy at an early date.

9. In order to prevent too great a time-lag before they were examined (*i.e.*, too long an interval for an intending aggressor to increase his armaments unobserved), the closed accounts must be sent in within fourteen months from the

end of the financial year.    This was agreed to be both practicable and reasonable.

10. If necessary, the international officials should be free to ask for "internal documents" (*i.e.*, the books of a national Ministry), as well as published accounts, if these "internal documents" were needed to enable them to verify what expenditure had actually been made.

11. A government might improve the efficiency of its forces in various ways which would increase its military strength, without exceeding its permitted sum of annual expenditure.    For example, a change in military organisation might cut out waste; a technological improvement in arms manufacture might lower costs, and permit a government either to increase the quantity of weapons it purchased, or to improve their quality; a reduction in the level of profit allowed on arms manufacture might have the same result.

These last considerations suggest that an absolute obligation must be imposed on every government not to lower the nominal cost of the arms it purchases by subsidies of any kind.    This would be a difficult matter to control, and might cause the international inspectors a lot of trouble, for subsidies may take many forms; they could be given, for example, by capital investment allowances to arms-producing firms; by paying higher prices for civil goods to a firm with "mixed production," on condition that the prices for its arms were lowered; or by granting export subsidies to arms firms, so as to increase their scale of production, and lower their average costs and prices.

No doubt a government could make corrupt bargains with arms firms in many forms.    The international inspectors, if they had access to "internal documents," as they should have, would have some opportunities to find these bargains out.    But it must be admitted that there might be *some* leaks, *some* opportunities for evading the loyal application of a budgetary limitation treaty, if a government so desired.    As has been said above, this is another reason why budgetary limitation by itself is not a satisfactory basis for a disarmament plan. But at least budgetary limitation, with continuous international supervision and investigation, would greatly reduce the risk of such disloyal evasion.

This, in outline, is the system which the budgetary experts proposed to the Preparatory Commission. The experts were constantly surprised by the unanimity of the conclusions which they hammered out, and their sense of the value of the work they did. They not only laid down the principles and framework of a system; they actually drew up the model statement, drafted the necessary instructions and " reconciliation tables," and prepared the material in such a way that, on the basis of their work, actual treaty clauses could quite easily be framed. They presented in all essentials a sound, ingenious, and workable system for restricting national armaments by agreed budgetary limitations on the sums which States might spend on national defence.

## The Disarmament Conference

The Disarmament Conference, when it met in 1932, proceeded to test in practice how the scheme would work. It set up a Technical Committee in which M. Jacomet and other experts still served, and this Technical Committee invited twenty-nine States, including Britain, the U.S.A., France, Italy, Germany and *Russia*, to submit their current annual military expenditure for examination; these States filled in the " model statement " which the experts had prepared; they furnished their estimates, their budgets, their closed accounts; they sent their leading Treasury and Defence officials to confer with the Committee, to explain how they had filled in the model statement, and to elucidate any obscurities or difficulties that might appear.

The Technical Committee's deliberations lasted for a year; they held 140 meetings; with the help of the most competent national experts—for every government sent their best and most trusted men—*they examined the budgets and accounts which covered 90 per cent. of the whole military expenditure of the world in 1931–32.* They " examined a documentation amounting to tens of thousands of pages "; their Report " was discussed three times, page by page." [8]

As a result the Technical Committee:

1. Unanimously declared that—

> " for the practical purpose for which such verification is required, it will be possible to verify *with a high degree of accuracy*, by means of the accounts, whether the rules proposed by the Committee for calculating the total national defence expenditure are being applied by the States." [9]

This was a most important finding; it showed that their system of exchange of information, and of supervision and verification, as they had framed it, was workable and sound.

2. Unanimously agreed that the principles of a satisfactory system of budgetary limitation had been established.

## The Advantages of Budgetary Limitation

The system, then, could be made to work, and to work as the Preparatory Commission and the budgetary experts had proposed. Its advantages were best stated by M. Palmade, the French delegate, in his final speech to the Conference. His argument may be summarised as follows:

The examination of defence estimates, budgets and closed accounts would constitute both " audited supervision " and " preventive supervision " of military expenditure. Evasions of the Disarmament Convention could be detected and checked at an early stage.

There would be " continuous observation," and not " accidental observation," of the governments' armament policies. Thus the means would be " provided of ascertaining any well-considered attempt at aggression," which,

---

[8] M. Vasconcellos, Minutes of the General Commission, Vol. II, p. 613.
[9] Report of the Technical Committee, p. 218. See also pp. 82–83.

of course, would require the time needed for careful preparation.

Budgetary limitation would be an important supplementary guarantee that States would not evade the other quantitative and qualitative limitations that might be laid down. It would, in particular, help to prevent the illegal intensive training of armed forces and their reserves (as had happened in Germany in the 1920s); illegal expenditure on buildings; illegal subsidies to private firms to enable them to prepare for "industrial mobilisation"; the illegal building up of stocks of semi-manufactured arms and ammunition, and of spare parts; the illegal "improvement" of the quality of arms; and it would in time help to reduce the stocks of arms and ammunition kept in reserve.

Budgetary limitation would also greatly assist in the technical supervision of armaments themselves. For example:

(i) The checking of expenditure would quickly discover if a State were keeping more effectives with the colours than it was allowed—pay, cost of maintenance, etc., are all known, and violations could be easily detected.

(ii) Similarly, the cost of arms per unit could be found out, and a similar check on purchases of arms established.[10]

The budgetary limitation and publicity would be a supplementary counter-check or guarantee for the observance and stability of the new system established by a disarmament treaty. This was the broad conclusion that emerged from eight years' expert study and debate, by men of the highest competence, in which, as one delegate observed, "there was nothing left unconsidered and unsaid that *could* be considered and said."

## *Budgetary Limitation Today*

The budgetary methods of Russia and the other major Powers have not changed, and since the system was tested

[10] Minutes of the General Commission, Vol. II, pp. 615–616.

satisfactorily on the Russian estimates and closed accounts
of 1932, it could be expected to work just as well in 1958.
In her plan of May 10, 1955, Russia accepted all the obligations required to make it work [11]; in particular, she agreed
that UN Inspectors should have " unimpeded access to
records relating to the budgetary appropriations of States for
military needs, including all decisions of their legislative
and executive organs on the subject." [12]   Thus the reduction
and limitation of national defence expenditure is one
important part of a disarmament treaty in which, as between
the West and Russia, no special difficulty, political or
technical, should now arise.

[11] See pp. 540–541.
[12] Cmd. 9636, pp. 41–42.

# 41

## *" Disengagement" :*
## *Demilitarised Zones*

In September 1955, a year before the Israeli attack on Egypt, General Burns, the head of the UN Truce Supervision Organisation in Palestine, reported to the Security Council on recent "incidents" between Israel and Egypt in the region of the Gaza strip. He said:

> "I am now of the opinion that a repetition of the incidents of firing between Egyptian outposts and Israeli motor patrols which have precipitated several crises since February, 1955, will only be avoided if the forces of the opposing sides are separated by an effective physical barrier along the demarcation line; and if, in addition, defensive positions and motorised patrols are kept at least 500 metres from the demarcation line on either side." [1]

This proposal was made by a UN representative seeking to avert the danger of war, in a situation which had long been menacing. It was not accepted, and a war followed which might have been averted, if it had been. It was based on a principle which has never been discussed in any UN body since 1945, but which played a considerable part in the debates of the League of Nations; much more will be heard of it, if serious plans for disarmament are ever prepared.

### Demilitarised Frontier Zones

Writers and governments have often spoken of " neutral " or " neutralised " zones, but the plan discussed in this

[1] *The Times*, September 8, 1955.

chapter is better described as the establishment of " demilitarised zones," *i.e.*, zones in which governments agree to
make no fortifications, barracks, depots or other preparations
for military action.  A number of demilitarised zones have
been established in the past, both on land frontiers and in
coastal areas, in international waterways, and in certain
areas of the open sea.

## Advantages of Demilitarised Zones

In League debates it was generally agreed that demilitarised zones might serve:

(i) To assist in preventing war by removing the forces
of potentially hostile States from immediate contact
with each other (General Burns' purpose in 1955).

(ii) To assist in determining, under a general security
scheme, which State had committed an act of
aggression.

(iii) To delay an aggressive attack, and thus to give more
time for procedures of pacific settlement, and for
effective mutual assistance to the victim, if the attack
goes on.

How far these purposes are actually achieved by a
demilitarised zone will depend on many things; the three
most important are the width of the zone; the nature of the
armaments possessed by the States concerned; and whether
the zone is on one side of a frontier only, or on both.

## Width of the Zone

The zone established between Greece and Turkey on the
River Maritza by the Treaty of Lausanne in 1922 was sixty
kilometres across—thirty on each side.  With the kind of
armaments then possessed by Greece and Turkey, this was
wide enough effectively to separate the forces of the two
countries and thus to minimise the risk of a collision; it
would also have seriously hampered an aggressive attack by
either party on the other.

## Nature of the Armaments Possessed by the Parties

Every increase in the speed of army transport or of the weapons used in an attack (aircraft, tanks, motorised artillery, etc.) means that the width of the zone must also be increased, if it is to be effective. When army transport was horse-drawn, five miles was the equivalent of forty when horses were replaced by motors; forty with the weapons and transport of 1918 were the equivalent of, perhaps, 200 today.

## Bilateral or Unilateral Zones

A zone which is freely accepted by the nations on both sides of a frontier, and which includes territory belonging to each, is much more likely to serve its purpose, and to endure, than a zone which is imposed by one party on the other. The Treaty of Versailles imposed on Germany the obligation to demilitarise all the German territory to the west of the Rhine, together with a zone fifty kilometres wide to the east of the Rhine. There was no corresponding demilitarised zone on the French side of the frontier; this inequality was deeply resented in Germany, and was regarded as inequitable by a large body of world opinion. If the zone had been voluntarily agreed to by France and Germany, with an equal width of demilitarised territory on each side of the frontier, it would have been a far better protection for France, and Hitler's violation of the Treaty in 1936 might have met with a very different world response.

# Success of Demilitarised Frontiers

Three examples of the success of demilitarised zones may be given:

## United States–Canadian Frontier

As the result of the Rush-Bagot Agreement of 1817 between the British and United States Governments, the whole frontier between Canada and the United States was demilitarised. The story of the Agreement, and of its results, can best be told by extracts from leading historians:

Sir Charles Webster:

"The war of 1812 had clearly shown that the *strategic situation on the Canadian frontier depended almost entirely on the command of the Lakes. Wellington had insisted on it as the key to the situation, when invited to take command in 1814.* It was only natural, therefore, that, immediately peace was obtained, both countries should show the keenest anxiety to secure their *position by establishing naval superiority. Castlereagh had from the first, however, desired an arrangement to prevent so dangerous and ruinous a competition. He had in 1814 been overruled by the military advisers*, and the British Government adopted the view that as they were the ' weaker party ' in North America they ought to be allowed control of the Lakes as a measure of defence. Naturally the Government of the United States could not agree to a suggestion which would have left them open to attack, while Canada was almost completely protected. Nevertheless, Madison and Monroe were no less anxious than Castlereagh to avoid the construction of rival fleets. . . . In April 1816 he (Castlereagh) reopened negotiations, and at once agreed that no new construction should be begun until the matter had been discussed further. *The ship-building race was thus at once stopped.* . . . Monroe . . . made the definite suggestion that naval armaments should be limited to the few vessels necessary for customs and police. Castlereagh obtained the agreement of the Cabinet. . . .

"*This was a positive achievement and the greatest contribution to the establishment of good relations between the two peoples during this period.*" [2]

---

[2] *The Foreign Policy of Castlereagh*, pp. 446–447.

*The Cambridge History of British Foreign Policy:*

*" Since complete disarmament would appear to leave the Canadian Colonists defenceless against a sudden American attack,* the British Cabinet was somewhat loth to consider the proposal. . . . Ultimately, however, Castlereagh expressed his readiness to enter upon negotiations. . . . It (the Rush-Bagot Agreement) was very short and *provided only for mutual disarmament upon the Lakes. . . . It had the most important effects; for in the temptation to naval rivalry on the opposite shores of the Lakes lay the germ of infinite mischief.* Its removal *set a precedent for the management of the frontier between the United States and British North America which has saved both Powers from great expense in fortifications and military guards and has deprived the frontier disputes of much of the acute danger they might otherwise have caused."* [3]

G. M. Trevelyan:

*" Before Castlereagh's career as Foreign Secretary ended, the fortunes of Anglo-American peace had been established on the sound basis of disarmament along the Canadian border, enabling future generations to weather many fierce storms, and to settle a frontier problem that no other two Great Powers would have been able to decide without war. . . .*

" The problem before Great Britain and Canada on one side and the United States on the other was nothing less than to fix a frontier of four thousand miles, which, except in the region of the Lakes, was not indicated by any natural boundary. It was perhaps the greatest operation that has ever been achieved in the interest of peace, and it took many years and many statesmen to accomplish and perfect it. But the most important stage of the whole proceeding came in 1817, when, after a sharp struggle inside the British Cabinet, the

---

[3] Vol. II, pp. 223–224.

British and American Governments agreed to abolish their navies on the Great Lakes, and forthwith dismantled, sold or sank the warships on Erie and Ontario. These fleets have never been reconstructed. From that moment forward, 'the long, invisible unguarded line' that divides Canada from her neighbour has been successfully defended by the sole garrison of trust and good will, even during the frequently recurring periods of acrimonious dispute as to its whereabouts. *If there had been armaments there would some time have been war."* [4]

These three long quotations have been made, not only because of the immense importance in the twentieth century of the consequences that flowed from the Rush-Bagot Agreement, but because the quotations bring out the following points:

The disarmament was effected in the area which was regarded as of vital strategical importance.

It was opposed by the military advisers of both Governments, and for some years their views prevailed.

It was only agreed to after " a sharp struggle " in the British Cabinet (later " sharp struggles " about disarmament ended differently).

Those who opposed it said that it left one party (the weaker) " defenceless."

It was not, as is so often said, the fact of common race, or a common language, that saved Britain and the United States from war throughout the nineteenth century and made war unthinkable in the twentieth; those factors may have helped, but, according to the consensus of opinion among the historians, the vital and decisive factor was the total abolition, and the immediate " scrapping," of the armaments which each of the two parties then felt to be " especially efficacious against its national defence."

[4] *British History in the Nineteenth Century*, pp. 177-178.

Later generations of Britons have owed a great debt of gratitude to Castlereagh and his colleagues for their persistence in their sharp but victorious struggle for disarmament.

## Swedish-Norwegian Frontier : Karlstad Convention of 1905

When Norway separated from Sweden in 1905, an outbreak of hostilities between the two countries was averted by the wisdom and authority of Nansen, and by a Convention in which a demilitarised frontier zone was an important factor. Under this Convention the two nations agreed to destroy all existing fortifications in a zone twenty miles across (ten on each side of the frontier) and 200 miles long.[5] The Convention said:

> " In order to ensure peaceful relations between the two States, a territory (neutral zone), which shall enjoy the advantages of perpetual neutrality, shall be established on either side of the common frontier. The neutrality of the said zone shall be absolute. The two States shall therefore be prohibited from . . . stationing . . . or concentrating armed military forces therein. . . . No fortifications, naval ports or depots of stores for the army or navy may be retained in the neutral zone, or may be established therein in future." [6]

The acceptance of this demilitarised zone not only helped to secure a peaceful settlement in 1905; it has continued to contribute to the growing friendship and peaceful co-operation of the Swedish and Norwegian peoples. It is, indeed, indisputable that in these two cases of the United States–Canadian and the Swedish–Norwegian frontiers, disarmament has been the prime factor in establishing peace on so firm a basis that the fear of war between the neighbouring nations has been banished. The two cases constitute a

---

[5] This included the whole area in which an armed conflict was a danger.
[6] Cited by Maj.-Gen. J. H. Marshall Cornwall, *Geographic Disarmament*, 1935, pp. 86–87. This book is the standard work on Demilitarised Zones; the author discusses numerous other examples with learning and judgment.

substantial answer in themselves to the allegation that disarmament has always failed. The historical importance of the Rush-Bagot Agreement can be measured by what the present relations between the United States and the British Commonwealth mean to the world today.

*Greco-Turkish Frontier: Treaty of Lausanne, 1923*

The Maritza Zone was only less notably successful. When it was established, Greece and Turkey were just emerging from a disastrous war, in which terrible events had taken place, and bitter hatreds had been engendered. The mutual acceptance of the zone was the first step towards the Greco-Turkish Entente which followed ten years later.

## *The Essential Features of a Demilitarised Zone*

The provisions required to make a zone seem fair and safe to the nations concerned may be summarised as follows:

(i) Its width must be reasonable and effective in the light of the armaments they possess; the exact width would have to vary with local geography.

(ii) All permanent fortifications and field works within the zone should be disarmed and dismantled.

(iii) No depot of war material, or other offensive or defensive installation should be organised, or manufacture of war material carried on.

(iv) No military camps or barracks should be stationed therein.

(v) Only the gendarmerie, police, customs officers and frontier guards necessary for internal order should be stationed in, or moved into, the zone.

(vi) The Maritza Convention provided that " military or naval aircraft of any flag whatsoever are forbidden to fly over a demilitarised zone."

(vii) It further provided that only the railway lines and sidings necessary for commercial traffic should be allowed; the legitimate requirements were to be determined by impartial experts appointed by the Transport Committee of the League.

An agreement for a demilitarised zone should also provide that any complaint of non-observance should be brought before a Standing Commission of the UN Assembly; this Commission should appoint a UN officer or officers to reside in every zone and to report on the observance of the agreement. The mere presence of such an officer would be a guarantee against aggression; his impartial report would be conclusive proof of guilt against any government that made a treaty-breaking attack.[7]

The above provisions would be an effective supplementary guarantee of peace, if the kind of disarmament described in this book were carried through, and if the modern weapons of mass destruction were abolished. If military aviation and missiles were retained, a zone would have to be much wider, and, even so, its restraining value would be reduced.

It must be repeated that the system of demilitarised zones cannot be universally applied. On mountain frontiers the advantages of a zone might be outweighed by the loss of strong defensive military positions. But on many land frontiers demilitarisation would be of value; it might permit large reductions of existing armaments, might relax tensions and perhaps, in due course, as in North America and Scandinavia, definitely eliminate the danger of war. Wherever they are appropriate, therefore, agreements for frontier zones should be included as part of a general disarmament treaty. If governments really want security against aggression from without, this is one way in which their chance of getting it can be increased.

---

[7] *e.g.*, there was a UN Commission under an Indian Chairman on the boundary between North and South Korea when the Communists attacked. The Commission's allocation of guilt to the Communists was accepted as decisive.

## Demilitarisation of International Waterways and of the Open Sea

### Waterways

The Suez Canal was " neutralised " by the Convention of Constantinople of 1888, which provided that the Canal was to be open in time of peace and war to merchantmen and warships of all nations; that it should never be blockaded; that no act of war should be committed in the Canal or within three sea miles from its ports; that belligerent men-of-war might not stay in the Canal more than twenty-four hours, except in case of absolute necessity; and that no fortifications should be made.

It is difficult to argue that these Treaty obligations were faithfully observed in the two World Wars, or in November 1956. In any case, they would need to be modified under a true system of collective security; international canals and waterways should obviously be open to the forces of UN nations co-operating against a Charter-breaking aggression. This change was, in fact, made for the Bosphorus and the Dardanelles by the Straits Convention adopted at the Lausanne Conference in 1923; it laid down that:

> " the present provision, which forms an integral part of those relating to the demilitarisation and to the freedom of the Straits, does not prejudice the rights and obligations of the High Contracting Parties under the Covenant of the League of Nations."

This provision was clearly right, and should now, in terms of the UN Charter, be applied to any demilitarised waterways or bordering zones, and, indeed, to demilitarised zones on land.

### The Open Sea

Straits are only of indirect importance to disarmament. The question of the open sea is different.

So far, only the Black Sea has ever been demilitarised. It was done by the Treaty of Paris of 1856, which declared that its ports and waters were to be forever *open to merchant ships* of all nations, and forever *forbidden to the warships* both of the riverain, and of all other, States.[8] This provision, which might have been of great importance, was abrogated in 1871. But it is possible that the principle which gave such good results in the Rush-Bagot Agreement might have a wider application. In 1924, the League convened a Conference in Rome to secure the application to all navies of the system established by the Washington Treaty of 1922.[9] The Conference quickly failed, largely because Russia demanded a capital ship tonnage of 490,000 tons; the United States tonnage under the Washington Treaty was only 525,000 tons, and as the Russian Navy was negligibly small in 1924 the other nations thought the Russian claim absurd. Russia offered to reduce it to 280,000, if it were agreed:

" (i) That the Bosphorus and Dardanelles (Straits) are closed.
" (ii) That vessels of war belonging to non-riparian States of the Baltic are forbidden access to the Baltic by the Sound and Belt.
" (iii) That the Straits of Korea are demilitarised (disarmed)." [10]

This proposal was urged repeatedly by the Russian delegate in Rome. The British Government strongly opposed it, as, at the Conference of Lausanne in the previous year, they had opposed the " neutralisation " of the Black Sea. In the Baltic Britain has always demanded an absolute right of entry for British ships in unlimited numbers, both in peace and war. But this traditional policy has lost its force, now that Russia, besides a multitude of bombers, has the second largest navy in the world and a fleet of submarines more numerous and powerful than the submarines of all the other maritime nations combined. It might well

[8] Treaty of Paris, 1856, Art. 18.
[9] See p. 451, n. 13.
[10] L.N. Document C.76, 1924, IX, p. 15.

be worth accepting some measure of demilitarisation in the Baltic and the Black Sea if Russia in return would reduce her navy. In any case, this is a bargaining counter of importance; and the West will need such counters when naval disarmament is discussed. In general, consideration should be given to the principle of securing reductions of naval strength in return for the demilitarisation of certain portions of the Open Sea.

## *Place of Demilitarised Zones in a Disarmament Treaty*

Many proposals have been made in recent years for what is called "disengagement" in Europe, among them the Rapacki plan for a nuclear-weapon-free area on both sides of the Iron Curtain. Since this was put forward as a measure to be taken apart from a general disarmament treaty, it does not fall properly within the scope of this book. In any case, it seems unlikely that it will be accepted, unless all armaments within the zone, nuclear and conventional alike, are reduced, limited and controlled. But if serious negotiations for a general disarmament treaty are begun, the demilitarisation of specific areas on land and sea might be made an important part of a system of general world armament reduction and limitation. Article 9 of the Geneva Protocol of 1924 "recommended" the establishment of "demilitarised zones" as "being calculated to prevent aggression"; it provided that they might be "placed under . . . permanent supervision" by the League; and it was intended to lead to a systematic effort to incorporate agreements for such zones as annexes to the disarmament treaty which the Protocol was intended to bring about.[11] There are various parts of the world—the Middle East, the Balkans—where such zones might be

[11] See P. J. Noel-Baker, *The Geneva Protocol*, pp. 104–106 and 219.

particularly useful. Demilitarisation is not only one method of reducing the armaments themselves, but, what is more important, it may be a means of removing the dangers which they involve.

# 42

## Bases

### The Number, Cost and Military Importance of Bases

MR. HANSON BALDWIN says that the United States " maintains and utilises at least 150 air and naval bases or installations overseas, in addition to hundreds of ground installations." Russia has a great many, and so have Britain, France and other countries, both on their own territory and abroad.

These bases represent a substantial part of the total military effort of the world. The installations of the British base at Suez were the result of the investment, over many years, of £500m. They included ports, railways, power plants, manufacturing capacity, repair facilities, and immense storage space. In the 1939 War the Suez base was the centre of a traffic to all the ports of Palestine, Egypt, and the Persian Gulf; it handled half-a-million tons of stores a month.[1]

The United States have recently established four air bases and one naval base in Spain; they cost $400m., and their oil supplies were assured by the building of 475 miles of pipeline, most of it underground. The air bases have runways long enough for jet bombers loaded with H-bombs; but they can only be used if Spain, after consultation, is willing to consent.[2]

The military importance of bases has always been great. Up till 1945 British bases, in many countries, were both the foundation and the symbol of British imperial power. They helped to keep world peace, and to defeat autocratic

[1] Lt.-Gen. W. G. Lindsell, *Sunday Times*, December 30, 1956.
[2] *The Times*, July 13, 1957; N.Y.T., July 16, 1957.

aggressors in two World Wars. British and United States bases are still of great and, some people would say, of growing importance.

"Overseas bases," says Mr. Hanson Baldwin, "tremendously simplify the logistic problem of . . . defence." The United States air bases save hundreds of refuelling tanker aircraft; they provide distant warning and fighter defence in depth; they mean " dispersion—one of the new requirements of the atomic age." They are no less important for offence.

"It is impossible, of course, to assess with mathematical precision the strategic value of our overseas bases. But it is probable that United States offensive power would be reduced by anywhere from 25 to 50 per cent. in the first month of an atomic war if we had no overseas bases. . . . In a limited war, these bases are essential for the use of conventional weapons and to support ground forces, either our own or our allies. In a ' cold war,' they can act as a deterrent to any aggressor or a stabilising factor in an area of instability. There is no present prospect that these assets of our overseas bases will diminish as new weapons are developed." [3]

In any case, the new weapons that may replace aircraft are by no means fully operational. In all probability manned bombers will still for years to come be an important, perhaps a very important, means of delivering nuclear, incendiary, chemical and biological weapons, not to mention conventional high explosive. Fighter aircraft may also have a considerable life. Both bombers and fighters must have bases on home territory, so long as national air forces exist. The United States bases overseas, the NATO bases in Germany, Italy and elsewhere, the Russian bases in the satellite countries, all serve the defensive purposes mentioned above—early warning, " dispersion," " tracking " missiles, fighter defence in depth against a sustained bomber campaign; while, still more important, they add greatly to the

[3] N.Y.T. *Weekly Review*, February 17, 1957.

range and offensive striking power of a strategic bombing
force.

The importance of naval bases is no less. Between the
Wars, the operations which fighting ships could carry out
depended in great measure on the naval bases from which
they worked. A base could enable them to dominate a
large area of sea; the absence of a base could more or less
effectively demilitarise that area. In lesser degree their
offensive and defensive power depended on the protection
of shore fortifications. These propositions still hold good
today; a glance at a map of the world shows what the
United States naval bases in Spain, in North Africa, at
Naples and in Japan mean to the United States navy.

As warships are given nuclear propulsion, the importance
of bases in the sustaining of operations will be diminished.
The ships will be able to cruise indefinitely without coming
into port; they will probably be able to carry all the missiles
they will require; and they could be supplied with food by
submarines or from the air. But for a good many years
bases will remain a vital factor in naval strength.

The same is true, *mutatis mutandis*, of army bases. In
order to adapt themselves to " nuclear strategy," every
general staff is trying to reduce the dependence of its land
forces on fixed bases; yet it inevitably remains true that
every nation which keeps an army must have bases on its
own territory; if it is pledged to take part in collective action
abroad to protect a victim of aggression, it must have the use
of bases on other nations' soil. These bases will add both to
the defensive and offensive strength of armies.

## The Present Threat to Bases

But, in spite of their military importance, the future of bases
is obscure. The point is admirably explained in the
following racy passage by Sir Stephen King-Hall:

> " Moving Bases. The confusion into which tech-
> nical developments have thrown orthodox defence

thinking during the past twenty-five years is well illustrated by the story of British bases. Throughout the nineteenth century the British overseas bases, nestling in a well-run colony, the dockyard (good money for the natives), the Service club, the barracks, were a well-known feature of the world's landscape. The bugle notes at sunset as the Union Jack was hauled down rolled steadily round the world keeping step with the earth's revolution. But since the 1950s what changes! Singapore, hardly completed at great expense, was a useless trap. The Canal Zone, evacuated on condition we could re-activate it, has been de-activated by the Egyptians who have also pinched all our stores, the value of which seems to depend upon how the Minister responsible is feeling. Cyprus (where great building is going on), was said to be useless when we were in the Canal Zone, then said to be essential, now regarded as doubtful. Malta in rapid decline. Trincomalee taken over by the Ceylonese. Simonstown handed over to the South African Nationalists. . . . As for that famous trio of British home bases, Plymouth (Guzzle!), Portsmouth (Pompey) and Chatham, the intermediate-range missile has made them singularly insalubrious residential areas." [4]

Bases on foreign soil are menaced by the new force of anti-colonialism. The British base at Suez had rendered great service to Egypt and the Middle East. It had twice saved Egypt from conquest by foreign dictators. It had helped to free most of the Arab peoples from Turkish domination, and to make them self-governing, independent members of the UN. It gave large-scale employment to the local population, and provided foreign exchange for the Egyptian Government. It was sited in the desert, where it was least likely to infringe Egyptian liberty or offend Egyptian pride. Yet five years after the menace of Hitler

[4] *King-Hall Newsletter*, No. 1093, July 3, 1957.

and Mussolini had been removed, Egyptians were fighting a guerrilla war against the forces which had saved them. This means that the hatred of foreign bases springs from a powerful human impulse, which is one of the important facts of international life today.

Russia intends to exploit this hatred, despite the fact that she herself has huge military installations and forces in many countries outside her frontiers. In the Sub-Committee in 1957 Mr. Zorin said:

> " Liquidation of bases on foreign territory is one of the problems which must be solved before there can be any question of strengthening the peace and security of peoples and States. The presence of foreign bases, now numbering several hundred and dispersed over the entire globe, is one of the principal sources of tension in relations between States. This tension and suspicion are intensified today by the fact that many of these bases are either already used or are intended to be used for stationing atomic units. . . . *It cannot be denied that the existence of foreign bases in a country's territory creates for that country a threat that it may be dragged into a new war against its will and desire.*" [5]

But even if Russia took no interest in the subject, bases on foreign soil would often arouse keen political resentment. A simple list of place-names shows how true that is: Suez, Cyprus, Singapore, Bizerta, Okinawa, Hungary, Poland.

All bases, both at home and abroad, are also menaced by the possibility of nuclear attack. One or two well-placed Hiroshima bombs would dispose of almost any of them. This has encouraged general staffs to aim at " dispersion " of base facilities and installations as well as forces, in spite of the fact that, with bases, dispersion is both costly and inefficient.

---

[5] Sub-Committee, August 15, 1957, pp. 23–24.

## *Bases and Disarmament*

In any case, in spite of this double menace to their future, bases, both at home and on foreign soil, still remain an important element of military strength. Mr. Zorin was, therefore, right when, recalling a passage in the Russian proposal of May 10, 1955, he said in the Sub-Committee in 1957:

> " The Soviet delegation maintains that any agreement on disarmament, whether broad or partial . . . must include appropriate provisions for the progressive liquidation of foreign bases." [6]

It will not be possible to reach agreement on a disarmament treaty unless it deals with bases. And probably it must deal with *all* bases, both those on a signatory nation's own territory and those abroad.

With some kinds of armaments, and in certain geographical situations, the question of bases may, indeed, be the crux of an agreement to disarm. It was so at Washington in 1922. Since a naval base may enormously increase the attacking strength of a given naval force, and greatly extend its range, Article 19 was a vitally important part of the Naval Treaty, upon which the rest depended. By its terms, the United States, Britain and Japan agreed that, in all their respective territories and possessions within a specified area of the Pacific Ocean, they would maintain " the *status quo* at the time of the present Treaty with regard to fortifications and naval bases." This meant that they might make no new bases or fortifications, nor increase the facilities for naval repair and maintenance at their existing bases, within the area. The area was so defined as to include all the islands and mainland ports from which an aggressive attack could be made upon Japan; but it left the United States and Britain legally free to improve their naval bases at Hawaii and Singapore.[7]

[6] August 15, 1957, p. 26.
[7] Art. 19 can be found in United States *Green Book*, 1955, p. 16.

The effect of Article 19 was thus expressed by a leading authority:

" For any attack on Japan, as matters now stand, the enemy must be in possession of a fleet about three times as powerful as that of the defence, because no other country has a fully equipped modern naval base and arsenal in the Western Pacific." [8]

It was in return for this arrangement, which greatly increased her immunity from naval attack, that Japan agreed to reduce and limit the number of her capital ships and aircraft carriers.[9]

Similar propositions may be true of army, air and missile bases.  All of these must, therefore, be dealt with in a disarmament treaty.  What can be done will obviously depend on the reductions and limitations of armaments which the treaty secures.  The following points may be suggested:

1. Even in the most " partial " of agreements, it would be necessary to insert a clause like Article 19 of the Washington Treaty, namely, an undertaking to maintain the *status quo*.  This should present no practical difficulty, so far as naval, air and army bases are concerned.  The question of missile bases is more difficult, for the Russians already have a large number of their bases and launching sites organised and ready, while the Western Governments are less advanced.

2. If missiles are abolished by the treaty, as Russia has proposed, and common sense dictates, this problem will disappear; existing missile bases and launching sites must be demolished, and no new ones made.

3. If national air forces are abolished, the problem of air bases will also be solved.  If air forces are simply reduced, or if bombers but not fighters are abolished, a reduction in the number of permitted bases should be made.  Bases take a long time to construct and they greatly facilitate the

---

[8] Ballard, *The Influence of the Sea on the Political History of Japan*, p. 291.
[9] See Buell, *The Washington Conference*, pp. 163 *et seq.*

expansion of an air force; if an air force is limited, therefore, the number of bases should be that which its permitted squadrons legitimately require.

4. The number of naval bases permitted will similarly depend on the reduction of navies which the disarmament treaty effects; and the same is true of army bases.

5. The creation of demilitarised frontier zones might mean the demolition of some army and air bases. If a wide demilitarised zone were created in Central Europe, as has been proposed, embracing Germany, parts of Poland, Czechoslovakia and Hungary, the NATO bases in Western Germany, and the Russian bases in the satellites would disappear. But if United States and British troops were to remain on the continent, new bases in France, Belgium, Holland and Italy might be required.

6. If proper arrangements were made in the disarmament treaty for collective security, some army and navy bases might be internationalised under the authority and management of the UN, for use in case of collective action against aggression; some might be handed over to a standing UN international force, if that is created by the treaty. Cyprus, Gaza or Suez, Trincomalee and Okinawa might be most suitable. This proposal may seem " unrealistic " while the arms race goes on; it would, in fact, be the symbolic recognition of the realities of the world community in which all nations now live.

# 43

## *Inspection and Control*

THE inspection and control of nuclear, chemical and biological disarmament have been dealt with in earlier chapters. This chapter is, therefore, primarily concerned with the inspection and control of conventional disarmament. But every part of a disarmament system would depend on, and be closely linked to, every other part; there would be only one UN service of inspectors, with specialist experts controlling different parts, but all organised on common principles, and under a single central direction. To describe fully the development of thought on the subject, and the course of the debates of recent years, would require much more space than can be given here. All that can be done is to bring out the salient points of past and recent proposals, and to outline the kind of system that is needed.

## The Importance of Inspection and Control

It has for long been a commonplace to say that inspection and control are the " crux " of the disarmament problem. It is often added that plans for disarmament in the past have always failed because the provisions for inspection broke down; and it is widely believed that no progress has been made in the UN since 1952 because Russia has rejected all the proposals for inspection and control which the Western Governments have made. There is no justification in past history for these assertions.[1] Nor is it even true that inspection has been the greatest difficulty in the UN since 1952. It was disagreement about substantive measures of armament reduction which led to deadlock in that year, and again in the Sub-Committee in 1954, 1955, 1956 and 1957.

[1] See pp. 20–21 and 534–537.

Nevertheless, while it is necessary to keep the matter in proper perspective, it is also true that inspection must constitute a vitally important part of any general disarmament system. It has been agreed ever since the League of Nations began its work in 1920 that no general scheme would inspire confidence, without guarantees that its undertakings would be observed; and that these guarantees must be founded on a mutual right of investigation and control.

## The Two Purposes of Inspection

Until 1955, proposals for inspection and control were simply concerned with the detection of violations of the disarmament treaty. In that year, Russia put forward the Bulganin proposal for the establishment of ground control posts; this had quite a different purpose, namely, to prevent surprise attack. With the same end in view, President Eisenhower replied with his plan for " Open Skies."

In present circumstances, both purposes are important, and they can be served by the same corps of UN Inspectors. But as they are in their nature different, it may be better, if they are separately discussed.

### PREVENTION OF SURPRISE ATTACK

It has been argued in earlier chapters that the best way to reduce the risk of surprise attack is to abolish the weapons which would help an aggressor to achieve surprise. But the measures proposed by Mr. Bulganin and President Eisenhower cannot, for that reason, be dismissed; they would be of great value in the interval which must elapse before abolition is actually carried out; if they induced a sense of security, they might even help to persuade the governments that abolition could be safely agreed to.

### Ground Control Posts

Mr. Bulganin started from the danger of a secret nuclear stock. He argued that no aggressor would venture an attack by nuclear weapons alone; he would have to mobilise all his conventional forces, too; this mobilisation could be readily detected by international teams of UN Inspectors stationed at railway centres, important road-routes, airfields, ports and docks, etc.[2] The task of these inspectors would be to follow all movements of troops and war-material, and to ensure that at transport centres no undue concentration should take place. This was a useful proposal, if Mr. Bulganin's main hypothesis is accepted, *i.e.*, if it is agreed that general mobilisation would be required before an aggressive war was launched. A relatively small number of UN Inspectors, stationed as he proposed, could detect the mobilisation of land, of sea, and perhaps of air, forces at an early stage. This would be a real guarantee against surprise attack, unless the aggressor decided to risk everything on a nuclear blitzkrieg, without mobilising his conventional forces until a decisive advantage had been won.

### Aerial Photography

It was to guard against the danger of nuclear blitzkrieg that President Eisenhower proposed the systematic air photography of the territory of the United States and Russia, and of other areas in Europe, the Arctic and elsewhere.[3] The proposal was not new; the UNAEC had proposed it in 1946,[4] and it had often been urged in the UN Disarmament Commission and Sub-Committee. But in 1955, the President put it forward as the most important of all measures, both for the prevention of a nuclear blitzkrieg, and for the creation of " confidence "; United States delegates in the Sub-Committee called it the " gateway to the reduction of armaments." [5] It is necessary, therefore, to consider how effective it might be.

During the 1939 War, the R.A.F. first discovered Hitler's

---

[2] See pp. 290–291. The proposal was first made in the Russian plan of May 10, 1955. See Cmd. 9636, pp. 39–42.

[3] The President made his proposal at the Geneva Summit Conference on July 21, 1955. See Cmd. 9636, pp. 48–50.

[4] 1st Report to the Security Council, 1946, Part V, Chap. 6, pp. 59–63.

[5] Sub-Committee, September 9, 1955, Cmd. 9651, p. 811.

preparation of his V 2 by the study of an aerial photograph of Peenemünde.[6] Since then, the speed of aircraft and the technique of photography have both enormously improved. In a test in 1956, four aircraft photographed the whole of Italy in an hour; the photographs showed clearly a poodle standing on the steps of St. Peter's, and a man, with his back to the camera, carrying a baby.[7] Photography of all the strategically important areas of the world is practicable; though, if repeated at frequent intervals, it would be very expensive.

As a normal part of a disarmament inspection system, it would discover all existing or newly constructed nuclear plants; new factories, which might be built for making war material; it could check the buildings provided for troops, and detect new building of barracks, bases or depots. It would thus help in the effective maintenance of reduced levels of armament or manpower.

It might help in detecting a normal mobilisation of armies, navies and air forces. Mr. Lodge claimed in 1956 that it " could undoubtedly detect major preparations, without which great efforts could not be undertaken. Had there been aerial inspection at the time," he said, " there probably would not have been any Pearl Harbour or any Hitlerite attack on the U.S.S.R." [8]

This may be true; but it may be doubted whether air photography could discover preparations for a nuclear blitzkrieg. It could detect nothing of what was going on under the roofs of hangars, barracks or depots. It could not find underground storage depots for nuclear bombs; camouflage and concealment could effectively hide even fairly extensive surface installations.[9] Nor could it detect what kind of bombs were being loaded on to aircraft. The bombers taking part in a nuclear blitzkrieg would operate from their normal bases. The bombers go up several times a week for

---

6 See Churchill, *The Second World War*, Vol. V, pp. 202-204.
7 Gen. Fanali, N.Y.H.T., October 15, 1956.
8 UN Disarmament Commission, July 3, 1956.
9 Hanson Baldwin, N.Y.T., July 22, 1955.

training flights; the crews practise bombing with dummy bombs which, in design, shape, size and weight must be identical with the nuclear bombs which they would use in war. It is not clear, therefore, how air photography could discover secret preparations for a surprise nuclear attack. The ground control posts would have a better chance, though even ground observers could hardly hope to detect the difference between a dummy practice bomb and a genuine nuclear weapon. This leads back to the conclusion that the best way to prevent surprise attack is to abolish the weapons which help surprise.

Nevertheless, both ground control posts and air photography are desirable parts of an inspection system. Since 1955 the Russians have gone some way towards accepting air photography, and their objections might be wholly withdrawn if it were put forward as an integral part of a general plan for more considerable armament reductions.

### DETECTION OF VIOLATIONS OF A DISARMAMENT TREATY

But the other purpose of inspection, the detection of violations of a disarmament treaty, is of greater long-term importance than the prevention of surprise attack; and there is a better hope that it will prove effective.

The doubt so often expressed about its efficacy is chiefly based on the experience of the Western Allies in Germany between the Wars. In virtue of the Treaty of Versailles the Allies sent a mission of 400 officers, headed by a French general, to ensure that the Treaty was carried out. They had wide powers, and the German Government accepted sweeping obligations to give them help. As a result, Germany was very effectively disarmed, and she remained incapable of aggression until Hitler had spent some years in rebuilding her forces, and re-equipping them with up-to-date weapons. But from 1919 onwards the German General Staff did everything in their power to evade their Treaty obligations, to deceive the Allied mission, and to prepare for the day when Germany could openly re-arm. Their methods and their success have been described by two authorities: Brigadier-General Morgan, who was a member of the Allied mission,[10] and Mr. J. W. Wheeler Bennett, who has a profound knowledge of Germany and of recent German history, and who has made a careful study of the German Government documents which have been published since 1945.[11] As these authors show, the German Staff built up a cadre of N.C.O.s, and a body of trained reserves, greater than the Versailles Treaty allowed [12]; they prepared the economic mobilisation of the State to equip an army of sixty-three divisions; they encouraged Krupp to cheat the Allied mission, to maintain his arms-making capacity in Germany, and to purchase a large interest in firms abroad, *e.g.*, Bofors in Sweden [13]; they created aircraft and chemical industries in Russia— the German Air Mission were the true founders of the Russian aircraft industry, which has developed Bisons and Sputniks and ICBMs; they built submarines in Spain and Russia, guns and tanks and other weapons in Sweden, Switzerland and Turkey.[14] All this powerfully assisted Hitler's rearmament when it began.

But what does this history prove? *Not* that the system of inspection failed in Germany; but simply that after 1925 it was never enforced. Sir Winston Churchill regards this as a fatal error:

" The strict enforcement at any time till 1934 of the disarmament clauses of the Peace Treaty would," he says, " have guarded indefinitely, without violence or bloodshed, the peace and safety of mankind. But this was neglected while the infringements remained petty, and shunned as they assumed serious proportions. Thus the final safeguard of a long peace was cast away." [15]

10 *Assize of Arms*, 1945.          11 *The Nemesis of Power*, 1954.
12 Wheeler Bennett, *op. cit.*, pp. 98, 102 *et passim*.
13 Wheeler Bennett, *op. cit.*, p. 146.
14 G. Scheele, *The Weimar Republic*, 1946, pp. 112 *et passim*.
15 *The Second World War*, Vol. I, p. 15.

This happened, not because it would have been difficult to enforce the Treaty, if the other nations had desired to do so, but because there was no general will to enforce it. The true "final safeguard of a long peace" was not the unilateral disarmament of Germany, but the multilateral disarmament of all nations, which Germany had been promised in 1919. If that promise had been fulfilled, and if the system of Inspection devised for Germany had been accepted by all nations, there would have been no difficulty in making it effective. The main lesson of experience in Germany is that compulsory *unilateral* disarmament will not endure, because the general body of the nations will regard it as inherently unjust.

There is, however, another lesson to be drawn. Brigadier-General Morgan, after an ample exposure and denunciation of the German military caste, reaches this conclusion:

> "Four years' experience have convinced me that you cannot hope, by anything short of military occupation, to limit the effectives of the armed forces of a great nation, unless you can carry the opinion of the nation with you." [16]

But in *Assize of Arms* he shows that in 1920 the German people, acting through their trade unions and under the leadership of their political chiefs, had defeated the *Kapp Putsch*—an attempt by a German military clique to seize power.[17] He describes how the German Staff hired an office underneath one of the offices of the Allied mission, and how they tried to persuade a German postman to deliver the Allied mail to them, so that they might read it first; the postman delivered the German Staff's letters to the Allies instead.[18] There is much other evidence to show that, so long as the hope of general disarmament remained alive, many Germans were ready to help in ensuring that

[16] *The Present State of Germany*, 1924, pp. 96–97.
[17] *Assize of Arms*, pp. 62–78.
[18] Morgan, *op. cit.*, p. 51.

their Government observed its Treaty obligations.[19] If this spirit could be created among the nations whose governments sign a disarmament treaty, the success of the system of inspection would be assured.

## Proposals between the Wars

As was said above, everyone agreed in theory from 1919 onwards that there must be *some* form of Inspection and Control. As discussion progressed, the proposals made became more ambitious. Unfortunately, the British Government, whose influence was great, were reluctant to accept an effective system; the Chapter on Control was the weakest part of their Draft Convention of March 1933. But the United States, who had begun by rejecting all proposals for Inspection, so changed their attitude that in 1933 President Roosevelt's delegate declared that " adequate measures of supervision were an essential part of any effective system of disarmament"; and that " *means of effective, automatic and continuous supervision* " must be found.[20] Mr. Litvinoff repeatedly insisted for Russia that " very rigorous supervision should be established." [21]

It was from these ideas that the UN discussions began in 1946.

## Western and Russian Proposals : 1946—1957

The first UN Assembly *unanimously* adopted a Resolution asking the Security Council to " expedite consideration of a draft convention . . . for the creation of an international system of controls and inspection," which it regarded as " essential to the general regulation and reduction of armaments . . . to protect complying States against the hazards of violations and evasions." [22]

[19] P. J. Noel-Baker, *Private Manufacture of Armaments*, p. 202.
[20] *Minutes of the General Commission*, Vol. II, p. 583.
[21] *Minutes of the Bureau*, Vol. I, p. 17.
[22] Resolution adopted on December 14, 1946.

Starting from this emphatic mandate, the delegates of the leading Western Powers gave the subject continuous attention until 1956. Indeed, there has been more debate about Inspection and Control in the UNCCA, the Disarmament Commission and the Sub-Committee than about all the other issues of conventional disarmament put together. It is the *only* issue on which any attempt has been made to write down the detailed provisions required in a disarmament treaty.

Not everything put forward by the Western delegates has been well inspired. But there has been much of lasting value, in particular in the detailed and constructive plans laid before the Sub-Committee by the United States delegate, Mr. Patterson, in 1954 [23]; by M. Moch in September 1955 [24]; by Mr. Nutting in the same month [25]; and jointly by M. Moch and Mr. Nutting in May 1956.[26] The two last papers proposed the creation of a disarmament organisation, modelled closely on the institutions of the UN, with an assembly, an executive council, and a secretariat, besides the actual control administration to be established in every country. This may seem to be a costly duplication; the assembly and council would perform duties which could more properly and adequately be performed by the UN itself. But in all these four papers there are valuable suggestions which should be retained.

Their authors were all agreed that the Control system must be administered, under the authority of the UN, by a central administration, with branch offices and an international corps of inspectors in every country; the inspectors would be recruited and paid by the UN and would owe the UN their exclusive loyalty; they would be in permanent residence, their inspection would be continuous, they would have wide powers of access to " objects of control," and full freedom of movement and communication. The signatory

23 Cmd. 9204, pp. 17–23.
24 Cmd. 9636, pp. 56–61.
25 Cmd. 9636, pp. 61–62.
26 Cmd. 9770, pp. 40–46.

governments would undertake to give them every assistance they might require.

Since everything depends upon the detailed obligations which are accepted, it may be worth while to set out a statement of the essential features of an effective system made in the Sub-Committee by Mr. Nutting in 1955:

" I. In our view the control organ must have the right of full information and inspection of the following 'objects of control' . . .

" (1) numbers of armed forces and their equipment;

" (2) conventional land, sea and air armaments, including certain categories of civilian aircraft and shipping;

" (3) military installations, including barracks, ordnance depots, dockyards and airfields;

" (4) factories capable of making armaments (including aircraft), explosives, and propellants;

" (5) nuclear installations and reactors;

" (6) plants capable of making chemical and biological weapons.

" II. The control organ should be able to make use of the following methods of inspection and supervision:

" (1) aerial reconnaissance;

" (2) inspection on the ground;

" (3) budgetary controls;

" (4) observation at strategic points.

" III. The control organ should also have the following rights:

" (1) unrestricted rights of freedom of movement to, from and within all States party to the treaty;

" (2) the right to make full use of the communication systems of the State which it is inspecting and to possess suitable transport and communications of its own;

" (3) the right of access to all the objects which I have just mentioned; advance notice would be given of routine visits, but the right of inspection without warning would also be essential;

" (4) the right to investigate alleged or suspected breaches of the treaty in any establishment or installation in the territory of any State party to the treaty; and, perhaps, in some respects, the most important of all,

" (5) the right to use all necessary technical devices which may assist supervision and detection."

Mr. Nutting added:

" I do not suggest that this list of rights and powers is final or fully comprehensive. I do suggest that anything less than this would be inadequate." [27]

In the debates of 1955 to 1957 the Russians went a long way to meet the Western Governments' demands. The best statement of their proposals is contained in the Control Chapter of their abortive plan for conventional disarmament put forward in March 1956. It may be useful to reproduce the text of what they said:

" II. Rights and Powers of the International Control Organ.

" With a view to the establishment of effective international control over the fulfilment by States of the above-mentioned obligations with respect to the reduction of conventional armaments and armed forces, an international control organ shall be established having the following rights and powers:

" 1. (This deals with surprise attack and the establishment of ground control posts.)

" 2. The international control organ shall exercise control, including inspection on a permanent basis, to the extent necessary to ensure implementation of the agreement by all States.

" 3. The control organ shall have permanently in all States parties to the agreement its own staff of

[27] Cmd. 9651, pp. 671–672.

inspectors, recruited on an international basis, having, within the bounds of the control functions which they exercise, unimpeded access at all times to all objects of control.

" The objects of control are : military units; stores of military equipment and ammunition; land, naval and air bases; factories manufacturing conventional armaments and ammunition.

" 4. At a specified stage of the execution of the general disarmament programme, when confidence among States had been strengthened, the countries concerned shall consider the possibility of using aerial photography as one of the methods of control.

" 5. The control organ shall have unimpeded access to records relating to the budgetary appropriations of States for military needs, including all decisions of the legislative and executive organs on the subject.

" 6. The control organ shall establish in the capitals of States parties to the agreement branches whose functions shall include maintaining liaison with the governmental organs of States, directing the work of the control posts and inspectors operating in the territory of the State concerned, and analysing the information furnished by States.

" 7. The international control organ shall be established within the two months following the entry into force of the agreement. It shall establish its local branches, set up the control posts and position its inspectors in good time to ensure that they are able to begin carrying out their functions at the moment when States begin the execution of the measures provided for in the agreement.

" 8. The international control organ shall make recommendations to the Security Council on measures of prevention and suppression with regard to violators of the agreement on the reduction of conventional armaments and armed forces.

" 9. The States parties to the agreement shall submit to the international control organ within one month after its establishment complete official figures of their armed forces, conventional armaments and expenditures for military requirements." [28]

It must be noted that these proposals related to conventional armaments alone, nuclear disarmament being excluded [29] (since the Russians at that time thought that this was what the Western Governments desired [30]), and no mention being made of chemical or biological weapons. This may explain the inadequacy of the definition of " objects of control " in paragraph 3.   Mr. Nutting's list is evidently much more satisfactory; in particular, it is clear that the definition must include not only " factories manufacturing " armaments, as the Russians proposed, but also, in Mr. Nutting's phrase, " factories *capable* of making armaments."   It should also include, in a comprehensive disarmament treaty, as M. Moch proposed in a later paper, " all nuclear and scientific research," which Mr. Nutting had omitted; and " all enterprises suspected by the control organ of engaging in any of the above-mentioned activities." [31]

But, subject to this, and to a point about sanctions which will be dealt with in a moment, the Russian proposal went very far.   The UN Inspectors were to be " recruited on an international basis," and to reside permanently in the State they control; they were " within the bounds of the control functions which they exercise " (a phrase not open to objection) to have " unimpeded access at all times to all objects of control "; their inspection was to be " on a permanent basis "; it was to be established in advance, so that it would be effective immediately the process of armament reduction began; above all, " *the international control organ shall*

[28] Proposal of March 27, 1956, Cmd. 9770, pp. 33–34.
[29] See pp. 281–282 for Russian proposals on Inspection and Control of nuclear disarmament.
[30] See pp. 228–230.
[31] Paper dated October 6, 1955, Cmd. 9636, p. 63.

*exercise control . . . to the extent necessary to ensure implementation of the agreement by all States.*" This principle would surely cover most of the points which Mr. Nutting mentions, and which the Russian plan omits.

In short, the difference between Russia and the West on Inspection and Control seemed in 1955 and 1956 to be less wide than was generally believed. The Russian proposal, involving, as it would, the permanent admission to Russian military and industrial plants and installations of many hundreds, if not thousands, of UN agents, would constitute a major renunciation of the policy of the Iron Curtain. The Russians still stand by what they said in 1956; it is difficult to believe that, if there were on both sides a genuine desire for armament reduction, agreement on an inspection system could not be secured.

## Inspection and Intelligence

There is every reason to expect, moreover, that an inspection system such as the Russians propose would be able to discover all but the most petty infringements of the treaty.[32] For it must be remembered that the UN system would supplement, and not replace, the secret services which most countries maintain. The General Staffs are rarely in error about the military preparations which other States are making. It is said that the NATO Intelligence Service has known about every Russian nuclear test, about Russian progress in guided missiles, about the development of Russian submarines and the detailed disposition and equipment of Russian troops. Governments could make available to the UN Control Administration any information obtained by their agents about violations of a disarmament treaty; with this guidance the UN Inspectors could hardly fail to establish the facts.

---

[32] Excluding, of course, the question of a secret nuclear stock, which is discussed on pp. 288 *et seq.*

## Sanctions for Violations

There was an important difference between the Russian and the Western proposals of 1955 about sanctions. The Russians suggested that the control organ should only be empowered to " recommend " the necessary measures to the Security Council, where, of course, Russia would have a veto.

This is clearly unsatisfactory; but the point may be of less practical importance than it seems. If Russia or a Russian ally were proved to have infringed the treaty, the most important sanction would lie in the fact that the other nations would forthwith cease to disarm; and it seems improbable that anything could prevent them from taking the collective economic measures against the criminal State which they might judge to be required. *In any case, collective economic and financial measures are the right preliminary answer to a violation of a disarmament treaty, and they should be organised in advance.*[33]

## Inspection and Disarmament

The Russians have always urged that it would be easier to settle the detailed provisions of an inspection system when the detailed reductions of armaments have been agreed.[34] There is force in this contention; certainly the Western Governments will be in a better position for urging the importance of control when they have made bolder and more definite proposals for the reductions which are to be controlled. In any case, it is certain that the United States delegate was right when he urged in 1952 that the further disarmament is carried, the simpler and more effective control will become. A single illustration will suffice. It was tentatively suggested by the United States in 1957 that a 10 per cent. reduction in conventional weapons should be made. This would have meant for the United States air

[33] See p. 551.
[34] Sobolev, Sub-Committee, September 13, 1955, Cmd. 9651, p. 826.

force, army and navy a reduction from approximately 41,000 aircraft to 37,000; and for the Russian forces from 20,000 to 18,000. It would probably prove impossible for UN Inspectors to determine whether these reductions had, in fact, been made. But if each power were allowed a maximum of 500 aircraft of a specified maximum unladen weight, as in the British Government's Draft Convention of 1933, a violation of this limit could easily be detected.

The Western Governments have urged a very drastic system of inspection and control over many years. In 1957 they beat an undignified and unexplained retreat.[35] Their attitude towards the mutual inspection established by the West European Union Treaty and the European Nuclear Energy Agency shows that their General Staffs are still reluctant to accept the " sacrifices " of sovereignty which inspection must involve.[36] It remains true, however, that without provision for effective inspection, a disarmament treaty will never be signed.

Inspection must be founded on the principle of distrust. " If we trusted each other," said M. Moch, " this Sub-Committee would not need to meet." [37] But once the system of inspection is established, it should help to remove distrust, and to create true confidence that the epoch of wars and competitive armaments is at an end. The mere presence of UN inspectors in every country, supervising an actual reduction in the burden of armaments, might produce a profound psychological effect. When the mind of the peoples has been won to support of the inspection system—and this might happen, even in Russia, more quickly than now seems probable—the long-term success of disarmament will be assured.

---

[35] See p. 29.
[36] *e.g., The Times* reported on October 12, 1956, that, under the W.E.U. system five days' notice must be given of any inspection, and that component parts of armaments were excluded. These restrictions would make inspection a farce.
[37] April 4, 1956, p. 27.

# 44

## *Collective Security*

"We cannot and will not condone aggression, no matter who the attacker, no matter who the victim."

President Eisenhower on the
Suez War.
November 1, 1956.

It has been accepted since the early days of the League of Nations that disarmament and collective security must go together. At present States are free to make the maximum military effort of which they are capable to defend themselves against attack; they will not renounce this freedom, unless they receive other guarantees instead.

The guarantees will be of various kinds; some of them have been dealt with in earlier chapters, but a brief recapitulation may be worth while.

### 1. The Restraining Power of the Law

Disarmament is the logical consequence of the decision to substitute the rule of law for the rule of armed force. The system of the UN is founded on the fundamental obligations of paragraphs 3 and 4 of Article 2 of the Charter:

" 3. All Members shall settle their international disputes by peaceful means in such a manner that international peace and security, and justice, are not endangered.

" 4. All Members shall refrain in their international relations from the threat or use of force against the territorial integrity or political independence of any State, or in any other manner inconsistent with the purposes of the United Nations."

For the eighty-two Nations who are Members of the UN, these obligations are binding law; they have all renounced the right to use armed force as an instrument of their national policy, or to impose their national will, and the Charter permits no reservations and no exceptions to this basic rule.

The restraining power of this law must depend on the degree to which the Member nations honour their obligations, and on the general authority and prestige of the UN. This is increased by every case in which the judgments of the International Court or the Resolutions of the Assembly and the Security Council are accepted; and there have been many such cases. It is diminished by the fact of the arms race, and by the existence of the rival alliances to which the arms race gives rise. But even today it is very considerable; in the autumn of 1956 an attack on Egypt by Israel, Britain and France was halted within a week after the UN Assembly declared it, with only two contrary votes, to be a violation of the Charter. If a general disarmament treaty were made, the restraining power of the law against aggression would be significantly increased.

## 2. DISARMAMENT AND SECURITY

(i) If the general disarmament treaty brought about a fair and balanced all-round reduction of armaments, with demilitarised zones in dangerous places, and an effective system of inspection, it would itself increase the security of the signatory nations.

(ii) This would be particularly true if the treaty abolished the weapons that are " specifically offensive " and " especially efficacious against national defence," *e.g.*, nuclear, chemical, incendiary and biological weapons, missiles, military aircraft, tanks, aircraft carriers, submarines.

## 3. A UN INTERNATIONAL FORCE

Paper plans for an international force have been prepared and debated for many years. In 1956 the UN Emergency

Force was established in Sinai as an *ad hoc* measure to deal with a dangerous situation in which war had broken out. The agreement to establish UNEF was a vital factor in bringing the fighting to an end; its presence in Sinai has brought tranquillity to an area where conflict had been for long endemic. It has worked so efficiently and so smoothly that the real difficulties of an international force have passed largely unperceived. Its success makes it certain that a permanent UN international force should form part, and an important part, of the security system which disarmament requires. Had such a force existed from the start of the UN, it might have helped powerfully to prevent fighting, and to secure stable settlements, in Palestine, Kashmir, Korea and other places.

Most of those who have studied the problems of a permanent international force are agreed that it should be organised on the principles suggested for an international air police in Chapter 35. Thus:

(i) The force should consist of long-term volunteers, recruited individually by the UN.

(ii) It should be organised on an international basis, with quotas for different nations, to ensure a fair balance.

(iii) Preferably, and in any case at the beginning, the commanding officer and staff should be chosen from among nationals of the middle and smaller States.

(iv) It would probably be wise to apply the same principle to all ranks.

(v) The force should have exclusive loyalty to the UN, and should be paid, equipped and armed with funds borne on the UN budget.

(vi) To begin with, at any rate, it should not be furnished with heavy arms.

(vii) It should have permanent bases, training depots, leave stations, etc., of its own, in a number of different countries.[1]

---

[1] See p. 529.

(viii) To begin with, its numbers should be relatively modest: 10,000 or 20,000 are figures sometimes proposed. (UNEF never exceeded 6,100.) It should be rapidly expanded as disarmament progresses and needs demand.

(ix) Its main function should be to perform, wherever they might be required, the kind of services rendered by UNEF in Sinai.

(x) It should also provide whatever resident UN commissioners, officers or guards might be needed for the supervision of demilitarised zones,[2] and for the protection of the stockpiles of fissile material which the International Atomic Energy Agency is to maintain. These stockpiles must, under the Statute of IAEA, be given a " strategic " distribution in different regions of the world, and IAEA must ensure their safety; it would be an ideal solution if the Director-General could use the UN international force. This would be still more appropriate if UN stockpiles of nuclear weapons were added.[3]

(xi) The Commander-in-Chief should be responsible to the Secretary-General of UN: the Secretary-General should be advised by a Standing Commission elected by the Assembly. This is the system adopted for UNEF, and it has worked well.

The existence of a permanent UN international force would be a further important guarantee for the security of States which loyally carried out their obligations under a disarmament treaty. If the government of any country believed itself to be threatened by a neighbouring State it could call on the UN force to send contingents to occupy and patrol its frontier. This would deter all but the most reckless aggressors; for example, if there had been such a force to occupy North Greece from 1945 to 1950 much disastrous fighting would have been avoided.[4]

2 See p. 517.                                    3 See pp. 304–308.
4 Earl Attlee in the House of Lords: " One interesting point was brought out by the noble Earl, Lord Selkirk (First Lord of the Admiralty) in dealing with NATO. He stressed . . . the integration at the United Nations of this

#### 4. UN International Air Police

If, as proposed in Chapter 35, a UN international air police is created, the principles suggested in the preceding section would equally apply. When the first draft of the Charter was being prepared at Dumbarton Oaks, the Russians " proposed that an international air force should be created, ready at a moment's notice to spring into action whenever the Security Council gave the word of command." [5]    Sir Winston Churchill said of this plan:

> " I do not consider that we should turn down the Russian proposal. . . . The matter raises very large questions of principle, and cannot be decided on purely military grounds. . . .  The introduction of an international air force is an event of the utmost importance and cannot possibly be settled on departmental considerations." [6]

Nevertheless, the British delegation opposed the Russian plan, and the Kremlin withdrew it.  It should now form part of a comprehensive system of disarmament and security.

#### 5. Sanctions and Collective Action

But even if all the above measures were adopted a determined aggressor might still take the risk of increasing his armaments above the treaty level, or even of going to war. This may seem unlikely, if the treaty reduces armaments by stages to the low levels suggested in earlier chapters, and abolishes the weapons which help attack.  But the risk of

force drawn from so many different nations.  I remember well that between the wars I was a strong advocate of an International Police Force.  We were always told that it was quite impossible, and that forces from different nations would never work together.  As a matter of fact, we saw it done in Lord Alexander's Army in Italy; and now we have a repetition of it. Members who have been there have seen how you can form an international force.  It seems to me encouraging to those who have always advocated that the United Nations should have a force of its own to see that in practice it is found to be possible."  *Hansard*, January 22, 1958, col. 156.

[5] W. H. McNeill, "America, Britain and Russia; their Co-operation and Conflict, 1939–45," *Survey of International Affairs, 1939–45*, p. 505.

[6] Minute dated August 29, 1944.

aggression, either during the process of reduction, or even after it is complete, must be considered.

To meet that danger, it should be agreed by all the nations which sign the disarmament treaty that they will take collective action by all the means at their disposal to halt the aggression, or to crush it, if it goes on. This obligation should be world-wide, though the use of some kinds of armed force might be organised on a regional basis.

This sounds like an onerous commitment. But:

(i) "Sanctions mean the pooling of self-defence. It means nothing else." [7] If each nation agrees to defend the others against attack, it is ensuring that all others will come to its defence; it is securing the maximum possible support against aggression.

(ii) Tendencious propaganda has made the word "sanctions" seem to many people the equivalent of "war." But there are sanctions short of war; and if disarmament had been carried through these sanctions could be progressively applied, and might well prove effective without any use of force.

(iii) The first and obvious sanction is diplomatic: the simultaneous withdrawal by all other States of their ambassadors from the aggressor's capital. This would constitute a warning to the aggressor, and would certainly, in many cases, produce a profound effect on his public opinion, since it would drive home in a dramatic form the collective condemnation of his action by the opinion of the world.[8]

(iv) If opinion by itself should fail, the next graduated deterrent would be the organised interruption of all means of transport and communication—postal, telegraphic, shipping, railway, aircraft, road—between the aggressor and the outside world. This would need careful preparation in advance; detailed plans for its execution should be

---

[7] S. de Madariaga, *Disarmament*, p. 231.

[8] See Maj.-Gen. Temperley, *The Whispering Gallery of Europe*, p. 333, on the Japanese aggression in Manchuria in 1931.

annexed to the disarmament treaty. It would cause loss and trouble to all the co-operating States, but there are few potential aggressors who would not find it an embarrassing sanction to have to face.[9]

(v) The suspension of transport and communication would, of course, involve, in effect, an economic and financial boycott of the aggressor. To make it fully effective, however, this boycott should be prepared in detail in advance, and the co-operating States should make arrangements to support each other by trade and banking measures, so that the loss involved should be spread, as far as possible, evenly over them all. In particular, arrangements should be made, on the lines of Draft Conventions prepared by the League of Nations, to assist any State or States at whose trade and commerce the aggressor might be able to strike effective blows.

Economic sanctions, if they were world-wide, organised in advance, and applied without delay, might in many cases prove decisive. There are few States, for example, which could defy an oil-sanction. An international Committee of Board of Trade and Ministry of Commerce experts reported to the League of Nations in February 1936 that even as late as that, when the fighting had already lasted six months, and the Fascist troops had penetrated far into Abyssinia, an embargo on oil would nevertheless have compelled Mussolini to abandon his aggression.[10] Unfortunately, the French and British Governments failed to give the required lead.

(vi) The imposition of economic sanctions might cause the aggressor to resort to violent measures in reply, in which case the co-operating Members of the UN would be involved in war.[11] In some cases, the only way to save the victim of aggression from defeat and, perhaps, extinction, would be, as in Korea, to resist the attack from the start by

[9] Plans of this kind are contained in the "Report on Collective Action," adopted by the UN Assembly in 1951.
[10] See Temperley, *op. cit.*, p. 332.
[11] *Ibid.*, p. 330.

the collective use of armed force. In any case, it would be useless to try to create a security system, unless the signatory States were willing to pledge themselves in advance to pool their strength, and to act against an aggressor by whatever means were needed to defeat him. There has always been an inexplicable reluctance on the part of leading States to give this pledge. If Britain and the United States had been willing to do it in 1932 the Disarmament Conference would have succeeded; they both refused to give guarantees to France and Poland, with the result that within a short period of years they were fighting for their very lives to defeat aggressors whose first victims had been Poland and France.

## Russia and Sanctions

It has been said that the sanctions described above would be effective against any State but Russia. Russia, it is argued, has such great resources, she is so impervious to world opinion, so independent of world trade, so self-sufficient in oil and vital raw materials, so defended by geography and nature against naval action, economic boycott, or even joint military pressure, that she could safely venture to defy the world.

No doubt there is force in this argument, particularly in the circumstances of today. But if Russia signed and ratified a disarmament treaty, and then violated her obligations by attempting to build up secret armaments, and was discovered by the UN inspectorate to have been guilty of this crime, she would find that she stood alone in her guilt, with the world against her. Every year her intercourse with the outside world is gradually growing; the presence of UN Inspectors on her soil would make her more susceptible to the pressure of world opinion; it will become increasingly difficult for her to resist the combined pressure of the rest of mankind.

## *The Risks of Sanctions*

The above is a sketch of the kind of Security system that might be set up to guarantee the faithful observance of a disarmament treaty.[12]   It is founded on three principles, which the experience of the last half-century has shown to be true:

1. " Peace is indivisible." [13]   The only stable foundation for peace is the law that makes *all* resort to war an international crime.   That law will only have binding force if it is universally applied.   If a small war in one continent (*e.g.*, in Manchuria) is allowed to happen, it will lead to other wars in other continents (the Gran Chaco, Abyssinia, Spain, Albania), and so in the end to a general conflict.

2. " Just as prisons are erected not so much to lock people in as to induce people to stay out, so sanctions must be devised in order that nations should not have to undergo them.   The most efficient system of sanctions is that which will never be applied." [14]

The stronger the sanctions, the less the danger that anyone will defy them.

3. Britain and the United States have now recognised the truth of these principles, and have accepted the onerous obligations of the NATO, SEATO and Baghdad Pacts. When real disarmament has been begun—but not till then —these Pacts can be merged into a world-wide security system, in which each gives guarantees to all, and all give guarantees to each.   There will be risks in such a system of world-wide collective security; but they will be slight compared to the stupendous risks of the arms race and the rival alliances of today.

---

[12] There is a large body of literature about Security, including standard works on the Covenant and the Charter and books such as *The Problem of Security* by J. W. Wheeler Bennett, *The Geneva Protocol* by P. J. Noel-Baker, etc.
[13] Litvinoff in Geneva, 1933.
[14] S. de Madariaga, *Disarmament*, p. 229.

# PART EIGHT

# CONCLUSION

# 45

## *The Best Military Defence*

" No military man is pleased with the present *status quo*—two armed camps sitting opposite each other. That would be a hell of a state of affairs to perpetuate."

General Lauris Norstad,

Supreme Commander,

NATO Forces in Europe.[1]

GENERAL NORSTAD's words admirably sum up the main thesis of this book: the arms race must be stopped. It has become too dangerous for the nations to allow it to go on.

Since the earlier chapters of the book were sent to press two other eminent Americans have made statements which supplement what General Norstad said.

Mr. Thomas K. Finletter has a large personal experience of high-level international negotiation [2]; he speaks about armaments with great authority, for he was head of the United States President's Air Policy Commission from 1947 to 1948, and Secretary of the Air Force from 1950 to 1953, the U.S.A.F.'s period of peak expansion. Writing in March 1958 Mr. Finletter said:

" We know more than ever that arms control cannot safely be deferred. . . . Will we persist stubbornly in the sterile London formula? . . . In my opinion, we should start with the proposition that the first-stage-only approach to disarmament came to an end in London in 1957. It did not go very far. In fact, it could not. . . . It has proved to be impractical,

---

[1] N.Y.T., July 17, 1957.
[2] He was Special Assistant to the United States Secretary of State during the 1939 War, and Minister in charge for Marshall Aid in Britain from 1948–49.

for the following reasons. . . . A first-stage-only plan does not reveal to the negotiators on either side where they are supposed to end. . . . [They] do not know if the final objective is to do away with war entirely, or only to mitigate its horrors, or if indeed there is any real intention to do anything at all significant about the problem of war or of weapon control. Therefore . . . [they] have to proceed on the assumption that war *may*, and if history is a guide, *will* occur again. The arms race may be made somewhat cheaper, but the game will go on."

This method, Mr. Finletter argues, must always fail. We must make a new start, on a totally different basis " before the weapons get geometrically worse than they are now, and before they get into the hands of governments all over the world. . . . We need *a grand design, an overall plan,* which will strike at the major causes of tension between the Communist and non-Communist worlds, including the greatest cause of tension of all, the massive and fantastically destructive armaments which are building up in the rival camps." We must " hit hard and daringly at this business of arms control. Essential is that we put forward in the UN a *complete proposal. This would consist of a first-stage plan in detail, and then, in the same document, a specific description of each of the successive steps down through the final one.* . . . The plan should create such enthusiasm and support from the peoples of the West and the uncommitted areas of Asia and Africa that . . . it would make it very difficult for them [the Communists] to resist."

The title of Mr. Finletter's article is " *Disarmament should be total.*" [3]

Dr. Leo Szilard was one of the leading pioneers in atomic energy research, and a member of the team that

[3] *Western World,* April 1958, pp. 32–36.

produced the first atomic bomb; Mr. Arthur Compton calls him " a most remarkable genius." [4] In 1958, Dr. Szilard wrote:

> " I am not one of those who believe that much of importance may be accomplished by halting the bomb tests, or even the further manufacture of bombs. I believe that, if the solution of our problem can be achieved through disarmament at all, then *nothing short of getting rid of the stock-piles of bombs, as well as the means suitable for their delivery, can be regarded as an adequate measure.*" [3a]

Mr. Finletter and Dr. Szilard have re-stated, with their great authority, the argument of the preceding chapters. Attempts at " partial " disarmament, with very small reductions, have failed, as they were bound to fail. Everyone would welcome " partial " measures, if they were generally agreed, and if they were certainly to be followed by further, more drastic, steps. But, as Mr. Finletter argues, it is far harder to get agreement on " partial " measures; how hard is shown by the fact that the 1957 London " package " plan had no figures, no clear or definite proposal, on any single part of a disarmament programme; and no proposals for how inspection and control should work. Proposals for a very small cut in manpower, and perhaps in military budgets, with the retention of great stocks of nuclear, chemical, biological and other weapons of mass destruction, and of missiles, bombers, tanks, aircraft carriers and submarines, and the continuation of military research, are most likely to succeed. Against the great evil of the present arms race and the modern weapons, small remedies would not produce a small result; they would probably produce no significant result at all. Even if they were signed and ratified, they would be so difficult to control that, in all probability, they would soon break down.

3a *The Times*, March 22, 1958
4 *Atomic Quest*, p. 83.

What is needed is a new " grand design, an over-all plan." This book has not discussed the possible introductory steps that might be taken, nor the smaller issues that will arise: at what intervals of time the successive reductions of armaments should be made; how many, and what, nations must ratify the treaty before it enters into force; the mechanism for suspending the reductions, if a violation of the treaty should occur. These are important matters, but they will cause no difficulty when agreement on the substance of disarmament has been reached.

In the " grand design " we must write out " the first-stage plan in detail," preparing it in draft treaty clauses, the precision and clarity of which leave nothing vague. We must propose at least as much disarmament as was offered by the Western Governments in the Anglo-French Memorandum of 1954: " major reductions " of all armed forces and conventional armaments, together with the total and rapid abolition of all weapons of mass destruction, including the conversion of all nuclear stocks.[5] To make the first-stage safe we must " hit hard and daringly at this business of arms control "; we must adopt whatever safeguards may be necessary to avert the danger of an illicit nuclear stock, abolishing the " means of delivery," the missiles and the bombers; even accepting a UN international force with a UN nuclear stock.

When we draw up the details of this " major " first-stage reduction we must also set out the later measures by which, within a limited period of years, all the " offensive " weapons which assist attack against defence (the bombers, the tanks, the aircraft carriers, the submarines),[6] shall be progressively abolished, and by which national armed forces shall be reduced " to the levels strictly necessary for the maintenance of internal security and the fulfilment of the obligations of signatory States under the terms of the UN Charter." [7]

---

[5] See pp. 15–19 and 301–312.
[6] See Chap. 33.
[7] Para. 8, Anglo-French Memo., 1954.

Above all, we must provide for the abolition of military research. We have been promised an anti-missile missile, to avert the latest danger which science has produced; but while this anti-missile missile still remains a distant dream, claims are made that the manned bomber can be given a protective shield of electrons which will " ward off any attacking missiles," [8] and enable it, as hitherto, to " get through " to the vital population centres of an enemy land. This electron shield may also be a dream; but what is certain is that, as Dr. Rabi said,[9] the next seventeen years of military research would add as many new and terrible " improvements " as the years since 1941. Military research, like the " offensive " weapons, must be abolished, and the scientists transferred to peaceful work.

It has been shown in detail in earlier chapters that there are no technical difficulties in these proposals which cannot readily be overcome. The detailed technical provisions of a disarmament treaty will certainly be complex, as anyone can see who looks at the Washington and London Naval Treaties, or at the British Government's Draft Convention of March 1933. But the broad issues are quite simple; technical solutions will cause relatively little trouble when the political decisions have been made.

These proposals are not " starry eyed " idealism. They are plain, realistic common sense. The romanticists are those who still believe that modern armaments can make a nation safe. There is no military defence today for any nation except in drastic measures of disarmament, embodied in a multilateral treaty to which all governments subscribe. From the first day that this treaty enters into force, and the UN inspectors take up their posts in the countries which they will control, the security of every nation will at once, and notably, be increased. The acceptance of inspection means the end of military secrets; it is the greatest of the " surrenders of sovereignty " which disarmament must

[8] N.Y.H.T., January 25, 1958
[9] See p. 3

mean; but, in itself, it will do much to end the " nightmare fear " of sudden and unprovoked attack; it will gradually, but profoundly, change the whole character of the inter-national relations between States.

Will Russia ever have a genuine inspection, or accept the drastic means of armament reduction proposed above? The Kremlin say they will, and in recent months have gone far beyond the Western Governments in declaring their readiness to accept whatever measures of inspection are required to ensure that a disarmament treaty is faith-fully observed. Their sincerity can only be tested by offering them the detailed text of a controlled disarmament system that would translate into reality the measures which they say they will accept. But there are solid grounds for thinking that the men in the Kremlin are genuinely afraid of nuclear war.[10]

Many people, who ardently desire disarmament, will think it facile optimism to believe that a *multilateral* treaty might soon be signed and ratified. But the harsh fact of world politics today is that nothing less than such a multi-lateral treaty can now encompass the safety of mankind. No one who has closely followed disarmament negotiations since 1919 is likely to be guilty of facile optimism about the prospect of success. But no one who understands the present arms race should be guilty of facile pessimism, which is by far the graver fault. Defeatism about the feasibility of plans for disarmament and ordered peace has been the most calamitous of all the errors made by democratic governments in modern times. It has betrayed the hopes of the vast majority of the people of every nation, who actively desired, as they actively desire today, the end of war.

The end of war is historically, by many decades, overdue. Scientists and engineers have eliminated the barriers of time and space, and all nations now form one society, bound by

[10] See pp. 225–231.

bonds of common interest which they cannot break. In 1919 Field-Marshal Smuts said: " We want a League which will be real, practical, effective as a system of world government." In 1941 Sir Winston Churchill and President Roosevelt made a joint declaration: " All of the nations of the world, for realistic as well as spiritual reasons, must come to the abandonment of the use of force." [11] These two statements, made under the impact of world war, embody what has been the professed objective of the foreign policy of the democratic governments for forty years. The facts set out in this book show that, as world wars recede into the past, their lessons fade and are forgotten; but they show, too, that unless this professed objective can be achieved within an early future, the policies mis-named " defence " may bring the final consummation of the use of force: the end of man.

Lasting peace and justice will only come from the gradual, cumulative inter-action of many new policies and many great reforms: a conscious, persistent effort to strengthen the deliberative institutions of the UN; the submission of all legal conflicts to the International Court; the building up of international legislation and administration for the greater happiness and prosperity of mankind. But these new policies can never triumph until the arms race has been ended, and the nations have thus decided that they will finally abandon the use of force.

[11] The Atlantic Charter, August 14, 1941.

# *Principal Documents Quoted*

## *United Nations Publications*

Atomic Energy Commission:
  1st Report to the Security Council, December 30, 1946.
  2nd Report to the Security Council, September 11, 1947.
  3rd Report to the Security Council, May 17, 1948.

Disarmament Commission [1]:
  2nd Report, October 13, 1952.

Report of the Preparatory Commission of the International Atomic
  Energy Agency, New York, 1957. GC.1/1. GOV/1.

## *League of Nations Publications*

Records of the Conference for the Reduction and Limitation of
  Armaments, Geneva, 1932–33:

| | |
|---|---|
| Verbatim Records of Plenary Meetings, Vol. I. | 1932.IX.60 |
| Minutes of the General Commission, Vol. I. | 1932.IX.64 |
| Minutes of the General Commission, Vol. II. | 1933.IX.10 |
| Conference Documents, Vol. I. | 1932.IX.63 |
| Conference Documents, Vol. II. | 1935.IX.4 |
| Conference Documents, Vol. III. | 1936.IX.4 |
| Preliminary Report on the Work of the Conference, prepared by the President. | 1936.IX.3 |
| National Defence Expenditure Commission, Report of the Technical Committee, Vols. I and II. | 1933.IX.3 |

## *H.M. Stationery Office Publications*

First Report of the Disarmament Commission of the UN. May 28,
  1952. UN No. 2 (1952) Cmd. 8589.

Report on the Proceedings of the Sub-Committee of the UN Disarmament Commission, May 13–June 22, 1954. UN No. 2 (1954)
  Cmd. 9204.

---

[1] The Verbatim Records of the Disarmament Commission, and of the Sub-
Committee 1956 and 1957, in mimeographed form, can be seen at the London
Information Office of the UN. For other Commission and Sub-Committee
documents, see under HMSO Publications.

Report on the Proceedings of the Sub-Committee of the UN Disarmament Commission 1955. UN No. 2 (1955) Cmd. 9636.

Report on the Proceedings of the Sub-Committee of the UN Disarmament Commission, March 19–May 4, 1956. UN No. 7 (1956) Cmd. 9770.

Report on the Disarmament Talks 1957. Misc. No. 17 (1957) Cmd. 228.

Report on the Proceedings of the Sub-Committee of the UN Disarmament Commission. UN No. 2 (1957) Cmd. 333.

Verbatim Records of the Meetings of the Sub-Committee of the UN Disarmament Commission:

    May 13–June 22, 1954. UN No. 3 (1954) Cmd. 9205.

    February 25–March 18, 1955. UN No. 1 (1956) Cmd. 9648.

    March 22–April 6, 1955. UN No. 2 (1956) Cmd. 9649.

    April 19–May 18, 1955. UN No. 3 (1956) Cmd. 9650.

    June 1–September 13, 1955. UN No. 4 (1956) Cmd. 9651.

    September 14–October 7, 1955. UN No. 5 (1956) Cmd. 9652.

*First Report from the Select Committee on Estimates*, Session 1953–54, on Civil Defence. (December 2, 1953. Reprinted 1954.)

*Fire and the Atomic Bomb*. Fire Research Bulletin No. 1. Published for the Department of Scientific & Industrial Research and Fire Offices' Committee. (1954.)

*Medical Manual of Chemical Warfare*. Published for the Admiralty, War Office and Air Ministry. (4th ed., 1955.)

*Biological Warfare*. Manual of Basic Training, Vol. II. Pamphlet No. 7. Home Office, Civil Defence. (1955.)

*The Hazards to Man of Nuclear and Allied Radiation*. Medical Research Council Report. (June 1956) Cmd. 9780.

*Nuclear Weapons*. Manual of Civil Defence, Vol. I. Pamphlet No. 1. Published for the Home Office. (1956.)

*Statute of the International Atomic Energy Agency*. New York, October 26, 1956. Misc. No. 4 (1957) Cmd. 92.

*Decision of the Council of the Organisation for European Economic Co-operation establishing a European Nuclear Energy Agency and Convention on the Establishment of a Security Control in the Field of Nuclear Energy*. Paris, December 20, 1957. Misc. No. 2 (1958) Cmd. 357.

*Report of the Committee appointed by the Prime Minister to examine The Organisation for Control of Health and Safety in the United Kingdom Atomic Energy Authority*. Atomic Energy Office. (January 1958) Cmd. 342.

## United States Publications

Lilienthal Report       *A Report on the International Control of Atomic Energy.* Dept. of State Publication 2498. March 16, 1946.

United States Hand-     *Atomic Energy: A General Account of the*
book, 1945              *Development of Methods of Using Atomic Energy for Military Purposes under the Auspices of the United States Government,* by H. D. Smyth. August 1945 (Reprinted by HMSO).

United States Hand-     *The Effects of Nuclear Weapons.* Prepared
book, 1957              by the United States Department of Defence. Published by the USAEC. June 1957.

United States Green     *Disarmament and Security: A Collection of*
Book                    *Documents 1919–1955.* 84th Congress, 2nd Session. United States Government Printing Office. 73652.

## Other Publications, Periodicals, etc.

Indian Government       *Nuclear Explosions and Their Effects.* Pub-
Report                  lished by the Ministry of Information and Broadcasting, Government of India. (1956.)

*Foreign Affairs*       The Council on Foreign Relations, 58 East
(Quarterly)             68 Street, New York.

*Bulletin of the Atomic*   Educational Foundation for Nuclear Science,
*Scientists* (Monthly)  Inc., 5734 University Avenue, Chicago 37, Illinois.

*The New Scientist*     Cromwell House, Fulwood Place, High Hol-
(Weekly)                born, W.C.1.

Brighton Conference     59 Bryanston Street, London, W.1.
Association

# Who's Who

| | |
|---|---|
| BALDWIN, Hanson | Military Correspondent, *New York Times.* |
| *BLACKETT, Prof. P. M. S. | Professor of Physics, Imperial College, London. President of the British Association, 1957–58. |
| BUSH, Dr. Vannevar | Chief Wartime Scientific Adviser to the United States Government. |
| BUZZARD, Rear-Admiral Sir Anthony | Director of Naval Intelligence, 1951–54. |
| CHISHOLM, Maj.-Gen. Brock | Former Director-General, Royal Canadian Army Medical Corps; Director-General, World Health Organisation, 1948–53. |
| COCKBURN, Dr. R. | Controller of Guided Weapons and Electronics, Ministry of Supply. |
| *COCKCROFT, Sir John | Director of Atomic Research in the United Kingdom. |
| *COMPTON, Arthur Holly | Director, United States Government's Plutonium Research Project, 1942–45. |
| DEAN, Gordon | Chairman, USAEC, 1950–53. |
| FRISCH, Prof. O. R. | Jacksonian Professor of Natural Philosophy at Cambridge. |
| JAY, Kenneth E. B. | Principal Scientific Officer, Atomic Research Establishment. |
| LAPP, Dr. Ralph E. | Former Consultant to the USAEC. |
| *LAWRENCE, Dr. Ernest O. | Director, University of California Radiation Laboratory. |
| LIBBY, Dr. Willard F. | Professor of Chemistry, University of Chicago. Member of USAEC. |
| LIDDELL HART, Capt. B. H. | Military Correspondent, *Daily Telegraph*, 1925–35; *The Times*, 1935–39. |
| MADDOX, John | Scientific Correspondent, *Manchester Guardian*; contributor to *The New Scientist*. |
| *MULLER, Dr. Hermann J. | Professor of Genetics, University of Indiana. |
| MURRAY, Thomas E. | Former member of USAEC. |
| OLIPHANT, Prof. Marcus | Director, School of Physical Sciences, Australian National University. |

569

| OPPENHEIMER, Dr. J. Robert | Wartime Director of Atomic Bomb Project Laboratory at Los Alamos; former Chairman of Advisory Committee, USAEC. |
|---|---|
| *PAULING, Dr. Linus | Professor of Chemistry, California Institute of Technology. |
| PETERSON, Val | United States Civil Defence Administrator, 1953–57. |
| PRENTISS, Augustin M. | Brigadier-General, United States Army (Retired). |
| *RABI, Prof. Isidor | Chairman, President Eisenhower's Science Advisory Committee. |
| ROSEBURY, Dr. Theodor | Was actively associated with the United States Government's Biological Warfare project. |
| ROTBLAT, Prof. Joseph | Professor of Physics, University of London. Worked on Atomic Energy at Los Alamos. |
| STRAUSS, Admiral Lewis S. | Chairman of USAEC since 1953. |
| TELLER, Dr. Edward | Member of General Advisory Committee, USAEC. Often called "the father of the H-bomb." |
| TEMPERLEY, Maj.-Gen. A. C. | War Office Adviser to the United Kingdom Delegation, League of Nations Preparatory Disarmament Commission and Disarmament Conference. |
| *THOMSON, Sir George | Emeritus Professor of Physics, University of London. Chairman of first British Committee on Atomic Energy, 1940–41. |

* = Winner of Nobel Peace Prize.

# Index